DATE DUE

DEMCO 38-296

LATIN AMERICA IN THE WORLD-ECONOMY

LATIN AMERICA IN THE WORLD-ECONOMY

EDITED BY
Roberto Patricio Korzeniewicz
and William C. Smith

STUDIES IN THE POLITICAL ECONOMY
OF THE WORLD-SYSTEM
Immanuel Wallerstein, SERIES ADVISER

CONTRIBUTIONS IN ECONOMICS AND
ECONOMIC HISTORY, NUMBER 181

GREENWOOD PRESS
Westport, Connecticut • London

HC 125 .L3449 1996

Latin America in the world-economy

Library of Congress Cataloging-in-Publication Data

Latin America in the world-economy / edited by Roberto Patricio
  Korzeniewicz, William C. Smith.
        p.   cm.—(Contributions in economics and economic history,
  ISSN 0084-9235 ; no. 181)   (Studies in the political economy of the
  world-system)
     Includes bibliographical references and index.
     ISBN 0-313-29814-9 (alk. paper)
       1. Latin America—Economic conditions—1982- 2. Latin America—
  Social conditions—1982- I. Korzeniewicz, Roberto Patricio.
  II. Smith, William C., 1946-   . III. Series. IV. Series: Studies
  in the political economy of the world-system.
  HC125.L344   1996
  337.8—dc20   96-5794

British Library Cataloguing in Publication Data is available.

A paperback edition of *Latin America in the World-Economy* is available from
Praeger Publishers, an imprint of Greenwood Publishing Group, Inc.
(ISBN 0-275-95423-4).

Library of Congress Catalog Card Number: 96-5794
ISBN: 0-313-29814-9
ISSN: 0084-9235

First published in 1996

Greenwood Press, 88 Post Road West, Westport, CT 06881
An imprint of Greenwood Publishing Group, Inc.

Printed in the United States of America

The paper used in this book complies with the
Permanent Paper Standard issued by the National
Information Standards Organization (Z39.48-1984).

10 9 8 7 6 5 4 3 2 1

CONTENTS

FIGURES AND TABLES

FIGURES

TABLES

Series Foreword

Immanuel Wallerstein

The Political Economy of the World-System Section of the American Sociological Association was created in the 1970s to bring together a small but growing number of social scientists concerned with analyzing the processes of world-systems in general, and our modern one in particular.

Although organizationally located within the American Sociological Association, the PEWS Section bases its work on the relative insignificance of the traditional disciplinary boundaries. For that reason it has held an annual spring conference, open to and drawing participation from persons who work under multiple disciplinary labels.

For PEWS members, not only is our work unidisciplinary, but the study of the world-system is not simply another "specialty" to be placed beside so many others. It is instead a different "perspective" with which to analyze all the traditional issues of the social sciences. Hence, the themes of successive PEWS conferences are quite varied and cover a wide gamut of topics. What they share is the sense that the isolation of political, economic, and sociocultural "variables" is a dubious enterprise, that all analysis must be simultaneously historical and systemic, and that the conceptual bases of work in the historical social sciences must be rethought.

PREFACE

Latin America is in the midst of great transformations. Institutional reforms in the 1980s and 1990s have sought to promote a more competitive position for the region in the world-economy. These reforms have sought to achieve greater economic efficiency by curtailing the ability of states to regulate the production and distribution of wealth. Often, these reforms have been perceived as entailing painful social adjustments (as manifested, for example, in the persistence of poverty and the exacerbation of income inequalities). At the same time, Latin America has experienced the consolidation of democratic transitions and the emergence of new political dynamics characterized by distinct organizational arrangements and novel forms of collective action. To probe the contours, scope, and implications of these dramatic transformations, the North-South Center at the University of Miami hosted the nineteenth annual Conference on the Political Economy of the World-System. The essays included in this volume were originally presented at the conference, which was held in Coral Gables on April 20–22, 1995.

We would like to thank all the conference participants for their contributions during three exhausting, but highly stimulating, days of discussion and debate. In addition to the authors of the chapters included in this volume, conference participants included Caren Addis, Frank Bonilla, Marcelo Cavarozzi, Norma Stoltz Chinchilla, Paul Ciccantell, Susan Eckstein, Nancy Forsythe, Walter L. Goldfrank, Ramón Grosfoguel, Nora Hamilton, Jeffery Paige, Edward Mc-Caughan, John M. Talbot, Richard Tardanico, Beatrice Wallerstein, and Immanuel Wallerstein.

On behalf of all the conference participants, we wish to express our great appreciation to those who made this project possible. For the necessary financial support for the conference and the simultaneous publication of hardback and paperback editions, we owe special thanks to the North-South Center, particularly to Ambler H. Moss, Jr.; Robin Rosenberg; and Jeff Stark.

This volume would not have been possible without the collaboration of our respective institutions, colleagues, students, and staff. We would like to acknowledge the help provided by the Department of Sociology (especially Kevin Barth, Darrin Helsel, Cyndi Mewborn, Timothy Moran, and Mildred Yen) and the Latin American Studies Center at the University of Maryland in College Park. At the University of Miami, the assistance of students at the Graduate School of International Studies (particularly Holly Pierce, Julie Diehl, Vanessa Gray, María Eugenia Mujica, and Mariela Córdoba) was essential in the organization and smooth operation of the conference. We also appreciate the support and encouragement of Immanuel Wallerstein, editor of the Political Economy of the World-System (PEWS) series, and the the patient work of James Ice, the book's editor at Greenwood Press. Above all, this book was made possible by the critical assistance of Nancy Forsythe.

LATIN AMERICA IN THE WORLD-ECONOMY

1

A GREAT TRANSFORMATION?

Roberto Patricio Korzeniewicz and William C. Smith

Latin America is in the midst of dramatic transformations. Stabilization and structural adjustment programs are dismantling state regulation of the economy in an effort to extend the reach of markets and construct a new framework for growth and development. Advocates of these programs expect neoliberal restructuring to enhance economic efficiency by shifting responsibility for the allocation of resources from states to markets, enterprises, and households.[1] Simultaneously, the consolidation of the democratic transitions of the 1980s has been followed by the emergence of a new and distinct (albeit still inchoate) matrix of political dynamics and modes of organization, as some of the most influential forces of the past (such as trade unions or the military) have experienced a significant erosion of their bargaining power, while other actors (such as nongovernmental organizations [NGOs]) have found a new voice. Together, these political and economic changes signal the emergence of new institutional arrangements.[2]

Not all observers share the optimism of advocates of current reforms as they evaluate the depth and resiliency of these new arrangements. Some critics fear that economic restructuring will expose vulnerable sectors of the population to rising levels of poverty and that market mechanisms ultimately will fail to ensure the sustainable development of human and natural resources under democratic conditions (Bresser Pereira, Maravall, and Przeworski, 1993, 1994). Others cast doubt on the extent to which the consolidation of democratic regimes has enhanced full citizenship (particularly in contexts of increased economic hardship among the poor), or the degree to which democratic institutions have overcome enduring legacies of authoritarianism and privilege in many spheres of public and private life (O'Donnell, 1994b; Smith, 1993).

The chapters included in this book provide a critical evaluation of several crucial dimensions of the institutional transformations experienced in Latin America during the 1980s and 1990s. Some contribute to such an evaluation by providing detailed insights into the organizational changes undergone within the region by households, enterprises, and states. Other chapters focus more closely on changes in world-economic flows (e.g., the movement of people or capital across national borders). This introductory chapter reviews the contributions made by the essays in this volume, focusing on the conceptual areas in which a world-systems perspective might be particularly useful in advancing our understanding of emerging patterns of social and political change in Latin America.

ECONOMIC GROWTH, SOCIAL EQUITY, AND DEMOCRACY

The 1990s have witnessed a strong endorsement of stabilization and structural adjustment programs throughout Latin America. The implementation of these programs has had a profound impact on prevailing institutional arrangements. At a superficial level, market mechanisms have continued to displace state regulation in coordinating the production and distribution of resources. More profoundly, new institutional arrangements privilege a greater separation in the spheres of action of enterprises, states, and households. These patterns of institutional change in Latin America during the 1990s are intricately linked to the unraveling and collapse of import-substitution industrialization and state-centric models, as manifested in three legacies of the 1980s: stagnant economic growth, an exacerbation of social inequalities, and the consolidation of democratic transitions. Among these, economic crisis and stagnant growth were perhaps the most important legacy, as they led to a thorough reevaluation of existing institutional arrangements.

Characterized by unprecedented levels of economic crisis and instability, the 1980s in Latin America came to be termed a "Lost Decade" (see Table 1.1). The cumulative change in gross domestic product (GDP) per capita between 1981 and 1990 was −7.9 percent in the region as a whole, including, for example, −21.2 percent in Argentina, −18.6 percent in Bolivia, −3.6 percent in Brazil, −4.3 percent in Mexico, −33.5 percent in Nicaragua, −28.9 percent in Peru, −19.4 percent in Venezuela, and −1.4 percent in Uruguay (ECLAC, 1994, 1995; see also World Bank, 1993b: table 1). Only two countries in mainland Latin America experienced an increase in their cumulative GDP per capita during this period: Chile (11.7 percent) and Colombia (17.9 percent) (ECLAC, 1994; for similar data on GNP per capita, see World Bank, 1993c: table 1).

Economic crisis in many of the Latin American countries in question was often accompanied by traumatizing bouts of hyperinflation. In Argentina, for example, the average annual rate of inflation between 1980 and 1993 was 374.3 percent, and it reached the astonishing rates of 3,079.2 percent in 1989 and 2,314.0 percent in 1990. Likewise, annual inflation rates in Brazil reached an average of 423.4 percent between 1980 and 1993, and moved into four-digit

Table 1.1
Some Leading Economic Indicators, Selected Latin American Countries,
1980–1995

	Cumulative Growth, GDP per Capita		Urban Unemployment	Average Inflation
	1981–1990 (percent)	1991–1995 (percent)	1995 (percent)	1995 (percent)
Argentina	-21.1	23.6	18.6	1.8
Bolivia	-17.4	6.1	5.8	10.7
Brazil	-4.6	4.8	4.7	22.0
Chile	12.4	29.7	5.6	8.3
Colombia	17.9	13.2	8.6	20.0
Costa Rica	-5.8	10.1	4.3	24.9
Cuba	27.8	-33.4	NA	NA
Ecuador	-6.6	6.0	8.4	22.2
El Salvador	-18.8	16.0	7.5	11.4
Guatemala	-18.2	5.8	4.3	8.6
Honduras	-8.2	1.6	4.5	28.6
Mexico	-4.3	-5.8	6.4	48.5
Nicaragua	-33.5	-11.1	20.2	10.8
Panama	-2.4	14.6	14.3	0.8
Paraguay	-0.8	0.9	4.8	10.4
Peru	-28.9	19.3	8.2	10.4
Uruguay	-1.4	14.8	10.7	36.8
Venezuela	-19.4	2.5	10.3	52.9
Latin America & Caribbean	-7.5	5.1		

Source: ECLAC (1995).

territory in 1989, 1990, and 1992–1994. In Bolivia, the average annual rate of inflation between 1980 and 1993 was 187.1 percent, and it reached an average rate of 1,300.0 percent in 1984 and 11,804.8 percent in 1985. Similarly explosive bouts of inflation were experienced prior to 1992 in Nicaragua and Peru (for these figures, see Inter-American Development Bank, 1994: 284; World Bank, 1995: 163).

There is considerable evidence that macroeconomic instability and inflationary spirals produced an environment that led to a deterioration of virtually all indicators of social equity. During the "Lost Decade," poverty became accentuated throughout the region (CEPAL, 1992). Bonilla (1990: 215), for example, has indicated that the incidence of poverty among households in Latin America increased from 33 percent to 39 percent between 1980 and 1985 alone. Furthermore, the data suggest a rapid increase in the incidence of poverty during recessionary periods, but a slow reduction of poverty during periods of economic growth (CEPAL, 1992: 5). For these reasons, compared to the 1970s, there came to be a significantly higher number of households lacking sufficient income to meet basic needs (CEPAL, 1992: 7).[3]

Similar patterns characterize recent changes in the distribution of income. Available data indicate that inequalities became significantly more pronounced in Argentina, Bolivia, Brazil, Guatemala, Mexico, Peru, and Panama. On the other hand, the distribution of income became slightly more equitable in Colombia and Uruguay. Reviewing the evidence on changes in income distribution in Latin America since the early 1980s, Morley (1994: 10) argued, "Inequality in almost every case is strongly countercyclical, rising in recession and falling in recovery."[4] Providing some support to such an interpretation, recent patterns of income distribution in Chile, Costa Rica, and Venezuela appear to have shifted according to the economic cycle (CEPAL, 1994; see also Lustig, 1995; Fiszbein and Psacharopoulos, 1995; Morley, 1995b; Psacharopoulos, 1993; Raczynski and Romaguera, 1995).

The profound impact of economic stagnation and hyperinflation gave a number of governments throughout the region considerable political leeway in their efforts to implement adjustment and restructuring programs. Using this leeway, administrations such as those of Carlos Menem in Argentina, Fernando Collor in Brazil, and Alberto Fujimori in Peru were able to implement reforms that had been considered impossible only a few years before (Acuña, 1994; Sola, 1994; Roberts, 1995).[5] The implementation of these reforms has generated considerable opposition from forces claiming to represent those sectors most affected by the adjustment and restructuring programs, including, most notably, the Chiapas insurrection in Mexico, but no coherent alternative agenda had emerged on a regional basis by the middle of the 1990s (Zermeño, 1996).

What are the long-term political concomitants of these trends in poverty and inequality? More specifically, how can we explain why stabilization plans and market-driven restructuring associated with recent patterns of poverty and inequality have been implemented so aggressively by democratic leaders chosen in competitive elections? Are not widespread poverty and growing social inequality antithetical to the consolidation of democratic regimes?

Although common sense would lead us to expect economic "hard times" to threaten new democracies (and economic prosperity to facilitate democratic transition and consolidation), the relationship between democracy and economic conditions is not so simple or linear. In fact, Latin America's conjunction of democratic transitions and a context of economic crises and regressive income distributions is consistent with a broader pattern experienced elsewhere in the semiperiphery of the world-economy since the 1970s. For example, the transitions of the southern European semiperiphery (Spain, Greece, and Portugal) took place precisely in a context of economic stagnation. Moreover, current political transitions elsewhere in the semiperiphery (e.g., Eastern Europe and Russia) are occurring in even more desperate circumstances of crisis, austerity, and the collapse of living standards. If anything, economic growth and employment (as well as salary levels) appear typically to have fallen during transitions from authoritarian rule to more open, competitive polities. In these cases, macroeconomic conditions adverse to the social welfare of the majority of the population posed a challenge to democratic stabilization, and it is tempting simply to conclude that democratic "consolidations" have taken place in spite of economic hardships. This conclusion is true as far as it goes, but an alternative formulation might highlight a less obvious, but more interesting, relationship; namely, that profound economic restructuring has been advanced despite its high social costs and precisely *because* new democracies have both legitimated harsh economic policies and demobilized much of the anti-systemic opposition.[6]

This somewhat counterintuitive relationship between democracy and economic trends is complemented, in contemporary Latin America, by the equally paradoxical elective affinity between neoliberal restructuring and neopopulism, as well as the more obvious linkages of poverty, inequality, and personalistic governing styles, with the symbols and formal rituals of representative democracy. In contrast with the emphasis on *substantive* reforms designed to assure social equality, economic justice, and the broadened political participation characteristic of previous waves of democratization, the democratic discourse of the 1980s and 1990s has generally stressed the "Schumpeterian" or *procedural* components of the competitive struggle between rival elites for the people's vote. Concomitantly, demands for fundamental structural reform and expanded participation take a back seat and are frequently portrayed as leading to excessive and inefficient state intervention, predatory rent seeking, and ungovernability. In these circumstances, dominant economic and political actors, as well as many less privileged sectors, come to share the conviction that dictatorial regimes are unpredictable and that democracies are more reliable in securing adequate conditions for capitalist growth. Citizenship and political participation are thus largely limited to elections and the act of voting, while the market is enshrined as the most efficient means through which consumers can express economic preferences.[7]

In these circumstances it is perhaps hardly surprising that "the most natural political correlate to the neoliberal era may actually be populism, the option most widely seen as its antithesis" (Roberts, 1995: 112).[8] As O'Donnell recently observed, under such conditions, powerful plebiscitarian and majoritarian tendencies are likely to prevail over weak liberal and representative impulses. As a result,

the more properly political, *democratic* freedoms are effective: uncoerced voting, freedom of opinion, movement, and association. . . . But for large sections of the population, basic *liberal* freedoms are denied or recurrently trampled [and] . . . individuals are citizens in relation to the only institution that functions close to what its formal rules prescribe, elections. In the rest, only the members of a privileged minority are full citizens. (O'Donnell, 1996: 45)

Personalist mobilization of the populace is the counterpoint to the weakness of representative institutions such as legislatures, political parties, and labor unions. Moreover, the rapidity of economic restructuring erodes traditional social and political identities and accelerates the disarticulation of forms of social organization that, during the previous state-centric model of development, had formed the basis for the collective action of the subaltern sectors of society. Along with the emergence of "national saviors," particularistic interests flourish and the weakening of the "state-as-law" allows archaic authoritarian practices to reassert themselves, thereby reinforcing, in the strongly hierarchical societies, already egregious asymmetries in power and privilege.

While these transformations may facilitate the emergence of more efficient and dynamic circuits of production and distribution, they are probably incompatible with the broad-based type of class compromise (e.g., New Deal or social democracy) that characterized the historical consolidation of democracies in the core of the world-economy. Nevertheless, neoliberal reforms are not only compatible with democracy but may even facilitate the eventual consolidation of a democratic political order in much of Latin America. The key question is no longer authoritarianism versus democracy, but precisely what *type* of democratic systems are likely to develop in the near future in such semiperipheral areas of the world-economy.[9]

The specific institutional arrangements and the social bases of posttransition democratic regimes in Latin America will vary considerably. A variety of alternative politico-economic scenarios is possible (Smith and Acuña, 1994).[10] As institutional arrangements in each nation are transformed by the implementation of market-oriented reforms, collective outcomes may not produce a modal pattern for the region as a whole. In this sense, profound alterations in social and economic structures probably foreshadow growing social, economic, and political diversity within the region.

Diversity can also be found in recent patterns of economic growth (see Table 1.1). At one end of the spectrum, Chile has continued to be characterized by extremely high rates of economic growth and a similar, if less dynamic, pattern has characterized the case of Colombia. At the other end of the spectrum, a considerably slower pace of economic growth has characterized cases such as Bolivia, Brazil, and Mexico. The most striking pattern of change has characterized countries such as Argentina and Peru, where the profound recession and instability of the 1980s was followed by considerable growth (although, as in other countries in the region, with considerable susceptibility to shifts in financial flows, as demonstrated by the recessionary tendencies manifested in the so-called "Tequila effect" following the Mexican crisis in 1994). In most of these cases, structural reforms have achieved considerable success in reducing inflation to historical lows, thus providing considerable legitimacy to the regimes in question. Nevertheless, in some countries, such as Argentina, structural reforms continue to be accompanied by painful social costs (i.e., excessive unemployment rates and measures of income inequality, which recently reached historically high levels), while in other countries, such as Chile, most of these social indicators have improved.

Notwithstanding these divergencies, the region as a whole has undergone major changes in existing institutional arrangements, including a new hegemonic ascendancy of liberal ideology in the design and implementation of economic policies, far-reaching changes in the regulatory capacity of the state, and an apparent erosion in the bargaining power of established political parties, social movements, and collective actors. Are these new institutional arrangements indicative of a "Great Transformation"? A little over 50 years ago, Karl Polanyi (see Polanyi, 1957) introduced the term to describe the rise and demise of a self-regulating market economy.[11] According to Polanyi, the rise of a self-regulating market economy in the middle of the nineteenth century generated social and political responses that led to its eventual demise between World War I and World War II, to be succeeded by new forms of state regulation and class compromise, as embodied in the "Keynesian" formulas of core countries and the statist and populist strategies pursued in the semiperiphery. Are the current changes in Latin America of such a magnitude that they indicate a new Great Transformation reintroducing a self-regulating market economy? The chapters in this volume serve to outline three key areas of inquiry that a world-systems perspective can explore to answer this question.

EVALUATING STRATEGIES FOR GROWTH: COMMODITY CHAINS IN THE WORLD-ECONOMY

From different perspectives and disciplines, scholars have observed that the trends that characterized Latin America during the 1980s are particularly striking when compared to regional patterns of development in East Asia. In comparison to the crisis, instability, and precipitous deterioration in economic performance that most of Latin America experienced during the "Lost Decade," the East Asian nations indeed appeared as success stories. Between 1980 and 1993, in the midst of the Latin American crisis, the average annual growth rate of gross national product (GNP) per capita was 8.2 percent for South Korea, 5.4 percent in Hong Kong, and 6.1 percent in Singapore (World Bank, 1993c: table 1). This striking divergence stimulated a large of body of empirical and comparative studies seeking to distill the strategies and policies that explain East Asian success (e.g., Amsden, 1989; Appelbaum and Henderson, 1992; Balassa et al., 1986; Evans, 1995; Gereffi, 1989, 1995; Wade, 1990; Whitehead, 1989; World Bank, 1987, 1993a).

We should be cautious about our ability to abstract recipes for such success. After all, in the 1960s and 1970s, there came to be considerable consensus that industrialization and self-reliance were important ingredients for growth, and the "economic miracles" that served as models in those decades were countries such as Yugoslavia or Brazil. Industrialization prescribed very clear strategies (e.g., in terms of investments, tariff and trade arrangements, and infrastructure) to be pursued by enterprises, households, and state agencies in order to promote economic growth and development. True, there were already conflicting interpretations over the specific mechanisms that should be implemented to promote effective industrial growth (e.g., in regard to the precise extent of state regulation of trade or the degree to which price supports or taxes were to be extended to agriculture or manufacturing). In overall terms, however, and particularly as compared to later developments in the 1980s and 1990s, there was relative consensus over the importance of industrialization as an engine of growth to drive the whole model of development.[12]

The postwar model of development that prevailed until the 1980s, which was based on industrialization and statist/populist modes of regulation, had clear difficulties in delivering its promise of promoting economic growth and rapid convergence with high-income nations. Already apparent, these difficulties prompted many debates in the 1960s and 1970s (e.g., Suttcliff, 1972, 1984). Until the 1980s, however, these debates did not fundamentally challenge the premise of industrialization as an engine of development. After the debt crisis and Latin America's "Lost Decade," on the other hand, the Asian experience became widely perceived, in policy-making circles and elsewhere, as providing a contrasting pattern of development and growth. In this new model, the pursuit of industrialization as a general strategy was displaced by a more specific emphasis on particular modes of organization (e.g., flexible specialization) and market integration (e.g., export-oriented growth rather than continued reliance on protected internal markets).

Efforts to derive a new model of development from the East Asian experience are tempered by considerable debates over how to interpret the role of enterprises and the state in promoting growth. For advocates of neoclassical prescriptions for economic restructuring, the East Asian experiences serve as an indictment of state regulation and inward-oriented industrialization (e.g., Balassa et al., 1986; World Bank, 1987, 1993a). For example, the World Bank suggested that in the East Asian experience, government regulation "was subjected to international competition and market-related checks and balances," trade regimes "remained highly outward-oriented," and government regulation of markets was "more moderate than in most other developing countries" (1991: 39). Some critics have countered that successful development did entail active intervention in markets on the part of effective state bureaucracies (Amsden, 1989; Evans, 1992, 1995; Wade, 1990).[13] For yet others, countries in East Asia and Latin America underwent distinct paths of industrialization, some of which (e.g., import-substitution industrialization oriented toward domestic markets) generated institutional constraints that made it difficult for states and enterprises to promote greater economic integration or move into more complex areas of production (Appelbaum and Henderson, 1992; Gereffi, 1989, 1995; Whitehead, 1989). Such a range of interpretations reflects considerable disagreement as to the crucial variables that might explain the success of the East Asian experience.

Often inherent in the effort to scrutinize the East Asian experiences in search of an effective model of growth is the assumption that success in the economic arena is derived from the *replicable* construction of certain capabilities (e.g., at the level of the firm or state agencies) that are best suited to exploit available opportunities. Alternatively, a world-systems perspective emphasizes the *relational* character of the economic transformations that have alternatively led to economic growth and/or stagnation. "Success" and "failure," from such a perspective, are related outcomes of a *singular* process of world-economic accumulation.

Historically, social and economic rigidities and institutional constraints operating in some areas of the world-economy have generated competitive opportunities that could be exploited by enterprises and state agencies in countries where innovations could be adopted relatively free from these rigidities and constraints.[14] These innovations sometimes have involved new organizational linkages to production and/or market niches within Global Commodity Chains (GCCs).[15] Innovative practices, however, have not been limited to enterprises, as they often have involved the organization of state regulation around new strategic objectives.

This type of focus on innovation allows us to emphasize the relational character of world-economic processes, thus focusing on the spatial dimensions of the processes of competition and exploitation shaping GCCs.[16] Such a perspective primarily emphasizes the fact that the relative command over wealth secured by specific patterns of organization and exchange (or by particular configurations of production processes, commodities, and services) is likely to change significantly over time. In this sense, successful growth policies in the 1980s and 1990s, as generated by both enterprises and states, have been characterized, not by specific forms of organizing production and/or trade, but by the organizational capacity to mold and shift strategic goals according to rapidly changing opportunities and constraints. The nature and characteristics of these patterns must be assessed empirically, which is the concern of several of the articles in this volume.

Amy E. Bellone, for example, carries out a detailed study of the organization of the cocaine commodity chain in Chapter 2. As in previous world-system studies of this chain (e.g., Wilson and Zambrano, 1994), Bellone points out that although the final product within this commodity chain commands a high value, wealth is very unevenly distributed within the chain. Overall, growers and agents involved in the earlier, labor-intensive stages of production and distribution are able to capture only a relatively small share of profit. However, some agents have been more successful than others in extending their role and share of profits. To illustrate this point, and also to identify the characteristics that made some agents more successful than others, Bellone compares coca producers in Bolivia and Peru. She indicates that these efforts by farmers and intermediaries to expand their role were often well received by the actors involved in the higher stages of refining and distribution, for risks were more diffused by the active role of small firms. However, Bolivian producers were better able than their Peruvian counterparts to control the refining of coca paste into cocaine. Bellone argues that this was because in Bolivia, there was an already-existing group of local elites in possession of the trade networks and capital required to engage in refining.

Changing patterns of competitive pressures are also highlighted in Chapter 3 by Miguel E. Korzeniewicz. The author begins by focusing on the success of Brazilian shoe manufacturers in capturing substantial niches in the global shoe market. He draws a comparison to shoe producers in Argentina in order to highlight several variables that help account for the comparative success of Brazilian producers. First, their concentration in geographically specific industrial districts has facilitated the emergence of organizations and informal ties that facilitated collective action on behalf of their interests. Second, a growing specialization in women's shoes allowed these shoe producers to target production to a specific world market niche. Third, the state played an important role in promoting these exports. Finally, Brazilian business firms were particularly successful in developing effective linkages, both backward (e.g., securing access to raw materials and labor) and forward (e.g., developing formal channels for marketing and distribution). However, although organizational choices along each of these dimensions served to enhance the competitiveness of Brazilian shoe producers prior to the 1990s, Korzeniewicz observes that this competitive edge began to erode in the 1990s, as producers in other countries (such as mainland China) made significant inroads in the market niches in question.

In Chapter 4, David Spener enhances our understanding of the competitive pressures that characterize GCCs by highlighting the importance of social capital in providing competitive advantages to small firms. As indicated by the author, "ethnic Mexican entrepreneurs' reliance on transborder social capital to extend commodity chains from the United States into Mexico was as much a strategy to compensate for their lack of other kinds of capital—human, physical, and financial—as it was a strategy that built on their natural strengths." Spener's study helps us to develop a better understanding of the conditions that are likely to strengthen and weaken this type of social capital: with the North American Free Trade Agreement (NAFTA), for example, as "state rules are lifted or made less stringent, the demand for the kinds of social network conditions that permitted the circumvention of the old trade barriers is reduced." Social capital is very important, but it is more unstable and vulnerable than usually assumed in the literature.

In Chapter 13, Alvaro Díaz tackles the case of Chile, which (along with Colombia, as indicated in Table 1.1) was among the few countries in Latin America to experience economic growth during the 1980s; moreover, high rates of growth have prevailed in the 1990s. The Chilean case has often become appealing as a model of development because its trajectory since the early 1980s can be used to justify the often-painful costs of adjustment and restructuring as temporary, and yet necessary, steps on the road to economic recovery. After all, in the early 1980s, Chile was characterized both by stagnant economic growth and by rapidly growing unemployment and poverty. In the 1980s, however, rates of economic growth achieved record heights, unemployment and poverty rates underwent a steady decline, and real wages grew rather substantially from the troughs they had reached in the early 1980s. Nevertheless, overall levels of income inequality remain essentially unchanged (Raczynski and Romaguera, 1995).

The Chilean case has been hailed as a model of development in order to emphasize the need to use exports as a platform for economic growth, to replace the state regulation of economic activities with entrepreneurial efforts regulated primarily by the market, and to reshape the political sphere so that state policies cease to respond to centralized decision making, unproductive rent seekers, and particularistic claims on resources. Advocates of the model claim that it alone provides the substantial reforms necessary to sustain economic development into the twenty-first century. Opponents of the model, however, argue that its social costs were such that they could only be incurred in Chile by a military dictatorship, and that efforts to implement a similar model under democratic regimes are only likely to undermine democratic rule by generating profound discontent or undermining the historical rights endowed by citizenship (Vergara, 1986, 1994).

Díaz suggests that the very success of strategies of economic growth in Chile is generating new constraints. First, while the adoption of technological and organizational innovations has provided enterprises in Chile with a considerable competitive edge in world markets, the very growth of exports and the accompanying influx in foreign investments have exposed the country to "Dutch Disease," in which the overvaluation of the currency can have a severe negative impact on other economic activities (particularly manufacturing). Second, income distribution remains highly skewed, an asymmetry that may undermine the future pace of economic growth. Finally, the persistence of many of the same authoritarian enclaves that allowed for the initial implementation of the prevailing model of economic growth may undermine the ability to continue the political and institutional reforms required for continued growth. These constraints represent a growing asymmetry between internationalization and democratic transition, on the one hand, and on the other, "the rigidity and obsolescence of the political and economic institutions inherited from the previous authoritarian regime and its neoliberal economic policies." Resolving such an asymmetry, according to Díaz, will be required to consolidate economic growth and deepen democracy.

The insights gained from these chapters on patterns of competition speak for caution in endorsing export strategies as the centerpiece of a model for economic growth. Furthermore, the magnitude of the changes required to *initiate* an export-centered strategy of growth in countries such as Argentina, Brazil, or Mexico (where exports account for a relatively small proportion of overall economic activity) is likely to be significantly greater than the *maintenance* of such a strategy is in countries such as Chile or Costa Rica, where exports have come to play a central role in the overall economy.[17] Furthermore, the overall size of the economy in countries such as Argentina, Mexico, or Brazil implies that increasing the relative importance of exports to the degree achieved in countries such as Chile would require a much larger transformation.

The promise that wealth would be forthcoming through the adoption of specific combinations of production processes, trade patterns, and institutional arrangements has often encouraged enterprises and states to pursue an impossible race. In fact, this was the most important lesson drawn from the failure of postwar industrialization to deliver greater approximation to the standards of wealth enjoyed in high-income or core nations (Arrighi, 1991). If greater control over wealth has been an outcome of innovation rather than specific commodities or production processes, there is no single model or specific strategy to be derived from the successful experiences (e.g., East Asia, Spain, or Chile).[18] In fact, the very implementation of innovative practices initiates their diffusion, their inevitable (albeit eventual) elimination as innovations, and the emergence of new technological, organizational, and institutional rigidities. However, this skepticism regarding the ability of the world-economy to deliver a more even distribution of wealth between nations in the near future should not distract us from the profound changes accompanying economic restructuring.

One of the most significant changes has involved the emergence of new world-economic organizational networks coordinating the production and distribution of goods and services. Observers in recent decades have frequently proclaimed these global economic networks to constitute a "new international division of labor" and have generally attributed the creation of these linkages to the action of multinational enterprises based in core countries. Regardless of the extent to which this "international division of labor" is actually "new" (such an argument is certainly challenged by the world-systems literature), the chapters in this volume suggest that enterprises in peripheral and semiperipheral nations should also be considered as crucial actors in the creation of these new arrangements.[19]

To some extent, the new role of peripheral and semiperipheral enterprises within GCCs is linked to changes in the organization of markets (hence following Adam Smith's dictum that the division of labor is determined by the extent of the market). Future world-systems research, however, might explore the degree to which the extent of markets is itself a consequence of the space allowed by an existing division of labor. In this sense, comparatively slow organizational changes among local enterprises outside the core prior to the 1980s might have prepared the terrain for the accelerated transformations of the 1980s and 1990s.[20]

Both Bellone and Korzeniewicz suggest in their respective chapters that the adoption of organizational innovations allowed local enterprises to capture important production niches within GCCs. Corroborating the findings of the broader literature on export strategies in East Asia, these contributions also suggest that local enterprises play an active role in gaining greater access to core markets (either directly or by developing new links to multinational corporations). However, beyond the crucial role of these local enterprises in allowing for the formation of the new production and distribution networks that are often characterized as a "new" internationalization, networks of peripheral and semiperipheral enterprises might themselves be moving in the direction of becoming large multinational corporations. For example, large business conglomerates in Chile have used direct foreign investments to expand elsewhere in the continent (particularly in Argentina, Bolivia, and Peru). As suggested in this volume and elsewhere by Alvaro Díaz (1996), the new control gained by these enterprises over processes of accumulation (following restructuring and privatization), represents, not so much a growing prevalence of market arrangements, but a shift from one type of command (as previously exercised by state agencies) to another (as currently deployed by large corporations).

THE LOGIC OF RULE AND THE RECASTING OF STATE POWER

Although states play an important role in shaping processes of accumulation, they are often driven by the dynamics of a separate logic of rule. As indicated by Arrighi (1994) in his recent contribution to world-systems theory, the relationship between accumulation and rule can be more effectively probed by acknowledging these distinctions. The essays included in this collection make an important contribution in probing the logic and processes of rule and the recasting of state power at different levels of action and organization.

In Chapter 9, Bruce M. Podobnik uses a comparison between Peru and Cambodia to probe the processes giving rise to revolutionary violence. He argues that the emergence and expansion of the Khmer Rouge in Cambodia and the Shining Path in Peru were tied to the linkage between sectarian dissident groups and a generation of youth that found few employment opportunities. A political vacuum (resulting, to some extent, from the failure of reformist efforts in previous decades) and the existence of institutional and geographical spaces (such as universities or isolated rural areas) allowed for the relatively free operation of the new groups. Regardless of the relative appeal or rejection inspired by the organizations involved, Podobnik suggests that revolutionary violence will remain one of the forms adopted by those in resistance to world-economic processes of accumulation and rule.

Dealing with a different arena of political demands, J. Timmons Roberts, in Chapter 10, focuses on the current deterioration of the environment in Latin America. Roberts indicates that this deterioration can be traced back at least to import-substitution industrialization and argues that future changes in environmental conditions will be shaped by several variables. For example, the initiatives associated with export-led strategies of growth certainly have a potential for further environmental degradation, but economic growth might generate resources that can be channeled (given sufficient pressure from interested parties) to improve the environment. A similar ambivalence is likely to result from the adoption of global environmental standards (for example, as dictated in international trade agreements). Most important, according to Roberts, will be the pressures brought to bear on governments, enterprises, and state agencies by an environmental social movement that has become increasingly international in character.

Such a perspective, which calls attention to the unhinging of the logic of rule from the logic of accumulation, can play an important role in clarifying contemporary political changes and the impact of market-oriented restructuring. In Chapter 11, A. Douglas Kincaid and Eduardo A. Gamarra examine the political challenges stemming from the illegality, huge profits, and violence manifested, for example, in Brazilian *favela* gangs or Bolivian coca growers. They argue that efforts to come to terms with the interaction between drug-trafficking networks and the erosion of state capacity, both of which are manifestations of particularly perverse forms of integration into the world-economy, are key to understanding emergent patterns of reorganization of the means of violence. A chief characteristic of a "new Latin American mode of public security," according to the authors, is growing recourse to military intervention in support, or in place, of the conventional roles of the police. Their case studies of Bolivia, Brazil, and Honduras probe three fundamental features of this redefinition of state and the market with regard to the provision of public security: a process of *militarization*, in which threats of major civic disorder are repressed but crime flourishes and citizen security erodes; a simultaneous *informalization* of some security functions, including the formation of paramilitary neighborhood groups and the rise of a "parallel state" of shantytown criminal organizations; and a *privatization* of security as a commodity to be purchased on the market by the privileged and powerful. Kincaid and Gamarra warn that despite initiatives to promote the demilitarization of public security, the toll exacted by neoliberal reforms and the transnational drug economy threatens to bring about a generalization of public disorder that will prove deeply inimical to democratic politics.[21]

A more nuanced understanding of the relations between the logics of accumulation and rule can also contribute to a more adequate interpretation of the recasting of state power as national political institutions are whipsawed between the growing hegemony of marketplace logic, which is reinforced by the exigencies of the world-economy, and by pressures to expand citizenship rights and popular participation. It is generally recognized that the collision between globalization and national and local actors has resulted in a sharp erosion of the national state's capacity to manage major macroeconomic variables. The difficulty is that such affirmations to the effect that state power is "weakening" actually say very little.[22]

Underlying the question of state and societal power, there is, in fact, a striking contradiction (Kahler, 1990, 1992; Bierstekker, 1995). On the one hand, neo-utilitarian and neoclassical prescriptions call for rolling back the state and weakening governmental mechanisms of macroeconomic regulation; on the other hand, the state apparatus must argument its power capabilities to impose a market-driven model of accumulation under conditions of growing globalization and intranational competition. Greater economic orthodoxy, under these circumstances, may well require, not less, but *more* autonomy, particularly from specific entrepreneurial and trade union interests. Similarly, greater orthodoxy may imply, not less, but *more* effective coordination and regulation of the private sector (e.g., overseeing the stock and financial markets, broadening the tax base, upgrading skills of workers, promoting technological innovations and competitiveness, and so on). Similarly, "market-friendly" growth strategies frequently seem to go hand-in-hand with the concentration of augmented administrative power in the hands of state managers and technocratic elites.[23]

To go beyond a simple recognition of this neoliberal paradox, we need carefully crafted comparative studies of state reform focusing on particular agencies and institutional arrangements. Sergio Berensztein's discussion of taxation policies in Chapter 12 is a valuable example of this needed research. Berensztein eschews the Manichean rhetoric surrounding the debate on neoliberalism and the state in which some tout the efficiency of international financial markets while others warn that the implacable discipline imposed by the globalization of financial flows has deprived states—even those at the core of the world-economy—of the instruments and resources to regulate the economy. Without ignoring these constraints, the author focuses on the institutional design of the semiperipheral Latin American states. On the basis of a detailed analysis of fiscal reforms in Argentina and Mexico, the author argues that theoretical perspectives emphasizing shifts in the international division of labor, the peripheralization of industrial activities, and the logic of competition in the world-economy should give greater weight to the continuing importance of domestic actors, state agencies, and processes of rule. By the same token, however, Berensztein is fully cognizant of the fragility of institutional reforms intended to enhance state capacity. Of course, as the Mexican collapse of 1994 reminds us, speculative movements of capital can wreak havoc in the form of recessions and political instability, and rising interest rates can spark a surge of tax evasion capable of threatening to reverse all efforts to bolster state capacity.[24]

These chapters illustrate that, while obeying their own separate dynamics, the logic of accumulation and the logic of rule clearly remain intertwined. Seen from this perspective, the recasting of the state in Latin America should be understood, not merely in terms of the shrinkage and more "efficient" operation of state administrative agencies, but as a manifestation of a more fundamental redrawing of the existing boundaries between "politics" and "economics" and between the "public" and the "private." This will be a wrenching experience during which many organized societal interests are, in effect, "expelled" from the regulated spheres to fend for themselves as individuals in the market.[25] A state more impermeable to societal demands will require a more "authoritative" administrative apparatus capable of neutralizing the reaction of adversely affected groups. The concentration of power in the executive agencies of the state (characterized by *decretazos*, or presidential decrees, of dubious legality and with clear authoritarian overtones), which is characteristic of current market-oriented reforms in Latin America, highlights a central aspect of the political and economic dynamics present in the transition from the Keynesian and Fordist modes of reproduction of consent to more "liberal" models of accumulation and of political domination and rule.

However, once the transition has been completed, will the state be stronger or weaker than before the market-driven restructuring? In all likelihood, state institutions and public authority in the future will be *both* stronger and weaker.[26] Depending on the specific issue area or public policy arena, for example, neoliberal restructuring may lead to a severe retrenchment of the public sphere's traditional "entrepreneurial" functions that are related to direct ownership and the management of productive enterprises, thus resulting in a smaller and much "weaker" state apparatus. Simultaneously, however, in other arenas, such as the capacity of civilian elites to exercise civilian control over the armed forces (e.g., formulation of national security policies, severe cuts in military budgets, and so on) or to impose labor market flexibilization and other restrictions on the prerogatives of workers and trade unions, public authority may be strengthened significantly, surpassing even the power and autonomy achieved by state elites during earlier populist and authoritarian periods. Even with respect to the market, it is not clear that neoliberal strategies necessarily imply a weaker state. For example, in order for markets to function properly and with the efficiency and transparency required by private investors, strong legal norms protecting private property must be guaranteed and effective mechanisms of state regulation that were previously absent must be put into place.

These observations make it clear that rather than trying to formulate overarching generalizations regarding the relative strength of the state in Latin America following restructuring, it will be fruitful for future empirical research to examine particular state agencies and specific public arenas.[27] The key role of local actors and institutional arrangements across the region should be stressed, but without losing sight of the fact that the dynamics and logic informing the choices of local actors and the recasting of state power necessarily incorporate transformations in the world-economy.

EVALUATING HOUSEHOLDS, COMMUNITIES, AND RESISTANCE

Some observers attribute growing poverty and income inequality to changes in the structure of production. Clearly, and particularly among the wealthiest Latin American countries, manufacturing and industrial activities lost relative importance to services.[28] In Argentina, for example, the share of industry in the gross domestic product declined from 44 percent in 1970 to 31 percent by 1993 (and manufacturing, from 32 percent to 20 percent during the same period), while services enhanced their share from 47 percent to 63 percent over the same years. Similar patterns, albeit with different degrees of intensity, can be observed in Uruguay, Chile, and Brazil (World Bank 1995: 166–167). In effect, such trends constitute a form of deindustrialization that is strikingly familiar to any observer acquainted with the dramatic decline of industrial job opportunities in the Rust Belt of the United States or similar regions elsewhere in the core of the world-economy.[29]

Other analysts have sought to emphasize the relationship between social welfare and alternative long-term and short-term variables. As a long-run determinant of social welfare, some have sought to emphasize the crucial importance of education (Morley, 1994, 1995a, 1995b). The World Bank, for example, noted that "education is the most important single variable influencing income inequality," and asserted that "when markets work well, greater equity often comes naturally" (1991: 138). As a short-term determinant of social welfare, this interpretation emphasizes the importance of economic growth. Hence, Morley, for example, has argued that in the short term, "changes in the level of per capita income are the key determinants of changes in the level of poverty" (1994: 1).[30]

One of the most striking features of recent patterns of economic and political change in Latin America is the fact that the growth of poverty and unemployment, as well as rising income inequality, have often been accompanied by a demobilization of civil society. In Chapter 13, for example, Díaz refers to "the (apparent) silence of civil society" in Chile (see also Tironi, 1986). The author calls our attention to the fact that economic restructuring involves both an initial decomposition of existing social and political arrangements and the eventual ascendance of new social and political actors. He suggests that in the case of Chile, the highest levels of collective organization and mobilization have characterized the areas most affected by recession or decline. By the same token, areas characterized by rapid growth and profound social recomposition have so far been characterized by lower levels of mobilization—an outcome, for Díaz, of the "inchoate" character of "collective social actors still in the process of formation."[31]

Distinguishing the social impact of economic restructuring in terms of demobilization and recomposition makes sense within a world-systems analytical framework that has often emphasized differences in the types of resistance elicited by exclusion as opposed to exploitation (e.g., Arrighi, 1978: 20). Such a line of analysis opens interesting areas of research on current patterns of mobilization and protest. Are protest movements in Chiapas or the provinces of the interior of Argentina indicative of the type of resistance associated with areas in economic decline? Does the new importance of transnational NGOs (e.g., organized around gender or environmental issues) reflect new modes of organization among the social actors most affected by processes of growth and reconstitution?

Several chapters in this volume focus on alternative efforts by households to gain greater leverage. In Chapter 5, José Itzigsohn focuses on economic strategies within the informal sector, differentiating four types of activities: petty marketers, suppliers, subcontractors, and the informal proletariat. To what extent do linkages to multinationals prevail in the new informal economy of the 1980 and 1990s, and to what extent are different patterns associated to the extent of state regulation? Itzigsohn calls for a nuanced study of these issues, as market conditions (for labor and products) and patterns of state regulation vary a great deal across different types of economic activities. Thus, product market opportunities are restricted for Costa Rican garment producers (who move into supplying and subcontracting arrangements), but not for their Dominican counterparts (who have greater bargaining power due to the existence of alternative outlets). For craft producers oriented to the tourist trade, on the other hand, state regulations lead to a restricted market for Dominican producers, while greater opportunities enhance the bargaining power of their Costa Rican counterparts. Thus, the ability of producers to maintain autonomy and capture a greater share of income is related to their relative bargaining power vis-à-vis purchasers.

In fact, the strategies adopted within the informal sector bear considerable similarity to the entrepreneurial strategies reviewed in the first section of this chapter. In both cases, "success" entails the adoption of organizational strategies that can exploit the opportunities and constraints of prevailing institutional arrangements. The successful deployment of such a strategy suggests that what is generally read as a "silence" of civil society might actually reflect the viability (under current conditions and for some sectors of the population) of what Albert Hirshman (1970, 1994) would characterize as an exercise of "exit" rather than "voice."

An alternative form of practicing the "exit" option involves migration, and several of the chapters included in this volume analyze patterns of change in this particular arena. For example, Susanne Jonas, in Chapter 6, argues that the migration patterns of some Latino communities (such as those of Salvadorans or Guatemalans) are transforming certain regions into "trinational spaces" that include the home countries of these migrants, Mexico, and areas of the United States. Furthermore, Jonas argues that these transnational spaces are constructed through informal networks that are particularly impervious to state regulation, and for this reason, she expresses skepticism regarding the likelihood that current efforts in the United States to restrict migration from Latin America will succeed in their larger objective. Jonas also warns that such policies might lead to exclusionary politics that restrict the practice of citizenship among important sectors of the population and undermine more generally the consolidation of democratic practices in the region as a whole, including the United States.

In Chapter 8, reproducing his noteworthy keynote address to the PEWS conference, Alejandro Portes argues that the current emphasis on processes leading to the globalization of capital should be complemented with a better understanding of the constitution of transnational communities. While analyses of transnationalization generally emphasize how geographic mobility enhances the bargaining power of capital, Portes seeks to call equal attention to the manner in which communities may use migration to exploit the opportunities that result from "the differentials of advantage created by political boundaries." These opportunities are generally exploited through "grassroots transnational enterprises" that rely on informal social ties centered around kin and friendship networks. For Portes, this is a relatively new phenomenon in both scale and relative importance. The potential significance of these communities is that they might serve to challenge "a strategy of capitalist accumulation based on wage differential and information asymmetries between different regions of the world."

Focusing on Garifuna migration to the Los Angeles metropolitan area, Linda Miller Matthei and David A. Smith, in Chapter 7, argue that gender relations constitute a crucial dimension of the way in which households participate in the world-economy. Their chapter highlights shifting migration patterns, characterized by declining opportunities for male workers (as a consequence of falling demand for manufacturing labor) but rising opportunities for female workers (particularly in service occupations and new types of manufacturing jobs). According to the authors, networks developed among women allowed their households (and the individuals contain therein) to expand their social capital and served as transnational linkages to the United States. These networks often included child care in Belize when parents migrate to the United States (in exchange for a share of remittances). In short, households appear as active as enterprises in constructing the transnational linkages that have emerged as a striking feature of recent decades.

A focus on shifts in the construction of gender is particularly important to understanding social movements and communities of resistance. Much of the theorizing on social movements in Latin America was built on the specific features that these movements appeared to exhibit through the course of the twentieth century: they seemed to be built primarily around class interests, they were geared primarily to alter the rule of states, and their principal sphere of action appeared to involve a public (rather than private) arena. The incorporation of gender as an important (if not central) concern in the contemporary social sciences has led to a reevaluation of these premises, highlighting the importance of cleavages other than class in guiding the construction of social identities, probing into the crucial impact on politics of everyday and informal organizational networks, and challenging the boundaries between public and private arenas (Bose and Acosta-Belén, 1995; Folbre, 1994; Jaquette, 1989; Jelin, 1990; Moser, 1993; Ward, 1993). This shifting analytical focus does not merely make visible what was always there, but also responds to a shift to women as the epicenter of a different "kind" of transnational community (Forsythe, 1995).

CONCLUSION

The institutional arrangements that prevailed in Latin America for most of the postwar period are being disassembled at a precipitous pace, to be replaced by a deepening differentiation in the arenas of operation of enterprises, states, and households (Korzeniewicz, 1996). Enterprises appear to exercise greater control over processes of accumulation, in a shift that has entailed the organization of new networks linking production and market niches within global commodity chains.[32] However, the adoption of neoliberal strategies does not necessarily imply a weaker state, as state agencies generally become involved in implementing effective mechanisms of state regulation and strong legal norms guaranteeing private property. Markets, in this sense, continue to require state regulation for their very survival. Social actors affected by such changes seek to maintain or enhance their relative bargaining power by alternatively moving among strategies designed to enhance "exit" and/or "voice" options.

These institutional transformations are reshaping the fundamental questions that currently guide intellectual discourse in the social sciences. What is the path to sustainable growth, and through what mechanisms can it ensure improvements in social welfare? What is the likely future of democracy, and to what extent does its strength depend on the practice of citizenship and the assertion of social rights? What are the new categories of identity emerging in the region, and to what extent are they likely to promote either existing or new social movements? In short, what are the crucial elements of the new constellation of institutional arrangements and social practices currently emerging in Latin America?

Returning to a question posed earlier in this chapter, the magnitude and simultaneity of the changes at hand do reveal a critical juncture that closely resembles a "Great Transformation" of Latin America. However, it is far too early to assess the extent to which new institutional arrangements and social practices will come to revolve around a self-regulated market "directed by market prices and nothing but market prices" (Polanyi, 1957: 43), or what will be the precise role of the state and political institutions in regulating the production and distribution of wealth. A world-systems perspective, with its emphasis on space and time as delineating the boundaries of change, does not offer definitive predictions but suggests instead useful and interesting ways of raising the pertinent questions, expecting the answers to be contingent on the courses of action and strategic choices adopted by the relevant actors.

NOTES

This chapter has benefited from comments by Nancy Forsythe and Aldo Vacs.

1. See Cavarozzi (1992, 1994) for illuminating analyses of the collapse of state-centric models of development. For authoritative statements of the so-called "Washington Consensus," see Williamson (1990a, 1993). See Fannelli, Frenkel, and Rozenwurcel (1994) and Bresser Pereira, Maravall, and Przeworski (1994) for criticisms.

2. Douglass North, who is grounded in neoclassical economics and focuses on the analysis of transaction costs, argues: "Institutions are the rules of the game in a society or, more formally, are the humanly devised constraints that shape human interaction. In consequence they structure incentives in human exchange, whether political, social, or economic" (1990: 3). A more "sociological" definition is advanced both by the French

Regulation school (e.g., Aglietta, 1979; Brenner and Glick, 1991) and the "social structures of accumulation" (SSA) school, which is advanced by some U.S. economists (cf. Kotz, McDonough, and Reich, 1994).

3. The data suggest differences between urban and rural areas during the 1980s, as in several countries (e.g., Argentina, Brazil, Costa Rica, Guatemala, Mexico, and Peru) poverty indicators rose in urban areas while declining in rural areas (CEPAL, 1992: 6). Moreover, while the *relative* incidence of poverty is still generally higher in rural areas, most of the poor in Latin America today reside in urban areas.

4. Similar conclusions had been provided earlier in a preliminary report of the World Bank that included Samuel Morley as an author (see Psacharopoulos et al., 1993).

5. For a review of the variety of political and economic features (e.g., hyperinflation, the political "honeymoon," etc.) that facilitate the adoption of free-market reforms, see Williamson and Haggard (1994).

6. For a discussion of recent transitions in southern and Eastern Europe and Latin America that call attention to these points, see Linz and Stepan (1991) and Przeworski (1991). See Acuña and Smith (1994) for an analysis focusing on the microfoundations of individual and collective responses under conditions of market-oriented structuring implemented by democratic regimes.

7. See Vacs (1994a) for a detailed exploration of these questions, which contrasts the contemporary period with earlier waves of democratization.

8. Roberts (1995) provides an extensive discussion of the similarities and differences between the classic populism of Juan Perón, Getúlio Vargas, and Lázaro Cárdenas, and the recent "new caudillos," such as Carlos Menem, Fernando Collor de Mello, Carlos Salinas, and Alberto Fujimori. In addition, useful analyses of the affinity between neoliberal reform and this new-style neopopulism can be found in Zermeño (1989, 1996), Dresser (1991), Cavarozzi (1994), Vacs (1994b), and Weyland (1994). For a broader analysis of the collapse of the "national-popular" model in Latin America and its consequences for modes of rule, see Touraine (1989).

9. Guillermo O'Donnell's recent work (1994a, 1994b, 1996) offers a provocative theorization of what he refers to as "informally institutionalized" polyarchies.

10. For detailed analyses of neoliberal reform and democratization in Argentina, Bolivia, Brazil, Chile, and Mexico, see the country studies in Smith, Acuña, and Gamarra (1994). On Venezuela, see Karl (1995) and McCoy and Smith (1995); and on Peru, see Roberts (1995), Mauceri (1995), and Pastor and Wise (1992). For a provocative treatment of the Andean region, which stresses broader comparative implications, see Conaghan and Malloy (1995).

11. Polanyi argued that in all modes of social organization prior to the nineteenth century, human interactions (e.g., economic transactions) had been regulated through customary moral arrangements, maintaining economies "submerged in . . . social relationships" (1957: 46). The Great Transformation of the nineteenth century involved the construction of a self-regulated market, with transactions becoming "directed by market prices and nothing but market prices" (1957: 43), and where "social relations are embedded in the economic system" (1957: 57). This self-regulating market revolved around three principal commodities (labor, land, and money), which were entirely fictitious, in that "[n]one of them is produced for sale" (Polanyi, 1957: 72). The use of these resources as commodities "subordinate[d] the substance of society itself to the laws of the market" (Polanyi, 1957: 71).

12. This model of development, which emphasizes industrialization as a key engine

of growth, also suggests rather clear paths of political transformation. Both the modernization and dependency literatures, for example, have tended to agree that industrialization should produce the various agents that would generate democracy over the long run. Of course, there were crucial differences in the interpretation of who were the key new agents of democratization (e.g., the middle class or the labor movement) and in their view of what would be the final appearance of democratic rule (e.g., capitalism with electoral democracy or socialism with "popular participation"). Most interpreters agreed, however, that industrialization and economic growth would generate or strengthen precisely those social classes, interest groups, and organizations that would, over the long run, promote greater electoral participation or generate more democratic styles of policy making and state organization (O'Donnell, 1973; Borón, 1977, 1995; Moore, 1966; de Schweinitz, 1964; Dos Santos, 1971).

13. There is a long tradition of studies that have emphasized the active role played by states in promoting industrialization among the later-developed nations (Hirschman, 1965; Gershenkron, 1962; de Schweinitz, 1964). Later, similar notions were incorporated into the literature on dependent development (Evans, 1979; Cardoso and Faletto, 1979) and the Bureaucratic-Authoritarian state (O'Donnell, 1973; Collier, 1979), as well as into literature on developmental states (Amsden, 1989; Evans, 1995; Wade, 1990).

14. To draw on Hirschman, "[T]he very process of decline activates certain counterforces" (1970: 4).

15. These GCCs are networks of households, enterprises, and states that serve to articulate production, distribution, and consumption as world-economic processes. Within these networks, the ability of individuals and organizations to appropriate wealth is unevenly distributed (Wallerstein, 1983; Hopkins and Wallerstein, 1986; Gereffi, Korzeniewicz, and Korzeniewicz, 1994; as well as the essays in Gereffi and Korzeniewicz, 1994). On innovations as new patterns of state regulation, see Cumings (1984) and Wade (1990).

16. Within these networks, production processes and commodities "have had 'production cycles,' starting off as core products and eventually becoming peripheral products" (Wallerstein, 1983: 36; see also Cumings, 1984; Arrighi and Drangel, 1986; Arrighi, 1991). This interpretation shares similarities with Schumpeter (1934, 1942), for whom innovative processes were at the root of the "creative destruction" that characterizes capitalism as a system. More recently, this focus on innovation (rather than industrialization) as the basis for comparative advantages in the world-economy has been at the fore of influential studies on economic organization (Vernon, 1979; Porter, 1985, 1990).

17. In Argentina, the value of exports rose 61.6 percent between 1984 and 1993 (from $8.1 to $13.1 billion), but accounted for a mere 5.1 percent of GDP by 1993. Likewise, exports in 1993 accounted for merely 8.7 percent of GDP in Brazil, 8.8 percent in Mexico, and 8.3 percent in Peru. On the other hand, in Chile, for example, the value of exports rose 152.1 percent between 1884 and 1993 (from $3.6 to $9.2 billion), to account for 21.4 percent of GDP by 1993 (likewise, exports account for 22.1 percent of GDP in Venezuela, and 38.4 percent of GDP in Costa Rica) (World Bank, 1995).

18. Even within countries, efforts to imitate successful strategies will often fail to produce the expected results. For example, farmers in Chile in the early 1990s sought to replicate the successful experience of grape exporters by engaging in kiwi production, but the outcome was a world glut and falling prices of kiwis in subsequent years.

19. This is not to diminish the role that the reduction of exchange risks has played in increasing the willingness of global investors to expand their exposure in Latin American markets.

20. For example, this is the argument implicit in Evans (1995), who discusses the role of local firms, in the 1990s, in allowing for new linkages to transnational corporations.

21. Likewise, Bellone, in Chapter 2, suggests that core-like activities may be pursued by organizations that challenge the monopoly of the state over the means of violence.

22. In fact, such generalizations obscure differences between those countries in which the state is unable to carry out the neoliberal policies favored by state elites and others in which, notwithstanding its "weakening," the state still possesses sufficient power to impose economic reform and disarticulate unruly social actors. See Acuña and Smith (1994) for an effort to rethink the relation between politics and economics in the context of economic restructuring.

23. For a discussion of the neoliberal prescriptions for shrinking the state advanced by the International Monetary Fund and the World Bank, see Bierstekker (1990).

24. In view of Latin America's recent authoritarian past (and the persistence of authoritarian enclaves under the current democracies), many critics of economic orthodoxy are perhaps rightly suspicious of the recent discovery (by institutions such as the World Bank) of the need for augmented state capacity. Nevertheless, as O'Donnell (1994b) has pointed out, the sharp erosion of the "state-as-law" in Latin America and the former socialist bloc vitiates any notion of genuine democratic politics and is particularly detrimental to the poor and powerless, who are left to the predations of powerful and unaccountable political elites and economically dominant classes.

25. The social and economic intervention of the Keynesian welfare state blurred the "liberal" limits between politics and economics and between the public and private spheres. As Offe (1974, 1975, 1984) and Przeworski (1990) have pointed out, this intervention (in fiscal and monetary policy, public investment, labor market regulation, educational and social welfare policies, the public production of goods and services, and so on) removed the market as the main mechanism for the resolution of conflicts of interest, and placed them under state tutelage in response to priorities determined by political and electoral objectives. The post-1930s politicization of the market prompted the mobilization and organization of societal interests to influence state policies. Conversely, the marketization of politics in the contemporary period frequently results in the erosion of traditional collective identities and the disarticulation of political and social organization, along with a decline in capacities for collective action. See Acuña and Smith (1994), Díaz (1996), and Zermeño (1996) for discussions of the implications of these trends for democratic politics in Latin America.

26. A (physically) "smaller" state can be "weaker" (control fewer resources, lose entrepreneurial functions, etc.) but simultaneously more autonomous, more coherent, and more effective in regulating macroeconomic and microeconomic behaviors. For an evaluation of some of these issues, see Huber (1995).

27. In carrying forth this effort, much is to be gained by developing closer linkages between the world-systems literature and other critical theoretical perspectives, such as those developed in international political economy or the field of economics proper.

28. Among the poorer Latin American countries, despite the explosion of the tertiary sector, the share of industrial and manufacturing activities has continued to increase, particularly in relation to a declining agricultural sector.

29. Such trends have generated a considerable amount of literature focusing on the impact of economic adjustment programs on household reproductive strategies (e.g., Benería and Roldán, 1987; De Vos, 1987; Folbre, 1994; García and Oliveira, 1994; Jelin, 1991; Moser, 1993; Pérez-Sáinz and Menjívar Larín, 1994; Roberts, 1994).

30. Regardless of the analytical framework used to explain trends in poverty and income distribution, the literature at hand suggests a noticeable shift in the underlying agenda. Partly as an outcome of the resource constraints imposed by structural reforms, but also reflecting some of the concerns raised by NGOs at both the local and international levels, the social sciences in Latin America have begun to evaluate more systematically the extent to which social programs funded by states can effectively reach their intended beneficiaries (e.g., the "truly disadvantaged").

31. On the possibilities of collective action under neoliberal restructuring, see Díaz (1996), Roxborough (1996), and Acuña and Smith (1994).

32. As suggested by scholars such as Arrighi (1995), the emergence of these new networks are also indicative of a broader shift in hegemony from the United States to Asia.

REFERENCES

Acuña, Carlos H. 1994. "Politics and Economics in the Argentina of the Nineties (Or Why the Future No Longer Is What It Used to Be)." In *Democracy, Markets, and Structural Reform in Latin America: Argentina, Bolivia, Brazil, Chile, and Mexico*, ed. William C. Smith, Carlos H. Acuña, and Eduardo A. Gamarra, pp. 31–74. New Brunswick, NJ: North-South Center/Transaction.

Acuña, Carlos H., and William C. Smith. 1994. "The Political Economy of Structural Adjustment: The Logic of Support and Opposition to Neoliberal Reform." In *Latin American Political Economy in the Age of Neoliberal Reform: Theoretical and Comparative Perspectives for the 1990s*, ed. William C. Smith, Carlos H. Acuña, and Eduardo A. Gamarra, pp. 17–66. New Brunswick, NJ: North-South Center/Transaction.

Aglietta, Michel. 1979. *A Theory of Capitalist Regulation: The U.S. Experience*. London: Verso.

Amsden, Alice H. 1989. *Asia's Next Giant: South Korea and Late Industrialization*. New York: Oxford University Press.

Appelbaum, Richard P., and Jeffrey Henderson, eds. 1992. *States and Development in the Asian Pacific Rim*. Newbury Park, CA: Sage.

Arrighi, Giovanni. 1978. "Towards a Theory of Capitalist Crisis." *New Left Review* 111: 3–24.

———. 1991. "World Income Inequalities and the Future of Socialism." *New Left Review* 189: 39–65.

———. 1994. *The Long Twentieth Century: Money, Power, and the Origins of Our Times*. London: Verso.

Arrighi, Giovanni, and Jessica Drangel. 1986. "The Stratification of the World-Economy: An Exploration of the Semiperipheral Zone." *Review* 10: 9–74.

Balassa, Bela, Gerardo Bueno, Pedro-Pablo Kuczynski, and Mário Henrique Simonsen. 1986. *Toward Renewed Economic Growth in Latin America*. Washington, DC: Institute of International Economics.

Benería, Lourdes, and Martha Roldán. 1987. *The Crossroads of Class and Gender: In-*

dustrial Homework, Subcontracting, and Household Dynamics in Mexico City. Chicago: University of Chicago Press.

Bierstekker, Thomas J. 1990. "Reducing the Role of the State in the Economy: A Conceptual Exploration of IMF and World Bank Prescriptions." *International Studies Quarterly* 34: 477–492.

———. 1995. "The 'Triumph' of Liberal Economic Ideas in the Developing World." In *Global Change, Regional Response: The New International Context of Development*, ed. Barbara Stallings, pp. 174–198. New York: Cambridge University Press.

Bonilla, Elssy. 1990. "Working Women in Latin America." In *Economic and Social Progress in Latin America: 1990 Report*, pp. 207–256. Washington, DC: Inter-American Development Bank.

Borón, Atilio. 1977. "El fascismo como categoría histórica. En torno del problema de las dictaduras en América Latina." *Revista Mexicana de Sociología* 39.

———. 1995. *State, Capitalism, and Democracy in Latin America*. Boulder, CO: Lynne Rienner.

Bose, Christine E., and Edna Acosta Belén, eds. 1995. *Women in the Latin American Development Process*. Philadelphia: Temple University Press.

Brenner, Robert, and Mark Glick. 1991. "The Regulation Approach: Theory and History." *New Left Review* 11: 45–119.

Bresser Pereira, Luiz Carlos, José María Maravall, and Adam Przeworski. 1993. *Economic Reforms in New Democracies: A Social-Democratic Approach*. New York: Cambridge University Press.

———. 1994. "Economic Reforms in New Democracies: A Social-Democratic Approach." In *Latin American Political Economy in the Age of Neoliberal Reform: Theoretical and Comparative Perspectives for the 1990s*, ed. William C. Smith, Carlos H. Acuña, and Eduardo A. Gamarra, pp. 181–212. New Brunswick, NJ: North-South Center/Transaction.

Cardoso, Fernando Henrique, and Enzo Faletto. 1979. *Dependency and Development in Latin America*. Berkeley: University of California Press.

Cavarozzi, Marcelo. 1992. "Beyond Democratic Transitions in Latin America." *Journal of Latin American Studies* 24: 665–684.

———. 1994. "Politics: A Key for the Long Term in Latin America." In *Latin American Political Economy in the Age of Neoliberal Reform: Theoretical and Comparative Perspectives for the 1990s*, ed. William C. Smith, Carlos H. Acuña, and Eduardo A. Gamarra, pp. 127–156. New Brunswick, NJ: North-South Center/Transaction.

Comisión Económica para América Latina y el Caribe (CEPAL). 1992. *El perfil de la pobreza en América Latina a comienzos de los años 90*. Santiago: CEPAL.

Collier, David, ed. 1979. *The New Authoritarianism in Latin America*. Princeton, NJ: Princeton University Press.

Conaghan, Catherine M., and James M. Malloy. 1995. *Unsettling Statecraft: Democracy and Neoliberalism in the Central Andes*. Pittsburgh: University of Pittsburgh Press.

Cumings, Bruce. 1984. "The Origins and Development of the Northeast Asian Political Economy." *International Organization* 38: 1–40.

de Schweinitz, Karl. 1964. *Industrialization and Democracy: Economic Necessities and Political Possibilities*. New York: Free Press.

De Vos, Susan. 1987. "Latin American Households in Comparative Perspective." *Population Studies* 41: 501–517.

Díaz, Alvaro. 1996. "New Developments in Social and Economic Restructuring in Latin America." In *The Politics of Social Change and Economic Restructuring in Latin America*, ed. William C. Smith and Roberto Patricio Korzeniewicz. Boulder, CO: North-South Center/Lynne Rienner.

Dos Santos, Theotonio. 1971. *Socialismo o fascismo: El nuevo carácter de la dependencia y el dilema latinoamericano*. Santiago: Centro de Estudios Sociales.

Dresser, Denise. 1991. *Neopopulist Solutions to Neoliberal Problems*. San Diego, CA: Center for U.S.-Mexican Studies.

Economic Commission for Latin America and the Caribbean (ECLAC). 1994. *Preliminary Overview of the Economy of Latin America and the Caribbean 1994*. New York: United Nations.

———. 1995. *Preliminary Overview of the Economy of Latin America and the Caribbean 1995*. New York: United Nations.

Evans, Peter. 1979. *Dependent Development: The Alliance of Multinational, State and Local Capital in Brazil*. Princeton, NJ: Princeton University Press.

———. 1992. "The State as Problem and Solution: Predation, Embedded Autonomy and Structural Change." In *The Politics of Adjustment: International Constraints, Distributive Justice and the State*, ed. Stephan Haggard and Robert Kaufman, pp. 139–181. Princeton, NJ: Princeton University Press.

———. 1995. *Embedded Autonomy: States and Industrial Transformation*. Princeton, NJ: Princeton University Press.

Fanelli, José María, Roberto Frenkel, and Guillermo Rozenwurcel. 1994. "Growth and Structural Reform in Latin America: Where We Stand." In *Latin American Political Economy in the Age of Neoliberal Reform: Theoretical and Comparative Perspectives for the 1990s*, ed. William C. Smith, Carlos H. Acuña, and Eduardo A. Gamarra, pp. 101–126. New Brunswick, NJ: North-South Center/Transaction.

Fiszbein, Ariel, and George Psacharopoulos. 1995. "Income Inequality Trends in Latin America in the 1980s." In *Coping with Austerity: Poverty and Inequality in Latin America*, ed. Nora Lustig, pp. 71–100. Washington, DC: Brookings Institution.

Folbre, Nancy. 1994. *Who Pays for the Kids?* London: Routledge.

Forsythe, Ann Elizabeth. 1995. "Old and New Anti-Systemic Movements: Accumulation, Rule and Resistance in Latin America." Paper presented at the nineteenth Annual Conference of the Political Economy of the World-System, University of Miami, Coral Gables, FL.

García, Brígida, and Orlandina de Oliveira. 1994. *Trabajo femenino y vida familiar en México*. México, DF: El Colegio de México.

Gereffi, Gary. 1989. "Rethinking Development Theory: Insights from East Asia and Latin America." *Sociological Forum* 4, 4: 505–533.

———. 1995. "State Policies and Industrial Upgrading in East Asia." *Revue d'economie industrielle* 71: 79–90.

Gereffi, Gary, and Miguel Korzeniewicz, eds. 1994. *Commodity Chains and Global Capitalism*. Westport, CT: Greenwood Press.

Gereffi, Gary, Miguel Korzeniewicz, and Roberto Patricio Korzeniewicz. 1994. "Introduction: Global Commodity Chains." *In Commodity Chains and Global Capitalism*, ed. G. Gereffi and M. Korzeniewicz, pp. 1–14. Westport, CT: Greenwood Press.

Gerschenkron, Alexander. 1962. *Economic Backwardness in Historical Perspective*. Cambridge: Harvard University Press.

Hirschman, Albert O. [1958] 1965. *The Strategy of Economic Development.* New Haven, CT: Yale University Press.

———. 1970. *Exit, Voice, and Loyalty: Responses to Decline in Firms, Organizations, and States.* Cambridge: Harvard University Press.

———. 1995. *A Propensity to Self-Subversion.* Cambridge: Harvard University Press.

Hopkins, Terence K., and Immanuel Wallerstein. 1986. "Commodity Chains in the World-Economy prior to 1800." *Review* 10: 157–170.

Huber, Evelyne. 1995. "Assessing State Strength." In *Latin America in Comparative Perspective: New Approaches to Methods and Analysis,* ed. Peter H. Smith, pp. 163–194. Boulder, CO: Westview Press.

Inter-American Development Bank. 1994. *Economic and Social Progress in Latin America: 1994 Report.* Washington, DC: Johns Hopkins University Press.

Jaquette, Jane, ed. 1989. *The Women's Movement in Latin America: Feminism and the Transition to Democracy.* Winchester, MA: Unwin Hyman.

Jelin, Elizabeth, ed. 1990. *Women and Social Change in Latin America.* London: Zed.

———. 1991. *Family, Households, and Gender Relations in Latin America.* London: Kegan Paul International.

———. 1996. "Emergent Citizenship or Exclusion? Social Movements and Non-Governmental Organizations in the 1990s." In *The Politics of Social Change and Economic Restructuring in Latin America,* ed. William C. Smith and Roberto Patricio Korzeniewicz. Boulder, CO: North-South Center/Lynne Rienner.

Kahler, Miles. 1990. "Orthodoxy and Its Alternatives: Explaining Approaches to Stabilization and Adjustment." *In Economic Crisis and Policy Choice,* ed. Joan Nelson, pp. 33–62. Princeton, NJ: Princeton University Press.

———. 1992. "External Influence, Conditionality, and the Politics of Adjustment." In *The Politics of Economic Adjustment: International Constraints, Distributive Conflicts, and the State,* ed. Stephan Haggard and Robert R. Kaufman, pp. 89–138. Princeton, NJ: Princeton University Press.

Karl, Terry Lynn. 1995. "The Venezuelan Petro-State and the Crisis of 'Its' Democracy." In *Venezuelan Democracy under Stress,* ed. Jennifer McCoy, William C. Smith, Andrés Serbin, and Andrés Stambouil, pp. 59–76. New Brunswick, NJ: North-South Center/Transaction.

Korzeniewicz, Roberto Patricio. 1996. "The Deepening Differentiation of Enterprises, States and Households." In *The Politics of Social Change and Economic Restructuring in Latin America,* ed. William C. Smith and Roberto Patricio Korzeniewicz. Boulder, CO: North-South Center/Lynne Rienner.

Kotz, David, Terrence McDonough, and Michael Reich. 1994. *Social Structures of Accumulation: The Political Economy of Growth and Crisis.* Cambridge: Cambridge University Press.

Linz, Juan J., and Alfred Stepan. 1996. *Problems of Democratic Transition and Consolidation: Southern Europe, South America, and Post-Communist Europe.* Baltimore: The Johns Hopkins University Press.

Lustig, Nora, ed. 1995. *Coping with Austerity: Poverty and Inequality in Latin America.* Washington, DC: Brookings Institution.

Mauceri, Philip. 1995. "State Reform, Coalitions, and the Neoliberal Autogolpe in Peru." *Latin American Research Review* 30, 1: 7–38.

McCoy, Jennifer L., and William C. Smith. 1995. "Democratic Disequilibrium in Venezuela." *Journal of Inter-American Studies and World Affairs* 37, 2: 113–180.

Moore, Barrington, Jr. 1966. *Social Origins of Dictatorship and Democracy: Lord and Peasant in the Making of the Modern World.* Boston: Beacon Press.

Morley, Samuel. 1994. *Poverty and Inequality in Latin America: Past Evidence, Future Prospects.* Washington, DC: Overseas Development Council.

———. 1995a. *Poverty and Inequality in Latin America: The Impact of Adjustment and Recovery in the 1980s.* Baltimore: The Johns Hopkins University Press.

———. 1995b. "Structural Adjustment and the Determinants of Poverty in Latin America." In *Coping with Austerity: Poverty and Inequality in Latin America,* ed. Nora Lustig, pp. 42–70. Washington, DC: Brookings Institution.

Moser, Caroline O. N. 1993. *Gender Planning and Development.* New York: Routledge.

North, Douglass C. 1990. *Institutions, Institutional Change and Economic Performance.* New York: Cambridge University Press.

O'Donnell, Guillermo. 1973. *Modernization and Bureaucratic-Authoritarianism: Studies in South American Politics.* Berkeley, CA: Institute of International Studies.

———. 1994a. "Delegative Democracy." *Journal of Democracy* 5 (January): 55–69.

———. 1994b. "On the State, Democratization and Some Conceptual Problems (A Latin American View with Glances at Some Post-Communist Societies)." In *Latin American Political Economy in the Age of Neoliberal Reform: Theoretical and Comparative Perspectives for the 1990s,* ed. William C. Smith, Carlos H. Acuña, and Eduardo A. Gamarra, pp. 157–181. New Brunswick, NJ: North-South Center/ Transaction.

———. 1996. "Illusions About Consolidation." *Journal of Democracy* 7 (April): 34– 51.

Offe, Claus. 1974. "Structural Problems of the Capitalist State." *German Political Studies* 1: 31–56.

———. 1975. "The Theory of the State and the Problem of Policy Formation." In *Stress and Contradiction in Modern Capitalism,* ed. Leon Lindberg, pp. 124–144. Lexington, KY: D. C. Heath.

———. 1984. *Contradictions of the Welfare State.* Cambridge: MIT Press.

Pastor, Manuel, and Carol Wise. 1992. "Peruvian Economic Policy in the 1990s: From Orthodoxy to Heterodoxy and Back." *Latin American Research Review* 27, 2: 83–117.

Pérez-Sáinz, J. P., and R. Menjívar Larín. 1994. "Central American Men and Women in the Urban Informal Sector." *Journal of Latin American Studies* 26: 431–447.

Polanyi, Karl. 1957. *The Great Transformation: The Political and Economic Origins of Our Time.* Boston: Beacon Press.

Porter, Michael. 1985. *Competitive Advantage: Creating and Sustaining Superior Performance.* New York: Free Press.

———. 1990. *The Competitive Advantage of Nations.* New York: Free Press.

Przeworski, Adam. 1985. *Capitalism and Social Democracy.* Cambridge: Cambridge University Press.

———. 1990. *The State and the Economy under Capitalism.* New York: Academic Publishers.

———. 1991. *Democracy and the Market: Political and Economic Reforms in Eastern Europe and Latin America.* Cambridge: Cambridge University Press.

Przeworski, Adam, et al. 1996. "What Makes Democracies Endure?" *Journal of Democracy* 7: 39–55.

Psacharopoulos, George, et al. 1993. *Poverty and Income Distribution in Latin America:*

The Story of the 1980s. Latin America and the Caribbean Technical Department Report No. 27. Washington, DC: World Bank.

Raczynski, Dagmar, and Pilar Romaguera. 1995. "Chile: Poverty, Adjustment, and Social Policies in the 1980s." In *Coping with Austerity: Poverty and Inequality in Latin America*, ed. Nora Lustig, pp. 275–333. Washington, DC: Brookings Institution.

Roberts, Bryan. 1994. "Informal Economy and Family Strategies." *International Journal of Urban and Regional Research* 18: 6–23.

Roberts, Kenneth M. 1995. "Neoliberalism and the Transformation of Populism in Latin America: The Peruvian Case." *World Politics* 48: 82–116.

Roxborough, Ian. 1996. "Citizenship and Social Movements under Neoliberalism." In *The Politics of Social Change and Economic Restructuring in Latin America*, ed. William C. Smith and Roberto Patricio Korzeniewicz. Boulder, CO: North-South Center/Lynne Rienner.

Schumpeter, Joseph A. 1934. *The Theory of Economic Development.* Cambridge: Harvard University Press.

———. 1942. *Capitalism, Socialism and Democracy.* New York: Harper and Row.

Smith, William C. 1992a. "Hyperinflation, Macroeconomic Instability, and Neoliberal Restructuring in Democratic Argentina." In *The New Democracy in Argentina*, ed. Edward C. Epstein, pp. 3–21. New York: Praeger.

———. 1992b. "State, Market and Neoliberalism in Post-Transition Argentina: The Menem Experiment." *Journal of Interamerican Studies and World Affairs* 33, 4: 45–82.

———. 1993. "Neoliberal Restructuring and Scenarios of Democratic Consolidation in Latin America." *Studies in Comparative International Development* 28, 2: 3–21.

Smith, William C., and Carlos H. Acuña. 1994. "Future Politico-Economic Scenarios for Latin America." In *Democracy, Markets, and Structural Reform in Latin America: Argentina, Bolivia, Brazil, Chile, and Mexico*, ed. William C. Smith, Carlos H. Acuña, and Eduardo A. Gamarra, pp. 1–28. New Brunswick, NJ: Transaction.

Smith, William C., Carlos H. Acuña, and Eduardo A. Gamarra, eds. 1994. *Democracy, Markets, and Structural Reform in Latin America: Argentina, Bolivia, Brazil, Chile, and Mexico.* New Brunswick, NJ: Transaction.

Sola, Lourdes. 1994. "The State, Structural Reform, and Democratization in Brazil." In *Democracy, Markets, and Structural Reform in Latin America: Argentina, Bolivia, Brazil, Chile, and Mexico*, ed. William C. Smith, Carlos H. Acuña, and Eduardo A. Gamarra, pp. 1–28. New Brunswick, NJ: Transaction.

Suttcliff, R. B. 1972. *Industry and Underdevelopment.* London: Addison Wesley.

———. 1984. "Industry and Underdevelopment Reexamined." *Journal of Development Studies* 21: 121–133.

Tironi, Eugenio. 1986. "Para una sociología de la decadencia: El concepto de disolución social." *Proposiciones* 6 (October–December).

Touraine, Alain. 1989. *Palavra e Sangue: Política e Sociedade na América Latina.* São Paulo: Editora da UNICAMP.

Vacs, Aldo C. 1994a. "Convergence and Dissension: Democracy, Markets, and Structural Reform in World Perspective." In *Latin American Political Economy in the Age of Neoliberal Reform: Theoretical and Comparative Perspectives for the 1990s*, ed. William C. Smith, Carlos H. Acuña, and Eduardo Gamarra, pp. 67–100. New Brunswick, NJ: North-South Center/Transaction.

————. 1994b. "The Unanticipated Merger of Liberal Democracy, Neo-Liberalism, and Neo-Populism in Argentina." Paper presented at the annual meeting of the American Political Science Association, New York, September 1–4.

Vergara, Pilar. 1986. *Auge y caída del neoliberalismo en Chile.* Santiago: Facultad Latinoamericana de Ciencias Sociales.

————. 1994. "Market Economy, Social Welfare, and Democratic Consolidation in Chile." In *Democracy, Markets, and Structural Reform in Latin America: Argentina, Bolivia, Brazil, Chile, and Mexico,* ed. William C. Smith, Carlos H. Acuña, and Eduardo A. Gamarra, pp. 237–262. New Brunswick, NJ: North-South Center/Transaction.

Vernon, Raymond. 1979. "The Product Cycle Hypothesis in a New International Environment." *Oxford Bulletin of Economics and Statistics* 41: 255–267.

Wade, Robert. 1990. *Governing the Market: Economic Theory and the Role of Government in East Asian Industrialization.* Princeton, NJ: Princeton University Press.

Ward, Kathryn. 1993. "Reconceptualizing World System Theory to Include Women." In *Theory on Gender/Feminism on Theory,* ed. Paula England, pp. 43–68. Hawthorne, NY: Aldine.

Wallerstein, Immanuel. 1983. *Historical Capitalism.* London: Verso.

Weyland, Kurt. 1994. "Neo-Populism and Neo-Liberalism in Latin America: Unexpected Affinities." Paper presented at the annual meeting of the American Political Science Association, New York, September 1–4.

Whitehead, Laurence. 1989. "Tigers in Latin America?" *The Annals* 505: 142–151.

Williamson, John, ed. 1990a. *Latin American Adjustment: How Much Has Happened?* Washington, DC: Institute for International Economics.

————. 1990b. *The Progress of Policy Reform in Latin America.* Washington, DC: Institute of International Economics.

————. 1993. "Democracy and the 'Washington Consensus.' " *World Development* 21, 8: 1329–1336.

Williamson, John, and Stephan Haggard. 1994. "The Political Conditions for Economic Reform." In *The Political Economy of Policy Reform,* ed. John Williamson, pp. 525–596. Washington, DC: Institute for International Economics.

Wise, Carol. 1994. "The Politics of Peruvian Economic Reform: Overcoming the Legacies of State-Led Development." *Journal of Interamerican Studies and World Affairs* 36, 11: 75–126.

Wilson, Suzanne, and Marta Zambrano. 1994. "Cocaine, Commodity Chains, and Drug Politics: A Transnational Approach." In *Commodity Chains and Global Capitalism,* ed. G. Gereffi and Miguel Korzeniewicz, pp. 297–315. Westport, CT: Greenwood Press.

World Bank. 1987. *World Development Report 1987.* New York: Oxford University Press.

————. 1991. *World Development Report 1991.* Washington, DC: Oxford University Press.

————. 1993a. *The East Asian Miracle: Economic Growth and Public Policy.* New York: Oxford University Press.

————. 1993b. *Social Indicators of Development 1993.* Baltimore: Johns Hopkins University Press.

————. 1993c. *World Development Report 1993.* New York: Oxford University Press.

————. 1995. *World Development Report 1995.* New York: Oxford University Press.

Zermeño, Sergio. 1989. "El regreso del líder: Crisis, neoliberalismo y desorden." *Revista Mexicana de Sociología* 51 (October–December).

———. 1996. "State and Society in Dependent Neoliberalism: The Mexican Case." In *The Politics of Social Change and Economic Restructuring in Latin America*, ed. William C. Smith and Roberto Patricio Korzeniewicz. Boulder, CO: North-South Center/Lynne Rienner.

2

THE COCAINE COMMODITY CHAIN
AND DEVELOPMENT PATHS IN PERU
AND BOLIVIA

Amy E. Bellone

Between 1980 and 1985, the amount of cocaine hydrochloride consumed by North Americans tripled from 34 to 100 metric tons per year (Healy, 1986: 110). In 1986, by the time the chemical reached the circulatory system of users, each metric ton generated an estimated $250 million in profits (conservatively) for an intricate network of producers, processors, traders, and transporters throughout the hemisphere (Healy, 1986: 110; Hargreaves, 1992: 159; Henkel, 1986: 59).[1] A crop traditionally cultivated for use in rituals enforcing social cohesion has been transformed into an international commodity funnelling an estimated $.8 to $1.5 billion a year into the Bolivian economy and $1.2 billion into the Peruvian economy (Henkel, 1986: 75; Morales, 1989: 48). The cocaine commodity chain generates more revenue than any other Bolivian product or enterprise (Healy, 1986; Henkel, 1986; Hargreaves, 1992; Blanes, 1989). The value of cocaine exports from Bolivia was twice that of all legal Bolivian exports in 1984 and 1987 and almost equal to that of all legal exports in 1989 (De Franco and Godoy, 1992: 376). Already in 1986, 5 percent of the Bolivian labor force was involved in harvesting coca leaves, and it is now estimated that one in five Bolivians receives income somehow associated with the production and trade of coca or cocaine (Healy, 1986: 110; Hargreaves, 1992: xi; De Franco and Godoy, 1992: 376). In 1987 an estimated 200,000 Peruvians (or 2.9 percent of the labor force) were directly employed in cocaine production (De Franco and Godoy, 1992: 376).

The expansion of cultivation, processing, and trade occurred in a context of severe economic crisis in the national economies of Peru and Bolivia. Bolivia's debt of almost $5.8 billion in 1987 represented between 45 and 50 percent of its GDP (Queiser Morales, 1992: 156). This debt burden was accompanied by a cycle of insufficient foreign exchange earnings, hyperinflation, and severe unemployment (Queiser Morales, 1992: 155–160; Healy, 1986). Peru's economy was also debilitated by high rates of inflation, a decline in export earnings, and decreased access to foreign credit and exchange.

Coca producers in both Bolivia and Peru have differed in their ability to engage the higher value-added niches of the cocaine commodity chain. These differences are explored through the use of the "commodity chain" approach (see Gereffi, 1989; Gereffi and Korzeniewicz, 1990, 1994; Truelove, 1992) to conduct a systematic analysis of the links between the local processes and the regional economic and social structures. Like that of Wilson and Zambrano (1994), this analysis places the cocaine trade in a framework of global exchange by employing a commodity chain framework to uncover the local and international links involved in production and distribution. Unlike the 1994 analysis, which focuses on implications for eradication and law enforcement efforts, this chapter seeks to explain how the "white gold rush" can be characterized and conceptualized in terms of uneven organizational development. In doing so, this analysis focuses on the early stages of the cocaine commodity chain rather than international trafficking and sales, topics on which most discussions of the drug trade focus. The cocaine commodity chain presents an interesting case because it encompasses agricultural production, transport, chemical processing, export, and trade in a chain operating outside government regulation in a manner which, unlike most agricultural commodities, has proven to be quite flexible in terms of production processes.

Placing the coca trade in the context of the global capitalist system is more than an academic exercise. If the international goals of control of the cocaine trade and development in Latin America are to be seriously considered, the precedents to, and operation of, the trade need to be identified. Furthermore, how we conceptualize the trade in terms of the type of enterprise it represents conditions the solutions advocated to curb efforts to cultivate the leaves, process them into cocaine, and market the final product. The world-system's commodity chain approach provides a framework clearly illustrating the aspects of the trade that are characteristic of dependent development and the junctures and characteristics that divert from traditional conceptualizations. Analyzing the structure of the cocaine commodity chain illustrates the proliferation of a global demand for cocaine, the accumulation of economic surpluses, how new actors and political environments contribute to the dynamism of particular production processes, and the futility of supply-side solutions. Such analysis also shows how relationships emanating from political culture and the organization of labor contribute to the form of cultivation, processing, sale, and trafficking of the coca leaf and cocaine in Peru and Bolivia and the ways that they are inserted into the global production process.

COLONIZATION AND THE BURGEONING COCAINE COMMODITY CHAIN

The often-harsh economic and social forces influencing life in the Andean Mountains have been mediated through time by the use of coca leaves as a traditional vehicle for regulating these forces at the individual, community, and spiritual levels. To those from the highlands of Peru and Bolivia, coca mastication is a ritual affirming individual identity and fostering social cohesion. Allen (1988, 1986) and other authors (Mitchell, 1991; Morales, 1989) have documented the importance of the coca leaf as a symbolic vehicle acting as an intermediary between the people and deities associated with the earth. It is seen as having a power that, when directed through prayer to specific places or deities, invokes these powers to aid the group. The physiological effects of coca mastication allow an individual to endure the hardships of poverty; of long, intense working days at high altitudes; and of limited resources. As a central element of Andean society, coca is also widely used for medicinal purposes and as a veritable prerequisite for celebrations (Morales, 1989: 19–24). In addition, coca leaves are often part of the wages received for day labor and of reciprocal labor arrangements whereby employers supply music, rations of coca, alcoholic beverages, and food (Morales, 1989: 147).

Prior to the beginning of the coca "boom" of recent decades, coca cultivation was confined primarily to the satisfaction of domestic demand in Peru and Bolivia. In Peru, cultivation was concentrated in the eastern slope of the Andes (known as the "Ceja de Selva" or "eyebrow of the jungle"), in the valley of the Huallaga River. In Bolivia, Las Yungas, a small region in the department of La Paz, supplied most of the coca for that country until the 1960s (Healy, 1986: 102). The Chapare region, in the department of Cochabamba, has become the primary area of cultivation and now supplies 90 percent of the leaves grown in Bolivia (Hargreaves, 1992: 32). The coca plant is native to these regions, as they provide the lower altitudes necessary for growth (500 to 2,000 meters above sea level depending on the variety) (Plowman, 1986). Thus, the primary locational constraint involved in the cocaine commodity chain has traditionally been, and continues to be, the climate necessary for the growth of the plant.

The first steps toward the international commodification of the coca leaf occurred with the parallel commencement of colonization efforts in Peru and Bolivia and the increasing U.S. demand for cocaine. Both Peru and Bolivia embarked on government-led efforts to colonize the jungle regions east of the Andean plateau, which was accompanied by spontaneous colonization (primarily because of land pressures in the highlands) and the growth of the coca trade. In Bolivia, the 1953 agrarian reforms, coupled with later assistance from the U.S. Agency for International Development, initiated colonization projects directed at Las Yungas, the Chapare region, and the department of Santa Cruz in order to promote national integration and self-sufficiency in staple crops (Sanabria, 1986: 82, 86; Healy, 1986: 102). Many highland farmers were granted titles to land in these target areas, while others either bought land or accompanied and worked for other landowners (Sanabria, 1986). Because the agricultural cycles of traditional highland crops and the coca plant are complementary, coca quickly became the primary crop in the colonized valleys.

Expanding cultivation of the plant required an increased labor supply: one hectare of coca requires about 260 days of labor annually, while rice and coffee, the next two most labor-intensive crops appropriate to the valleys of the Andean plateau, require, respectively, only 84 and 88 days (Sanabria, 1986: 92, 95). As more highlanders permanently moved to the Chapare, the system of bizonal cultivation declined and was coupled with an "influx of peasant laborers from different parts of Bolivia without secure access to land in the lowlands" (Sanabria, 1986: 99). By 1981, the net stock of migrants to the Chapare region was 68,000, and "as many as 420,000 people—7 percent of Bolivia's total population—travelled to the Chapare to work in coca cultivation or cocaine production" (De Franco and Godoy, 1992: 383). Thus, locational constraints and an inability to manipulate the rate of production dictated the organization of the labor needed to cultivate coca leaves, resulting in intensive travel in and out of the Chapare region.

During the agrarian reforms of the 1950s, large cattle ranchers in the department of Beni and owners of sugar and cotton estates in the department of Santa Cruz not only avoided the expropriation of their land, but enjoyed "favorable pricing, export, credit, marketing and investment policies of the Bolivian state" (Healy, 1986: 105, 107). These enterprises served as a platform for the boom of agricultural exports in the 1960s and 1970s. While these estates are north and east of the area that is appropriate for growing coca, the power and international export experience developed by these entrepreneurs created a powerful elite whose resources were available when the illicit market for coca emerged in the 1970s (Hargreaves, 1992: 52–56; Healy, 1986: 104–107; MacDonald, 1989: 67–70).

Similar changes in patterns of migration and human settlement characterize the case of Peru. In the late 1950s, increasing land pressures led the Peruvian government to seek a solution to excessive migration to Lima and the coast through the colonization of the less-populated land available in Eastern Peru. Upon being promised credits for citrus, coffee, and cattle production (as well as a highway to Lima), many residents of the highland areas voluntarily moved to the Ceja de Selva. Many migrants were unfamiliar with the agricultural techniques necessary for the climate and soil of the jungle, and the promised credit, marketing channels, and technical assistance never materialized. Nevertheless, the population density in the upper Huallaga Valley (now Peru's center for coca cultivation) grew from one person per square kilometer in 1961 to ten in 1981 (Morales 1990: 631).

The increases in population density in both the Huallaga Valley in Peru and the Chapare region in Bolivia are directly related to an increase in the cultivation and processing of coca leaves. Between 1962 and 1972, land devoted to coca

Figure 2.1
Commodity Chain for Cocaine

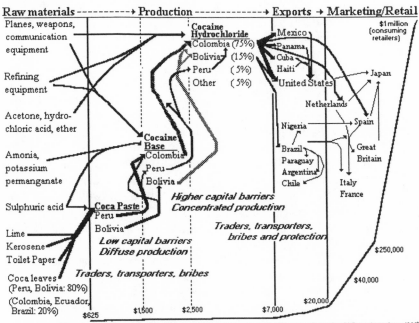

Line represents the rough value of inputs used at each stage to make 1 kilogram of cocaine (U.S. market prices, 1986)

in the Huallaga Valley doubled to 3,000 hectares, and by 1989, at least 75,000 hectares were used to grow coca (the amount of land needed to harvest leaves to make at least 85 tons of cocaine, or 40 percent of the world's supply) (Kaswell, 1989a: 24, 1989b: 13; Campodonico, 1989: 235; Craig, 1987: 13). Arable land devoted to coca cultivation in Bolivia's Chapare region *exploded* to 48 percent in the period between 1977 to 1985, compared to only 24 percent of land between 1970 and 1977 (De Franco and Godoy, 1992: 395).

TRACKING THE TRAFFICKING

Tracing the cocaine commodity chain from the cultivation of the initial raw material (the coca leaf) to the marketing and distribution of cocaine demonstrates how this international commodity links small farmers and landless entrepreneurs to the world capitalist system, offering opportunities, at various junctures, to exploit forward linkages and value-added profits. The productive structures involved in the various stages of the commodity chain illustrate the ways that this particular commodity chain encompasses aspects of both agricultural and industrial production, the nonmarket forces involved in its operation, and the reasons for its growth and resiliency.

The commodity chain for cocaine is illustrated in Figure 2.1, in which estimates of the degree of profits enjoyed at the various stages are included.[2] Key aspects of this chain include the informal nature of each node and connection, narrow roles for actors involved in the chain, continuous exchanges between inputs, and expenditures for bribes, transport, and trade, which are encountered at every link and connection. In addition to bribes, individuals receive coca-related profits through a vast array of activities in coca-growing regions. Among these activities are the transport and resale of inputs by a host of landless entrepreneurs in the regions, as well as the resale of confiscated goods by government personnel trying to augment extremely low salaries. Therefore, all inputs in the chain are essentially illegal goods.

The effects of the commodity chain may also be witnessed outside its direct operation in terms of forfeited taxes, degraded working environments, the growth of contraband markets, and capital flight. In Bolivia, "[a]ccording to some economists, the size of illegal economic transactions is comparable to that of the official balance of trade" (Blanes, 1989: 139; see also Wilson and Zambrano, 1994). Even though the aggregate effect of informal trade of this magnitude is a destabilization of the national economies, the informal diffusion of profits to virtually all elements in the society makes unlikely the existence of a collective will to dismember the cocaine commodity chain. Furthermore, without such a will, pursuit of a path of development more strongly based on welfare seems quite elusive.

Raw-material supply networks for the cocaine commodity chain may be characterized as "procurement networks," based "upon personal ties, common ethnic backgrounds, and a history of previous common transactions," as opposed to vertically integrated networks (Gereffi and Korzeniewicz, 1990: 57). The narrowly defined productive roles of each link and, at the raw material and initial production stages, the use of exchange (both of which are characteristic of the trade) are not only the result of an exploitation of comparative advantages as suggested by Gereffi (1989), but also brought about by the relatively small amounts of capital necessary at most nodes of production and by the entire enterprise's illegality. As a commodity chain operating outside regulation and constantly pursued by legal authorities, actors in each link of the chain minimize risks by sticking to one or few roles, and production is carried out in small quantities, thus impeding market domination by one actor.

Although yields of coca crops cannot be increased significantly through technology or other inputs, and although large amounts of labor are needed for harvesting, its ability to grow interspersed with other crops and the fact that these plants, which last 20 to 35 years, may be harvested up to six times per year after only twelve months, make the crop particularly attractive and easy to manage (Plowman, 1986). Unlike most other agricultural commodities for export, coca is generally grown on plots of only a few hectares. Additionally, because of the bulkiness of the dried leaves, they are generally processed into coca paste and sometimes further refined before being transported for final processing into cocaine and export. In this sense, the locational constraint of a limited area appropriate for cultivation enables agricultural production to be linked to the first steps of refining. This initial processing, along with the need for secret transport in small quantities, provide value-added profits for the Peruvians and Bolivians involved. In comparison to the profits enjoyed by *narcotraficantes* (drug traffickers), however, the commodity resembles other traditional exports more closely (with only 0.5 percent of the final value accruing to farmers) (McClintock, 1988: 128; Hargreaves, 1992: 38).

The low capital barriers involved in cultivating coca leaves and procuring and selling other raw material inputs result in the existence of widespread small-scale enterprises. Even once the coca leaves enter the production stages of the commodity chain, networks of buyers, sellers, and transporters are employed with relatively low amounts of capital and high profits. With the exception of planes and refining and communications equipment, the bulk of raw materials needed to make and market coca paste (the first stage of refining after harvesting the leaves) are supplied from within Bolivia and Peru. This demonstrates the generation of backward linkages throughout the national economies within the cocaine commodity chain. Another very unique feature of the cocaine commodity chain is the fact that inputs are often exchanged in place of cash, as for example, in the common exchange of coca paste for weapons (Hargreaves, 1992).

The cultivation and harvest of coca plants, along with their preparation for transport, generate employment and income for a whole set of laborers. Clearing land before planting, preparing seedlings, planting, and harvesting are all activities that could be done by individual farmers yet, because of the influx of workers to the jungle, tend to be done by specialized workers (see Morales, 1989; Healy, 1986). Transforming coca leaves into coca paste not only requires labor, but materials such as toilet paper (used as a filter), kerosene, sulfuric acid, and lime. The prices of these products are high, due in part to demand, but also because the final price includes bribes, transport costs, and markups incurred in the journey to the coca pits, where leaves are transformed into coca paste.[3] Therefore, forward and backward linkages involved in the chain include numerous exchanges rather than one transfer at each node. Furthermore, the linkages involved in providing raw materials illustrate how individuals who are considered otherwise employed become integrated into the illicit commodity chain.

Once the leaves are harvested, the first stage of processing consists of turning the coca leaves into coca paste. Because the leaves are bulky, 80 percent of all coca paste is made in Peru and Bolivia (Henkel, 1986: 54). Coca paste is made in a pit, which can be constructed simply of plastic sheets and tree branches, thus requiring little capital. Paste making, however, is a labor-intensive and risky activity, which involves serious health hazards.[4] Thus, it is relegated to the vast labor supply of native individuals willing to take such risks with little profit compared to the final value of cocaine. Bolivian *pisacocas*, or leaf stompers (many of whom are ex-miners), receive seven to fifteen dollars for a night's work, amounting to wages four times those of other agricultural labor associated with coca and eight to twelve times greater than those of labor for other agricultural crops (Hargreaves, 1992: 39; Healy, 1986: 123; K. Healy, personal communication, March 28, 1995).

In conceptualizing the production networks of commodity chains, the size of firms and the labor patterns and organization of production are key (Gereffi and Korzeniewicz, 1990). According to Morales (1989) and Kaswell (1989a, 1989b), coca farmers in Peru's upper Huallaga Valley are economically and socially stratified according to the extent to which the leaves are processed. Some farmers only cultivate and dry coca leaves and are therefore excluded from value-added profits gained from linking with the production node of the commodity chain. Others remain involved in the process until the leaves have been converted to coca paste and are ready to be sold to refiners and traffickers. To date, the proportion of farmers engaging in different levels of processing in Peru and Bolivia is unknown.

Prior to the 1980s, the decision to make coca paste was not an issue for Bolivian and Peruvian farmers, who instead tended to sell their leaves to intermediaries for resale to traffickers and refiners (Morales, 1989). In Bolivia, operating "paste pits went against the way of thinking of many campesinos who were used to subsistence on the land, not being entrepreneurs" (Hargreaves, 1992: 36). While difficult to investigate empirically, this kind of social consideration is key in understanding how nonmarket factors condition a commodity chain. In Bolivia, increasing cultivation in the 1980s led to a drop in the price of leaves and an influx of labor to the jungle regions (Hargreaves, 1992). Because transforming the leaves into paste offered considerable profits and labor was abundant, many farmers were willing to take the risk of venturing into the blatantly illegal stage of production (Hargreaves, 1992).

The shift by Peruvians and Bolivians to a forward link and increased value-added profits was not perceived as competition by actors in the nodes further along in the commodity chain but rather as a boon, as the further refined the product is before they buy it, the less risk there is (Hargreaves, 1992: 36). The value-added profits for links farther away from the retail stage are insignificant compared to the profits received from transporting and selling refined cocaine hydrochloride. Diffusing risks associated with early stages of production among small entrepreneurs in the jungles decreases those of future links which, in turn, allows the latter to operate on a larger scale. In this way, participants from peripheral economies receive less profit because they are far removed from the final sale of the commodity, while their engagement allows participants closest to the consumption stage to earn greater profits.

The networks and labor relations involved in harvesting leaves and transforming them into coca paste are based on mutual reliance, ensuring that the farmers and paste-making "chemists" act as links in the productive process rather than dominant powers in a vertically structured commodity chain (Gereffi and Korzeniewicz, 1990). Even if a farmer is a chemist, the inability to farm large tracts of land with coca, the need for a diverse pool of material inputs, and the illegal sale and transport of the paste mean that the individual is intimately linked to a complex production process, which includes "infrastructure sharing," pooling for the purchase of the necessary inputs, and the sharing of "coca pits."

When choosing a level of processing, the decisions of farmers are influenced in part by their access to production networks and their level of risk-acceptance or -aversion. Even though the additional inputs and labor needed to make paste are expensive, the profits for the value they add are comparatively high, and coca farmers may usually pay for them in leaves, thus lessening the need for large capital outlays. Price fluctuations, as well as the possibility that the paste could be confiscated after investing in its production, create a "risk factor" that individual farmers must weigh. Unlike coca leaves, coca paste cannot be stored because it loses weight and thus drops in value (Morales, 1989). Furthermore, although selling leaves is easy because they may readily be exchanged or sold to a large group of landless individuals and entrepreneurs for processing, selling paste (to which value has been added with low capital barriers) limits the market for the farmer's product.

Entrepreneurs who buy leaves from farmers and then process them also receive a relatively large profit because, since the leaves are dried and thus can last longer, they are able to engage in year-round processing. "Besides constant production, this type of operation is often connected to the next chemical step, refining centers" (Morales, 1989: 74). Year-round processing offers this type of entrepreneur more opportunities to establish forward and backward linkages in processing and to exploit economies of scale, making up for the costs of not cultivating coca. Since processing does not only occur in the coca growing regions, these entrepreneurs are also liberated from the locational constraint associated with agricultural production. Coca pits can be set up virtually anywhere, including the back of trucks, to allow for mobility in escaping law enforcement personnel (Hargreaves, 1992).

The refining of coca paste into "cocaine base" is the next stage in the production process. Making cocaine base (and then cocaine hydrochloride) tends to be done on a larger scale than paste-making because it requires more tools (lamps, tables, bowls), an indoor location, additional chemicals, and planes for transport of the base and refined cocaine (Hargreaves, 1992: 65). In August 1991, the price of the amount of coca paste needed to make a kilogram of cocaine was $250, while refining this paste into base earned the seller six to seven times that amount (Hargreaves, 1992: 66; Henkel, 1986). In August of 1991, a kilogram of cocaine hydrochloride could be sold to traffickers in Bolivia for anywhere from $1,600 to $2,500 (Hargreaves, 1992: 66). This same kilo might cost $7,000 in Colombia; $20,000 in Miami; $40,000 in Detroit; and $250,000 by the time it is sold to dealers (Hargreaves, 1992: 159). Once it has been broken into batches as small as an eighth of a gram and cut with baking soda or other substances, consumers in the United States may end up paying about a million dollars.

The transition to refining stages represents a larger scale of production, a less labor-intensive organization, an increased need for capital investments, and significantly higher risks and value added. This chapter argues that the extent to which this transition included an internationalization of the commodity chain was a consequence of the availability of local organizational capacities. In this sense, the transition represents the point in the chain where cross-national differences emerge between Peru and Bolivia due to factors such as the strength of local elites and existing political climates.

FORWARD LINKAGES AND POSITIONS IN THE INTERNATIONAL NETWORK

In 1989 and 1990, a law enforcement clampdown in Colombia resulted in difficulties for Peruvians and Bolivians in selling their paste at high prices (Hargreaves, 1992: 66). Up until this point, Bolivia and Peru had been restricted to the raw material and primary processing stages. Paste was then flown to Colombia, where it was further refined and then smuggled to its international destinations. Even though the Colombian drug traffickers had the networks needed to operate the chain, the fact that coca appropriate for cocaine grows only in Peru and Bolivia required that international networks be created to gain access to those leaves—but why Colombia? Why did Peruvians and Bolivians fail to seek such greater value-added profits? To answer this, we must once again consider nonmarket factors influencing production. Henkel has suggested that Colombia's domination of the later links of the commodity chain was the result of an already-existing and highly organized supply network of marijuana for the United States (Henkel, 1986: 54; Hargreaves, 1992: 65–66). Not only were the chemicals needed for later refining stages available in Colombia, this network also ensured direct connections by air and sea to the United States (Henkel, 1986: 55).

By the late 1980s, however, the law enforcement efforts in Colombia and the increasing availability of chemicals and technical expertise in Peru and Bolivia led to a shift in the productive structure of the cocaine commodity chain. More and more labs for refining coca paste into cocaine were erected in Bolivia and, to a lesser extent, in Peru (Henkel, 1986; Hargreaves, 1992; Morales, 1989). The involvement of Peruvians in the commodity chain is primarily through the generation of raw materials and the first productive process (Morales, 1989: 86). Since only 5 percent of the world supply of cocaine hydrochloride is estimated to be produced in Peru, while Bolivia (which cultivates about half the amount of leaves) generates 15 percent of all cocaine, it can be reasonably inferred that refining is much more prevalent in Bolivia than in Peru (Hargreaves, 1992: 54; Henkel, 1986: 56; Strug, 1986). While this may have changed in recent years, one distinct feature of the production network in Peru is that subsequent production stages beyond the stage of paste making are dominated by either Colombians or Peruvians working under close Colombian supervision (MacDonald,

1989: 59–60; Morales, 1989: 89; Kaswell, 1989b). Hence, Peru has been less successful in exploiting opportunities for value-added profits enjoyed in the later links of the commodity chain.

The nature of the *narcotraficantes* is somewhat different in Bolivia. The booming market for cocaine was accompanied by U.S. pressure to control coca production in the Chapare (Sanabria, 1986: 57). The effect of this increased enforcement was to drive coca paste production into the Beni and Santa Cruz departments. In these departments, colonization projects and the promotion of agro-industry and ranching had solidified the political and economic hegemony of a rural elite during the 1960s and 1970s, whose cotton, soy, and cattle enterprises had received credit and marketing assistance, largely through foreign loans (Healy, 1986: 105; Sanabria, 1986: 108–109).[5] By the late 1970s, these elites had developed both a strong experience in international trade and local political clout. Many of the cattle ranches in the remote Beni region, which were established through colonization projects, faced a troubled export market for cotton and therefore became involved in refining operations (K. Healy, personal communication, March 28, 1995).

The linkages between raw materials and production were facilitated by the remoteness of the regions and the capital available from local elites. The capital enabled the Bolivian actors to extend forward linkages into refining facilities, thereby decreasing their reliance on Colombian export connections, capital, and transportation networks (Sanabria, 1986; Hargreaves, 1992; Healy, 1986; Henkel, 1986). These Bolivian labs were able to exploit a number of locational advantages, including proximity to raw materials, avoidance of law enforcement personnel, and availability of infrastructure (such as airstrips that had been originally constructed to develop agro-industrial production in the regions). Air transport to Colombia was much easier from these areas than via land from the Chapare, enabling the Bolivian refining "industry" to engineer productive arrangements to exploit their locational advantages (Henkel, 1986; Hargreaves, 1992). Furthermore, unlike the cartels controlling the Colombian end of the trade, the Bolivian "narcobourgeoisie" have avoided violence with the community outside the commodity chain and have often financed public works projects, thus solidifying their support in their communities of operation (Hargreaves, 1992: 58).

The results of this control of forward linkages in Bolivia are manifested in several ways. Though much of the capital earned by the higher value contributed to the Bolivian product probably flees the country or is reinvested in the illicit economy, it still has a greater chance of remaining in Bolivia than in Peru (where Colombian cartels capture these profits). Nevertheless, the effects of the cocaine trade were extremely deleterious for Bolivia's economy. The weakness of the state, coupled with escalating trade and economic crises, has caused significant portions of the economy to go "further underground" (Blanes, 1989). The acute financial crisis experienced by Bolivia between 1982 and 1985 severely restricted credit for legitimate businesses, some of which sought "narcodollars" to continue their operations which, due to their secure access to foreign exchange, increased the political and economic influence of the narcobourgeoisie (Henkel, 1986: 66). The power this narcobourgeoisie gained throughout the 1980s crippled efforts to control and capture traffickers and strengthened the efforts of the traffickers themselves. Not only were they protected by high-level contacts and economic power, but the thousands of Bolivians working for them were somewhat protected as well.[6] In contrast, the absence of an indigenous elite in Peru meant that the government was less intimately tied to the interests of traffickers.

This is not to suggest that the forces with which the Peruvian government must contend are manageable. Sendero Luminoso, a Maoist Peruvian guerrilla group, has presented a completely separate and forceful variable in Peruvian efforts to control the cultivation and processing of coca leaves. Speculations about its uncertain role in the commodity chain range from categorical declarations by state agencies that towns engaged in the production and transport of coca leaves and paste are under the "de facto political authority" of Sendero Luminoso (Kaswell, 1989a) to speculations that absolutely no influence is enjoyed by the group (Morales 1989, 1990).[7] Whether Sendero Luminoso enjoys an ideological influence in the coca-growing areas of Peru almost becomes a moot point when one considers that the mere perception of a powerful guerrilla threat facilitates the networks of the illicit commodity chain, because the Peruvian military (in charge of controlling Sendero) has adopted a laissez-faire stance toward the drug trade as a means to contain guerrilla movements (Reid, 1989: 158). For the drug traffickers, framing terrorist actions as if they were committed by guerrilla groups shifts attention away from the violence they commit and reinforces a fear of the spread of Sendero Luminoso (Morales, 1989). Thus, efforts to contain guerrilla movements can result in a relaxation of efforts to control the coca trade and facilitate its functioning.

The resistance to eradication efforts in Bolivia takes a very political form, including hunger strikes, protest marches, and roadblocks.[8] The Confederation of Peasant Worker Unions of Bolivia (CSUTCB) operates at the community, regional, and national levels to express peasant interests (Healy, 1986).[9] Since the 1970s, membership in CSUTCB organizations in the Chapare region has included an increasing number of coca farmers. These groups have proven very strong relative to other branches of the confederation, as members have not only more income to support leaders and activities, but also strong interests to defend (i.e., the right to grow coca). With the development of coca cultivation on a large scale, peasant organizations have become extremely vocal and effective in expressing opposition to Bolivian and U.S. governmental efforts to quell the trade.

Each initiative by either the Bolivian or U.S. government to reduce the amount of coca being cultivated has been met with opposition from CSUTCB and other concerned unions and organizations (Healy, 1986; Henkel, 1986; Hargreaves, 1992). In recent years, union activity has gone beyond defensive measures and now includes coca leaf "chew-ins," rallies, and large-scale marches to bring the issue of the right to grow coca to the forefront of the national agenda (Healy, 1991). These mobilizations undoubtedly hinder government efforts to take strong and effective eradication measures. Not only does the coca growers' militancy improve their ability to grow the leaf, but CSUTCB's efforts have been framed in terms of cultural preservation and revitalization, national themes with an appeal beyond the population receiving profits from the coca trade (K. Healy, personal communication, March 28, 1995). Furthermore, the traffickers working with the growers are well aware of the benefits that accrue to them because of CSUTCB's activism. Thus, they often make concessions to the growers. Hargreaves reported that each time a plane lands in a village to pick up paste or base, the traffickers donate about $120 to the local union for "public works" (1992: 63).

The experiences of Peru and Bolivia illustrate how political culture, historical circumstances, and class structure may condition a commodity chain. These factors determine the extent to which otherwise similar actors are able to exploit differing degrees of locational advantages, forward linkages, and value-added profits. The experiences described here also illustrate the flexible nature of productive organization that is inherent to the production and exporting stages of the commodity chain. As the chain thrives despite efforts to curb the trade, modifications may constantly be made to adapt to the new environments to which its structure is subjected. Adjustments are made through human agency, modifying productive structures, sharing of infrastructure and power, and exploiting locational advantages, all of which are central elements of the structure of industrial, and not necessarily agricultural, production.

CONCLUSION: FIVE PENNIES FOR A DIME OR A NEW DEVELOPMENT PATH?

In examining the effect of the cocaine commodity chain in Peru and Bolivia, the focus has been on the first two of the chain's four stages. These stages (raw material supply and production) are characterized by low capital barriers, small-scale enterprises, continuous exchanges between actors, extensive forward and backward linkages, and diffuse production. Informal links are pervasive throughout the chain, as both the final commodity (cocaine) and its principal components (cocaine paste and base) are illegal. Compared to the profits enjoyed in the postproduction stage, profits for the growth of coca and for the production of cocaine and its components are very low. Like other commodity chains, the value of the product in peripheral areas is lower than in core nations (Gereffi and Korzeniewicz, 1994).

Unlike other commodity chains, however, the differential profits are only partially attributable to increased value added and higher capital barriers. The cocaine commodity chain is conditioned, not only by the labor and materials necessary for its operation, but also by social networks, political conditions, and social attitudes about the actual product. This demonstrates the importance of considering factors not directly related to production when using the commodity chain approach to examine the distribution of profits among core and peripheral economies. As Wilson and Zambrano (1994) have pointed out, the bulk of profits are in the nodes of the chain that occur in core countries, despite the fact that production is complete before export.

The cocaine commodity chain challenges traditional conceptions about development that suggest the nation-state is the primary motor and unit of the development of growth strategies and a capital base. While the nation-state is certainly an important actor in the operation of the cocaine commodity chain, its role is primarily in reaction to the chain's operation. Regulation and taxation are not the responses to its growth but, rather, international political and legal issues. The tangible products of the commodity chain and the accumulated profits remain largely informal, illegal, and transnational in nature. For countries such as Peru and Bolivia, the effect has been that national efforts to plan development must be made in response to the illegal classification of the commodity rather than efforts to incorporate its enormous profits into national revenues.

Examining cocaine as a transnational commodity also demonstrates the way its production process diverts from traditional agricultural-export crops. While supplying the primary input of the final commodity resembles agricultural production, it is also unique in the hardiness of the plant, the large amounts of labor necessary for harvesting, the small plots on which it is grown, and the highly inelastic demand for cocaine as an international commodity. Moreover, cultivators of the leaf have found it relatively easy to insert themselves into later links of the commodity chain, thus affording them more control over the type of production in which they engage.

Locational constraints conditioning the cocaine commodity chain demand extensive transportation costs and the development of routes and vehicles. Because this must be done outside the law, it tends to occur on a small scale and involves narrow roles for participants. This results in the creation of significant forward and backward linkages for local producing economies that are involved in the international commodity chain. In the sense that the coca trade is a response to externally generated demand, it resembles traditional commodity exports fairly closely. Production for the exclusive purpose of export results in the trade's removal from the consumption needs of the producing society. However, as Healy observed: "[F]armers control the raw material within an economic structure of small-plot agriculture. This point appears to contradict the theory that treats peasant farmers as passive and manipulated 'masses,' victimized by a dependent development process dominated by the State and the national and international bourgeoisie" (1986: 126). It can also be argued that because of the highly inelastic demand for cocaine, the market is (at least so far) much less affected by external constraints of market dependence. While coca producers are price takers, the high demand usually ensures a high price and secure market.

Furthermore, as the Bolivian case suggests, the commodity chain is so flexible that it can sometimes be manipulated so as to be internally controlled. The procurement of other raw materials necessary to make cocaine; the production of coca paste, cocaine base, and cocaine hydrochloride; and the mechanisms governing the export and sale of cocaine resemble an industry more closely than an agricultural enterprise. The locational constraints conditioning cultivation are not as strong in these later stages, nor is the need for intensive labor. The production of coca paste and cocaine can occur wherever the law does not disable it and the capital is available. For the later stages in production (refining paste into base and cocaine), the necessary social connections and capital result in its operation in a more concentrated manner, also making it more closely resemble an industry.

Although the organization of labor in the chain is constrained by the location of the main raw input, the contrast of these networks in Peru and Bolivia suggests that there is some latitude in the chain's establishment. Elite structures are, therefore, key to understanding the geography of the cocaine commodity chain. While the business in Peru has been dominated by a Colombian power structure and production that is relatively contained in the Huallaga Valley, in Bolivia, the organization of labor has become controlled by a national elite spread all over the remote areas of the Beni and Santa Cruz regions. In turn, through their participation in the cocaine commodity chain, these elites have reconfigured themselves into a new group, termed the "narcobourgeoisie."

If coca cultivation did more closely resemble that of traditional crops, controlling the coca trade would consist of isolating the area of cultivation. Instead, the small plots, low capital barriers, large profits, and flexibility of organizational and production networks render this strategy futile. "Like any business, it responds to changing market conditions by altering management and location. . . . Finding employees to run the gauntlet of smuggling cocaine supplies across international borders, however risky, will never be difficult given the enormous sums the druglords can afford to pay" (Hargreaves, 1992: 188). As can be seen in Figure 2.1, given the remarkably higher profits in the export and marketing stages, the structure of the commodity chain is such that any decrease in the final consumer prices can be absorbed by the links closer to the retail stages without rendering the chain unprofitable. As long as the demand for coca remains relatively inelastic, and the price many times higher than that of alternative crops, the cultivation of this export crop will be the choice for many. Furthermore, eradication and control efforts aimed at curbing the drug supply seem to ignore the flexibility of the productive structure following the stage of raw material supply.

Even though the U.S. market for cocaine seems to be shrinking, recent evidence suggests that other, more profitable ones are opening up. "Between 1989 and 1990 the amount of cocaine confiscated in Europe more than doubled, from 6 to 14 tons. Given that police estimate they seize a maximum of 10 percent of the total, that means that in 1990 Europe was awash with at least 140 tons of [the drug]'' (Hargreaves, 1992: 8). Moreover, cocaine entering the rapidly expanding markets in Japan and Europe fetches up to three times more than that exported to the United States (Hargreaves, 1992: 188). Human agency is certainly involved in finding networks and processes to satisfy the incredible demand. Furthermore, given recent increases in illegal synthetic drugs, the eradication of the coca used for cocaine will probably neither end these international networks nor erase demand for illicit drugs. Given the impracticality of supply-side solutions demonstrated in this chapter, a government wishing to address a national drug problem would be wiser to focus on demand and, as recommended by Wilson and Zambrano (1994), on efforts at making it more difficult for cocaine to penetrate national borders.

Clearly, the cocaine commodity chain is of tremendous economic importance in both Peru and Bolivia. De Franco and Godoy reported that ''work as an unskilled labourer in cocaine production pays 20 times more than work as a public employee'' and that ''landless rural labourers in the Chapare earn three to five times more by working in the drug industry than working in their homelands'' (1992: 386). Thus, even though only about 0.5 percent of $1 million that cocaine users may pay for a kilogram of cocaine goes to the growers of the main raw material, for many, the cocaine commodity chain appears as the most viable development path in the face of a lack of alternate export crops and economic destitution. As explained by a U.S. Drug Enforcement Agency official, ''These people are not addicted to coca, they are addicted to eating'' (quoted in Hargreaves, 1992: 190).

NOTES

The author wishes to thank J. Timmons Roberts for several sets of comments and numerous ideas; John Hite, Bill Smith, and Roberto P. Korzeniewicz for comments and editorial assistance; and Tulane University for supporting travel to the Political Economy of the World-System (PEWS) conference.

1. Due to the illicit nature of the cultivation, processing, and trade of the coca leaf, these and virtually all the other figures used in this chapter are largely speculative: they are derived through local surveys, information collected by law enforcement agencies in the United States and Latin America, satellite photos, estimates derived from seizures, and development agencies. Here, every effort has been made to compare statistics with as many sources as possible. The data and descriptions of the social relations of production presented here are drawn heavily from ''micro'' analyses. Therefore, regional generalizations made on the basis of specific anecdotes and particular cases, while extremely illustrative, are also primarily speculative.

2. While the line representing the price of the components necessary to produce a kilogram of cocaine is a very rough estimate, the proportion of profits enjoyed at each stage is represented fairly accurately.

3. For example, in 1986 a roll of toilet paper cost nine times more in Chapare than in the nearby city of Cochabamba, and about 2,000 individuals made a living buying, selling and transporting toilet paper in Bolivia alone (Healy, 1986: 118).

4. Those who stomp on the leaves mixed with sulfuric acid may experience burns on the soles of their feet, often resulting in amputation (Hargreaves, 1992: 39).

5. In 1975, when prices of cotton dropped, the "Cotton Growers' Association" (controlled by the Santa Cruz elites) was granted millions of dollars in credit as compensation (Sanabria, 1986; Hargreaves, 1992: 57). It is suspected that much of this money was funneled to finance the development of the cocaine-trafficking infrastructure (Hargreaves, 1992: 57).

6. While alignment with the Bolivian narcobourgeoisie allows for some degree of protection, in both Bolivia and Peru, arrests are primarily symbolic acts against agents in the early stages of the chain rather than against those who control refining and transport.

7. Morales argued that the ideologies of those involved in the drug trade are inherently opposed to those of a revolutionary movement and that Peruvians enjoying profits from the trade have little interest in Sendero Luminoso's radical ideological agenda (1990: 103, 136).

8. For a detailed account of the development of a political consciousness among coca growers in the Bolivian Chapare region, see Healy (1991). He reported that Bolivian growers are developing more sophisticated political tactics designed to preserve the legality of coca growing, gain legitimacy among national union groups, and advance issues such as international legalization and the preservation of Bolivia's sovereignty in the face of U.S. pressure for eradication.

9. "The peasant sindicato organizations [local CSUTCB groups] have employed sophisticated means of using the news media, print, radio and television to represent the interests of Bolivia's peasant majority and to embarrass and pressure the relevant government ministries" (Healy, 1986: 135).

REFERENCES

Allen, Catherine J. 1986. "Coca and Cultural Identity in Andean Communities." In *Coca and Cocaine: Effects on People and Policy in Latin America*, ed. Christine Franquemont and Deborah Pacini, pp. 35–48. Boston: Cultural Survival.

———. 1988. *The Hold Life Has: Coca and Cultural Identity in an Andean Community*. Washington, DC: Smithsonian Institution Press.

Blanes, José Jiménez. 1989. "Cocaine, Informality and the Urban Economy in La Paz, Bolivia." In *The Informal Economy: Studies in Advanced and Less Developed Countries*, ed. Alejandro Portes, Manuel Castells, and Lauren Benton, pp. 135–149. Baltimore: Johns Hopkins University Press.

Campodónico, Humberto. 1989. "La política del avestruz." In *Coca, cocaína y narcotráfico: Laberinto en los Andes*, ed. Diego García-Sayán, pp. 225–258. Lima: Comisión Andina de Juristas.

Craig, Richard B. 1987. "Illicit Drug Traffic: Implications for South American Source Countries." *Journal of Interamerican Studies and World Affairs* 29, 2: 1–34.

De Franco, Mario, and Ricardo Godoy. 1992. "The Economic Consequences of Cocaine Production in Bolivia: Historical, Local, and Macroeconomic Perspectives." *Journal of Latin American Studies* 24: 375–406.

Gereffi, Gary. 1989. "Rethinking Development Theory: Insights from East Asia and Latin America." *Sociological Forum* 4, 4: 505–533.

Gereffi, Gary, and Miguel Korzeniewicz. 1990. "Commodity Chains and Footwear Exports in the Semiperiphery." In *Semiperipheral States in the World Economy*, ed. William G. Martin, pp. 45–68. Westport, CT: Greenwood.

————, eds. 1994. *Commodity Chains and Global Capitalism*. Westport, CT: Greenwood.

Hargreaves, Clare. 1992. *Snowfields: The War on Cocaine in the Andes*. New York: Holmes and Meier.

Healy, Kevin. 1986. "The Boom within the Crisis: Some Recent Effects of Foreign Cocaine Markets on Bolivian Rural Society and the Economy." In *Coca and Cocaine: Effects on People and Policy in Latin America*, ed. Christine Franquemont and Deborah Pacini, pp. 101–144. Boston: Cultural Survival.

————. 1991. "Political Ascent of Bolivia's Peasant Coca Leaf Producers." *Journal of Interamerican Studies and World Affairs* 33 (Spring): 87–121.

Henkel, Ray. 1986. "The Bolivian Cocaine Industry." In *Drugs in Latin America*, ed. Edmundo Morales, pp. 53–80. Williamsburg, VA: College of William and Mary.

Kaswell, Jo Ann. 1989a. "The Addict Economies." *NACLA Report on the Americas* 22, 6: 33–38.

————. 1989b. "The Real Green Revolution." *NACLA Report on the Americas* 22, 6: 12–19.

Macdonald, Scott B. 1989. *Mountain High, White Avalanche: Cocaine and Power in the Andean States and Panama*. New York: Praeger.

McClintock, Cynthia. 1988. "The War on Drugs: The Peruvian Case." *Journal of Interamerican Studies and World Affairs* 30, 2/3: 127–142.

Mitchell, William P. 1991. *Peasants on the Edge: Crop, Cult, and Crisis in the Andes*. Austin: University of Texas Press.

Morales, Edumundo. 1989. *Cocaine: White Gold Rush in Peru*. Tucson: University of Arizona Press.

————. 1990. "The Political Economy of Cocaine Production: An Analysis of the Peruvian Case." *Latin American Perspectives* 17, 4 (Fall): 91–109.

Plowman, Timothy. 1986. "Coca Chewing and the Botanical Origins of Coca (Erythroxylum SPP) in South America." In *Coca and Cocaine: Effects on People and Policy in Latin America*, ed. Christine Franquemont and Deborah Pacini, pp. 5–29. Boston: Cultural Survival.

Queiser Morales, Waltraud. 1992. *Bolivia: Land of Struggle*. Boulder, CO: Westview Press.

Reid, Michael. 1989. "Una región amenazada por el narcotráfico." In *Coca, cocaína y narcotráfico: Laberinto en los Andes*, ed. Diego García-Sayán, pp. 133–169. Lima, Peru: Comisión Andina de Juristas.

Sanabria, Harry. 1986. "Coca, Migration and Social Differentiation in the Bolivian Lowlands." In *Drugs in the Americas*, ed. Edumundo Morales, pp. 81–124. Williamsburg, VA: College of William and Mary.

Strug, David L. 1986. "The Foreign Politics of Cocaine: Comments on a Plan to Eradicate the Coca Leaf in Peru." In *Coca and Cocaine: Effects on People and Policy in Latin America*, ed. Christine Franquemont and Deborah Pacini, pp. 73–88. Boston: Cultural Survival.

Truelove, Cynthia. 1992. "The Fetishism of Commodity Chains: Social Embeddedness, Social Regulation and Economic Restructuring Reconsidered." Unpublished paper presented at the American Sociological Association's 87th Annual Meeting, Pittsburgh, PA, August 20–24, 1992.

Wilson, Suzanne, and Marta Zambrano. 1994. "Cocaine, Commodity Chains, and Drug Politics: A Transnational Approach." In *Commodity Chains and Global Capitalism*, ed. Gary Gereffi and Miguel Korzeniewicz, pp. 297–315. Westport, CT: Greenwood Press.

3

Uncertainty, Innovation, and Global Competitiveness: The Brazilian Footwear Industry

Miguel E. Korzeniewicz

In the 1990s, Latin America has undergone profound economic, social, and political transformations. Many governments in the region have implemented policies involving the privatization of state assets, an emphasis on the role of free markets, and trade liberalization, thus seeking a greater integration into the international economy. The global landscape itself has changed dramatically in the past few years. New capitalist markets have surfaced in Eastern Europe and the former Soviet Union, North America and Western Europe have established trading blocs, and greater East Asia (including the People's Republic of China) has emerged as the most dynamic and fastest-growing economy in the world.

The nature and evolution of these global trends, and their consequences for individuals and communities, can only be grasped by an analytical framework that integrates local, national, and international dimensions. This chapter examines the Brazilian footwear industry to illustrate the linkages between industrial districts, state export policies, and world-market competitiveness.

In the 1970s and 1980s, Brazilian footwear manufacturers became highly successful exporters. In those two decades, the U.S. domestic production of shoes declined drastically as factories closed or became distributors of imports. During the 1980s, U.S. consumption of footwear grew rapidly, and this demand was met largely by production sites in Brazil, South Korea, and Taiwan. Within a cluster of small towns in southern Brazil, a tightly knit industrial district with the support of governmental export-promotion policies captured the profitable niche of mid-priced women's leather shoes. In the 1990s, however, competition from the People's Republic of China and the decline of state support has atomized firms within the district and eroded the communitarian character that had led to its success.

The objective of this chapter is to explore the nature and consequences of insertion in the global economy by specifying the conditions that underlie the emergence, transformation, and eventual decline of export-oriented manufacturing industries in semiperipheral countries such as Brazil. I suggest that the study of local organization and state support shows that they play an important role in competitive success. A Global Commodity Chains (GCC) approach helps cast light on the critical importance of the integration of backward and forward linkages. However, new theoretical and conceptual insights are needed to understand the conditions that lead to industrial decline.

The first section of this chapter reviews theoretical issues associated with the study of transnational linkages and manufactured exports. Next, I summarize data on three components of Brazilian export success: consumption patterns in the core, the consolidation of industrial districts, and the role of state incentives. The third section reviews the concept of GCC and its application to the case study. In the fourth and final section, I discuss both the empirical and the conceptual challenges of trends of global competitiveness in the 1990s.

TRANSNATIONAL ECONOMIC LINKAGES AND EXPORTS

In 1965 and 1966, Fernando Henrique Cardoso conducted a survey of firms and firm managers in Argentina and Brazil. The results were published in 1972 under the title of *Ideologias de la burguesia industrial en sociedades dependientes (Argentina y Brasil)*. The study was a very nuanced exploration of the relationship between the degree of "internationalization" of firms and their ideology and political orientation. Among other conclusions, Cardoso wrote that "from the moment in which the international capitalist system of industrial production becomes 'internationalized,' there is no longer a necessary relation between 'development, national independence and industrial bourgeoisie'" (1972: 221). A few years later, in *Dependency and Development in Latin America*, Cardoso (1979) defined both the extrinsic and intrinsic dimensions of dependency: "[I]mperialist penetration is a result of external social forces.... [T]he system of domination reappears as an 'internal' force, through the social practices of local groups and classes which try to enforce foreign interests" (1979; cited in Brown, 1994: 7).

Even in their subtle and sophisticated formulation, Cardoso's interpretations of the international economy and the international system reflect the perceptions prevalent in the intellectual and political agendas of the Latin American left in the 1960s and 1970s. From the standpoint of both history and contemporary trends, societal linkages to the outside world were cast in a detrimental light. In the twentieth century, the most visible manifestations of external linkages were the penetration of multinational corporations in domestic economies and foreign aid (in currency and arms) tied to U.S. political objectives of promoting and supporting "friendly" regimes. Even linkages originating at home (exports, primarily of raw materials) were seen as part and parcel of the overall structure of domination by core countries.

Thirty years after his earlier publications, Fernando Henrique Cardoso reformulated his assessment of external linkages:

The international system is a field of opportunities, of resources that must be sought. . . . The process of liberalization of the economy and opening toward the outside world will continue, not an objective in and of itself, but as a strategic element in the modernization of our economy. (cited in Brown, 1994:7)

Currently, the majority of sociologists and the political leaders, especially those from developing countries, identify the integration to, and the participation in, the international system with the solution to their problems rather than with the cause of their difficulties. (cited in Grosfoguel, 1995: 2)

Such a reassessment of the possibilities of development is characteristic of broader trends within the development literature. In the 1970s and 1980s, the impressive growth and relative equity of the development patterns of some East Asian nations led to a reevaluation of the role of external linkages in national development (Evans, 1987; Gereffi and Wyman, 1990). National ties to the world economy were defined as transnational economic linkages (TNELs) and categorized as consisting of four types: foreign aid, exports, direct foreign investment, and loans. The main argument underlying these types of analyses is that the specific conditions of dependency and inequality are contingent on both the mix and the management of these international linkages. In Latin America, foreign direct investment (primarily by U.S. multinationals) and commercial loans have been predominant, whereas in the East Asian nations, foreign aid and exports have driven their insertion in the world economy.

The "lost decade" of the 1980s in Latin America stood in sharp contrast with the growth of GNP per capita and trade in South Korea and Taiwan. There have been two different readings of the East Asian success. A "market" approach argues that the reason for their success lies in free and open merchandise and financial markets, a minimal role of the state, and the reliance on comparative advantages for their insertion in the world economy. An alternative reading of the success of East Asian economies focuses on the historical and institutional conditions that shaped its incorporation into the world economy (Johnson, 1982; Haggard, 1989; Cummings, 1987).

These theoretical interests coincide with an effort to study the institutional causes and effects of successful export strategies in Latin America (CEPAL, 1990, 1991; Goldfrank, 1989, 1990; Schwartz, 1991) and an interest in lessons that can be learned from other nations that have engaged in export-led development strategies (Fishlow, 1989; Gereffi and Wyman, 1990; Whitehead, 1989). To approach such themes, scholars from a variety of fields have called for a cross-disciplinary approach to the study of comparative development and organizational behavior (Evans and Stephens, 1988; Scott, 1983; Pfeffer, 1987; Starr, 1988).

Manufactured exports have come to be increasingly regarded as critical influences on national economies, and for several interrelated reasons. An export orientation may increase employment, provide currency, and force manufacturers to become competitive. Rubinson and Holtzman examined several studies of trade and found that a concentration on export commodities and reliance on raw-materials exports have a negative effect on development (Rubinson and Holtzman, 1982). Trade and international competitiveness have been related to issues of distribution and equity (Krueger, 1985; Baer and Gillis, 1983). Some scholars have argued that "patterns of trade in manufactured goods provide better insights into the efficiency of the institutions and policies of a country than do patterns of trade in primary products or services" (Olson, 1987: 252–253). Others indicate that the expansion of manufactured exports involves an expansion of overall employment and industrial activity, by contributing to the achievement of economies of scale (Tavares de Oliveira, 1987; Baldinelli, 1990; de Paula Pinto, 1983) and by exposing exporting firms to theoretically quasi-infinite markets (Lim, 1981). A detailed study of exports in Brazil found a substantive contribution of exports to savings and investment (Baumman Neves, 1985). The need to generate foreign currency to meet debt payments and interests has stimulated interest in manufactured exports because they are considered to be more stable in the long run, compared to the price and demand fluctuations that affect primary-product exports (CEPAL, 1989).

In previous studies, colleagues and I have identified cases of successful export industries in Latin America and analyzed the various social and economic factors that underlie their performance (Korzeniewicz et al., 1995; Goldfrank, 1994; Korzeniewicz, 1990; Lee and Cason, 1994; Wilson and Zambrano, 1994). Brazilian footwear is an archetype of a successful export commodity. Exports grew from U.S. $6 million in 1970 to $390 million in 1980 and $1.4 billion in 1992 (see Figure 3.1). Placed in the context of footwear exporters to the U.S. market, Brazil has maintained a share of between 10 and 15 percent of the total, which in 1994 amounted to almost $10 billion (see Table 3.1). What are the sociological insights that help account for this growth? The following two sections explore the role of industrial communities, state policies, and global commodity chains.

BRAZILIAN FOOTWEAR EXPORTS IN THE 1970s AND THE 1980s

During the 1980s, U.S. consumption of imported shoes grew at an astounding rate. Shoe imports tripled between 1975 and 1995 (U.S. Department of Commerce, various years–c). Twenty-five years ago, one out of every five pairs of shoes purchased in the United States was imported; fifteen years ago, one out of every two pairs was imported; and by 1989, four out of every five pairs of shoes purchased in the United States were made abroad (FIA, 1990; Mutti, 1980; U.S. Department of Commerce, various years–a).[1]

Table 3.1 shows the total current dollar value amount of footwear imports and the distribution of market share by country where exports originate. Between

Figure 3.1
Exports of Brazilian Footwear, 1970–1992

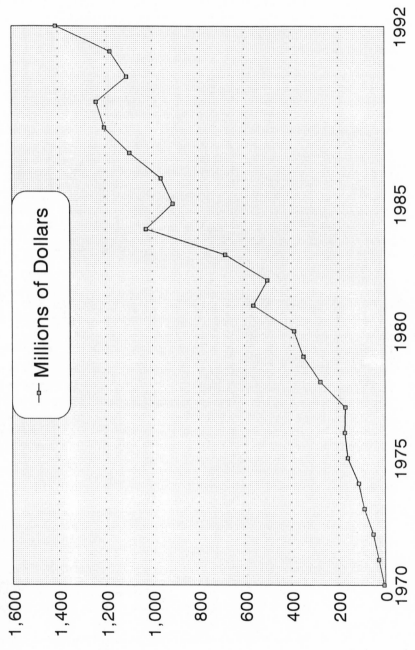

Source: United Nations, *International Trade Statistics Yearbook* (various years).

Table 3.1
Market Share of U.S. Footwear Imports, Selected Countries, 1967–1994 (Thousands of Dollars)

Year	TOTAL	Japan	Spain	Italy	Korea	Taiwan	Brazil	Indonesia	P.R.C.
1967	263,220	23	9	39	3	3	0	–	–
1968	388,135	21	12	41	3	4	1	–	–
1969	488,172	17	15	41	2	4	0	–	–
1970	629,402	15	13	42	2	6	1	–	–
1971	758,095	13	17	38	4	9	3	–	–
1972	915,014	6	19	37	5	11	5	–	0
1973	1,079,166	2	18	34	6	13	8	–	–
1974	1,153,391	1	17	28	9	15	8	–	0
1975	1,301,404	2	18	26	10	16	9	–	0
1976	1,724,547	1	14	20	16	21	8	–	0
1977	1,805,824	1	12	20	16	24	7	–	0
1978	2,584,979	2	11	22	15	23	7	–	0
1979	2,859,446	1	10	28	13	21	8	–	1
1980	2,807,937	1	7	19	17	30	9	–	1

Year	Value								
1981	3,019,374	1	7	17	18	27	12	–	1
1982	3,437,455	1	7	18	22	27	10	–	0
1983	4,009,541	1	6	17	21	30	13	–	0
1984	5,034,436	1	7	16	19	29	17	–	–
1985	5,955,634	–	7	15	19	30	15	0	1
1986	6,472,891	0	6	14	23	32	13	0	1
1987	7,546,765	0	5	11	23	32	13	0	2
1988	8,406,340	–	4	10	28	29	12	0	4
1989	8,380,755	–	4	10	26	24	12	1	9
1990	8,408,472	–	4	11	26	16	12	3	15
1991	8,311,911	–	4	9	20	12	11	5	27
1992	8,587,509	–	3	9	12	8	13	7	35
1993	9,256,221	–	3	8	7	5	15	8	42
1994	9,889,570*	–	2	7	4	3	14	7	46

*Projected.

Sources: U.S. Department of Commerce, U.S. General Imports (various years); Foreign Trade Highlights (1987, 1989); National Trade Data Bank (April 1991); U.S. International Trade Commission, Nonrubber Footwear Quarterly Statistical Report (various years).

1967 and 1994, the distribution of exports shows a distinct pattern. In the late 1960s, Japan, Italy, and Spain were the dominant exporters to the U.S. market, accounting for 74 percent of total imports in 1967. As these countries' economies matured and labor costs increased, the production of footwear relocated to Korea, Taiwan, and Brazil. By the mid-1980s, these three countries accounted for two-thirds of all imported footwear into the U.S. market.

The world footwear industry is segmented in terms of price and type-of-shoe niches. Data on shoe imports between 1970 and 1987 show that Korea has been highly specialized in the production of mid-priced athletic footwear; Taiwan concentrated on the lower-price plastic/rubber category; and Italy and Brazil were dominant in the women's leather shoes segment, at the high- and mid-price ranges, respectively. The consolidation of export niches in terms of type, gender, and cost of shoes is a key component of the success of Brazil and other semiperipheral countries in world markets. "Export niches help explain how South Korea, Taiwan and Brazil captured large shares of the American footwear market by specializing in products that were well suited to their raw material supply networks and domestic industrial capabilities" (Gereffi and Korzeniewicz, 1989: 24–25).

Women's footwear is the driving segment of the footwear industry. A majority of the dollars spent on shoes in the United States are spent on women's shoes, and a majority of the pairs of shoes bought in this country are women's shoes ("Footwear," 1989: 40–46). The growth in consumption of women's shoes helps explain the export success of Brazilian manufacturers. In 1970, Italian manufacturers were responsible for 70 percent of all the imported women's leather shoes sold in this country. By 1987, Brazil was the dominant exporter of women's leather shoes, accounting for 39 percent of the value and 50 percent of all the pairs sold. Within Brazil, footwear manufacturers have increasingly specialized in the women's shoe niche. In 1970, women's shoes comprised 41 percent of all the shoes Brazil exported to the United States; in 1980, the share was 67 percent; and in 1987, it was 83 percent (U.S. Department of Commerce, various years–b).

Two factors help account for the success of Brazilian exporters: industrial communities and state policies.

The Constitution of Geographically Bound Industrial Districts

Brazilian footwear producers are concentrated in distinct regional clusters. Data is drawn from a directory of Brazilian footwear firms (CTCCA, 1983), which, in its 1983 edition, lists 4,059 Brazilian firms. To identify geographical distribution, I first selected only those firms located in a city with ten or more producers, which yielded a sample of 3,140 firms, or 77.61 percent of the total directory.

Over 90 percent of producers are located in just five states (Minas Gerais,

Rio de Janeiro, Rio Grande do Sul, Santa Catarina, and São Paulo), and about 84 percent are located in only three states. The Brazilian footwear industry thrives in nonurban areas. In the state of São Paulo, only 265 firms, or 27 percent of the total, are located in the city of São Paulo, while 431 firms, or close to half the state total, are located in the smaller city of Franca. Finally, within the state of Rio Grande do Sul, only nine firms (1.19 percent) are located in its capital of Porto Alegre, while 309 (41 percent) are located in the smaller city of Novo Hamburgo. This regional concentration of the footwear industry also encompasses a range of suppliers of tanned leather, component parts, chemicals, and machinery (Schmitz, 1995).

The region of Vale dos Sinos is by far the most important footwear-exporting locality in Brazil. Total footwear exports in Brazil increased by 700 percent between 1973 and 1988. Throughout this period, the share of Rio Grande do Sul (RGS) over the Brazilian total has remained relatively constant, oscillating between 75 and 80 percent of the Brazilian total, although with a slight declining tendency. The region of Vale dos Sinos accounts for the overwhelming majority of RGS exports. In 1973, it accounted for 99.12 percent of all RGS exports. Since that year, however, it has declined slightly but consistently, and for the last four years of the series (1985–1988), it has accounted for about 90 percent of the state total. In sum, the region of Vale dos Sinos remains the preeminent exporting area in Brazil, accounting for well over two-thirds of all exports throughout the period of highest growth for the footwear-export business.

Brazilian firms are also very concentrated in terms of the type of products manufactured. Firms in the Vale dos Sinos area are highly specialized in the production of women's shoes for export, and this product concentration has increased over time. In 1974, about 85 percent of all shoes produced in the Vale do Rio dos Sinos area were women's shoes. In 1985, the share was closer to 98 percent (ACI, various years). On the one hand, specialization in ladies' shoes may be associated with highly dynamic organizational structures, since the quantity and quality of demand for ladies' shoes changes more and faster than for any other segment of footwear. On the other hand, a reliance on one segment hinders the capacity to diversify markets and renders producers dependent on specific marketing and distribution channels.

A critical component of industrial districts is what may be called *competitive collectivism*, which refers to the remarkable combination of collective-oriented actions—namely, the sharing of new technology and information—and competitive-oriented actions—namely, individual-firm production and marketing. One indicator is the consolidation of collective trade associations that provide benefits to their members, and a second is the existence of ethnically based informal ties that enhance economic competitiveness.

Brazil's collective organizations are old, effective, and consistent, particularly in terms of training and of research and development. There are two types of collective organizations: training/R&D organizations, and lobbying organizations. The Vale dos Sinos area, in southern Brazil, contains five well-established collective organizations. The Feira Internacional do Calçado (FENAC), or International Shoe Fair, organized its first fair in the Novo Hamburgo area in 1963 and became institutionalized in 1973. Its purpose has been to provide a showcase for Brazilian products and to serve as meeting point for Brazilian sellers and international buyers. The Serviço Nacional de Aprendizagem Industrial (National Industrial Apprenticeship Service) (SENAI) is a national organization in charge of instruction and training in technical areas, which maintains a footwear school (Escola do Calçado) in Novo Hamburgo. The Centro Tecnólogico do Couro, Calçado, e Afins (CTCCA), or Technological Center for Leather, Footwear, and Related Items, which is located in the city of Novo Hamburgo, is a private institution created by initiative of the producers of the Rio Grande do Sul area. Their main activity consists of ensuring quality controls of components and chemical products and lending technological assistance to their associates or to other firms requesting their services (Klein, 1986).

One example of interfirm networking is illustrated by the response to competitive challenges. At a time when Taiwanese shoe exports were beginning to be perceived as a potential threat because they were entering segments of the market in which Brazil had been dominant, the CTCCA chaired a roundtable with the participation of producers and importers to discuss the problem (Tecnicouro, 1987: 3–8). The Associação Comercial e Industrial do Novo Hamburgo (ACI/NH), or Industrial and Commercial Association of Novo Hamburgo, is the oldest trade association in Novo Hamburgo (founded in 1920). Most of its members (87 in 1989) are small- and medium-sized producers, and the main functions of the organization are lobbying, representing area industrialists, technical consulting, and maintaining a data bank. The Associaciao das Indústrias do Calçado do Rio Grande do Sul (ADICAL), or Association of Footwear Industries of Rio Grande do Sul, which was founded in 1983, consisted of 121 members as of 1989. ADICAL is primarily a lobbying group, and many of its members were among the largest firms in the Vale dos Sinos area at the time when ADICAL retained the services of Anthony Motley, former U.S. ambassador to Brazil and a former ranking State Department official, as a paid consultant to advance the interests of footwear producers in Washington.

Interviews with footwear industry people in Brazil and the United States indicate that a common German heritage of residents of the Vale dos Sinos area of Brazil has been a key component of the region's economic success in footwear manufacturing. The city of Novo Hamburgo—the largest in the Vale dos Sinos area—received its name after large numbers of Germans settled the area in the eighteenth and nineteenth centuries. Between the early 1800s and early 1900s, about 400,000 Germans migrated to Brazil, and by far the largest number settled in the state of Rio Grande do Sul, home of the Vale dos Sinos (Luebke, 1987: 14). In the late nineteenth and early twentieth centuries, many Germans or their second-generation descendants began to specialize in leather products. In the mid-1920s, Germans constituted about one-eighth of the overall population of nearby Porto Alegre, but they accounted for nearly one-third of the commerce and industry there. Even as far back as 1915, Germans and their descendants dominated the shoe and leather-goods businesses (Luebke, 1987: 29, 214). Today, a high percentage of Brazilians involved in the footwear industry are of German descent.

There is in the region a competitive spirit that is very healthy, but at the same time, we continue to have a gregarious spirit, of unity and collaboration, perhaps because of the German descent/colonization. Community action is impressive. You can easily manage to get the participation and the support of people for common activities. Large firms are conscious about the need of small and medium firms because of their agility in attending certain orders. (Klein, 1986)

The Role of the State

Governmental policies have played a key role in the development of footwear exports in Brazil. There are two fundamental types of policies through which the state carries out policies of export promotion: the administration of the exchange rate and the use of financial and fiscal incentives for exporters. Elsewhere (Korzeniewicz, 1990), I have shown that exchange rates and export incentives were relatively stable in Brazil throughout the 1970s and most of the 1980s. Virtually all producers interviewed in Brazil agreed that these were two stable features of their broader environment. The stability of these two variables is explained by the relative strength and cohesiveness of the Brazilian state.

The rate of foreign-currency exchange, or exchange rate, is of fundamental importance to the promotion of exports because it is one of the most important of the factors that determine the competitiveness of the locally produced good in the world market. Considerations about the exchange rate are a key aspect of a firm's decision to invest and produce. This is especially true of developing countries, such as Brazil. Throughout the 1970s and 1980s, the Brazilian state maintained its currency at a slightly undervalued rate, which favored exports of manufactures. Such a strategy was part of a broader Brazilian industrial policy designed to stimulate foreign trade.

Throughout the 1970s and 1980s, the promotion and management of exports in Brazil was concentrated in a relatively small but highly efficient agency: the Carteira do Comércio Exterior (CACEX), a division of Banco do Brasil. CACEX was characterized by an unusual degree of coordination with other agencies related to international economic policy making. Its effectiveness was due in part to its particular institutional configuration, as a "kind of strategic vertice of different governmental agencies and private interests . . . [with] evident dexterity to occupy 'empty spaces' in the administration . . . and assimilate entrepreneurial practices without losing its governmental mission" (Martins, 1985: 156). One of the institutional advantages of CACEX was its location, by virtue of its association with Banco do Brasil, vis-à-vis financial loci of power. The availability of resources allowed export programs to be financed consistently, and the bargaining power of CACEX in relation to both public and private interests was enhanced.

In summary, the Brazilian state's policies of export promotion in the 1970s and part of the 1980s met Meyer-Stamer's (1995: 5) definition of one condition of sustained competitiveness: "[T]he existence of stable framework conditions is crucial to industrial activity that goes beyond profit-maximization in the shortest possible term."[2] While the role of industrial districts and state policies are important components of the explanation of Brazilian success, a Global Commodity Chains approach helps shed light on the critical areas of backward and forward linkages.

COMMODITY CHAINS

Global Commodity Chains (GCC) are conceptual devices that examine related networks of organizations, activities, and social relations. They help illustrate and describe some of the master institutions underlying the structures of contemporary global capitalism.

A GCC consists of sets of interorganizational linkages, formed in the production and distribution of a commodity or product, that integrate trends in the global economy with their consequences on regions, nations, local industrial districts, communities, and the workplace. A "commodity chain," as defined by Hopkins and Wallerstein, refers to "a network of labor and production processes whose end result is a finished commodity" (1986: 159). In building a commodity chain, one begins with the final production operation for a consumable good and moves sequentially backward until reaching the raw-materials inputs (Hopkins and Wallerstein, 1986: 160–163).

The complexity of commodity chains for the kinds of export-oriented manufacturing industries in countries like Argentina, Brazil, and Chile requires extending the model proposed by Hopkins and Wallerstein (1986). It is extremely important to include forward as well as backward linkages from the production stage in the commodity chain. In the example of the global leather-footwear industry, a full commodity chain spans the entire spectrum of activities in the world economy: from Argentine raw materials to Brazilian manufacturing and then to the critical area of marketing and distribution in the U.S. market.

The concept of GCCs helps clarify the interplay of local, national, and international dimensions of organizations, classes, and politics. It can also help explore and explain the social, political, and economic dynamics that shape this global division of labor. By using a Global Commodity Chains perspective, we ask how and why firms, industries, localities, and/or countries incorporate themselves into the world economy and what the social consequences of these patterns of integration will be. GCCs help capture new trends in worldwide economic organization, as well as their consequences on society. The models focus on the organization of production in global industries enables us to make assessments about how and where wealth is generated and accumulated in the world-economy.

A GCC analysis also allows us to estimate the relative strength and importance of each of the chain's segments and to assess the possible consequences for the organizations and individuals involved. In the case of the leather footwear chain, while links are interdependent, U.S. importers and distributors have held the initiative in determining the volume and timing of purchases. The critical link provided by Brazilian marketing intermediaries illustrates the utility of Global Commodity Chains in highlighting simultaneously domestic and global dimensions of social and economic organization.

The commodity chains approach provides a helpful taxonomic device to understand how export networks are organized. However, these models tend to focus on the descriptive analyses of static components of particular chains, providing a snapshot of one point in time but neglecting processes and change over time (Humphrey, 1995: 151).

Backward Linkages

Tanned leather is one of the key inputs in leather footwear production. How, when, and what kind of tanned leather becomes available are fundamental factors underlying competitive export patterns. The processed leather must be of a quality appropriate to the intended quality and price of the finished product. The quantity of the leather must be sufficient to make the number of shoes required in a particular purchase order. Finally, the leather must be delivered in time to meet the appropriate deadlines.

Leather is by far the most important raw material utilized in the manufacturing of Brazilian shoes, and it is also an important component in the manufacturing of soles. The share of all-leather upper shoes in Vale dos Sinos exports (where the vast majority of Brazilian exports originate) has increased substantially between 1980 and 1987, from about half of all shoes produced to about 65 percent. In 1980, about 70 percent of all shoes exported from Vale dos Sinos had all-leather or nearly all-leather uppers, and by 1987, the share had risen to about 80 percent. Leather is the most important raw material supply for Argentine and Brazilian producers, and its importance has been increasing (ACI, 1980, 1985).

Interviews with Brazilian footwear producers show that informal as well as formal linkages allow them to purchase Argentine leather, which is considered more prestigious and of higher quality than Brazilian leather (Klein, 1986). Brazilian footwear producers have been successful in developing input networks to secure the best quality of processed leather in appropriate delivery schedules.

Labor is also an additional key input in the shoe industry of Brazil. The industry remains characterized by labor-intensive production, particularly as compared to related activities such as leather production. Among the firms interviewed in a recent study of shoe exporters (henceforth, the UIIC [Uncertainty, Innovation, and International Competitiveness] study),[3] where the labor force ranged from 262 to 2,200 workers, productivity levels showed no clear correlation with either the overall size or magnitude of sales of each particular enterprise. The largest firm, for example, had levels of productivity that placed it among the overall average of the sample, while one of the smallest firms (with 320 workers) had the second highest level of productivity. Without exception, all the firms reported no problems in securing a steady supply of labor and characterized their overall labor relations as stable.

Forward Linkages

Shoe manufacturers in Brazil have organized production primarily in terms of their export market. Among the seven enterprises interviewed in the UIIC study, for example, all except one derived over 90 percent of sales from the export market (and the remaining enterprise derived 73 percent of sales from exports). Such a pattern differs significantly from the industry's Argentine counterpart, where the export market constitutes, at best, a supplemental source of demand for firms that are primarily oriented toward their domestic market. Shoe producers in Brazil are also overwhelmingly directed toward the North American market. In the UIIC sample, for example, six of the seven producers cited the United States as their principal market (in most cases, capturing over 70 percent of overall exports), and the remaining producer cited Canada as the principal market (capturing 40 percent of overall exports). By contrast, only one of the shoe producers interviewed in Argentina had made any inroads into the North American market.

The differences between Brazil and Argentina are partially explained by the relative importance of their domestic markets. In the case of Argentina, domestic demand continues to constitute the principal market for shoe producers. In the case of Brazil, on the other hand, local market opportunities are characterized by greater constraints and export markets often provide the only available avenue to greater volumes of sales. These differences are reflected in the UIIC interviews: five of the seven Brazilian firms in the study cited the instability of the domestic market or the "low purchasing power of Brazilians" as the principal reason for moving into export markets, while none of their counterparts in Argentina mentioned the characteristics of the domestic market as an incentive for promoting exports.

The success of Brazilian footwear manufacturers is also explained by their ability to rely on an intermediary "corps" of individuals who act as linkages between the local producers and consumer markets in the United States and other destination markets. The seven Brazilian shoe producers interviewed in the UIIC study all identified these *intermediarios* ("intermediaries") or "export agents" as the primary channel used to gain access to markets in the United States and Europe.

These agents fulfill several key roles in the exporting sequence of the footwear industry in Brazil. Formally, they act as trading intermediaries between local domestic producers and foreign buyers, but in practice, they also cover a wide range of additional activities. For example, the agents act as product consultants; they study and follow fashion trends in Paris, Milan, New York, and other leading centers and then design shoes that meet changing consumer trends (Schuster, 1985). In a personal interview, an exporting agent in Brazil described his functions as including shoe design, cost estimation, production-sequence programming, leather quality control, raw-materials procurement, and economic and financial advice (Pochintesta, 1988).

The crucial role of intermediary agents is reflected in their symbiotic relationship with the tight-knit community of producers, particularly in the Brazilian Vale dos Sinos area. Comments made during the interviews in the UIIC study suggest that personal *trust* is a crucial component of the transactions conducted between local producers and export agents.

It is interesting to note differences between the cases of Brazil and Argentina. In Argentina, where shoe producers have been much less successful in capturing niches in the world market, the export agents that characterize the case of Brazil are altogether absent. In the UIIC study, the strategies used by four producers of shoes and related products in Argentina to seek markets abroad involved arrangements developed by either personal visits by firm owners to foreign stores or the use of appointed representatives abroad. A similar pattern characterized the strategies used by the Argentine leather exporters interviewed in the UIIC study. In these cases, the absence of formal channels of commercialization appears to be an important variable in explaining the limited access of Argentine producers to foreign markets.

The importance of analyzing the role of export agents lies in the fact that it allows us to link the success of exporters in Brazil to the changes experienced by the industry in the United States through a single organizational variable. That is, the two sets of observations—the success of exporters in Brazil and the decline of the industry in the United States—are equally central to the transformations experienced by this industry on a world-economic scale. Furthermore, both processes often arise out of a single shift in organizational strategy, as when corporations in the United States closed local production and replaced it with new contractual relations developed through agents abroad.

THE 1990s: GLOBAL COMPETITION, DEMISE OF THE DEVELOPMENTAL STATE AND THE LIMITS OF COMMUNITARIANISM

In the late 1980s and early 1990s, there have been three key developments in the global production of footwear. First, the People's Republic of China (PRC) has redrawn the map of the international division of labor in the production of light manufactures. The PRC now accounts for about half the value of all shoe exports to the United States (see Table 3.1).

The second major development of the 1990s is intrinsically related. Footwear firms have relocated from Taiwan and Korea to peripheral locations. Firms from Taiwan have relocated primarily to sites in the People's Republic of China, and Korean firms have relocated primarily to Indonesian sites. Part of the reason for this relocation is the increase in labor mobilization that accompanied the reinstitution of democratic regimes in Taiwan and South Korea. In addition, the pool of available labor for light manufacturing factories shrunk as these countries' economies became more diversified and the proportion of service activities increased. In contrast, the authoritarian regimes of Indonesia and the PRC have provided the appropriate combination of a low-paid workforce, incentives in the form of infrastructure and fiscal concessions, and the means for social control.[4]

A third characteristic that emerges from Table 3.1 is that in each of the first two waves of footwear exports, one country has maintained an important share of the market. Italian footwear firms continued to export a significant value of shoes through the 1980s. In the second wave of major exporters, the share of Korean and Taiwanese-made shoes dropped precipitously, but Brazil has not followed the trajectory of its semiperipheral counterparts. Instead, the data shows that Brazil has maintained its share of exports to the U.S. market.

The Demise of the Developmental State

The central question facing the Brazilian footwear industry is whether resources and actions can be mobilized to achieve "systemic competitiveness" (Meyer-Stamer, 1995: 7–8). Beyond labor cost advantages, supporting environments need to be consolidated and new patterns of state-firm relationships must be created. In 1994, the Brazilian state set in motion a set of programs designed to fundamentally transform the economic system and the trade regime. The basic cornerstone of these programs has been control over the inflation rate. Tight monetary policies, privatization of state-owned enterprises, and the influx of foreign capital have combined to substantially appreciate the domestic currency.

Domestic currency appreciation has two immediate consequences: first, it automatically renders locally produced goods more expensive in world markets (and, hence, less competitive) and second, it renders imported goods cheaper. The reduction in cost of the imported goods has two important consequences for industrial production and industrial exports: on the one hand, it can help industrial firms renovate or expand their capital goods and equipment, while on the other, it encourages imports of consumer goods. In other words, firms have the strategic option of either strengthening or weakening their competitiveness in global markets.

In terms of state incentives for exports, de Castro (1994) gave an excellent overview of what he calls the "Demise of State-Led Development" in Brazil (for a broader and compelling assessment of the dynamics involved in the social, economic and political outcomes of neoliberal reforms, see Smith, Acuña, and Gamarra, 1994). Over the past few years, there has been a gradual retrenchment of state expenditures on items like the promotion of manufactured exports (including the dissolution of CACEX). Many of the most important fiscal and financial incentives that gave that industry a boost in the late 1970s and early 1980s had been either phased out gradually or been subject to policy-originated fluctuations through the 1980s. Brazil's balance of trade has deteriorated in the mid-1990s. Between 1989 and 1993, Brazil's exports grew by $4.4 billion, but its imports grew by $7.4 billion (Brazil Country Report, 1994: 1–5).

The Limits of Communitarianism

The effect of competition from Asia and the loss of governmental incentives on the Brazilian footwear industry have been twofold. Some firms have found locations with relatively inexpensive labor and fewer labor organizations in the hinterland within the Brazilian borders. In the industry as a whole, there has been a process of atomization between firms able to compete successfully under these new conditions and those that have been unable to adjust.

Data from the 1980s already showed a pattern of firm relocation. In particular, the two most important municipalities in the area show a declining share of total Vale dos Sinos exports. Between 1976 and 1987, the share of exports originating in the municipality of Novo Hamburgo declined by 40 percent, while in the same period, the share of Campo Bom declined by about 25 percent. On the other hand, there was a cluster of four municipalities—mostly small—that noticeably increased their share of Vale dos Sinos exports. Sapiranga increased its share, between 1976 and 1987, by about 50 percent. The other three municipalities—Igrejinha, Dois Irmaos, and Ivoti—increased their share from a combined total of 5.3 percent to 15.5 percent—an increase of 300 percent. The relative increases and decreases in the two clusters are fairly consistent over time but became more accentuated throughout the 1980s.

This data suggests that these two clusters of municipalities reproduce, *within a single industrial district*, patterns of sequential change from manufacturing to service activities. Newer, less urbanized municipalities with lower labor costs become more industrialized, while older, more developed municipalities come to specialize in services. In the words of one Brazilian businessman, "Novo Hamburgo has become the New York of Vale dos Sinos" (Korzeniewicz, 1990: 125).

The Brazilian footwear industry is facing some of the constraints and challenges that the Italian footwear industry confronted in the 1970s. Faced with competition from lower wage sites in Brazil and Asia, producers strengthened their advantages in the areas of image, fashion content, and design, upgrading the average unit-value of their shoes (Rabellotti, 1995: 31). In Brazil, some of the larger firms are trying to modify their marketing in order to diversify both export destinations and distribution and retail patterns (Schmitz, 1995: 15). The central question facing the Brazilian footwear industry is whether resources and actions can be mobilized to achieve "systemic competitiveness" (Meyer-Stamer, 1995: 7–8).

While a number of small and medium producers are expected to downsize or close down in the near future, "a small handful of factories, well-financed and well-administered, have reinvested profits for decades and have thrived and grown. These factories will continue their path of perfecting their product, technology, skills and efficiency, with their average price climbing, to replace those surviving Italian factories in a specific quality level" (Geller, 1995: 2). Additionally, faced with changing trends in demand and foreign competition, firms may either attempt to move into different niches or to redefine their position within their commodity chain (Humphrey, 1995: 158).

During the 1970s and most of the 1980s, the cohesiveness of trade associations in the Brazilian footwear industry played a major role in the success of exports. However, in the course of interviews conducted in 1992, Brazilian shoe manufacturers reported almost unanimously that their entrepreneurial environment was characterized by a combination of confrontational and cooperative elements. One firm owner remarked that "our system is confrontational. We have a system of agents that buy from the cheaper supplier. Each time, Americans are getting lower and lower prices." According to another, "[S]mall firms are left aside when the most important decisions get made." Another explained: "Abicalcados [the Brazilian Association of the Footwear Industry] does not help us. It's only for an elite. They don't help with cancelled orders. . . . [T]he weak point in the system is the factory, but they don't help with the relationship between factories and buyers. I pay my dues, but what they talk about has nothing to do with me" (UIIC study).

CONCLUSION

Scholars in the areas of social and economic development have increasingly turned their attention to the role of external linkages (such as manufactured exports) in shaping local, regional, and national patterns of growth. This chapter described the success of Brazilian footwear in global markets during the 1970s and 1980s and the competitive challenges that have surfaced in the 1990s. It focused on three main explanations. First, the constitution of industrial districts based on cooperative and communitarian action facilitated effective and expedient economic transactions. However, these sets of relationships have become strained as firms atomize in the face of increased competition. Second, the Brazilian state's policies of export promotion through fiscal incentives and management of the exchange rate provided a stable macroeconomic environment conducive to trade transactions. However, by the mid-1990s, developmental policies and resources have become drastically curtailed in the context of major economic reforms, which also resulted in the appreciation of the domestic currency. Finally, the consolidation of commodity chains that linked production with backward and forward linkages played a major role in the success of the Brazilian footwear industry.

This chapter raised theoretical and conceptual issues that suggest venues for future research. Taxonomically, I highlighted the importance of integrating macro- and micro-levels of analysis by linking communities, state policies, and the global environment. The use of a commodity chains approach is particularly helpful in mapping out the geography and organization of transnational activities. For example, the focus on export agents as a component of forward linkages helps shed light on both the access of Brazilian manufacturers to global markets and the transformation of American footwear producers into importers and distributors.

Perhaps the most germane and promising questions, however, arise out of the dynamic changes that these global linkages and structures undergo over time. The rise of the People's Republic of China as a major exporter of footwear directs our attention to geographical cycles of competitiveness. The decline of the Brazilian state's policies of export promotion suggests that the relationship between state and industrialization in Latin America has changed drastically and needs to be analytically redefined. Last, but not least, recent data for the Vale Dos Sinos area show patterns of industry consolidation, firm relocation, product upgrading, and transition to service activities. These patterns indicate that semiperipheral, "newly industrializing" regions and countries can replicate, to some extent, the cycles of industrial growth, maturation, and decline typically associated with developed countries. Assessing and measuring these changes, their consequences, and the social and organizational responses that follow should prove to be a very valuable contribution to our understanding of development.

NOTES

1. Between 1988 and 1992, however, the consumption of imported footwear in the United States remained stagnant. It again grew in 1993 and 1994, but at a much slower pace compared with the 1980s.

2. By contrast, state policies in Argentina were characterized by considerable shifts over the past two decades.

3. This study is composed of 27 interviews with managers of firms associated with the shoe-exporting business in Brazil and Argentina.

4. While Taiwan and South Korea contend with a relatively confined geographical setting, Brazilian companies continue to expand within the national territory. In recent months, firms have relocated as far as northeast Brazil to take advantage of lower labor costs and concessions by local state and city governments (Geller, 1995: 3).

REFERENCES

Associação Comercial e Industrial do Novo Hamburgo (ACI/NH). 1980, 1985, 1989. [census data.] Novo Hamburgo, Brazil: Associação Comercial e Industrial do Novo Hamburgo.

Baer, Werner, and Malcolm Gillis, eds. 1983. *Export Diversification and the New Protectionism.* Champaign: University of Illinois Press.

Baldinelli, Elvio. 1990. *Exportar, el Camino de los Paises que Crecen.* Buenos Aires: Fundacion de Investigaciones Economicas Latinoamericanas.

Baumann Neves, Renato. 1985. *Exportacoes e Crescimento Industrial do Brasil.* Rio de Janeiro: Instituto de Planejamento Economica e Social.

Brown, Ken. 1994. "Having Left Campus for the Arena, Winner in Brazil Shifts to Right." *New York Times*, November 20, 1994, sec. 4.

Capecchi, Vittorio. 1989. "The Informal Economy and the Development of Flexible Specialization in Emilia-Romagna." In *The Informal Economy*, ed. Alejandro Portes, Manuel Castells, and Lauren Benton, pp. 189–215. Baltimore: Johns Hopkins University Press.

Cardoso, Fernando Henrique. 1972. *Ideologias de la Burguesia Industrial en Sociedades Dependientes (Argentina y Brazil).* Mexico: Siglo XXI editores.

Cardoso, Fernando Henrique, and Enzo Faletto. 1979. *Dependency & Development in Latin America.* Berkeley: University of California Press.

Centro Tecnologico do Couro, Calçados e Afins (CTCCA). 1983. *Anuario da Industria Nacional do Couro, Calçados, e Afins.* Novo Hamburgo, Brazil: CTCCA.

Comision Economica para America Latina y el Caribe (CEPAL). 1989. *Proceso de Industrializacion y Dinamica Exportadora: Las Experiencias de las Industrias Aceitera y Siderurgica en la Argentina.* Buenos Aires: CEPAL.

———. 1990. *Changing Production Patterns with Social Equity.* Santiago: CEPAL.

———. 1991. *Los Canales de Comercializacion y la Competitividad de las Exportaciones Latinoamericanas.* Santiago: CEPAL.

Cummings, Bruce. 1987. "The Origins and Development of the Northeast Asian Political Economy: Industrial Sectors, Product Cycles, and Political Consequences." In *The Political Economy of the New Asian Industrialism*, ed. Frederic Deyo, pp. 44–83. Ithaca, NY: Cornell University Press.

de Castro, Antonio Barros. 1994. "Renegade Development: Rise and Demise of State-Led Development in Brazil." In *Democracy, Markets, and Structural Reform in Latin America*, ed. William Smith, Carlos Acuña, and Eduardo A. Gamarra, pp. 183–209. Miami, FL: Transaction Publishers.

de Paula Pinto, Mauricio Barata. 1983. *Exportaçoes Brasileiras de Manufacturados: Crescimento e Mudanca de Estrutura.* São Paulo: Instituto de Pesquisas Economicas.

Economist Intelligence Unit. 1994. *Brazil: Country Report 1994.* London: The Economist.

Evans Peter. 1987. "Class, State, and Dependence in East Asia: Lessons for Latin Americanists." In *The Political Economy of the New Asian Industrialism*, pp. 203–226. Ithaca, NY: Cornell University Press.

Evans, Peter, and John Stephens. 1988. "Development and the World Economy." In *Handbook of Sociology*, ed. Neil Smelser, pp. 739–773. Beverly Hills, CA: Sage.

Fishlow, Albert. 1989. "Latin American Failure against the Background of Asian Success." *Annals* 505 (September): 117–128.

"Footwear." 1989. Fairchild Factfile. New York: Fairchild Publications, Market Division.

Footwear Industries of America (FIA). 1990. *Current Highlights.* Washington, DC: FIA.

Geller, Lawrence, President of Celerity-Comercio International Ltda., Novo Hamburgo, Brazil. 1995. Personal interview via fax.

Gereffi, Gary, and Miguel Korzeniewicz. 1990. "Commodity Chains and Footwear Exports in the Semiperiphery." In *Semiperipheral States in the World Economy*, ed. William Martin, pp. 45–68. Westport, CT: Greenwood Press.

Gereffi, Gary, and Donald Wyman, eds. 1990. *Manufacturing Miracles: Paths of Industrialization in Latin America and East Asia*. Princeton, NJ: Princeton University Press.

Goldfrank, Walter. 1989. "Harvesting Counterrevolution: Agricultural Exports in Pinochet's Chile." In *Revolution in the World-System*, ed. Terry Boswell, pp. 189–198. Westport, CT: Greenwood Press.

———. 1990. "State, Market and Agriculture in Pinochet's Chile." *Semiperipheral States in the World-Economy*, ed. William Martin, pp. 69–77. Westport, CT: Greenwood Press.

———. 1994. "Fresh Demand: The Consumption of Chilean Produce in the United States." In *Commodity Chains and Global Capitalism*, ed. Gary Gereffi and Miguel Korzeniewicz, pp. 267–279. Westport, CT: Greenwood Press.

Grosfoguel, Ramón. 1995. "From Cepalismo to Neoliberalism: A World-System Approach to Conceptual Shifts in Latin America." Manuscript presented at the Political Economy of the World-System XIX Annual Conference: Latin America in the World-Economy, University of Miami, April 20–22.

Haggard, Stephan. 1989. "The East Asian NICs in Comparative Perspective." *Annals* 505 (September): 129–141.

Hearn, Frank. 1988. "Part Three: Beyond the Management Model of Industrial Organization." In *The Transformation of Industrial Organization*, ed. Frank Hern. Belmont, CA: Wadsworth Publishing Company, pp. 193–204.

Hopkins, Terence K, and Immanuel Wallerstein. 1986. "Commodity Chains in the World-Economy prior to 1800." *Review* 10, 1: 157–170.

Humphrey, J. 1995. "Industrial Reorganization in Developing Countries: From Models to Trajectories." *World Development* 23, 1: 149–162.

Johnson, Chalmers. 1982. *MITI and the Japanese Miracle*. Stanford, CA: Stanford University Press.

Klein, Enio, Director of the Technologicial Center for Leather and Footwear (CTCCA). Novo, Hamburgo, Brazil. 1986. Personal interview.

Korzeniewicz, Miguel. 1990. "The Social Foundations of International Competitiveness: Footwear Exports in Argentina and Brazil." Ph.D. diss., Department of Sociology, Duke University, Durham, NC.

Korzeniewicz, Roberto P., Walter Goldfrank, and Miguel E. Korzeniewicz. 1995. "Vines and Wines in the World-Economy." In *Food and Agrarian Orders in the World-Economy*, ed. Philip McMichael, pp. 113–138. Westport, CT: Greenwood Press.

Krueger, Anne. 1985. "The Experience and Lessons of Asia's Super Exporters." In *Export Oriented Development Strategies*, ed. Vittorio Corbo, Anne Krueger, and F. Ossa, pp. 187–212. Boulder, CO: Westview Press.

Lazerson, Mark. 1988. "Organizational Growth of Small Firms: An Outcome of Markets and Hierarchies." *American Sociological Review* 53, 3 (June): 330–342.

Lee, Naeyoung, and Jeffrey Cason. 1994. "Automobile Commodity Chains in the NICs: A Comparison of South Korea, Mexico, and Brazil." In *Commodity Chains and*

Global Capitalism, ed. Gary Gereffi and Miguel Korzeniewicz, pp. 223–244. Westport, CT: Greenwood Press.

Lim, Youngil. 1981. *Government Policy and Private Enterprise: Korean Experience in Industrialization*. Berkeley: University of California Press.

Luebke, Frederick C. 1987. *Germans in Brazil*. Baton Rouge: Louisiana State University Press.

Martins, Luciano. 1985. *Estado Capitalista e Burocracia do Brasil Pos-64*. Rio de Janeiro: Paz e Terra.

Meyer-Stamer, Joerg. 1995. ''Governance in the Post-Import Substitution Era: Perspectives for New Approaches to Support Industrial Competitiveness in Brazil.'' Unpublished manuscript.

Mutti, John H. 1980. *Output and Employment in a ''Trade Sensitive'' Sector: Adjustment in the U.S. Footwear Industry*. Washington, DC: World Bank.

Olson, Mancur. 1987. ''Economic Nationalism and Economic Progress.'' *World Economy* 10, 3: 240–261.

Pfeffer, Jeffrey. 1987. ''Bringing the Environment Back In: The Social Context of Business Strategy.'' In *The Competitive Challenge: Strategies for Industrial Innovation and Renewal*, ed. David J. Teece, pp. 119–135. Cambridge, MA: Ballinger.

Piore, Michael J., and Charles F. Sabel. 1984. ''The Second Industrial Divide.'' New York: Basic Books.

Pochintesta, Alberto, President of STEPS, Inc. 1988. Personal interview, Ivoti, Rio Grande do Sul, Brazil, March 13.

Rabellotti, Roberta. 1995. ''Is There an 'Industrial District Model'? Footwear Districts in Italy and Mexico Compared.'' *World Development* 23, 1: 29–41.

Rubinson, Richard, and Deborah Holzman. 1982. ''Comparative Dependence and Economic Development.'' In *Comparative Sociological Research in the 1960s and 1970s*, ed. J. Michael Armer and Robert Marsh, pp. 86–101. Leiden, The Netherlands: E. J. Brill.

Schmitz, Hubert. 1995. ''Small Shoemakers and Fordist Giants: Tale of a Supercluster.'' *World Development* 23, 1: 9–28.

Schuster, Lynda. 1985. ''Brazil Captures a Big Share of the U.S. Shoe Market.'' *Wall Street Journal*, August 27.

Schwartz, Hugh H. 1991. *Supply and Marketing Constraints on Latin American Manufacturing Exports*. Washington, D.C.: Interamerican Development Bank.

Scott, W. Richard. 1983. ''The Organization of Environments: Network, Cultural and Historical Elements.'' In *Organizational Environments: Ritual and Rationality*, ed. John W. Meyer and W. Richard Scott, pp. 155–175. Beverly Hills, CA: Sage.

Smith, William L., Carlos H. Acuña, and Eduardo A. Gamarra, eds. 1994. *Latin American Political Economy in the Age of Neoliberal Reform*. New Brunswick, NJ: Transaction Publishers.

Starr, Martin K. 1988. *Global Competitiveness: Getting the U.S. Back on Track*. New York: W. W Norton.

Tavares de Oliveira, Carlos. 1987. *Exportaçao: O Modelo Ideal*. Rio de Janeiro, RJ, Brazil: Editors de Fundacao Getulio Vargas.

Tecnicouro. 1987. ''Brasilestá Começando a Perder Mercado nos Sapatos Baratos.'' *Tecnicouro* (Brazil) 9 (March-April).

U.S. Department of Commerce. Various years–a. *U.S. Foreign Trade Highlights*. Washington, DC: Bureau of the Census.

————. Various years–b. *U.S. General Imports.* Washington, DC: Bureau of the Census.

————. Various years–c. *U.S. Industrial Outlook.* Washington, DC: Bureau of the Census.

————. Various years–d. *Nonrubber Footwear Quarterly Statistical Report.* Washington, DC: Bureau of the Census.

Whitehead, Laurence. 1989. "Tigers in Latin America." *The Annals of the American Academy of Political and Social Science.* 505 (September): 142–151

Wilson, Suzanne, and Maria Zambrano. 1994. "Cocaine, Commodity Chains, and Drug Politics: A Transnational Approach." In *Commodity Chains and Global Capitalism,* ed. Gary Gereffi and Miguel Korzeniewicz, pp. 281–296. Westport, CT: Greenwood Press.

4

SMALL FIRMS, SOCIAL CAPITAL, AND GLOBAL COMMODITY CHAINS: SOME LESSONS FROM THE TEX-MEX BORDER IN THE ERA OF FREE TRADE

David Spener

The United States–Mexico border is a unique geographical zone of articulation between a dominant state in the capitalist core and a subaltern state in the traditional periphery of the world-system.[1] Social, cultural, economic, and political relations—indeed practically the entirety of social life in the region—are starkly colored by the international division of labor that is enforced by the militarized political boundary between Mexico and the United States. The last few years have been an especially interesting conjuncture for studying the border region as Mexico, under the administrations of Miguel de la Madrid and Carlos Salinas, attempted to move from the periphery and into the semiperiphery of the world-economy, becoming what the current U.S. administration deemed one of the world's major "emerging markets." During this period, the border region has received a great deal of attention in the research literature on globalization in capitalist development. Most of the effort has gone into studying the Border Industrialization (*maquiladora*) Program, and important insights have been gained for the export-oriented industrialization of Latin America as a whole. Much less attention has been paid, however, to the role played by small- and medium-scale enterprises in the region, which employ half or more of the private sector working population on both sides of the international border.

In this chapter, I relate the effects that Mexico's unilateral trade liberalization of the late 1980s and early 1990s had on entrepreneurs operating small businesses in the Texas portion of the U.S.-Mexico border region and explain how these entrepreneurs—most of whom were of Mexican ancestry—responded by using the social and cultural resources at their disposal.[2] The analysis will: (1) describe how Texas border entrepreneurs helped, not only U.S., but also Asian and European manufacturers to extend commodity chains into Mexico in the period prior to that country's trade opening in a limited, informal way; (2) how, subsequent to the trade opening, they played a crucial role in the rapid elaboration of more complete distribution networks for these goods in Mexico; and (3) how the same social and cultural resources that served Texas border entrepreneurs well in the initial period of Mexican liberalization soon proved inadequate to defend their traditional role as brokers of binational trading relationships.

There are several senses in which the border entrepreneurs discussed in this chapter occupied what Wright (1985) has referred to as a "contradictory class location." First, they were owners or managers of businesses, and hence, generally bourgeois in their outlook, yet in most cases they had only limited capital and labor at their disposal. They thus found themselves in an extremely vulnerable position relative to larger-scale enterprises, which had a much greater capacity to dominate the markets served by both. Second, most of the border entrepreneurs, as either Mexican-Americans or Mexican immigrants, were members of a U.S. minority group and binational diaspora that had suffered a long history of discrimination and subordination at the hands of the dominant Anglo majority in the United States. At the same time, they had been treated with great ambivalence by the Mexican ruling elites as well. Thus, their perspectives on the structure of U.S. society and their opportunities within it, as well as toward the Mexican state and society, were different than those of Anglo businesspeople in the United States and Mexican businesspeople across the border. Third, unlike many large U.S. manufacturers, most entrepreneurs in the Texas border region viewed Mexico mostly as a geographically accessible, coethnic market to be sold to, and not as a low-wage production site to either exploit or from which to fear competition. Amid these contradictions, the business organizations in which border entrepreneurs participated became strong advocates of the North American Free Trade Agreement (NAFTA). The agreement was viewed as beneficial for the Mexican consumers and firms who were their own customers, and they hoped it would strengthen the binational brokering role they had already been playing within the limits imposed by the restrictive trade regime that was in place prior to NAFTA.

By looking at the particular conjunctural situation of Texas border entrepreneurs in the period leading up to NAFTA, I also attempt to shed some theoretical light on the participation in general of small-scale retail/wholesale firms in global commodity chains. Gereffi, Korzeniewicz, and Korzeniewicz (1994) have described how in many industries it is not multinational manufacturers who direct the market in goods, but rather global merchandisers who organize, not only the promotion and distribution of goods sold under their auspices, but also their production through a system of flexible subcontracting. What remains undertheorized in this formulation are many of the forward commercial linkages of not only producer-driven, but also buyer-driven commodity chains. It is frequently forgotten that it is not always the manufacturer or global merchandiser who organizes the local distribution of globally traded products, but rather a plethora of small firms whose detailed knowledge of local markets is drawn from the many webs of socioentrepreneurial relationships in which their personnel are enmeshed. As Sayer and Walker (1992) and others (Crook, Pakulski, and Waters, 1992; Reich, 1991) have pointed out, small firms have traditionally carried out vital commercial, distribution, and maintenance/repair services that larger concerns cannot perform as profitably.

Moreover, these many small firms add considerable value to the final product by delivering it to the buyer and servicing it thereafter in what analysts of the post modern condition remind us is an increasingly fragmented global consumer market (Harvey, 1989). The existence of these firms and the persons operating them should not be assumed, nor should it be viewed as incidental to the overall process of elaborating commodity chains. Large corporations playing directive roles in global commodity chains do not simply conjure up these smaller firms; instead, small firms actively seek to insert themselves in these global commodity chains, and they do so for particular sets of reasons and with specific kinds of resources at their disposal. Finally, how successfully small firms are able to insert themselves or defend their existing positions in global commodity chains has serious repercussions for the local communities in which they are located, not only in terms of employment levels (since small firms are generally more labor intensive than their larger-scale counterparts) but also in terms of the social reproduction of the local (mostly petty) bourgeoisie. The experiences of Texas border entrepreneurs provide an interesting case study of this process.

THE TEXAS BORDER REGION BEFORE MEXICAN TRADE LIBERALIZATION

The urban areas of the border region of Texas have long been among the poorest in the United States (Cárdenas, Chapa, and Burek, 1993; Maril, 1989; Montejano, 1987; Valdez, 1993).[3] Geographically isolated from and economically marginal to the rest of the United States, the border region could be referred to as "Mexican" Texas as well, for the large majority of its nearly 3 million inhabitants are of Mexican ancestry (63 percent were Latinos, and 57 percent spoke Spanish at home in 1990).[4] Historically, the economies of the cities in this region were dependent on farm production, ranching, mining, and government employment (particularly the military), and in the case of El Paso, garments and other light manufacturing (Institute for Mining and Materials Management, 1991). As the population in northern Mexico grew between 1960 and 1980, brought about in part by the Border Industrialization Program (the *maquiladora* program), Texas cities on the international line itself also increasingly specialized in commerce and distribution services for production and consumption needs across the border (Corona Vásquez, 1990; Curtis, 1993; Savage and Blankmeyer, 1990; Tamayo and Fernández, 1983). While the San Antonio metropolitan area is not normally thought of as a "border town" (it is located more than 100 miles from the international line) the city serves as the economic and cultural capital of the region, and it has especially strong historical and contemporary ties to Mexico (Arreola, 1987; Dunigan, 1992; Landolt, 1976; "Casa San Antonia," 1994). San Antonio also increasingly attracted Mexican shoppers, tourists, and immigrants during this period and, as the region's largest city, was a net exporter of services to the border towns in its "hinterland" (Geyer, 1990; Gilmer, 1990).

Even though the Texas border region's trading relationship with Mexico was of a limited nature during this period, its urban economies were still quite dependent on sales to Mexican nationals, many of whom resided in Mexican border cities immediately across the international line and regularly shopped on the U.S. side. When the Mexican peso crashed in 1982, the effect on business revenues and employment in the Texas border cities was devastating (Harrell and Fischer, 1985), leading two commentators to note that the "monetary and fiscal policies of the Mexican government have a greater impact on the border merchant than do the fiscal and monetary policies of the United States" (Savage and Blankmeyer, 1990: 76). By that time, the avenues for new, autonomous economic growth in the Texas border region were quite limited. Mechanization had eliminated much of the need for farm labor in South Texas (Maril, 1989; Montejano, 1987); moreover, the region's existing manufacturing base was small (14.3 percent of workers in 1980) and government employment was large (24.6 percent) relative to other major Texan urban centers. Opportunities for industrial expansion in the region were limited by competition with the Mexican *maquiladoras* for assembly operations (low wages) and by already established manufacturing in Dallas and Houston (which benefited from existing plant and equipment and better access to U.S. and world markets, as well as sources of finance). The region was not blessed with abundant natural resources, nor did it have a vast potential as a tourist attraction for residents of either the United States or Mexico. The low education levels and poverty of the border region's workers compared to those in Dallas and Houston also limited the region's internal market for services (see Table 4.1), since the growth of retail trade and other personal services depends on high disposable incomes on the part of a substantial part of the population. The history of anti-Mexican racism in Texas (Foley, 1988; Maril, 1989; Montejano, 1987), as well as nearly continuous cross-border migration by Mexican nationals, resulted in poverty and lack of education being especially concentrated among Mexican-Americans and Mexican immigrants in the region.

Given these conditions, trade in goods with Mexico was one of the few viable entrepreneurial niches for nonelite members of the border region's majority Mexican ancestry population. This was especially so to the extent that such trade could be built on social network and cultural connections with Mexico—Mexican *social capital*—that could be substituted for other kinds of capital (financial, physical, and human), which were in short supply in the community.[5] Indeed, physical proximity to the border with Mexico and Texas's social and cultural connections to Mexico were not only what defined the Texas border region as a *region*, but also constituted its principal economic *resource* in the

Table 4.1
Selected Characteristics of the Employed Population, Texas Border Region,
Dallas, and Houston, 1980

Border Region Urban Areas			
Group	Percent with college degree	Percent living in poverty	Mean annual income*
All persons	17.2	10.7	$13,138
White Anglo natives	29.5	3.9	$17,103
Latino natives**	9.8	12.4	$10,974
Latino immigrants	4.9	24.9	$9,336

Dallas			
Group	Percent with college degree	Percent living in poverty	Mean annual income*
All persons	23.1	4.4	$16,594
White Anglo natives	25.6	2.9	$17,853
Latino natives**	8.7	7.7	$12,571
Latino immigrants	7.0	12.0	$11,064

Houston			
Group	Percent with college degree	Percent living in poverty	Mean annual income*
All persons	24.5	4.6	$18,119
White Anglo natives	28.9	2.6	$21,886
Latino natives**	7.9	6.5	$13,923
Latino immigrants	8.6	11.4	$10,697

*For persons who worked at least 1,600 hours in 1979 (40 weeks times 40 hours per week).
**Nearly all Latinos in the border region of Texas are of Mexican origin; however, many Mexican-ancestry persons identify themselves simply as "Hispanic" on the census questionnaire.
Source: U.S. Bureau of the Census (1980), 5 Percent Public Use Microdata Sample.

capitalist world-system. The hundreds of *maquiladora* plants in Ciudad Juárez, for example, were located in the middle of the Chihuahuan desert, isolated from major population centers, ports, and transportation hubs, *only* because the border existed and functioned as a peculiar zone of articulation between the capitalist core and periphery and featured both physical proximity to the U.S. market and cheap Mexican labor. In addition, many of the El Paso economy's producer and distributive services—which were mostly controlled by the same multinational corporations that run *maquiladoras* themselves—were ancillary to the *maquiladora* industry immediately across the border. Similarly, the central business districts in Laredo and McAllen owed their existence to the border and the way in which it served to divide two quite distinct economic spaces, one featuring a wide variety of high-quality consumer products at low prices, and the other with fewer and less appealing products at higher prices. Unlike the case of *maquiladora*-based development, however, commerce in the form of brokering U.S. commodities into Mexico offered the Texas border's regional population at least some chance to establish its own, autonomous enterprises.

Research literature on the Mexican diaspora in the southwestern United States in general, and in Texas in particular, has shown that throughout this century, active transborder social networks have abounded, connecting both Mexican Americans and Mexican immigrants to persons and places immediately across the border in northern Mexico (Alegría, 1992; Arreola, 1993; Martínez, 1994; Portes and Bach, 1985). It has also documented a significant entrepreneurial tradition among Mexicans, in spite of the fact that the global *rates* of entrepreneurship for the Mexican-ancestry population have tended to be dramatically lower than for Anglos and other ethnic groups and immigrants in the region (Alvarez, 1990; Cárdenas, De la Garza, and Hansen, 1986; Chapa and Cárdenas, 1991; Torres, 1990). Given (1) their geographic location on the border; (2) the binational nature of the social, cultural, and linguistic resources at their disposal; and (3) the lack of other lucrative alternatives in the region, playing a brokering role for U.S. goods flowing into Mexico seemed almost a "natural" role for border entrepreneurs to assume. In fact, Latino entrepreneurs in the region in 1980 were especially concentrated in retail/wholesale trade (50 percent operated businesses in this sector), which was heavily dependent on sales to Mexican firms and consumers.

Before undertaking trade liberalization in the mid-1980s, Mexico's policy of protecting domestic industries substantially limited its imports of consumer goods and many intermediate goods from other countries.[6] Imports were limited through tariffs of up to 100 percent, extensive import-licensing requirements, the government subsidy of some industries, and a system of official reference prices (Lustig, 1992; Pastor and Wise, 1994; Ros, 1992; Ten Kate, 1992; United States International Trade Commission, 1990; Wright, 1971). Exporters from the United States, which provided up to 70 percent of Mexican imports (Lustig, 1992; Weintraub, 1990), bore the brunt of these restrictions, which were quite onerous. They were so onerous, in fact, that most smaller enterprises seeking to access the Mexican market *legally* found it nearly impossible to do so, given the costs involved (both in terms of paying the tariffs and the resources that had to be invested in obtaining the required permissions).

Nonetheless, many small businesses in Texas border cities, such as Laredo, McAllen, and El Paso, did "export" substantial quantities of goods to Mexico in the period before trade liberalization was undertaken. These exports occurred in a peculiar and informal way, however. Texas entrepreneurs would open formal retail and wholesale establishments and receive customers and clients from the Mexican side, who would return to Mexico with their purchases. Much of the merchandise entered Mexico without being taxed (or counted as imported value) because it was carried by private consumers, whose purchases fell under the duty-free limit ($50 per person for border residents, $300 per person for residents of the interior). Goods purchased by Mexican businesses were frequently smuggled back across the border in small quantities or allowed to enter without proper authorizations or tariffs by Mexican customs officials who had been bribed. A leading wholesaler whom I interviewed in El Paso described the business environment there before trade liberalization as "a field of dreams: build it and they will come."[7] An electrical parts salesman in Laredo put it this way:

People, when they can't get something in Mexico, normally they come to the border. And that's how we've been in the business for forty years! So they know that we can get whatever they need. . . . We've never taken care of how things get back into Mexico. The customers themselves would take care of it. The Mexican government had a lot of barriers. And more restrictions on imports. . . . Before you had to get government permits and pay so much for the permit that by the time you got it across it'd cost you 100 percent in duties! But also, in those days, people had ways to go, without having to go through the big thing, you know, go around. . . . They would get the things across. (personal interview, August 12, 1993)

Of course, some entrepreneurs on the Texas side also actively smuggled goods into Mexico themselves and made a handsome profit doing so; their more colorful exploits have been documented in the popular press (see Miller, 1981, for example).

MEXICAN TRADE LIBERALIZATION AND THE TEXAS BORDER BOOM, 1988–1994

Although Mexico's restrictive trade regime created some specific and fairly lucrative opportunities for a few Texas border entrepreneurs, there is little doubt that more Texas border entrepreneurs would have been exporting far greater quantities of goods into Mexico had trade restrictions not been in place. Following the onset of its debt crisis and the collapse of the peso in 1982, Mexico abandoned its import-substitution development model and became a party to the General Agreement on Tariffs and Trade (GATT) in 1986. By 1988, Mexico had implemented measures that brought it largely into compliance with GATT norms, and in so doing it effectively ushered in the era of (so-called) free trade with the United States several years before negotiations of a formal free-trade pact were undertaken (Lustig, 1992; Pastor and Wise, 1994; Ros, 1992; Ten Kate, 1992). The elimination of formal trade barriers and the peso's subsequent recovery provoked a sharp increase in imports. As demonstrated in Table 4.2,

Table 4.2
Mexican Imports, 1980–1994, in Millions of U.S. Dollars

	Dollar Amount	Percent Change
1980	18,895	
1981	23,950	26.8
1982	14,436	-23.6
1983	8,549	-54.8
1984	11,255	-40.4
1985	13,219	-30.0
1986	11,135	-41.1
1987	12,223	-35.3
1988	18,895	0.0
1989	23,411	23.9
1990	29,799	57.7
1991	38,100	101.6
1992	62,100	228.8
1993	65,400	246.0
1st Qtr. 1993	15,400	---
1st Qtr. 1994	18,100	---

*Excludes *maquiladora* inputs.
Sources: Ten Kate (1992); Banco de México (1994): 281, 564.

by 1990 Mexico's non-*maquiladora* imports were nearly 60 percent higher than they were in 1980, and by 1993 they were nearly three and a half times higher than before the trade opening. U.S. exports to Mexico rose from just under $20 billion in 1988 to over $40 billion by 1993, and Texas's share of U.S. exports to Mexico grew from 40 percent to over 50 percent, as shown in Table 4.3. Not only did over half of U.S. exports originate in Texas by 1993, but nearly 80 percent of the dollar value of all U.S. surface exports to Mexico were funneled through the Texas border region (Stolp, 1994). From 1990 to 1992, annual growth in payrolls (8.4 percent), the number of business establishments (3.2 percent), and private sector employees (3.6 percent) in the border region far exceeded that experienced by Dallas and Houston, as the border became the first region in Texas to emerge from the 1980s recession.[8] The business press did not miss this development, and frequent articles began to appear describing the trade "boom" on the Texas border (Dunigan, 1992; "Mexican-American Border," 1991; "Texan-Mexican Trade," 1992; Holt, 1991; Palmieri, 1994; Schusler, 1991a, 1991b).

BORDER ENTREPRENEURS' SUPPORT FOR NAFTA

As the Bush and Salinas administrations began to discuss the accession of Mexico to a North American Free Trade Area (NAFTA), the Texas border

Table 4.3
U.S. and Texan Exports to Mexico, in Millions of U.S. Dollars

Year	U.S. Exports to Mexico	Texas Exports to Mexico	Texas Percent of Total
1983	$8,755	NA	---
1984	11,461	NA	---
1985	13,084	NA	---
1986	11,925	NA	---
1987	14,045	$5,659	40.3
1988	19,853	8,241	41.5
1989	24,117	11,011	45.7
1990	27,468	13,288	48.4
1991	32,279	15,485	48.0
1992	39,605	18,839	47.6
1993	40,265	20,380	50.6

Note: NA = not applicable.
Sources: U.S. Department of Commerce (1994); Texas Department of Commerce (1988–1994); U.S. International Trade Commission (1990).

region appeared to be at the cutting edge of free trade, and border entrepreneurs became some of its most ardent exponents. An official of the El Paso Hispanic Chamber of Commerce described his organization's support of a free trade agreement in the following terms:

One of the reasons we're grateful for NAFTA is the fact that because of NAFTA, all of a sudden we're getting noticed here on the border! And a lot of people are turning their attention to the border! . . . Our local Hispanic businesses, if they're not already doing business in Mexico, if they don't have joint ventures, then they've got sales people going into Mexico. We speak the language, we understand the culture. The majority of the time we've got relatives that are still in Mexico that can help us out as far as the networking aspect. So we've got a leg up on the rest of the business, on the rest of US business, we've got a leg up on them because of all these contacts. And NAFTA will give us an advantage! (personal interview with Hispanic business leader in El Paso, April 1, 1993)

Border entrepreneurs and their business organizations were active participants in the political action committee, Texans for NAFTA, which was instrumental in garnering nearly unanimous support for the agreement among members of the Texan congressional delegation. The Texas Association of Mexican American Chambers of Commerce and the U.S. Hispanic Chamber of Commerce lobbied other Latino/Hispanic organizations to endorse passage of NAFTA by the U.S. Congress. In the end, the leadership of organizations such as the National Council of La Raza and the Mexican American Legal Defense Fund were convinced of the benefits of NAFTA to Latino businesses and offered their qualified support for the agreement. The Latino Summit on NAFTA, a political event that was carefully orchestrated to hush voices from within these same organizations who opposed NAFTA (and who were generally from other areas of the country where unionized industries were likely to be hurt by the agreement), articulated the following justification for its conveners' endorsement of NAFTA:

Under the proper conditions, NAFTA can foster greater economic growth, job creation, and ownership opportunities in the Latino community. . . . NAFTA may very well stimulate Latino entrepreneurship. Small business, including Latino-owned enterprises, which are incubators for product and technological innovation, created most of the new jobs in recent years, and offer wealth and ownership opportunities. . . . NAFTA offers an obvious potential for Latino business formation and growth and greater involvement and participation, including joint ventures, with the mainstream economy. (Latino Summit on NAFTA, 1993: 23)

San Antonio, as the border region's economic and cultural capital, played a particularly important role in the push for NAFTA. Its Hispanic Chamber of Commerce was the largest Hispanic chamber in the state of Texas and, together with the Greater San Antonio Chamber of Commerce, the San Antonio World Trade Association, and the city planning department, it aggressively promoted San Antonio as a major North American trade hub via frequent missions to and from Mexico. The San Antonio Hispanic Chamber also organized commercial expositions, invited Mexican businesses and government trade delegations to locate in the city, lobbied the federal government for passage of NAFTA, and pressed for the location of key NAFTA institutions—mainly, the North American Development Bank—in San Antonio. The city's position was also enhanced by the fact that the Mexican government hired former mayor and future U.S. cabinet secretary Henry Cisneros to be one of its principal NAFTA lobbyists in Washington, D.C., a move that reflected Mexico's growing recognition that enlisting the support of ethnic Mexicans in the United States could advance its own interests before the U.S. government (De la Garza and Vargas, 1992). It was no accident, therefore, that San Antonio was the place where Presidents Bush and Salinas and Prime Minister Mulroney of Canada signed the draft NAFTA agreement in 1991 and was subsequently chosen as the site for the new North American Development Bank following NAFTA's approval by Congress.

The congressional passage of NAFTA was in doubt right up to the time of the final vote in November 1993. The lobbying efforts of Texas border businesspeople who believed their interests would be advanced by the agreement were ultimately a key force in assuring its passage, a point that was strongly emphasized by U.S. Representative Esteban Torres (a California Democrat who was one of the principal players in the last round of congressional wrangling on NAFTA) when he visited San Antonio shortly after the agreement was ratified (Torres, 1994). It is worth noting, in this regard, that the majority of Mexicans in Texas live in the border region, as do the majority of the state's Mexican-ancestry entrepreneurs. Moreover, while Mexican immigrants and Mexican Americans are not dramatically more likely to be entrepreneurs in the border region than elsewhere in Texas, their close proximity to Mexico has given many of them a better understanding of the potential of its market (Spener, 1995).

With the establishment of the North American Free Trade Area and the rise in the hemispheric status of Mexico to that of junior partner to the United States, Mexican-ancestry entrepreneurs in the Texas border region seemed poised to finally "cash in" on the advantages of their dual Mexican/American identity. Their position seemed to be ideal in many ways. They were geographically closer to the major Mexican industrial centers and consumer markets than anywhere else in the United States. They shared a common language and culture with the *madre patria* (mother country), and many maintained family and social ties on the other side of the border. Many already had considerable experience selling to Mexican private consumers and businesses at a time when relatively few other entrepreneurs in the United States did and they were a *known* site of provisioning for many Mexican businesses in the interior. With regard to free trade with Mexico, the Texas Mexican entrepreneurs seemed to be at the cutting edge: they were the right people in the right place at the right time.

TEXAS BORDER ENTREPRENEURS AND U.S. MEXICAN ECONOMIC INTEGRATION

Survey results and in-depth interviews conducted in 1993 tend to confirm that Texas border entrepreneurs built on their social networks and cultural knowledge to extend their businesses' sales into Mexico. Logit regression results (Spener, 1995; Spener and Roberts, 1994) from a survey of small business operators in El Paso, Laredo, and San Antonio showed that, net of other factors such as branch of industry, businesses were much more likely to make sales calls in Mexican territory if their operators had lived in Mexico as adults, had immediate family currently living in Mexico, were first- or second-generation Mexican immigrants, or spoke Spanish while growing up. In all three cities, Mexican-American and Mexican-immigrant entrepreneurs cited the importance of their social network connections in Mexico for conducting business in the major cities, particularly in light of a Mexican way of doing business that they viewed as both much more personalistic *and* more bureaucratic than in the United States. In this regard, they concur with the anthropologists (Alvarez, 1990; Lomnitz, 1977; Vélez-Ibáñez, 1983, 1988) on the importance of *confianza* (trust) and *compadrazgo* ("godfathering," a common male fictive-kinship relation) in economic relations among Mexicans, and with Lomnitz (1990) in particular on the persistence of informal modes of exchange within bureaucratic systems in Mexico. One Laredo wholesaler, for example, described his attempts to set up a joint venture with a company in Mexico City by investing not only his financial capital, but his social capital as well:

That's where culture comes [in]to play. And as you might know, in Mexico, *el compadrazgo*—and that's everybody getting a little bit of everything. . . . Because the *compadre le va a pasar la mano* [your *compadre* will give you a hand]. . . . The other thing that they have to do is they have to trust us. And I think that being *mexicano* is an advantage. Because you know my family, I have an uncle and extended family that live in Mexico City. Well, what I want to do, is I'll call my uncle and his family to make sure that I get, you know, straight information. That I have access to some officials, you know, when it's needed. Because he's a *judicial*, so he belongs to the *judicial*, which is the federal police. He's a functionary there, and he should make it easier for us to to get along. . . . He'll be able to tell us how to handle the bureaucracy and . . . it's *big*. And they'll all want something. And my uncle will tell me, you know, how to get to the right people. . . . He'll know which bureaucrats to talk to [to] get reports, to get reports, to get information, to get statistics, because those are very hard to come by in Mexico. You always need some contact to show you the way. . . . [Still] you're going to have to rely on a lot of friendships and other relationships to show you the ropes. (Personal interview)

With regard to the position of Mexican-ancestry entrepreneurs in the Texas border region in the period of "silent integration" (Ros, 1992) immediately preceding NAFTA, it is important to remember that the Mexican government's removal of formal restrictions on trade in the latter half of the 1980s did not by itself guarantee that new trade would proceed automatically (Alarcón González, 1994). Distribution networks for U.S. goods needed to be established in Mexico, and in many cases these networks had to be built using existing networks for Mexican goods of the same type. These existing networks, in turn, were often controlled by Mexican businesspeople who traditionally had obtained a variety of parts and supplies from merchants on the Texas border. By beginning to sell to the Mexican market via a "middleman" in the Texas border region, or by increasing the volume of Mexican sales passing through that border broker, U.S. manufacturers could meet rapidly expanding demand in Mexico without extending credit to Mexican firms of still unknown reliability and without either having to invest in establishing their own operations in Mexico or in recruiting an appropriate Mexican joint venture partner. Many U.S. companies had long known that their sales through distributorships or manufacturers' agents in the border region were much greater than the official sales territory being covered on the U.S. side could support. It was natural, therefore, for them to explore the Mexican market further by working through small companies that had already been serving Mexico for them. Similarly, the owners of many small Mexican firms knew that their most direct point of access to U.S. products was through Texas merchants. As a result, in the first years of the export boom to Mexico, thousands of traders flocked to Laredo, McAllen, and San Antonio, not only from Monterrey, but from as far away as Mexico City and Guadalajara, to supply the demand in Mexico for newly affordable consumer goods—a demand that was readily served by Texas entrepreneurs because of their unique geographical, cultural, and linguistic position. At the same time, the more forward-looking border entrepreneurs began to extend their own sales networks forward into the major Mexican cities, building on their existing networks of customers and other social or familial contacts across the border.

Although local entrepreneurs on the Tex-Mex border had pioneered the elaboration of many trans-frontier trade networks, by the eve of NAFTA's passage, their very success in doing so began to bring them significant new competition. First, major retail warehouses such as Wal-Mart, Sam's Warehouse, K-Mart, Best Buy, and Home Depot began to open mega-stores in border cities, mainly to serve the Mexican market. The low prices, large inventories, and high profile of such stores cut into the sales of smaller businesses, both wholesale and retail, as they had done elsewhere in the United States. In the huge parking lots of these stores in Laredo in the fall of 1992, one could see hundreds of cars with Nuevo León license plates, reflecting the extent to which Monterrey consumers and businesses stocked up on goods in Texas. Second, by 1993, many of these same companies had begun opening branches in Mexico, starting first in Monterrey and Mexico City but then fanning out rapidly to Guadalajara and many second-tier Mexican cities, such as San Luís Potosí, León, and Aguascalientes (for example, by the summer of 1994, Wal-Mart already had about 40 Mexican stores either in operation, under construction, or in the planning stages). While some Texas "middlemen" who served specialized market niches felt that this competition would not harm them, many others had already lost customers to the local branches of these mega-stores and worried about losing additional customers to the new stores opening in Mexico.

In addition to competition from discount chain stores, the take-off of the Mexican export market brought with it other threats to the position of Texas border traders. While the middleman role that these entrepreneurs played in the initial phases of the elaboration of distribution networks from the United States into Mexico may have been crucial, such a position was inherently precarious. The go-between who introduces two trading partners and mediates their relationship at the outset of commercial relations can soon become a costly "third wheel" in the transaction. Once U.S. manufacturers became convinced of the profitability and stability of the Mexican market, had workable distribution networks in place, and had established professional and personal contacts of their own in Mexico, their need for intermediaries on the border diminished. Indeed, one of the principal complaints of border middlemen was that they were being cut off by suppliers who decided either to contract with distributors in major Mexican cities or to open their own distributorships or factory outlets in Mexico. One angry Laredo businessman, who was a Mexican-American, put it this way:

Because if I buy from a company . . . and I was taking care of my customers and that company, I've built my sales for their product to this customer, and then all of a sudden they—a lot of companies are doing this, they jump me and go sell to the customer that I've built for them, without even asking me, "What are you going to do with Mexico? Can you do something better? Let's work together." They just jump me and go directly to my customers! And that's killing me after *I've* built the business! . . . A lot of companies are doing that, and we don't think it's fair. (Personal interview)

Efforts to cut out the middleman at the border were also initiated by Mexican businesses. Field interviews conducted with manufacturers and wholesalers in Mexico City, Guadalajara, and Monterrey in July and August 1994 revealed that even before trade liberalization was undertaken, the heads of small Mexican businesses frequently traveled to the United States to attend trade shows, visit suppliers, and vacation. They regularly received trade publications and company catalogues from the United States and, in spite of their often-weak English language skills and lack of familiarity with U.S. business practices, did not hesitate to make "cold calls" on U.S. suppliers in search of needed parts and equipment. When Mexican entrepreneurs were obliged to avail themselves of the services of a border wholesaler or manufacturer's representative, they often did so in the hopes that the relationship would be a temporary first step on the way to a direct relationship with a manufacturer.

In addition, a number of Mexican business operators whom I interviewed "confessed" to their own *malinchismo*; they maintained that they would rather deal with real *americanos* (i.e., Anglo businesspeople from the "real" United States, and not the border) than with Mexican businesspeople in Texas.[9] Their feelings stemmed in part from a desire to interact with the leadership of U.S. companies, whose headquarters were far from the border region, and in part from a general feeling that although they were more cold and ruthless, Anglos were also more reliable and trustworthy than Mexican businesspeople. Some of the Mexican businesspeople also reserved particular contempt and suspicion for Mexican-*American* entrepreneurs on the border, whom they regarded as unscrupulous in their business dealings with Mexico and who were, in their eyes, of doubtful cultural affinity. As one Mexico City manufacturer told me, "*Ni sabemos qué son, si son mexicanos o americanos u otra cosa, como les decimos: pochos.*"[10]

These entrepreneurs also discounted the importance of Mexican cultural sensitivity on the part of U.S. businesspeople, noting that "business is business" and that they understood that the *americanos* had different customs than their own. Moreover, they said, they were looking to the United States principally to do business, not to make friends.[11] A few Texas businesspeople whom I interviewed in 1993 themselves acknowledged that their Mexican "cultural capital" (i.e., general knowledge of language, customs, and business practices) was of limited value in a free-trade environment on the border, although they did not mention enmity between Mexican citizens and Mexican-Americans as a reason for this:

When you get down to brass tacks, and you talk business and you talk free trade, and you talk free enterprise, I don't think that [culture] is going to matter a lot, basically. I mean, businessmen do business where it's more convenient to do business. . . . And the bottom line always is—yes, we've got the language, and we've capitalized on that—but I think they [Mexicans] are always looking for good business. This is a place where a Mexican can come in and it's the fastest crossing point, he'll save money on the transaction and then, of course, it helps that we speak Spanish. But if we didn't speak Spanish, he'd still save money and he'd still do it. . . . Because once you become global, once you're dealing in a global community, those guys from Mexico now are trained in Harvard. I mean they know our system better than we do! [Laughs.] So now those guys are looking for the best deals. They can speak English, or find people who speak English for them, and that kind of thing. I think it's part of progress. (Mexican-American official of a border business organization, personal interview)

Of course, I also interviewed other Mexican businesspeople who professed affection for Texas and their *paisanos* living there; my point here is simply that the Mexican cultural capital of Mexican-ancestry entrepreneurs based in Texas is not uniformly valued in Mexico itself. Furthermore, it is important to recognize that free trade does not only involve U.S. businesspeople learning about how Mexicans do business, but also involves Mexican businesspeople learning how gringos do business. In fact, the asymmetrical power relationship between the two countries suggests that Mexicans must learn gringo ways to a greater extent than Texans must learn Mexican ways.

Following the opening of the Mexican market, in addition to contending with larger, better-financed competitors with a greater "global reach," entrepreneurs in the Texas border region experienced a depreciation of the fungibility of their Mexican social capital. There were several reasons for this. First, the lifting of certain kinds of trade restrictions by the Mexican government reduced the need for special favors from Mexican officials in order to get goods into Mexico. Principal among these changes was the elimination of most import-licensing requirements, which formerly had required intensive politicking of the government trade ministry with little certainty of obtaining the license unless one had the needed inside contacts (Wright, 1971). The reduction of tariffs on goods going into Mexico, like the lifting of import-licensing requirements, lowered incentives for smuggling goods into Mexico and, in so doing, also had the effect of diminishing the importance of *confianza* between Texas border traders and their Mexican customers who conspired to move goods into Mexico without paying duties on them. Second, some real advances were made by the Salinas administration in its efforts to eliminate corruption and increase the transparency of trade-related regulations. Business operators on both sides of the border gave Salinas particular credit for cleaning up the Mexican customs service by firing corrupt agents en masse and replacing them with new, better-paid, and more professional personnel (see also Holt, 1991; MacDonald, 1993). The reorganization of the Mexican customs service did not necessarily make it easier to get goods into Mexico (the new agents quickly developed a reputation for being overly stringent in enforcing the remaining import regulations), but it did make it much more difficult either to bribe or trade favors with agents in order to clear customs. Third, the formal trade-promoting activities of state and federal governments and business associations on both sides of the border made it considerably easier for smaller firms without Mexican social capital to enter the Mexican market. These activities included not only workshops and seminars, but also frequent trade missions and exhibitions, the opening of trade offices by various Mexican states in San Antonio and by the state of Texas in Mexico City, and the development of match making on-line databases for prospective traders. While state programs are perhaps ultimately not a substitute for *confianza*, they could facilitate the establishment of cross-border business relationships in the first instance, and thus substitute for a border "middleman" in some cases.

None of the depreciation of the Mexican social capital of border businesses contradicts Granovetter's (1985) assertion that all economic relations are embedded in social contexts. It suggests, rather, that the forms of state regulation of economic activity constitute an important element of those contexts and that changes in state policy also alter the *social* contexts in which economic activities take place. Portes (1994a, 1994b), Roberts (1978), and Lomnitz (1990) have all noted that state regulation and informal economic activity define one another in a dialectical relationship. As Portes put it:

By definition, informal economic activities bypass existing laws and the regulatory agencies of the state. It follows therefore that the more pervasive the enforcement of state rules and the greater the penalties for violation, the more socially embedded must informal transactions be. This is so because their success in highly repressive situations depends not only on preventing malfeasance by partners but in avoiding detection by the authorities. Secrecy in these situations demands a high level of mutual trust and the only way this can be created is through the existence of social networks. (1994b: 431)

In the context of trade liberalization on the border, the converse also seems to hold true: to the extent that state rules are lifted or made less stringent, the demand for the kinds of social network connections that permitted the circumvention of the old trade barriers is reduced. Other things being equal, the kind of social capital that is more fungible under conditions of relatively unrestricted trade has rather less to do with having useful personal contacts in the right places and rather more with one's professional reputation for honesty and reliability, a company's track record in the market, and the quality of the product being sold. This latter kind of social capital may be possessed (and put to good use in a free-trade environment) by the personnel of large, multinational corporations as well as by local entrepreneurs whose operations are of a much smaller scale.

We must also remember that the Texas border entrepreneurs' reliance on trans-border social capital to extend commodity chains from the United States into Mexico was as much a strategy to compensate for their lack of other kinds of capital—human, physical, and financial—as it was a strategy that built on their natural strengths. Moreover, while they are not perfect substitutes, different forms of capital may be substituted for one another in production such that an economic actor with greater endowments of human, physical, and financial capital may be able to get by with a smaller endowment of social capital. The implication of this formulation is that border entrepreneurs who are richly endowed with Mexican social capital can be outcompeted by rivals who are better trained, equipped, and financed. Once these competitors for the Mexican market appeared on the scene—essentially, as soon as the Texas border-region entrepreneurs had demonstrated the profitability of that market—the comparative advantages of the border entrepreneurs diminished considerably.

Although competitors for the Mexican market came from all over the United States, it seemed that the border entrepreneurs' chief competition came from Texas's two largest metropolitan centers, Dallas–Fort Worth and Houston. While trade liberalization and improved transportation and communications do, in principle, make borders and physical location less important to economic success, Texas's capture of the lion's share of U.S. exports to Mexico demonstrates nonetheless the continued advantages of physical proximity to markets. With large and diversified manufacturing bases, world-class transportation and warehousing facilities, and substantial concentrations of financial and other producer-services firms, Dallas and Houston are in a better position to benefit from NAFTA-related export activity than any other part of the state (Gilmer, 1990; Stolp and Weintraub, 1993; Weintraub and Boske, 1991). Indeed, as has been suggested by a number of books and articles in the popular press, Texas has been witnessing an economic expansion of the border region to include these two large "interior" Texas cities (Myerson, 1994; Orme, 1993; Palmieri, 1994). While Mexican-ancestry entrepreneurs in Dallas and Houston may able to take advantage of this reorientation of export activity away from the border, the majority of the state's Mexican-ancestry population and entrepreneurs live in the border region. Moreover, the wholesale, transportation, and manufacturing markets of Dallas and Houston are dominated by large-scale national and international companies, and the leading professional service firms are Anglo-owned and -operated.

CONCLUSIONS

It is an irony of the first order that the entrepreneurs in the Texas border region, who played such a crucial role in the initial opening of the Mexican market and the political push for passage of NAFTA, were already beginning to find themselves bypassed by the process of binational economic integration even before the formal consummation of the free trade pact. We must also bear in mind, however, that many kinds of border businesses have not been bypassed as a result of trade liberalization between the United States and Mexico.

- The many retailers in the Texas border cities on the international line itself who served the daily consumption needs of cross-border shoppers from the "twin" cities on the Mexican side of the border have been little affected by integration, though the competition from large-scale discount chains remains as serious a threat to them as to small merchants anywhere in the United States.

- Those border wholesalers who sold relatively small quantities of specialized parts and equipment for industry may have found niches in which to remain protected from competition from larger concerns, especially to the extent that they serve markets in smaller Mexican cities close to the northern border. Numerically speaking, however, such wholesalers employed less than 5 percent of the border region's workforce in 1990 (U.S. Bureau of the Census, 1990); their survival is probably not crucial to the region's overall economic well-being.

- Professional-service providers located in the border region—including engineers, architects, and management consultants, who accounted for a growing share of total employment (15.3 percent in 1990)—probably stood to benefit most from economic integration, as NAFTA allowed them to serve a binational market running in a 360-degree (instead of a 180-degree) radius around them, especially given that quality services of these kinds had been in short supply outside the major cities in Mexico. Entry into these professions, however, requires educational credentials that are in particularly short supply among the majority Mexican-ancestry population in the region—by 1990, only 12.3 percent of Mexican Americans and 6.0 percent of Mexican immigrants who were employed in the border region had graduated from college, compared to 35.9 percent among Anglo natives. (U.S. Bureau of the Census, 1990)

Perhaps the increased volume of goods passing through the border region would have made up for its decreased centrality to the overall process of integration had the Mexican import boom been sustained beyond the first year of the free-trade area's existence. Of course, the liquidity crisis that left the Mexican economy prostrate in 1995 rendered the question moot. In commercial terms, the Texas border region has seen a repeat of 1982, with retail sales in Laredo and El Paso down 60 to 80 percent in January 1995 compared with January 1994 (Texas Comptroller, 1995); moreover, it remains to be seen what significant role, if any, Mexican-ancestry and other border entrepreneurs will play in a future resurgence of exports to Mexico. Whether such a resurgence in exports occurs will most certainly depend on decisions made by members of elite social networks to which border residents barely have access.

At the theoretical level, the experiences of entrepreneurs in the Texas border region demonstrate several points about the role of small-scale firms in global commodity chains. First, the operators of such firms do, in fact, actively seek to insert themselves into global chains and do so in a way that is reflective, not of the will of the large firms directing the chains, but rather of their own social and economic trajectories. These trajectories, in turn, are bound up in contexts that are simultaneously local and transnational insofar as they are determined by both the personal networks of local community members and the impersonal forces of global political economy. Second, small-scale firms insert themselves into global chains in accordance with the resources they have at their disposal. Relative to larger firms, small businesses often depend more heavily on social capital deriving from the personal networks and lived experiences of their owners/operators and less heavily on financial, physical, and human capital investments or other types of social capital deriving from institutional rather than personal networks.

Finally, in the context of global free trade, social capital may be a more valuable substitute for other forms of capital as part of a *subsistence* strategy involving intrafirm relations (e.g., use of unpaid family labor) or exchange relations at a local, community level (e.g., rotating credit associations, in-kind barters, etc.) than as part of a *competitive* strategy for meeting challenges from rivals who are better endowed with those other forms. Thus we can see that the economic activities of small firms in global commodity chains are embedded in social contexts that involve, not only the "horizontal" exchange relations among members of local communities or migrant diasporas, but also the "vertical" power relations that are intrinsic to the capitalist world system. The latter relations exert an inexorable pressure on the former, while the former relations adapt and persist in ways that often place our assumptions about the functioning of the system in doubt.

NOTES

1. Research for this chapter was conducted with generous support from the Ford Foundation and the Institute for Latin American Studies of the University of Texas at Austin. Computing services were funded in part by the National Institute for Child Health and Development's core grant to the Population Research Center of the University of Texas. I also wish to acknowledge helpful comments on an earlier version of this chapter that I received from Robert G. Cushing, Rodolfo de la Garza, Roberto Patricio Korzeniewicz, Humberto González, Bryan Roberts, and Chandler Stolp.

2. In relating this story, I rely on results of my own field research in the Texas border region from 1992 to the present, as well as official statistics published or made available electronically by the governments of the United States, Mexico, and the state of Texas. For simplicity of presentation in the narrative I often use the terms "border business" and "border entrepreneur" as short-hand expressions for businesses that sell to Mexican firms or private consumers and the people who operate those businesses. Not all businesses located in the border region can be regarded as "border businesses," since many serve immediate local markets. Similarly, not all entrepreneurs in the region qualify as "border entrepreneurs," whatever their national heritage. In this regard it should also be noted that not all "border entrepreneurs" who use the cultural and social resources at their disposal to do business with Mexico are themselves of Mexican ancestry. Just as Mexican-ancestry entrepreneurs learn and become expert in the language and culture of business in Anglo-majority communities, Anglos and other non-Latinos can, and do, become expert in the language (Spanish) and culture (Mexican or Tex-Mex) of the border region. Indeed, in spite of the fact that the region's working population is mainly of Mexican ancestry, the entrepreneurial community is disproportionately composed of white Anglo natives, European Jews, and Asian immigrants.

3. By the "Texas border region," I refer to the urban areas of El Paso, Del Rio, Eagle Pass, Laredo, McAllen, Brownsville-Harlingen, and San Antonio.

4. Demographic data on the working populations of the border region, Dallas, and Houston are taken from the 5 Percent Public Use Micro Samples of the 1980 and 1990 United States Censuses of Population and Housing. Figures for the border region do not include Del Rio and Eagle Pass.

5. My use of the term "social capital" in this chapter derives from Coleman (1988).

6. *Maquiladora* inputs were of course exempted from this general policy. However, as noted earlier, inputs, and ancillary services to the *maquiladoras* on the northern border were not generally supplied by local entrepreneurs in the Texas border region. For my purposes here, the real story has to do with Mexico's *overall* policy on imports.

7. This characterization of the border business environment before Mexican trade liberalization is drawn from a popular Hollywood movie of the 1980s. *Field of Dreams* stars Kevin Costner as an Iowa farmer who is obsessed with baseball and who is visited by the ghost of a great player of the past. The ghost instructs him to clear one of his cornfields and create a baseball field so that the ghosts of other legendary players can appear and play there. When Costner states his skepticism about the plan, the ghost replies, "If you build it, they will come." This phrase is repeated at key moments throughout the remainder of the movie, as Costner does the ghost's bidding—and, being a Hollywood movie, the ghosts do indeed come.

8. These figures are derived from U.S. Bureau of the Census, *County Business Patters* (1990, 1992), electromagnetic tape data.

9. La Malinche was the Aztec mistress of Hernán Cortes, the Spanish conqueror of Mexico. To accuse a Mexican of *malinchismo* is to accuse him or her of treason to his or her own country and people.

10. Translation: "We don't know what they are, whether they're Mexicans or Americans, or something else, like we call them: *pochos*." The term *pocho* is a derogatory term used by Mexicans in Mexico to describe Mexican immigrants or Mexican Americans in the United States who have abandoned Mexican ways.

11. This comment is especially interesting given that many border entrepreneurs on the Texas side insisted on the importance of knowing the proper Mexican customs and way of socializing in a business context. This theme is overstated a great deal in the business press. See, for example, Barnstone (1993).

REFERENCES

Alarcón González, Diana. 1994. *Changes in the Distribution of Income in Mexico and Trade Liberalization*. Tijuana, Mexico: El Colegio de la Frontera Norte.

Alegría Olazábal, Tito. 1992. *Desarrollo urbano en la frontera México–Estados Unidos*. Mexico City: Consejo Nacional para la Cultura y las Artes.

Alvarez, Robert. 1990. "Mexican Entrepreneurs and Markets in the City of Los Angeles: A Case of an Immigrant Enclave." *Urban Anthropology* 19, 1–2: 99–124.

Arreola, Daniel D. 1987. "The Mexican American Cultural Capital." *Geographical Review* 77, 1: 17–34.

———. 1993. "Mexico Origins of South Texas Mexican Americans, 1930." *Journal of Historical Geography* 19, 1: 48–63.

Banco de Mexico. 1994. *Sumario Estadístico*. Mexico, DF: Author.

Barnstone, Robert. 1993. "Viva la diferencia!" *Texas Monthly*, October, pp. 66–74.

Cárdenas, Gilberto, Jorge Chapa, and Susan Burek. 1993. "The Changing Economic Position of Mexican Americans in San Antonio." In *Latinos in a Changing U.S. Economy: Comparative Perspectives on Growing Inequality*, ed. Rebecca Morales and Frank Bonilla, pp. 160–183. Newbury Park, CA: Sage Publications.

Cárdenas, Gilberto, Rodolfo O. De la Garza, and Niles Hansen. 1986. "Mexican Immigrants and Chicano Ethnic Enterprise: Reconceptualizing an Old Problem." In *Mexican Immigrants and Mexican Americans: An Evolving Relation*, ed. Harley Browning and Rodolfo O. De la Garza, pp. 157–174. Austin: Center for Mexican American Studies, University of Texas at Austin.

"Casa San Antonio: Blazing the Trail to Free Trade." 1994. *Public Management* 76, 8 (June): 23–24.

Chapa, Jorge, and Gilberto Cárdenas. 1991. *The Economy of the Urban Ethnic Enclave*. Austin: Lyndon B. Johnson School of Public Affairs and Tomás Rivera Center, University of Texas at Austin.

Coleman, James. 1988. "Social Capital in the Creation of Human Capital." *American Journal of Sociology* 94 (supplement): s95–s120.

Corona Vásquez, Rodolfo. 1991. "Principales características demográficas de la zona fronteriza del norte de México." *Frontera Norte* 3, 5: 141–155.

Crook, Stephen, Jan Pakulski, and Malcolm Waters. 1992. *Postmodernization: Change in Advanced Society*. London: Sage Publications.

Curtis, James R. 1993. "Central Business Districts of the Two Laredos." *Geographical Review* 83, 1: 54–65.

De la Garza, Rodolfo O., and Claudio Vargas. 1992. "The Mexican-Origin Population of the United States as a Political Force in the Borderlands: From Paisanos to Pochos to Potential Political Allies." In *Changing Boundaries in the Americas: New Perspectives on the U.S.-Mexican, Central American, and South American Borders*, ed. Lawrence Herzog, pp. 89–111. San Diego: University of California at San Diego, Center for U.S.-Mexican Studies.

Dunigan, Andrew. 1992. "Texas Looks South: The Lone Star State Meets Mexico, Once Again." *Business Mexico*, December, pp. 32–33.

Foley, Douglas E. 1988. *From Peones to Políticos: Class and Ethnicity in a South Texas Town, 1900–1987*. Austin: University of Texas Press.

Gereffi, Gary, Miguel Korzeniewicz, and Roberto P. Korzeniewicz. 1994. "Introduction: Global Commodity Chains." In *Commodity Chains and Global Capitalism*, ed. Gary Gereffi and Miguel Korzeniewicz, pp. 1–14. Westport, CT: Praeger.

Geyer, Anne. 1990. "Strengthening Trade Connections." *Business Mexico*, September, pp. 22–23.

———. 1991. "Credit Card Surge: Mexicans Are Finding Plastic to Be a Handy Way to Spend Money." *Business Mexico*, June, pp. 4–7.

Gilmer, Robert W. 1990. "Identifying Service-Sector Exports from Major Texas Cities." *Economic Review*, July, pp. 1–16.

Granovetter, Mark. 1985. "Economic Action and Social Structure: The Problem of Embeddedness." *American Journal of Sociology* 91, 3: 481–510.

Harrell, Louis, and Dale Fischer. 1985. "The 1982 Mexican Peso Devaluation and Border Area Employment." *Monthly Labor Review* 108, 10: 25–32.

Harvey, David. 1989. *The Condition of Post-Modernity*. Oxford: Basil Blackwell.

Holt, Stanley. 1991. "Clearing Customs: U.S. and Mexican Customs Services Struggle to Meet the Challenges of Increasing Trade." *Business Mexico*, May, pp. 46–48.

Institute for Mining and Materials Management. 1991. *Paso del Norte Regional Economy: Socioeconomic Profile*. El Paso: University of Texas at El Paso.

Landolt, Robert Garland. 1976. *The Mexican American Workers of San Antonio, Texas*. New York: Arno Press.

Latino Summit on the North American Free Trade Agreement (NAFTA). 1993. *Latino Consensus Position on NAFTA*. Washington, DC: Latino Summit on NAFTA.

Lomnitz, Larissa. 1977. *Networks and Marginality: Life in a Mexican Shantytown*. San Francisco, CA: Academic Press.

———. 1990. "Redes informales de intercambio en sistemas formales: Un modelo teórico." *Comercio Exterior* 40, 3: 212–220.

Lustig, Nora. 1992. *Mexico: The Remaking of an Economy*. Washington, DC: Brookings Institution.

MacDonald, Christine. 1993. "'Customs' Unsung Hero? Francisco Gil Díaz Cleans Up Customs." *Business Mexico*, April, pp. 27–29.

Maril, Robert Lee. 1989. *The Poorest of Americans: The Mexican Americans of the Lower Rio Grande Valley of Texas*. Notre Dame, IN: University of Notre Dame Press.

Martínez, Oscar. 1994. *Border People: Life and Society in the U.S.-Mexico Borderlands*. Tucson: University of Arizona Press.

"The Mexican-American Border: Hi, Amigo." 1992. *Economist*, December 12, pp. 21–25.

Miller, Tom. 1981. *On the Border: Portraits of America's Southwestern Frontier*. New York: Harper and Row.

Montejano, David. 1987. *Anglos and Mexicans in the Making of Texas, 1836–1986*. Austin: University of Texas Press.

Myerson, Allen R. 1994. "The Booming, Bulging Tex-Mex Border." *New York Times*, August 7, p. C1.

Orme, William A., Jr. 1993. *Continental Shift: Free Trade and the New North America*. Washington, DC: Washington Post Company.

Palmieri, Christopher. 1994. "Laredo's Giant Sucking Sound." *Forbes*, April 25, p. 78.

Pastor, Manuel, and Carol Wise. 1994. "The Origins and Sustainability of Mexico's Free Trade Policy." *International Organization* 48, 3: 459–489.

Portes, Alejandro. 1994a. "By-passing the Rules: The Dialectics of Labour Standards and Informalization in Less Developed Countries." In *International Labour Standards and Economic Interdependence*, ed. W. Sensenberger and D. Campbell, pp. 159–176. Geneva, Switzerland: Institute for Labour Studies.

———. 1994b. "Paradoxes of the Informal Economy: The Social Basis of Unregulated Entrepreneurship." In *Handbook of Economic Sociology*, ed. Neil Smelser and Richard Swedberg, pp. 426–449. New York: Russell Sage Foundation.

Portes, Alejandro, and Robert Bach. 1985. *Latin Journey*. Berkeley: University of California Press.

Reich, Robert B. 1991. *The Work of Nations: Preparing Ourselves for 21st Century Capitalism*. New York: Random House.

Roberts, Bryan. 1978. *Cities of Peasants: The Political Economy of Urbanization in the Third World*. London: Edward Arnold.

Ros, Jaime. 1992. "Free Trade Area or Common Capital Market? Notes on Mexico-U.S. Economic Integration and Current NAFTA Negotiations." *Journal of Interamerican Studies and World Affairs* 34, 2: 53–92.

Savage, V. Howard, and Eric Blankmeyer. 1990. "A Test of Purchasing Power Parity: Texas Border Retail Trade and the Value of the Peso, 1976–1987." *Journal of Borderlands Studies* 5, 1: 67–78.

Sayer, Andrew, and Richard Walker. 1992. *The New Social Economy: Reworking the Division of Labor*. Cambridge, MA: Blackwell Publishers.

Schusler, Ralph. 1991a. "Border Boom Town: Laredo Ready for Action as Free Trade Paves the Way for Growth." *Business Mexico*, November, 28–31.

———. 1991b. "Getting Ready: U.S. Businessmen on the Border Gear for Free Trade." *Business Mexico*, March, pp. 16–19.

Spener, David. 1995. "Entrepreneurship and Small-Scale Enterprise in the Texas Border Region: A Sociocultural Perspective." Ph.D. dissertation, University of Texas at Austin.

Spener, David, and Bryan Roberts. 1994. "Social Networks and Trade on the Texas-Mexico Border: The Role of Small-Scale Enterprise in the Integration of Transnational Space." Paper presented at the annual meeting of the Latin American Studies Association, Atlanta, GA, March 9–13.

Stolp, Chandler. 1994. "The LBJ School of Public Affairs Model of NAFTA Impacts." Unpublished mimeo, Austin, Texas.

Stolp, Chandler, and Sidney Weintraub. 1993. "NAFTA: Challenges and Opportunities for a 21st Century Texas." *Texas Lyceum* 10, 1: 16–23.

Tamayo, Jesus, and Jorge Luis Fernández. 1983. *Zonas fronterizas*. Mexico City: Centro de Investigación y Docencia Económicas.

Ten Kate, Adriaan. 1992. "El ajuste estructural de México: Dos historias diferentes." *Comercio Exterior* 42, 6: 519–528.

"Texan-Mexican Trade: Optimists All." 1991. *Economist*, August 17, pp. 25–26.

Texas Comptroller. 1995. "Peso Fiasco: Texas Exports Feel the Brunt of Mexico's Fiscal Woes." *Fiscal Notes*, March, pp. 3–6.

Texas Department of Commerce. 1988–1994. *Texas Exports*. Austin: Author.

Torres, David. 1990. "Dynamics behind the Formation of a Business Class: Tucson's Hispanic Business Elite." *Hispanic Journal of Behavioral Sciences* 12, 1: 25–49.

Torres, Esteban. 1994. "NAFTA Owes Texas." *Fiscal Notes*, June 1994, p. 6.

U.S. Bureau of the Census. 1980. *1980 Census of Population and Housing: 5 Percent Public Use Microdata Sample*. Washington, DC: Author. Electromagnetic tape data.

———. 1990. *1990 Census of Population and Housing: 5 Percent Public Use Microdata Sample*. Washington, DC: Author. Electromagnetic tape data.

———. 1990, 1992. *County Business Patterns*. Washington, DC: Author. Electromagnetic tape data.

U.S. Department of Commerce. 1994. *National Trade Database*. Washington, DC: Author. CD-ROM database.

U.S. International Trade Commission. 1990. *Review of Trade and Investment Liberalization Measures by Mexico and Prospects for Future United States-Mexico Relations. Investigation No. 332–282: Phase I: Recent Trade and Investment Reforms Undertaken by Mexico and Implications for the United States*. Washington, DC: United States International Trade Commission.

Valdez, Avelardo. 1993. "Persistent Poverty, Crime, and Drugs: U.S.-Mexican Border Region." In *The Barrios: Latinos and the Underclass Debate*, ed. Joan Moore and Raquel Pinderhughes, pp. 173–194. New York: Russell Sage Foundation.

Vélez-Ibáñez, Carlos G. 1983. *Bonds of Mutual Trust: The Cultural Systems of Rotating Credit Associations among Urban Mexicans and Chicanos.* New Brunswick, NJ: Rutgers University Press.

————. 1988. "Networks of Exchange Among Mexicans in the U.S. and Mexico: Local-level Mediating Responses to National and International Transformations." *Urban Anthropology* 17, 1: 27–51.

Weintraub, Sidney. 1990. *A Marriage of Convenience: Relations between Mexico and the United States.* New York: Oxford University Press.

Weintraub, Sidney, and Leigh Boske. 1991. *US.-Mexico Free Trade Agreement: Economic Impact on Texas.* Austin: University of Texas, Lyndon B. Johnson School of Public Affairs.

Wright, Erik Olin. 1985. *Classes.* London: Verso.

Wright, Harry K. 1971. *Foreign Enterprise in Mexico: Laws and Policies.* Durham: University of North Carolina Press.

5

GLOBALIZATION, THE STATE, AND THE INFORMAL ECONOMY: THE LIMITS TO PROLETARIANIZATION IN THE LATIN AMERICAN PERIPHERY

José Itzigsohn

Proletarianization is one of the central characteristics of the capitalist world-system. As the world-economy expands, it leads to the commodification of the labor force in the newly incorporated regions. As Wallerstein (1983) pointed out, however, the proletarianization of the peripheral labor force is always partial. Not all the labor force of the periphery of the world system is incorporated into modern wage relations, as this would put on capital's shoulders the full cost of its reproduction. The result of the process of partial proletarianization is the rise of a variety of non–fully proletarian income-producing activities that are commonly referred to as the informal economy.

Individual workers are rarely isolated economic actors. Instead, for most people, the basic economic unit is the household. Households in the periphery very rarely, in fact, depend totally on proletarian wages. The modal type of peripheral household usually depends on a combination of wages and petty market operations (Smith and Wallerstein, 1992). Peripheral households usually have different members working on a diverse array of formal and informal activities. The question arises, then, how these different types of activities are related to each other in the functioning of peripheral urban economies.

The focus of this chapter is on the roles of informal economic activities within the urban economies of Latin America and the Caribbean, and on how those informal activities are related to the process of proletarianization in the region. During the last two decades, Latin America and the Caribbean have gone through a process of social and economic change. This process, which has been alternatively labeled structural adjustment, economic restructuring, or export-oriented development (EOD), amounts to a restructuring of the mode of insertion of the region in the world-economy. In previous periods, the region was a provider of raw materials for core production and, in a few cases, a provider of some industrial products or markets for transnational companies. Presently, however, a central role of the region in the world-economy is that of a provider of cheap labor and services for an increasingly globalized production system. This chapter compares the articulations of formal and informal firms in the Dominican Republic and Costa Rica in order to address these questions. However, it should be asked whether linkages to multinationals prevail as a general pattern in the new informal economy of the 1990s, or whether there are alternative patterns of informal arrangements that reflect variables such as the particular extent and type of state regulation that prevail in different local environments. The two countries discussed here have applied export-oriented policies during the last fifteen years and have opened their economies to international trade. They have also emphasized a focus on the informal economy as a cornerstone of their social policies. This chapter examines different ways in which informal and formal economic activities are related to each other and explores the effects of the mode of insertion of these two countries in the world-economy and the action of their respective states on the boundaries between the formal and informal economies. The goal is to achieve an understanding of the functioning of peripheral urban economies and of the relationship between the processes of formation of a proletarian and an informal labor force in Latin America in the present period of globalization of the world-economy.

THE INFORMAL ECONOMY IN THE LATIN AMERICAN PERIPHERY

During the period of import-substitution industrialization, Latin America witnessed a growth in both formal proletarianization and the informal economy. Employment in manufacturing, the public sector, and modern services grew very fast. In spite of this, the informal economy did not disappear; on the contrary, it encompassed a large part of the economically active population. Moreover, the proletariat created by the process of industrialization did not always correspond to the image of factory wageworkers. Part of the proletariat was, in fact, an informal proletariat, which was employed in small workshops and lacked legal protection (Portes, 1985). Nevertheless, its members were still part of commodity chains that linked them to the formal economy. Several researchers have documented how informal, and apparently marginal, economic activities are linked to modern formal production or distribution (Birckbek, 1978; Bromley, 1978; Moser, 1994; Portes and Schauffler, 1994). These scholars have shown that the informal economy was part and parcel of peripheral capitalism.

The social and economic crisis that hit Latin America and the Caribbean in the beginning of the 1980s reversed the trends of the previous decades. Stable and protected employment in manufacturing and the public sector decreased, and the continent witnessed a rise in precarious forms of employment encompassing temporary, part-time, and unprotected jobs in sectors such as export manufacturing and in the public sector. This crisis also gave way to the rise of a large array of informal activities. The last decade, therefore, saw a partial reverse in the process of proletarianization in the Latin American periphery.

In this context, the informal economy has acquired a renewed interest. After years of being considered a result of an incomplete process of industrialization, the informal economy has come to be hailed as a reservoir of true market forces and a potential solution for the problems of unemployment and poverty in the region (De Soto, 1989; Rakowski, 1994). These views, however, do not take into account the roles that the informal economy plays in the process of capital accumulation. In order to understand the roles of the informal economy, it is necessary to examine the forms of articulation of informal and formal economic activities. This is, in fact, an old, but always present, question in political economy: how capitalism, as it expands, organizes production and distribution. In other words, it focuses on the types of labor relations, firms, and markets that emerge as the world capitalist economy searches for new forms of capital accumulation.

The informal economy is defined in this chapter as comprising those economic activities that are carried out in spite of existing regulations that restrict those types of activities. In order to reduce the scope of the definition, I will consider informal only those activities that violate existing labor regulations. This definition, however, is still very broad. The informal economy is, in fact, a label that encompasses a multitude of different economic actors and social relations. Its use is widespread because it is an easy way to refer to activities that depart from the legal and "expected" norms regarding working conditions and the structure of firms in industrialized economies. Nevertheless, the types of economic activities and linkages encompassed under this label vary in different contexts. In order to make sense of such diverse economic activities, we need to analyze their roles within the urban economy. The rest of this section relates the different functions of the informal economy to the particular types of linkages found between formal and informal activities. This, in turn, allows the development of a typology of informal economic actors in relation to those linkages and functions.

The informal economy performs two main functions within the urban economic system. The first function is to supply low-cost goods and services for working-class and middle-class consumers. In this way, the informal economy subsidizes the formal firms: by lowering the costs of consumption of basic needs, formal firms are able to pay lower salaries than they would have to pay if consumption were carried on only through formal means. The second function of the informal economy is to allow formal firms a direct reduction of labor costs through the practices of subcontracting parts of their production or marketing tasks and through off-the-books hiring (Portes and Walton, 1981). In this way, formal firms can avoid the burdens imposed by labor and social security laws concerning minimum wages, working conditions, and other fringe benefits that they are forced to pay their permanent formal workers.

The production and marketing of any good or service is the outcome of different sets of linkages that include, among others, securing sources of capital, raw materials, and supplies, as well as finding outlets for the final product. These linkages can be horizontal, such as arm's-length market relationships between different firms; they can also be vertical, as when a branch of a firm supplies or sells the goods of another branch of the same firm. They can be linkages of subordination (e.g., subcontracting relationships) or linkages of cooperation, such as those described for industrial districts (Portes and Schauffler, 1994). The sum of the linkages of a business constitutes its articulation with the urban economy.

The two different functions of the informal economy are associated with different types of linkages among formal and informal economic units. The subsidizing of consumption is related to two main types of linkages. The first is between informal sellers of goods or services and final consumer markets (e.g., the independent informal street vendors, informal workers who perform home services such as gardening or painting, or informal workshops that repair everything from tape recorders to cars). I call these informal actors *self-employed petty marketers*. The second type of linkage is between informal firms and formal markets (e.g., an informal shoemaker who supplies one or more formal shoe stores). I call these informal actors *suppliers*. In these ways, informal firms supply consumers with cheap goods and reduce the amount of money needed to meet the needs of the household.

The direct reduction of the labor-cost function is also related to two main types of linkages. The first involves subcontracting chains between a formal firm and one or more informal firms or self-employed people. The latter work for the formal firm, producing certain products, performing particular parts of the production process, or selling the final product. I call this group of informal actors *subcontractors*. The second type of linkage involves the hiring of informal workers by informal or formal firms. The latter often resort to the hiring of temporary or off-the-books workers who do not enjoy the wages and benefits of most of the firm's labor force. These informal workers constitute the *informal proletariat* proper.

Table 5.1 schematically presents the different types of articulation between the formal and informal economies. The basic difference between the linkages under the two functions is that those under function (1) are basically horizontal linkages; in other words, linkages between independent economic actors in different markets.[1] The linkages under function (2) are vertical linkages; that is, linkages where the informal economic actors are vertically articulated into formal commodity chains. In the two functions, however, the second type of linkage expresses a more subordinate relation than the first type. It is easy to see why this is so. The fact that two economic units are related by horizontal linkages does not necessarily mean that they have equal power. The markets of those informal firms that supply formal firms—the second type of linkage—are often oligopolic or oligopsonic. Hence, the informal entrepreneurs have a clear disadvantage vis-à-vis their formal partners. Furthermore, casual, "off-the-

Table 5.1
Articulations among the Formal and Informal Economies

	Function 1: Horizontal articulation. Subsidize consumption by formal workers and middle classes.	Function 2: Vertical articulation. Reduce labor costs of formal firms.
Less-Subordinated Articulation	"petty marketers"— Informal sellers, or producers selling informal products in consumer markets.	"subcontractors"— Informal producers performing part of the production process for formal firms, or informal sellers selling the products of formal firms.
More-Subordinated Articulation	"suppliers"— Informal producers supplying formal retailers with the goods they produce.	"informal workers"— Informal workers working temporarily off-the-books for formal firms, or employees of informal firms.

book'' workers are in a relation of more direct subordination than those informal producers who perform subcontracted work for other firms, as the latter can engage in such relations with several different firms or sell part of their product independently.

Table 5.1 underscores the heterogeneous character of the informal economy, which encompasses a continuum of economic actors from off-the-books workers to self-employed people and small entrepreneurs; the social relations include informal proletarians, independent workers, and informal employers. Therefore, in order to understand the functioning of peripheral urban economies, it is necessary to look at the types of activities and social relations that predominate at any particular moment of the expansion or contraction of the world-economy. In other words, it is important to examine what causes the rise of particular forms of informal activities and what role they fulfill. In this way, we can find out the forms, extent, and limits to the process of proletarianization in the periphery.

GLOBALIZATION, THE STATE, AND THE INFORMAL ECONOMY

As we analyze the interaction between global and local processes in the formation of particular forms of articulation between formal and informal activities, two issues are of particular interest: the presence and extent of international subcontracting linkages, and the role of the state in shaping the boundaries between formal and informal activities.

The existing literature often suggests that the globalization of the economy is accompanied by the proliferation of international subcontracting chains linking corporate headquarters in the core to informal producers or homeworkers in the periphery. Commodity chains of this sort were documented by several researchers (Beneria and Roldán, 1990; Portes and Schauffler, 1994). There is some evidence that during the last decade, informal firms with a certain capacity of accumulation due to their connections with producers or consumers in the United States have emerged in Latin America. My interest is in finding out to what extent commodity chains spanning from international firms to informal workshops are common within the new informal economy.

The role of the state in shaping the boundaries between formal and informal activities has been emphasized by Portes (e.g., Portes and Schauffler, 1994), who proposed that a state that regulates labor relations strictly will lead formal firms to try to evade those regulations through subcontracting or off-the-books hiring, thus creating a tight articulation in production or marketing between formal and informal activities. In a less regulated context, however, there will be fewer incentives to integrate informal activities in production or marketing, and therefore, their role will tend to be that of a supplier of cheap consumer goods. To evaluate these propositions, I assess whether a more regulated context accentuates the labor-cost reduction function of the informal economy, while a less regulated context accentuates the consumption subsidy function.

To permit analysis of these issues, this chapter compares the linkages between formal and informal firms in San José, Costa Rica, and Santo Domingo (the Dominican Republic). These two countries share a series of common characteristics due to similarities in their insertion in the world-economy (in terms of the structure of their trade) and social structures. Both countries were latecomers to industrialization, as serious industrialization efforts were not attempted until the 1960s. At that point, both countries had small economies that depended on the export of a few commodities for growth: sugar, in the Dominican case, and coffee and bananas in Costa Rica. Both countries applied an import-substitution industrialization (ISI) model during the 1950–1980 period, and both switched to an export-oriented development (EOD) model during the 1980s (Lozano and Duarte, 1992; Rovira Más, 1985). The two countries differ, however, in the type and degree of state regulation of economic activities and labor relations and in the size of their informal economies. Costa Rica has a more extensive regulation of economic activities and labor relations than the Dominican Republic. Moreover, in Costa Rica, the existing regulations are more consistently applied than in the Dominican Republic.[2]

The economic crisis of the early 1980s and the new, export-oriented model of development strongly affected formal sources of employment. The protected industries were hit by the opening of the economies to international trade, and employment and income in the import-substitution–manufacturing sector were reduced. During the economic crisis, the public sector performed a counter-cyclical function, absorbing some of the workers who were expelled from the private formal sector. This increase in employment caused a large reduction in the salaries of the sector. As the decade went on and structural adjustment programs were applied, employment in the public sector also decreased (Infante and Klein, 1991). On the other hand, the fastest-growing employment sectors have been export assembly manufacturing, tourism, and the informal economy. This general trend toward socioeconomic internationalization and informaliza-tion constitutes the context within which to analyze the articulations of the informal economy (Portes, Itzigsohn, and Dore, 1994.).

Based on a series of interviews with informal microentrepreneurs, this section contrasts what emerged as the most typical situations of articulation of formal and informal firms in the two cities.[3] The results have an exploratory character, and therefore, the conclusions should be taken as hypotheses for further research. In spite of these limitations, the access to direct sources provides important insights about the roles of informal economic actors in the urban economy. The interviews provide in-depth information on issues such as forward and backward linkages and the histories of the informal microenterprises and the microentre-preneurs. I focus on the results of interviews with informal microentrepreneurs producing garments and crafts (the latter refers to those crafts that are produced for selling to tourists). The choice of these two trades is due to their inclusion in two increasingly internationalized economic sectors: garment production and tourism. It is important to look at the formal-informal linkages in more than one sector. The articulations of formal and informal firms may vary, not only be-tween the two cities, but also within the two cities themselves (e.g., the contrast between the two cities in the articulations of informal garment production is different than the contrast among craftspersons). This occurs because the effects of different types of state regulations interact with the characteristics of the markets for the products of the different industries within each city (such as the openness of the local market to the import of goods that compete with informal production, or the presence or absence in the local markets of oligopolistic national producers). The remainder of this section presents the basic patterns of linkages found in each city.[4]

Garments

The garments sector is one of the most interesting in which to look at the economic articulations of informal businesses. The international garment and textile industry has been "globalized" during the last two decades. Large as-sembly factories have moved from the core to the periphery, where they are concentrated in export zones. In the core countries, garment production has moved underground to informal sweatshops (Portes and Sassen-Koob, 1987). Linkages have been found between formal factories in core countries and small,

informal workshops in peripheral countries, such as those described by Pérez
Sainz (1994) between formal garment firms in California and informal workshops in the Mayan village of San Pedro Sacatepequez (near Guatemala City).
Thus, in this trade we can expect to find a large array of different economic
actors, from people who make clothes for their neighbors to informal producers
engaged in international commodity chains.

In Santo Domingo, I found a certain progression in the forms of articulation
of the informal garment producers. Small producers begin selling to the public,
to informal peddlers, or to middlemen. They secure their position by obtaining
some secure contracts with formal shops. The latter stage of growth comes when
they are able to diversify their clientele and manage to have a number of vendors
going around the city or the country and sell their production. Thus, they begin
as sellers in final consumer markets (or selling to people who sell in final consumer markets), continue as suppliers or subcontractors, and then return as independent sellers in consumer markets.

Of course, not all of the informal garment producers go through these stages.
In fact, most of them do not, remaining instead at the first or second stage.
However, although the number of microenterprises that "make it" is small, the
results of the interviews indicate that there are several market options for garment producers in Santo Domingo. These options are related to the presence of
a large number of people trying to make a living by selling whatever they can.
There is, in fact, an informal producer–informal retailer articulation that provides
an outlet for informal products. Nevertheless, what seems to be a bonus for
informal producers may be a curse for informal retailers.

The interviews in San José show both a common element and a clear difference in comparison to Santo Domingo. The common element is that in both
cities, the subcontracting of garment production to informal workshops is extensive. The big difference is that in San José, the market for informal garment
production is much narrower than in Santo Domingo and the informal businesses
are in a much more subordinated position. The reasons for this are, on the one
hand, the much larger presence in Santo Domingo of informal retailers, who
offer an outlet for informal goods, and on the other hand, the lower purchasing
power of large segments of the population in the Dominican Republic, which
leads them to buy cheap goods that are produced locally. In Santo Domingo,
the informal producers provide the low-income consumer markets with cheap
goods that are marketed, to a large extent, through informal retailers. In San
José, due to the higher level of earnings and the presence of cheap imports,
people buy mainly in formal outlets. Informal retailers also provide cheap goods
for popular consumption, but the demand for them is lower than in Santo Domingo. Most informal products are marketed through formal outlets. In the terms
of Table 5.1, we can say that in Santo Domingo, there is a larger presence of
"petty marketers" within the informal economy, while in San José there is a
larger presence of "suppliers."

This explanation is based on variations in the consumer-goods markets that are caused by the different structures of the labor markets rather than differences in the burden of labor costs. In both cities, formal businesses subcontract their production to informal businesses. In Santo Domingo, though, informal businesses have more alternatives that allow them to escape the more subordinated type of relationships. It is important to note that most of the subcontracting work does not come from factories, but from retail chains. To be sure, in both cities there are factories that subcontract to small workshops. However, most of the subcontracting arrangements that I found were between retail chains or independent stores that cater to low-income sectors and the informal firms.

According to this interpretation, state regulation affects the linkages of informal microentrepreneurs in the garment sector more through its effects on the labor and consumer markets than through its effect on labor costs. Nevertheless, that is not the whole story. The informal labor force in San José is not entirely unprotected, as informal workers can use the threat of complaining to the ministry of labor in order to obtain better working conditions (a threat that is completely irrelevant in Santo Domingo). As a result, informal entrepreneurs in Costa Rica also need to escape high labor costs as well as the threat of an increase in their payroll that they cannot withstand. For this reason, the informal commodity chains in San José have more stages than in Santo Domingo. In San José I found two types of relationships that I did not find in Santo Domingo: (1) the subcontracting of production by the informal firms to homeworkers and (2) informal middlemen specializing in the design of products and the subcontracting of their production to informal firms.

All the examples presented so far concern cases of subcontracting by local firms. In both cities, I asked all my informants whether they had ever taken subcontracting jobs for international firms or knew about such cases. In all the cases but one, the answer was that small firms did not get those kinds of jobs because international firms have schedules and quality demands that small workshops cannot fulfill. For that reason, international subcontracting work is carried out in export zones in Santo Domingo and in big *maquila* factories in San José.[5] International subcontracting exists, but it stays at the level of the medium-sized firms and does not reach the level of the microenterprises and small informal workshops.

These results can be explained by the existence of a secondary labor market within the formal economy, which is composed mainly of cohorts of young women who were previously not employed. This sector offers international subcontractors access to a pool of cheap labor coupled with the advantages of large-scale production and tight control over the production process. The Dominican and Costa Rican states have encouraged this "informalization" of formal work through their policies of promoting export assembly-manufacturing, using cheap labor costs as an incentive for investment.

Craftspeople

Craftspeople linked to the tourism industry in the two cities provide an interesting counterpoint. In garments, we have seen a more favorable market situation for informal enterprises in Santo Domingo. In this sector, the situation is reversed. Most of the informal crafts producers in Santo Domingo find themselves pressed between an oligopsonic market for their products and monopolistic prices for their raw materials (Lozano, 1994). These craftspeople can sell only to a small number of gift shops, often through intermediaries who have connections with those shops. The latter, therefore, have the power to arbitrarily determine the prices of the products of the informal producers. Those informal entrepreneurs who have a direct connection with the gift shops have more power in the market because they are able to skip one link in the commodity chain: they are able to sell more when demand is up. Even those craftspeople, however, are in a position of subordination in relation to the gift shops.

The situation is different in San José, where the market for "souvenirs" is larger than in Santo Domingo. In San José, there are more outlets for crafts, and they are sold in more areas of the city than in Santo Domingo. Moreover, there is also the street selling of crafts products in San José—this is the one type of product that is not sold in the streets of Santo Domingo. In Santo Domingo, the link with the tourist sector is monopolized by a small number of shops, while in Costa Rica, crafts products for tourists have a larger and less controlled outlet. This is, in part, the result of the fact that the Dominican state has kept street sellers out of the main areas where tourists concentrate, and in that way it has precluded access to the market by craftspeople.[6]

In this sector, we find that the predominant type of actor in San José is the "petty marketer," while in Santo Domingo, "suppliers" predominate. These suppliers, however, confront a market that is so limited that they are almost totally subordinated to the buyers. In this case, the linkages between the global and informal economies are mediated through the domination of the market by local formal traders. The state intervenes in consolidating this subordination through its regulations and control of street trading. This subordination transforms these self-employed people into disguised workers of the traders. Nevertheless, even though their market situation and income are very unstable, the craftspeople whom I interviewed in Santo Domingo would not take up a formal job, since the income they could obtain in their trade was higher than any wage employment they could access. This suggests that in the present situation of general informalization of labor relations, partial or "disguised" proletarianization is, for many, a preferable alternative to full proletarianization (Itzigsohn, 1994; Murphy, 1990).

CONCLUSION

This chapter describes common trends between the two countries, as both respond to global pressures in quite similar ways. The qualitative interviews did not show major differences between the articulation of formal and informal enterprises in the two cities. In both cities, informal firms act mainly as suppliers or petty marketers. Most of the subcontracting chains that encompass informal microenterprises involve retailers who cater to the low-income sectors, rather than large multinational firms.

The sourcing by formal stores that cater to low-income sectors from informal enterprises may be explained by the need of the former to guarantee low prices, given the constraints of the markets in which they operate. As a result, they organize production in a sort of "putting-out" system in which formal stores provide informal enterprises with raw materials that are assembled by the latter at lower costs. Given the instability of the markets for informal goods, informal enterprises have no alternative but to accept the deals proposed by this type of formal business, which, in most cases, are unfavorable to informal producers. International subcontracting does not reach the small, informal workshops but rather remains at the level of the medium firms. In the two cities, international subcontractors have access to cheap labor in large factories—in the export zones in Santo Domingo and in the *maquilas* in San José. For that reason there is no incentive to extend the commodity chains to include informal microenterprises. Moreover, the latter lack the capacity to meet the quality and schedule demands of the international subcontractors.

The explanation of these similarities lies in a leveling between the formal and informal conditions of work in both cities. In Santo Domingo, the formal/informal divide is quite blurred due to the deterioration of formal working conditions during the last ten years. As a result, formal labor is not much more expensive than informal labor, and hence, there is no stimulus for formal firms to subcontract parts of their production (a finding that was expected). In San José, labor regulations make a difference even for informal workers, who are not completely unprotected. On the other hand, within the formal sector there is a secondary subsector whose working conditions differ little from those in the informal economy. Thus, for certain productive sectors (mainly light industries), the costs of secondary formal and informal labor are nearly the same.

What do these findings show concerning the relationship between informality and proletarianization? This chapter suggests a reorganization in the relationship between capital, the state, and labor in Latin America under the new mode of the insertion in the world-economy. By reducing labor regulations or their enforcement, states "informalize" the labor markets. In this context, capital has access to cheap sources of formal labor and is free of any pressure to "go informal." The role of the informal economy in this context is that of a subsistence sector that subsidizes the low cost of labor for capital. This role is not a new role for the informal economy, which fulfilled a similar role under import-substitution industrialization. The difference is that during the import-substitution period, although the informal economy partially subsidized the costs of proletarianization, access to formal wage work meant access to relatively decent wages and stable jobs. Thus, proletarianization implied an increase in the costs of the labor force for capital.

Under the new, export-oriented model, there is a process of general informalization of labor relations. The export-oriented development model that emerged during the last two decades is indeed associated with the formation of a global proletariat, but it is a heterogeneous rather than a "traditional" one, as the scattered productive units embedded in global commodity chains encompass different types of labor relations (Barkin, 1985; Broad, 1991; Sanderson, 1985). Access to formal employment in either the new, growing sectors or the public sector does not mean additional access to stable employment or a decent level of income. Income from informal activities, as well as remittances, has acquired a central role in the household economic strategies, while an increasingly precarious formal employment is being relegated to a secondary role (Itzigsohn, 1994).

As Smith and Wallerstein (1992) showed, in periods of economic contraction of the world-economy (such as the present), there is a reduction in wage employment opportunities and a rise in informal activities. This, however, is not the whole story. There is, in fact, a reversal in the importance of the different types of income for household subsistence. The incomes derived from formal and informal activities change in favor of the latter as shifting the costs of the reproduction of the labor force toward informal activities significantly cheapens the costs of wage labor. The growing process of informalization renders the use of full proletarian labor a cheap alternative for capital.

Peripheral proletarianization, thus, is not only a partial, but also an ever-shifting, process.[7] As capital searches for cheaper labor costs, it commodifies the labor of populations that were previously excluded from wage work. This process takes place by expanding industrial work into nonindustrialized peripheral areas or incorporating into industrial production populations that were not previously part of the active industrial labor force in industrialized areas. At the same time, new populations are proletarianized and segments of the population that were previously included in the labor force are deproletarianized and forced into informal activities to make their living. In the present context, these informal activities are mainly of the petty marketer and supplier type. The persons engaged in these activities participate in the reproduction of the newly proletarianized labor force. In this way, the creation of a cheaper proletariat, which combines the advantages of low cost as well as high control of the labor process, is related to the expansion of certain types of informal activities.

This process is occurring in both cities, as it is the result of global structural pressures. The process of informalization, however, is much more advanced in Santo Domingo than in San José. In the latter city, labor protections still make a difference in favor of formal employment. The action of the state is, after all, an important intermediary variable that affects the form that global processes take in each locale. This suggests that the growing calls for flexibilization of the labor market will not solve the problems of unemployment and underemployment. Therefore, the presence of effective state regulation, while not a solution, is needed to slow the pace of the deteriorating of living conditions of the popular sectors.

Since state action is a relevant variable, a final word is necessary with regard to the policies aimed toward the informal economy, which have been extremely popular in the last decade. The informal economy fulfills an increasingly important role in guaranteeing the reproduction of the labor force, suggesting that a policy focus on the informal economy is indeed necessary. Nevertheless, the results of this study show that the informal economy is not a panacea for growth, as suggested by De Soto (1989) and several international institutions. It does not seem that, under the present economic model, the informal economy can be absorbed by the formal sector. As shown by De Oliveira and Roberts (1994) rather than being more integrated into international chains of production and distribution, the informal economy is becoming increasingly marginalized. Therefore, a policy directed toward the informal economy cannot, and should not, pretend to transform informal activities into an engine of accumulation. The main tool available to informal economic actors to improve their situation, within the limits imposed by the local and global socioeconomic context, is their social networks. A successful policy directed toward the informal economy has to take into account, and promote, the organization of informal economic actors on the basis of their social networks and common interests.

NOTES

1. In fact, informal firms can often be classified as subcontractors or suppliers at the same time, or at different periods in the history of the business. Likewise, petty marketers often change their status between true self-employed and "disguised" workers. It is important to note that so-called suppliers do not always reduce the price of goods; sometimes, they retain an extra profit by acting as intermediaries.

2. In spite of these extensive regulations, or perhaps because of them, the informal sector in Costa Rica is considerably smaller than in the Dominican Republic (Itzigsohn, 1994).

3. The empirical base for the analysis is a series of semistructured interviews with informal microentrepreneurs conducted in the two cities during the summers of 1992 and 1993. The people interviewed were reached through the use of the snowball technique with multiple points of entry. I conducted 44 interviews in Santo Domingo, of which 9 were with microentrepreneurs and workers in the garments sector and 9 in the crafts sector. In San José, I conducted 46 interviews, including 22 with microentrepreneurs and workers in the garment sector and 4 in the crafts sector. These interviews cannot be taken as representative of the entire population of informal entrepreneurs in the two cities due to the limitations of the sample.

4. For a detailed description of the cases, see Itzigsohn (1994).

5. The only exception I found confirms this statement. It was a case of a cooperative of women in a popular area west of San José. The cooperative had 23 workers, most of them members, and the production process was organized with strict discipline as to working hours and production standards. Hence, more than an informal workshop, it was a small informal factory with the capacity to meet the tight standards of international firms.

6. The reference to the state here is not misguided, as, in the last ten years, Dominican president Joaquín Balaguer has taken on himself the management of the city of Santo Domingo.

7. This is a characteristic of proletarianization in general, as shown by the rise of temporary employment, sweatshops, and structural unemployment in the core regions. The differences are in the different forms that this process takes in the core and the periphery.

REFERENCES

Barkin, David. 1985. "Global Proletarianization." In *The Americas in the New International Division of Labor*, ed. Steven E. Sanderson, pp. 26–45. New York: Holmes and Meier.

Beneria, Lourdes, and Martha Roldán. 1987. *The Crossroads of Class and Gender: Homework, Subcontracting, and Household Dynamics in Mexico City*. Chicago: University of Chicago Press.

Birkbeck, Chris. 1978. "Self-Employed Proletarians in an Informal Factory: The Case of Cali's Garbage Dump." *World Development* 6: 1173–1185.

Broad, Dave. 1991. "Global Economic Restructuring and the (Re)Casualization of Work in the Center." *Review* 14, 4: 555–592.

Bromley, Ray. 1978. "Organization, Regulation and Exploitation in the So-Called 'Urban Informal Sector': The Street Traders of Cali, Colombia." *World Development* 6: 1161–1171.

Castells, Manuel, and Alejandro Portes. 1989. "World Underneath: The Origins, Dynamics, and Effects of the Informal Economy." In *The Informal Economy: Studies in Advanced and Less Developed Countries*, ed. Alejandro Portes, Manuel Castells, and Lauren A. Benton, pp. 11–37. Baltimore: Johns Hopkins University Press.

De Oliveira, Orlandina, and Bryan Roberts. 1994. "The Many Roles of the Informal Sector in Development: Evidence from Urban Labor Market Research, 1940–1989." In *Contrapunto: The Informal Sector Debate in Latin America*, ed. Cathy A. Rakowski, pp. 51–71. Albany: State University of New York Press.

De Soto, Hernando, 1989. *The Other Path*. New York: Harper and Row.

Infante, Ricardo, and Emilio Klein. 1991. "The Latin American Labour Market, 1950–1980." *CEPAL Review* 45 (December): 121–135.

Itzigsohn, José. 1994. "The State, the Informal Economy, and the Reproduction of the Labor Force." Ph.D. dissertation, Johns Hopkins University, Department of Sociology.

Lozano, Wilfredo. 1994. "La Vida Mala: Economía informal y pobladores urbanos en Santo Domingo." Unpublished manuscript, Johns Hopkins University, Department of Sociology.

Lozano, Wilfredo, and Isis Duarte. 1992. "Proceso de urbanización, modelos de desarrollo y clases sociales en República Dominicana 1960–1990." In *Urbanización en el Caribe*, ed. Alejandro Portes and Mario Lungo, pp. 213–349. San José, Costa Rica: Facultad Latinoamericana de Ciencias Sociales.

Moser, Caroline. 1994. "The Informal Sector Debate, Part 1: 1970–1983." In *Contrapunto: The Informal Sector Debate in Latin America*, ed. Cathy A. Rakowski, pp. 11–29. Albany: State University of New York Press.

Murphy, Martin. 1990. "The Need for a Re-evaluation of the Concept of 'Informal Sector': The Dominican Case." In *Perspectives in Economic Anthropology*, ed. M. E. Smith, pp. 161–181. Lanham, MD: University Press of America.

Pérez Sainz, Juan Pablo. 1994. "Apatía y esperanza: Las dos caras del área metropolitana de Guatemala." Unpublished manuscript, Johns Hopkins University, Department of Sociology.

Portes, Alejandro. 1985. "Latin American Class Structures: Their Composition and Change During the Last Decades." *Latin American Research Review* 20, 3: 7–39.

Portes, Alejandro, José Itzigsohn, and Carlos Dore. 1994. "Urbanization in the Caribbean Basin: Social Change during the Years of the Crisis." *Latin American Research Review* 29, 2: 3–37.

Portes, Alejandro, and Saskia Sassen-Koob. 1987. "Making it Underground: Comparative Material on the Informal Sector in Western Market Economies." *American Journal of Sociology* 93 (July): 30–61.

Portes, Alejandro, and Richard Schauffler. 1994. "Competing Perspectives on the Latin American Informal Sector." *Population and Development Review* 19 (March): 33–60.

Portes, Alejandro, and John Walton. 1981. *Labor, Class, and the International System*. New York: Academic Press.

Rakowski, Cathy A., ed. 1994. *Contrapunto: The Informal Sector Debate in Latin America*. Albany: State University of New York Press.

Rovira Más, Jorge. 1985. *Costa Rica en los años 80*. San José, Costa Rica: Editorial Porvenir.

Sanderson, Steven. 1985. "A Critical Approach to the Americas in the New International Division of Labor." In *The Americas in the New International Division of Labor*, ed. Steven E. Sanderson, pp. 2–25. New York: Holmes and Meier.

Smith, Joan, and Immanuel Wallerstein, eds. 1992. *Creating and Transforming Households: The Constraints of the World-Economy*. Cambridge: Cambridge University Press and Maison des Sciences de l'Homme.

Wallerstein, Immanuel. 1983. *Historical Capitalism*. London: Verso.

6

Transnational Realities and Anti-Immigrant State Policies: Issues Raised by the Experiences of Central American Immigrants and Refugees in a Trinational Region

Susanne Jonas

This chapter suggests an interdisciplinary, cross-border conceptual framework for research about the second and third largest groups of Latinos in California (after Mexicans): Salvadoran and Guatemalan immigrants and refugees of the 1980s and 1990s. The upsurge in the movement of Salvadorans and Guatemalans across borders in recent years is analyzed here in relation to the configuration of a "trinational region" or "space" that includes their home countries in Central America, the "intermediate space" of Mexico, and the United States (focusing here on California). In conforming transnational communities, Salvadorans and Guatemalans have established cross-border circuits and linkages that are difficult to break, even in the face of anti-immigrant state policies. Furthermore, their experiences in a "trinational region" are transforming the identities and behavior of Salvadoran and Guatemalan immigrants, making many of them actors in more than one nation (particularly as some return, by choice or coercion, to their countries of origin).

In addition to sketching the outlines of this specific research, the chapter explores the effects of anti-immigrant state policies in an age of transnational realities. Because the research draws on a particular case study and the policies in question are themselves changing rapidly, this chapter does not propose definitive or generalized conclusions. However, the research reported in the study, together with other recent contributions, does raise questions about both the effectiveness of restrictive state policies in actually stopping or controlling immigration and the collateral political effects of such policies (for the immigrants themselves as well as in their different sites of residence and action).

The approach presented here is regional in scope in that it draws on the experiences of Salvadoran and Guatemalan refugees and immigrants who have crossed two borders within a trinational region that is becoming ever more integrated. These two borders (Guatemala/Mexico and Mexico/United States) are becoming nodal points in the contradictory pressures between economic transnationalization, on the one hand, and restrictive immigration policies imposed by nation-states, on the other hand. Cross-border flows of capital and goods (many of them state-promoted or -assisted), as well as U.S. foreign policies affecting the case of Central Americans, are among the realities that have made these borders more porous and stimulated increased immigrant flows. At the same time, however, the U.S. government is attempting to stem the flow of migrants (both labor and political) through increasingly restrictive immigration and refugee policies and is pressuring the Mexican government to prevent Central Americans in particular from ever reaching U.S. soil. Hence, this chapter suggests broader questions about the contradictory roles of the state in relation to cross-border movements of capital and people—a central concern of immigration research within a world-systems framework.

Like the migrations being studied, this research adopts a regional, cross-border perspective. The backdrop for this study involves the rapidly changing economic and political conditions in all three parts of this region. During the 1980s, the prolonged civil wars in El Salvador and Guatemala, which were characterized by widespread violence and repression, both combined with and intensified economic crises that left over 85 percent of the population living below the poverty line in both countries. These conditions generated a new, much larger wave of immigrants to Mexico and the United States. In the 1990s, the prospects for and obstacles to stable peace and development in the home countries continue to appear as crucial variables in shaping the decisions of Salvadorans and Guatemalans about cross-border migrations in both directions. Within the region, Mexico has played a very particular (and increasing) role as a space and a player mediating between the United States and Central America—all the more so in the age of the North American Free Trade Agreement (NAFTA) and its projected extension to Central America. Today, the endless complexities and contradictions of Mexico itself are affecting the conditions for Central American transmigrants to the United States. Finally, rapidly changing events in the United States (in this case, in California) also continue to have repercussions for Salvadorans and Guatemalans throughout the region.

This chapter is organized in four principal sections. The first section establishes a structural context, referred to as the emergence of a trinational region. The second section describes briefly some of the insights about recent migration patterns derived from in-progress, empirical research projects. The third and fourth sections suggest that the study of the Salvadoran and Guatemalan experiences can contribute toward addressing two broader questions. First, how effective are anti-immigrant state policies in the face of transnational realities within an increasingly integrated region? Second, if their effectiveness is only relative, what are the other political consequences of these policies for the region? The chapter ends by suggesting briefly some theoretical implications for cross-border reconceptualizations of democracy in the Americas and for immigration research grounded in world-systems perspectives.

TRINATIONAL REGION AS THE STRUCTURAL CONTEXT

The structural context for changing migration patterns involves the emergence of a trinational region that is undergoing a process of integration, spanning the United States (particularly California), Mexico, and Central America, and becoming interlinked economically, politically, and socioculturally. With regard to economic integration, there is already an extensive literature written by world-systems scholars (e.g., Immanuel Wallerstein, Alejandro Portes, María Patricia Fernández-Kelly, Robert Bach, Saskia Sassen, Paul Ong, Edna Bonacich, and Lucie Cheng) that focuses on the complementarity of capital and labor flows, particularly within economic arrangements characterized by relations of unequal exchange. This topic has attracted wide discussion, most recently in relation to NAFTA (e.g., the linkages created by this agreement, as well as the disruptive and/or displacing effects of economic integration for some sectors of the population on each side of the border).

Throughout the 1980s, economic crises in the region increased migratory flows, and such trends are likely to continue in the 1990s. Of equal or greater importance, the demand continues for the low-waged labor of Central Americans as well as Mexicans (both in agricultural and urban/service activities), even at the height of economic recession and anti-immigrant sentiment in the United States. In this sense, economic integration is itself important in explaining the rise of migration from Central America over recent decades.

In this region, however, the process of integration includes political, social, and cultural dimensions, and not merely economic linkages. Politically, the civil wars in Guatemala and El Salvador during the 1980s contributed to the integration of the region through the deep involvement of both the United States and Mexico (each in its own way, and directly or indirectly) in those civil wars and their peace processes. These linkages are hence based primarily on security and diplomacy considerations. Ironically, the Reagan administration's policies of supporting counterinsurgency wars during the 1980s served indirectly to stimulate the exodus of Central Americans to Mexico and the United States. The role of Mexico as a site for Central American refugees, as well as Mexican diplomacy in the region, also increased significantly during the same period. Other political linkages were forged by opponents of U.S. policy (sanctuary cities, church activists, asylum lawyers, and human rights groups in the United States and Mexico). Today, the construction of peace (the volatile peace of El Salvador and the endlessly difficult efforts to reach peace in Guatemala) has become a factor whose progress will affect people's living conditions in their home countries and, in turn, their migration decisions.

Socially, the movement of people has itself become a structural factor. Prior Central American migrations have created "bridges" (based on kinship, household, and community networks) that new migrants are crossing today.[1] These prior relationships and interactive networks have increasingly contributed to the integration of the United States, Mexico, and Central America as a trinational social region through which people move north and return. As with other transnational communities, older generations of Salvadorans and Guatemalans frequently paved the way for the 1980s refugees, who in turn have laid the groundwork for the 1990s immigrants.[2] An important concrete indicator of the significance of these transnational family and community networks is the fact that remittance flows from the United States to the home countries have become a pillar of the economies of both El Salvador and Guatemala (estimated, respectively, at $1 billion and over $.5 billion a year); in the Salvadoran case, remittances have become far greater than revenues from coffee exports.

A final point about this region is that today it is a zone of multiple conflicts and growing instabilities—from the wars and uncertain peace in Central America to the compounded crises of 1994–1995 in Mexico and economic recession in California and elsewhere in the United States. Anti-immigrant initiatives, such as California's Proposition 187 (denying education, health, and social services to undocumented immigrants), can also be expected to increase social conflict and have destabilizing consequences. This entire complex, then, forms the material basis or framework for understanding the cross-border movements of Central American immigrants and refugees as social actors.

SALVADORANS AND GUATEMALANS IN CALIFORNIA AND MEXICO

Within this trinational region, most Salvadoran and Guatemalan migrants to the United States have had two borders to cross, generating two different sets of passage (and, in some cases, adaptation) experiences. Moreover, while some Central American migrants seek a rapid passage to the United States, others end up in California only after an extended stay in Mexico. Furthermore, taking households as the unit of analysis, some migrants (especially Guatemalans) have family members in all three countries. Our in-progress research seeks to establish how migrants are transformed by their trinational experiences and, to complete the circle, how those who return to El Salvador or Guatemala may play new roles there as a result of their experiences in Mexico and California. Our research suggests the constitution of new social actors (binational or even trinational), whose behavior and identities are being redefined in a variety of ways.[3]

The Salvadoran and Guatemalan immigrants/refugees of the 1980s and 1990s, as opposed to previous generations, are characterized not only by greatly increased numbers, but by a distinct class background (generally lower-middle class, working class, or peasant rather than professional or entrepreneurial). The vast majority of these Central American migrants entered the United States via Mexico and without documentation. In some cases of indigenous Guatemalans, entire communities came collectively and continue to live collectively in "daughter communities." Given the close association between the political and economic disasters leading to their emigration, as documented in the vast literature on Central America during the 1980s, the line between political and economic motivations is often blurred. (Hamilton and Chinchilla, 1991, and Stanley, 1987, address this question directly.) In general, however, we can say that political violence was a more important factor in the 1980s than in the 1990s, particularly for Salvadorans.[4]

Precise numbers regarding Central Americans in the United States are virtually impossible to establish because a high proportion of these residents are undocumented. All counts, however, show a dramatic increase in the number of Central American immigrants during the 1980s. Although estimates vary considerably, some mid-1990s approximations suggest that up to 1.2–1.5 million Salvadorans and 800,000–1 million Guatemalans (including permanent legal residents, those in legal limbo with temporary work permits, and undocumented migrants) have entered the United States.[5] The main increase in legal immigrants for both groups occurred in 1989 and 1990 (resulting from a combination of new admissions and legalizations). For both groups, at least half are estimated to be undocumented. The data provided by the U.S. Immigration and Naturalization Service (INS) greatly underestimate the numbers involved (because they are based on a count of "deportables apprehended"), but INS data do clearly show an increase in immigration, in the mid-1980s for Salvadorans, and in the late 1980s and early 1990s for Guatemalans. For both groups, by far the largest numbers of both documented and undocumented immigrants are in California. According to the 1990 U.S. Census, almost 60 percent of Salvadorans and Guatemalans resided in this state; 1992 INS statistics suggest that the shares are even higher for undocumented immigrants.[6]

Since the civil wars were a major factor in the exodus of the 1980s, many migrants originally came as refugees but entered the United States via Mexico without refugee status and without documentation of any kind. Such a pattern contrasts with the experience of refugees from other countries such as Cuba, who generally entered the United States directly and with refugee status. Among those who applied for asylum once they were in the United States, 97 percent of Salvadorans and 99 percent of Guatemalans were turned down during the 1980s—a situation that only began to be rectified with the ABC class action lawsuit (*American Baptist Church v. Thornburgh*), which was won in December 1990, and the granting of Temporary Protected Status (TPS) to Salvadorans in 1991.[7] Even at the end of fiscal year 1994, there were some 126,500 asylum cases pending for Guatemalans (30 percent of all pending asylum cases) and 72,000 for Salvadorans, plus 187,000 TPS cases (as explained in note 7). These numbers do not include the many thousands of immigrants who never applied for asylum out of fear. The accumulation of pending asylum cases suggests that restrictive U.S. immigration policies since the mid-1980s, and U.S. hostility toward these asylum seekers specifically, did very little to deter Salvadorans and

Guatemalans from deciding to leave their home country and undertake a violent and dangerous trip through Mexico and into the United States. In fact, the largest numbers of arrivals came during the years when the INS was systematically denying asylum to virtually all applicants from these two countries who sought such a status.[8]

The passage of immigrants through Mexico represents a crucial moment in the migration circuit, especially for Guatemalans. (This section builds on the extensive research about the largest group, Guatemalan migrants and transmigrants, which was conducted by Manuel Angel Castillo at the Colegio de Mexico and Rodolfo Casillas at FLACSO/Mexico during the last decade, and which focused primarily on Mexico's southern border, in Chiapas and the surrounding states.) Our research includes as many as 150,000 Guatemalan migrants and refugees of the 1980s who were never incorporated into the camps of the United Nations or recognized in Mexico as refugees.[9] Some have become integrated into Mexican society and its labor force, and do not plan to return to Guatemala. Many have gone from the southern border states of Mexico to the cities or other points north, and some end up in the United States. Given the instability of southern Mexico and their inability to attain refugee status in Mexico, some Guatemalans who initially remained in southern border areas may now be more likely to move on to the United States.

We also focus on Guatemalan transmigrants who consciously pass through Mexico in order in order to enter the United States—often through networks that are extremely exploitative and abusive, especially for women and children. Reliable statistics are even more difficult to obtain in Mexico than in the United States, but the studies by Casillas and Castillo leave no doubt that the number of transmigrants is also growing and that experiences in Mexico are significant for some migrants who end up in California.

We now turn from the migrants' initial decisions, to leave their home countries and traverse Mexico to the United States, to their decisions to remain in the United States, return to their home countries, or move back and forth. This is the focus of our collaborative study in northern and southern California.[10] The project involves interviews with 600 Salvadorans and Guatemalans in the metropolitan areas of Los Angeles and San Francisco, two of California's "global cities." This survey attempts to determine how a number of variables, including the winding down of the 1980s civil wars in their home countries, is affecting the decisions of these Central American migrants to stay in the United States or return home. Other variables include the legal status of the Salvadorans and Guatemalans in question, their arrival date and length of stay, the strength of their family and community networks, and the changing political-economic climate in California.[11]

The survey is beginning to suggest one possible trend: even after the war is over, many Salvadorans are not deciding to return to their home country in the near future.[12] The formal end of the war is no longer the primary consideration in making the decision to stay or return—for some, they have become incorporated here; for others, because of doubts about their economic future in El Salvador. If they came largely as refugees, the determinants of their decision to remain or return are far more complex, and may vary along gender and generational lines. The findings also suggest that Salvadorans have not been induced to return permanently by anti-immigrant policies or denial of asylum—even in California's current hostile political climate (although this climate might lead many residents to advise their friends and relatives not to come to California in the immediate future). Certainly, these migrants retain very close ties to El Salvador and closely follow events in their home country. Consequently, those residents who have the option may choose to move back and forth between El Salvador and the United States. However, the situation and mind-set of the Guatemalans are quite different since the low-intensity civil war there is not fully over and political violence remains widespread.

ANTI-IMMIGRANT STATE POLICIES AND TRANSNATIONAL REALITIES

What does this case suggest about the effectiveness of anti-immigrant state policies within an increasingly integrated region—particularly in the era of an expanded NAFTA that will incorporate Central America, and of state-promoted cross-border flows of capital and goods? Specifically, in the medium or longer range, how effective are U.S. anti-immigrant policies (now complemented by Mexican policies) in relation to Central American migration through Mexico to the United States? It will take many years to have definitive answers, but I can suggest some preliminary working hypotheses.

Since the mid-1980s, U.S. immigration policies have become increasingly restrictive.[13] During the 1980s, the denial of virtually all asylum requests from Salvadorans and Guatemalans in particular was largely a function of a U.S. foreign policy that supported the counterinsurgency armies of those two governments and regarded refugees as "subversives." In the post–Cold War era of the 1990s, it is primarily for domestic political reasons that these asylum seekers and immigrants are being treated as if they constituted a threat to U.S. "national security." The post–Cold War redefinition of U.S. national security doctrine actually includes immigration as a top priority concern. Salvadorans and Guatemalans are particularly affected by all the border-focused anti-immigrant measures and by increasingly restrictive "reforms" of asylum laws, as well as by the end of TPS for Salvadorans.

An additional component that has surfaced since the mid-1980s is growing U.S. pressure on Mexico to collaborate in keeping Central Americans out of the United States. The INS has been working with Mexican migration agents (particularly on Mexico's southern border) to turn back Central Americans before they can ever come through Mexico to cross into the United States, where some could exercise the right to seek asylum and others would find work. The Mexican government denies this collaboration, but it is documented in the United

States, with Congress openly allocating funds to reimburse Mexico for the expenses of interdiction and deportation (see Frelick, 1991, and more recent congressional documents). In any case, Mexican deportations (mainly of Central Americans) have increased one hundredfold, from 1,308 in 1987 to around 130,000 a year since 1990 (Casillas, 1995:12).

A word about Mexico itself: because of its historic role as a mediator between the United States and Central America, as well as its geographic position as an "intermediate space," Mexico is caught in a complex dilemma between its diplomatic and national security concerns vis-à-vis Central Americans. Within this trinational region, Mexico's relative weight in Central America has been on the increase throughout the 1980s and 1990s. Mexico has been not only a space through which Central Americans pass, but also a major player in the Central American peace negotiations, with its own interests and definitions of "national security" (and in this regard, often an opponent rather than a supporter of U.S. policy). In addition, Mexican business interests now project increasing investment, and therefore seek greater stability, in Central America. Today, however, the situation is vastly complicated by Mexico's own crises, especially in the context of the Chiapas uprising and greater militarization on the border with Guatemala. In short, just at the moment when Mexico is becoming the centerpiece of this trinational region, its policies toward Central Americans are more contradictory and less predictable than ever.

Despite the escalation of anti-immigrant measures by both the United States and Mexico, it is far from clear how effective state policies that treat immigration as a "national security" issue will prove in the medium or long range in actually keeping out Salvadorans and Guatemalans. Clearly, a hostile U.S. reception did not stop them from coming during the 1980s. Since then, the pace of regional economic integration has greatly quickened, while the demand for cheap labor in the United States remains as high as ever; and by now, preexisting immigrant social networks are already in place. As Espenshade (1994), Kossoudji (1992), and others have suggested, the threat of apprehension at the United States–Mexico border has only a limited deterrent effect unless it is applied massively and absolutely (which would make border areas literally a police state)—although we can expect that the deterrent effect will be greater for Central Americans, who risk deportation to their home country, than for Mexicans. Increased interdictions and deportations by Mexican authorities have not stopped the influx of Salvadorans and Guatemalans, although they have doubtless reduced the numbers. Moreover, in terms of those already in the United States, it seems likely that, short of massive deportations or the passage of extremist legislation, many individuals and families who have the option will do what they can to remain (including naturalization), while maintaining ties to their home countries.

In short, anti-immigrant state policies do not necessarily control the actual behavior of people whose lives have been transnationalized. These measures may temporarily affect the direction of the flow, but they will not decrease cross-border movements of people, disrupt the migration circuits, or stop the process of regional integration. In the case of Salvadorans and Guatemalans specifically, the numbers of new migrants will be significantly affected by the extent to which the end of the civil wars brings stable peace and economic opportunity—equitable, rather than neoliberal, development. Apart from that, migration will doubtless continue through established and, to some extent, self-perpetuating networks and patterns.[14] Furthermore, even if the end of the wars, combined with the crackdown in the United States, were to encourage a larger number of Central Americans to return home (by free choice or increased deportations), the binational or trinational practices and collective cross-border links and circuits that have developed during the last fifteen years are likely to persist, with Salvadorans and Guatemalans continuing to move back and forth across the borders in this trinational region.

The final contradiction of anti-immigrant state policies, which undermines or relativizes their effectiveness perhaps more than all other factors discussed here, is that labor migrants are not truly "unwanted" in the United States. Consequently, proposals for a new Bracero-type program are now emerging precisely at the height of anti-immigrant measures, which is an oft-repeated pattern in the immigration history of the United States. Today, as Portes remarks in Chapter 8 of this volume, "Core-bound immigration is not an optional process, but one driven by the structural requirements of advanced capitalist accumulation." Public perceptions in the United States that immigrants are "taking American jobs" or "over using public services" must be understood largely as a function of the fact that the costs of immigration are socialized (worse yet, at a time of economic recession), while the benefits are privatized. Clearly, there are many different agendas in regard to immigration policy, but those who advocate stopping the flow are less likely to prevail, in the long run, than those who seek to control it (in ways adverse to the immigrants themselves).

POLITICAL EFFECTS AND THEORETICAL IMPLICATIONS

All the issues discussed here raise serious questions about the medium- or long-range effectiveness of anti-immigrant state policies, but there are other consequences as well. The creation of an integrated region is already in process; but what kind of region will it be, politically? Treating immigration as a national security issue, I suggest, will likely have serious antidemocratic and destabilizing consequences. Specifically, it subjects the migrants involved to conditions of greater vulnerability, with diminished human and civil rights. Just as banning abortion only leads to coat-hanger abortions, so, too, the criminalization of border crossings does not stop them; bans might reduce border crossings, but above all, they make them far more dangerous and abusive to those involved. To put it another way, anti-immigrant state policies can certainly punish undocumented entrants, regardless of the effectiveness in restricting their entry.

More broadly, these anti-immigrant policies also lead to exclusionary politics in the United States. Castañeda (1993), writing about Mexican immigration, postulated a ''de-democratization'' of California, referring to the creation of a two-tiered system of citizens/non citizens as a form of electoral apartheid. Furthermore, de-democratization has had a spread effect in California and elsewhere in the United States. The measures began by treating undocumented immigrants as a national security problem, but they have rapidly spread to attacks on legal resident immigrant communities, and they could ultimately affect Latino citizens. (We should not forget the massive deportations of Mexican-American citizens during the 1930s). Even beyond that, however, given the multiple initiatives to change the Fourteenth Amendment of the U.S. Constitution so as to deny citizenship to children born in the United States of undocumented parents, a basic principle of ''American democracy'' is in danger of being profoundly undermined.

Anti-immigration policies also have broader implications for Latin America. Even in terms of the stated goals of U.S. policy for the hemisphere, both Mexico and Central America will be politically and economically destabilized rather than stabilized as a consequence of these measures. To cite only the most obvious example, cutting off remittances from immigrants (one of the survival mechanisms of economies in crisis) will surely undermine economic stabilization programs in both Mexico and Central America. By contrast, permitting free movement of peoples would build a more stable, as well as a more humane, integrated region. That is the European approach, at least among the European Community (EC) countries.[15] Nor can the economies of these countries absorb a major influx of deportee labor. Furthermore, treating immigration as a national security issue actually serves to undermine rather than promote democracy in Latin America, since it institutionalizes new forms of exclusionary politics in inter-American relations and in the countries involved (e.g., the militarization of Mexico's borders).

In the case presented here, Salvadorans and Guatemalans have begun to play a role in struggles for democratization in all three areas of this region and are engaging in ''transnational grassroots political practices,'' as some (e.g., Smith, 1994) have called them.[16] In addition, having begun as targets of exclusionary politics in their countries of origin, some of these Salvadorans and Guatemalans are carriers of resistance strategies, which they are learning to adapt and use against exclusionary politics in the United States (e.g., working in coalitions around immigration issues).

These immigrant groups will need solid support from progressive movements in the United States and Mexico. In the United States, this suggests the need to build a new civil rights movement with an internationalist orientation to fight for the rights of Latino and other immigrants and to build cross-border coalitions and alliances. Such a movement would go beyond defensive focuses (e.g., against restrictive legislation) to initiate campaigns for the strict application of international refugee conventions, an international charter or bill of rights (even an ombudsman), and international unions representing workers who move across borders (including their treatment at those borders). This movement would also push for hemispheric codes establishing and enforcing minimum wage rates, basic working conditions, and so forth—in short, setting limits on the degree of exploitation of Latin American workers within the United States as well as in their home countries. These should be among the priority concerns of twenty-first-century, U.S.-based citizens of an increasingly integrated transnational region.

Finally, let us consider briefly some of the theoretical implications. First, the great upsurge in cross-border immigration suggests the limitations of the nation-bound concept of democracy as nothing more than elections—and even more so, the neoliberal idea that the internationalization of capital will automatically "democratize" these regions (which is the working assumption of NAFTA and of U.S. policy in Latin America generally). On the contrary, free-trade agreements can only be compatible with a more integral notion of democracy that includes its social dimension if they are based on an upward harmonization of wage, environmental, and political standards rather than downward harmonization, as is currently the case. Furthermore, in a transnational era, democracy must include mechanisms to ensure the accountability of states to civil society across borders, and thus to counter the undemocratic tendencies of, and pressures from, transnationalized capital. More generally, as I argue in more detail elsewhere (Jonas, forthcoming), democracy and citizenship must be substantially reconceptualized for the twenty-first century in order to address the rights of people who move across borders and of transnational populations as de facto citizens of an increasingly integrated region.

Second, just as immigration research grounded in a structural world-systems framework has been greatly enriched by ethnographic and network research and perspectives, so too it can gain a new dimension from examination of the political implications of anti-immigrant state policies and the new opportunities for political action on this issue by individual and collective actors in civil society. This more explicit political focus can be useful, not only to activists, but also to researchers and theorists developing a multidimensional paradigm or approach to immigration. It can shed light on the contradictory roles of the state as it seeks to enhance cross-border flows of capital and goods while restricting cross-border movements of people, and on the intersection of transnational realities and state policies—both ongoing concerns of world-systems analysis.

Third, at a more general level, we need a thoroughly interdisciplinary approach. The project described here combines structural and policy analyses with survey research, ethnographic interviews, and statistical analysis. This particular study, and immigration research more generally, exemplifies the broader need and the opportunity (already identified by leading world-systems scholars) for a new paradigm for the social sciences—including its interaction with what has traditionally been considered the "humanities."[17]

A final note on levels of analysis goes back to our starting point: this chapter has attempted to present an approach that is multilevel—that is regional as well as global and local. By themselves, global structural analyses risk explaining too little by explaining too much. Strictly community or local focuses, on the other hand, can become problematic when their conclusions are generalized too readily. However, a combination of both that additionally incorporates a "middle," or regional, cross-border level permits a focus on the specific dynamics of a particular area, such as the trinational region examined here. This multidimensional spotlight seems particularly appropriate to illuminate the complex dynamics of immigration in the Americas of the twenty-first century.

NOTES

I wish to thank the North-South Center of the University of Miami and the Chicano-Latino Research Center of the University of California (UC) at Santa Cruz for the funding that made this research possible. Thanks also go to John Marshall for valiant research assistance on statistical materials, and many thanks go to the organizers and participants in the PEWS conference (especially Bill Smith), as well as colleagues at UC Santa Cruz (John Isbister, Pat Zavella) and elsewhere (particularly Nestor Rodríguez, Manuel Angel Castillo, and Frank Bonilla) for invaluable comments on earlier versions of this chapter. As always, they bear no responsibility for the final product.

1. As Fernández-Kelly and Portes (1992: 253) put it, "Migrants walk across the invisible bridges created by particular capital flows and political linkages." From a different vantage point, Basch, Schiller, and Blanc referred to "the creation of social fields that cross national boundaries," in which people link nations (1994: 22).

2. The pioneering work by Frank Bonilla and the Centro de Estudios Puertorriqueños (1986) about "circuits and cycles of migration" has proven useful for understanding transnational Latino communities. In the case of Salvadorans and Guatemalans, see note 10 below.

3. In a recent review of the immigration literature, Massey et al. referred to the emergence over time of a "culture of migration that is distinct from the culture of both sending and receiving countries" (1994: 738).

4. The importance of civil wars and political violence in the case of Salvadorans and Guatemalans (and Nicaraguans, although they are not included in our study) can be seen by contrasting their large wave of immigration during the 1980s with the far smaller migration from Honduras, where poverty levels were similar but were not accompanied by civil war or an equivalent level of political violence.

5. The 1990 U.S. Census reported 565,081 Salvadorans and 268,779 Guatemalans; in addition to generally recognized undercounting (in large part, because of the high proportion of undocumented migrants), this does not include post-1990 entrants—which is particularly problematic in the case of Guatemalans, because their migration increased more during the late 1980s and early 1990s.

6. Los Angeles has become the second capital city to both groups, with 300,000–500,000 Salvadorans and 250,000–400,000 Guatemalans by 1994 (estimates vary significantly)—in both cases, and especially for Guatemalans, far more than the number counted in the 1990 census.

7. The ABC class-action lawsuit (*American Baptist Church v. Thornburgh*), which was won in December 1990, established that the INS had "wrongfully discriminated" against Salvadoran and Guatemalan asylum applicants (by arbitrarily dismissing their

cases on foreign policy grounds), and called for their cases to be reheard. Several hundred thousand Central Americans were saved from deportation pending a new hearing; today, over four years later, they remain in a legal limbo but do have work permits. Given the huge backlog of cases pending, it is likely that some will find a way to regularize their status. Those who came after 1990, however, are not protected by the ABC decision. Between 1991 and 1994, Salvadorans had another avenue: Temporary Protected Status/ Deferred Enforced Departure (TPS/DED)—temporary safe-haven programs. However, as of 1995, the TPS program was ended, giving 187,000 Salvadorans thirteen months to find another way to legalize their status. Meanwhile, Guatemalans never enjoyed any TPS or DED program, and efforts to gain such a program failed—despite the lack of a peace accord to end the 35-year civil war, and despite the continuing high level of political violence and repression there. From 1992 through 1994, the number of Guatemalan asylum applications was by far the highest for any country in the world (42 percent of the total in 1992 and 23 percent in 1994). In a year when 44,000 applications were received (1992), only 63 were granted.

8. The influx of Salvadoran asylum seekers slowed in 1992, when the civil war was ended. With the termination of the TPS program in 1995, the number of asylum cases will likely increase, but the end of the war will make their cases far more difficult to win. Moreover, both Salvadoran and Guatemalan asylum seekers will face an even more difficult situation in the future: among the current asylum "reforms" is the denial of work permits to applicants awaiting a decision, and far more drastic proposals are making their way through the U.S. Congress.

9. In regard to Guatemalans in Mexico, this section does not focus on the seasonal contract laborers who come across the Guatemala/Mexico border "legally" (50,000–60,000 a year are involved in something like a bracero program) or border residents who move back and forth across that border (some on a daily basis). Nor does it focus on the 45,000 Guatemalan political refugees of the 1980s who have been living in the UN camps in southern Mexico and whose goal is collective and organized return to Guatemala (which is now in progress).

10. This study on Salvadorans and Guatemalans in California is being conducted by Nora Hamilton, Norma Chinchilla, Carlos Córdova, and myself. It will complement research being conducted by Nestor Rodríguez and Jacqueline Hagan in Texas, Allen Burns in Florida, Terry Repak in Washington, D.C., and Sarah Mahler on Long Island, New York—and previous and ongoing work being conducted in California by various researchers (see References).

11. Our questionnaire is quite broad and will yield much additional information about these transnational individuals, families, and communities. We are currently conducting the interviews (300 in each area)—primarily with those who came during the 1980s and 1990s, but also including some from earlier migrations, in order to see the contrast. Snowball sampling is used, with an orientation toward a stratified sample that will replicate data from the 1990 census with regard to national group and similar parameters. Our interviews include both documented and undocumented migrants and are drawn from a wide range of networks, including soccer clubs, business associations, refugee assistance organizations, and churches; moreover, they are distributed over gender and generational groupings, as well as between Salvadorans and Guatemalans. In addition to the interviews, we will be integrating available statistical information from the census, the INS, and other sources—despite the limitations of such information when taken by itself. A second phase of this project will attempt to assess the multiple impacts of the decisions

to either remain or return on families and communities, both in the United States and "back home," as well as the creation of transnational identities.

12. This confirms informal surveys reported in 1993 on Univisión (Spanish-language television news in the United States) in the *San Francisco Chronicle*, and in *La Opinión* (Los Angeles) to the effect that a very high percentage no longer considered themselves refugees. For earlier studies, see Chávez, Flores and López-Garza (1990) and Córdova (1987).

13. For the purposes of policy analysis, these observations shift from the California to the U.S. level because national laws have far greater impact than state laws; additionally, anti-immigrant initiatives that premiered in California are spreading to other states and being taken up in Congress.

14. Sarah Mahler (1995) went even farther, arguing that Salvadoran society has become so "vested in migration"—so permeated by the culture and industries of migration—that the flow will be only minimally deterred by restrictionist U.S. policies or the end of the war. Studies by Nestor Rodríguez and others have emphasized, in addition, the role of rapid travel and communications. On these points more generally, see Chapter 8 in this volume, by Portes, which focuses on the role of transnational entrepreneurs. The latter contribution and Massey et al. (1994: 699–751) have both referred to the "cumulative" and "self-perpetuating" nature of migration.

15. As Luis Guarnizo concluded in his study of Dominican return migration, "While the formal Dominican economy is restructuring itself to redefine its mode of insertion into the world economy, migrants are laying the groundwork to further this process of globalization: a growing Dominican population overseas with a thriving ethnic economy, plus a continuous flow of tangible and intangible resources between both countries, are apt pillars to support this process" (1993: 44).

16. To cite just one incipient example, a group of Guatemalan "Displaced Persons living in the United States" gained representation in the multisectoral Assembly of Civil Society in Guatemala, which is deeply involved in the peace process and the democratization of Guatemala; in the United States, this same group has been part of a coalition seeking to gain TPS status for Guatemalans. Like other transnational Latino communities described by Basch, Schiller, and Blanc, "by living their lives straddling several nation-states, they are affected by, pose special challenges to, and contribute to hegemonic processes in several separate states" (1994: 15).

17. See, among others, Gulbenkian Commission (1992), Quijano and Wallerstein (1992), and Bonilla (1994). On the last point, which has received increasing attention in cultural studies, Quijano and Wallerstein have noted that the Americas are undergoing a "growing decolonization of the production of culture, of the arts, and of scientific knowledge," despite the pressures from globalizing capital (1992: 549–557).

REFERENCES

Bach, Robert L. 1992. "Hemispheric Migration in the 1990s." In *The United States and Latin America in the 1990s: Beyond the Cold War*, ed. J. Hartlyn, L. Schoultz, and A. Varas, pp. 262–281. Chapel Hill: University of North Carolina Press.

Basch, Linda, Nina Glick Schiller, and Cristina Szanton Blanc. 1994. *Nations Unbound: Transnational Projects, Postcolonial Predicaments, and Deterritorialized Nation-States*. Langhorne, PA: Gordon and Breach.

Bonilla, Frank. 1986. "Ethnic Orbits: The Circulation of Capitals and Peoples." In *Industry and Idleness*, ed. Frank Bonilla and Ricardo Campos. New York: Centro de Estudios Puertorriqueños.

———. 1992. "Circuits and Cycles: A Century of Puerto Rican Migration." Connecticut Humanities Council.

———. 1994. "The Global Society and the Latino Community: Changing the Americas from within the U.S." Unpublished manuscript.

Burns, Allan. 1993. *Maya in Exile: Guatemalans in Florida*. Philadelphia: Temple University Press.

Casillas, Rodolfo. 1995. "Se mueve la frontera al Suchiate?" *Este País*, April, pp. 9–12.

———, ed. 1992. *Los Procesos Migratorios Centroamericanos y Sus Efectos Regionales*. Mexico, DF: Facultad Latinoamericana de Ciencias Sociales/Mexico.

Casillas, Rodolfo, and Manuel Angel Castillo. 1994. *Los flujos migratorios internacionales en la frontera sur de México*. México, DF: Secretaría del Trabajo y Previsión Social, Consejo Nacional de Población.

Castañeda, Jorge. 1993. "Mexico and California: The Paradox of Tolerance and Dedemocratization." In *The California-Mexico Connection*, ed. A. Lowenthal and K. Burgess, pp. 34–47. Palo Alto, CA.: Stanford University Press.

Castillo, Manuel Angel. 1995. "Politicas de Refugio y Politicas de Immigración: ¿Posibilidades de Conciliación?" Unpublished manuscript.

Chávez, Leo, Estevan Flores and Marta López-Garza. 1990. "Here Today, Gone Tomorrow? Undocumented Settlers and Immigration Reform." *Human Organization* 49, 3: 193–205.

Córdova, Carlos. 1987. "El Salvadorean Immigrants in the San Francisco Bay Area." *Journal of La Raza Studies* 1, 1: 9–37.

Espenshade, Thomas. 1994. "Does the Threat of Border Apprehension Deter Undocumented U.S. Immigration?" *Population and Development Review* 20, 4 (December): 871–892.

Fernández-Kelly, M. Patricia, and Alejandro Portes. 1992. "Continent on the Move: Immigrants and Refugees in the Americas." In *Americas: New Interpretive Essays*, ed. Alfred Stepan, pp. 248–274. New York: Oxford University Press.

Frelick, William. 1991. "Running the Gauntlet: The Central American Journey through Mexico." Washington, DC: U.S. Committee for Refugees.

Guarnizo, Luis. 1993. "Going Home: Class, Gender and Household Transformations among Dominican Returned Migrants." Report prepared for Commission for Hemispheric Migration and Refugee Policy, Georgetown University.

Gulbenkian Foundation Commission. 1992. "Report." *Fernand Braudel Center Newsletter* (State University of New York at Binghamton) 17 (August).

Hagan, Jacqueline. 1994. *Deciding to be Legal: A Maya Community in Houston*. Philadelphia: Temple University Press.

Hamilton, Nora, and Norma Chinchilla. 1991. "Central American Migration: A Framework for Analysis." *Latin American Research Review* 26, 1: pp 75–110.

Jonas, Susanne. Forthcoming. " 'National Security,' Regional Development, and Citizenship in U.S. Immigration Policy: Reflections from the Case of Central American Immigrants and Refugees." In *Transnational Realities and Nation States: Trends in International Migration and Immigration Policy in the Americas*, ed. M. Castro. Miami, FL: North-South Center.

Kossoudji, Sherrie. 1992. "Playing Cat and Mouse and the U.S.-Mexican Border." *Demography* 29, 2 (May): 159–180.

López, David, Eric Popkin, and Eddie Telles. 1995. "To Earn a Living: The Occupational World of Central American Immigrants in Los Angeles." Unpublished manuscript.

Mahler, Sarah. 1995. "Vested in Migration: Salvadorans Challenge Restrictionist Policies." Unpublished manuscript.

Massey, Douglas, Joaquín Arango, Graeme Hugo, Ali Kouaqci, Adela Pellegrino, and J. Edward Taylor. 1994. "An Evaluation of International Migration Theory: The North American Case." *Population and Development Review* 20, 4 (December): 699–751.

Ong, Paul, Edna Bonacich, and Lucie Cheng. 1994. *The New Asian Immigration in Los Angeles and Global Restructuring.* Philadelphia: Temple University Press.

Portes, Alejandro and Ruben Rumbaut. 1990. *Immigrant America.* Berkeley: University of California Press.

Quijano, Aníbal, and Immanuel Wallerstein. 1992. "Americanity as a Concept, or the Americas in the Modern World-system." *International Social Science Journal* 44, 4 (November): 549–557.

Rodríguez, Nestor. 1987. "Undocumented Central Americans in Houston: Diverse Populations." *International Migration Review* 21, 1 (Spring): 4–26.

Sassen, Saskia. 1988. *The Mobility of Labor and Capital.* Cambridge: Cambridge University Press.

Smith, Michael Peter. 1994. "Can You Imagine? Transnational Migration and the Globalization of Grassroots Politics." *Social Text* 39 (Summer): 15–33.

Stanley, William. 1987. "Economic Migrants or Refugees from Violence?" *Latin American Research Review* 22, 1: 132–153.

Torres Rivas, Edelberto and Dina Jiménez. 1985. "Informe sobre el estado de las migraciones en Centroamerica." *Anuario de Estudios Centroamericanos* (San José, Costa Rica) 11, 2: 25–57.

Wallerstein, Immanuel. 1992. "The Collapse of Liberalism." In *Socialist Register 1992,* ed. Ralph Miliband and Leo Panitch, pp. 96–110. New York: Monthly Review Press.

7

WOMEN, HOUSEHOLDS, AND TRANSNATIONAL MIGRATION NETWORKS: THE GARIFUNA AND GLOBAL ECONOMIC RESTRUCTURING

Linda Miller Matthei and David A. Smith

The world-system perspective provides a powerful conceptual framework for the analysis of global processes that give rise to and structure migration. Unlike "modernization" theories, which explain migration flows as the cumulative responses of individuals to "push" factors (e.g., high unemployment) in sending areas and unrelated "pull" factors (e.g., high labor demands) in receiving areas, world-system analyses focus explicitly on the structural inequalities that link societies in a single system: the capitalist world-economy (Portes and Walton, 1981; Sassen-Koob, 1981a). Migration, from this perspective, is generated by the penetration and expansion of capitalism and represents a mechanism for the allocation of labor in the global economy (Sassen-Koob, 1981b; Fernández-Kelly 1981).

Though the historical-structural approach developed in world-system analyses significantly advances our understanding of the linkages between migration and global economic forces, it is sometimes criticized for its singular emphasis on the economic *functions* of labor migrants in capitalist development and a lack of attention to migrants as active participants in the migration process (Bach and Schraml, 1982; Massey et al., 1987). As Bach and Schraml have pointed out, in historical-structural analyses, migration is often reduced to a purely economic process in which the migrants themselves are treated "like empty grocery carts, wheeled back and forth between origin and destination under the hungry intentions of world capital. The migrants themselves engage in very little action" (1981: 324).

World-system analyses are also criticized by feminist scholars who argue that macrostructural research often presents an impoverished view of women in international labor migration and in the world-system in general (Grasmuck and Pessar, 1991; Pedraza, 1991; Georges, 1990; Ward, 1993). In numerous studies of international labor migration, women are overlooked completely or treated as secondary migrants who move only at the behest of male decision makers (e.g., Massey et al., 1987; Portes and Bach, 1985; Piore, 1979). This neglect of gender issues in migration research, feminists argue, perpetuates the ideological assumption that "women do little worth writing about" (Pedraza, 1991: 302).

Those macroeconomic studies that *do* examine gender as a dimension of international labor migration generally focus on the global restructuring of production processes and the increasing demand for female labor in low-wage services and the garment and electronic industries (Morokvasic, 1983; Sassen-Koob, 1981a, 1988). The recognition that women are not simply "along for the ride" but are indeed labor migrants in their own right is a significant one. However, these studies, too, tend to limit their analyses to the economic functions of female migrants, and we are left with the impression that the only real difference between men's and women's migration lies in the fact that women represent a more exploitable source of labor. Still absent is any sense of women as active participants in the migration process. "The woman remains silent and invisible, present as a variable, absent as a person" (Morokvasic, 1983: 18).

This chapter is based on an ethnographic study of a "transnational community" (see Portes, Chapter 8 of this volume): the Garifuna of Belize, Central America and Los Angeles. It examines the political-economy of global restructuring and the way in which structural forces shape migration processes, but our primary focus is more "micro"—focusing on what Portes (Chapter 8 of this volume) terms the "everyday networks and patterns of social relationships" that develop in response to more global forces. More specifically, we question the adequacy of approaches that focus on the household as the fundamental unit of analysis in migration research. Such approaches, we argue, obscure women's roles in building and maintaining the transnational networks that pave the way for migration.

In seeking to establish a conceptual link between individuals and the macroeconomic forces that shape migration flows, many migration researchers settle on the household as the "appropriate" unit of analysis (e.g., Wood, 1981; Pessar, 1982). Typically, households are conceptualized as income-pooling and decision-making units that ensure their viability through the strategic allocation of labor (e.g., Wood, 1981; Smith, Wallerstein, and Evers, 1984). In migration research, this "generic" household model has been applied uncritically across societies to explain how migration is planned and how resources are marshaled at ground level. However, these efforts to fit a temporally and culturally specific model of household structure and behavior to all locales and times assume a uniformity and stability that do not hold up to empirical scrutiny (Guyer and Peters, 1987; Moser, 1993). Cross-cultural research indicates, for example, that there is a good deal of variability in levels of income pooling within households. Factors such as marital instability, ethnicity, individual household members' access to employment opportunities, and varying inheritance and marital patterns all contribute to patterns in which household members find it strategically beneficial to maintain "separate purses" (Treas, 1991; Fapohunda, 1988; Beneria and Roldan, 1987). The conceptualization of households as monolithic units in which members selflessly subsume their individual interests and desires for the good of the collectivity also fails to bring to light inequalities and competing interests that give rise to conflict between household members (e.g., Wolf, 1988, 1992; Blumberg, 1991; Wong, 1984). Feminist scholars are particularly critical of the model's lack of attention to the unequal gender distribution of resources and access to power within the household (e.g., Benería and Roldán, 1987; Blumberg, 1991; Wolf, 1992). Treated as a wholly cooperative unit, the household has been cast as *the* actor in migration decision making, and as a result, the negotiations and conflicts that characterize gender relationships within households are left unexamined. Consequently, any woman "who seeks a paying job, earns a wage, or migrates is interpreted as doing so as part of a household strategy" (Wolf, 1992: 12). In fact, however, numerous studies from a variety of migration-sending societies show that women often use migration as an avenue of escape from marital relationships that are exploitative and oppressive (e.g., Chávez, 1992; Grasmuck and Pessar, 1991: 146–147; Foner, 1986: 139).

Recent efforts to address international migration as a social process have resulted in renewed attention to migration as "a process of network-building" (Portes and Walton, 1981: 60) through which migrants organize their moves, gain access to the economic opportunities that await in receiving societies, and pave the way for a subsequent return to sending communities (Portes and Bach, 1985; Massey et al., 1987). However, as Monica Boyd pointed out:

To date much of the recent research on networks is indifferent to gender. Some studies emphasize the experiences of male migrants or all migrants undifferentiated by sex, while others emphasize group behavior as represented in household decisionmaking [*sic*] strategies. Such emphasis is consistent with a general research orientation which assumes that women migrate as part of family migration. As a consequence, little systematic attention is paid to gender in the development and persistence of networks across time and space. (1989: 655)

This lack of attention to female participation in migration networks, we argue, is perpetuated by studies that fail to examine migration as a process of *intra*-household negotiation and decision making, and to question the long-held assumption that migration and migration decision making are, by and large, the province of males (e.g., Massey et al., 1987: 124; Portes and Bach, 1985: 60). Even feminist scholars often treat women as "passive victims" of patriarchal domination (Wolf, 1992: 20). Kathryn Ward, for example, in summarizing research on the impact of migration on women, emphasized their "disadvantaged" status relative to males and suggested that when women accompany their migrant mates, they "lose access to kin-support networks that were essential for economic subsistence and social support in the rural areas" (1985: 308). Moreover, nonmigrant women, if they are considered at all, are characterized simply as "women who wait" (Peattie, 1977: 126), or "women left behind" (Gordon, 1978).

Limiting the focus of research on migration and gender to the social and economic "consequences" for women fails to recognize their active participation in the process of transnational network building. A large body of cross-cultural literature documents the central role that "women-centered" networks play in facilitating the flow of goods, services, and information between households in both industrialized and less-developed societies (e.g., Yanagisako, 1977; Neuhouser, 1989; Grieco, 1987; Stivens, 1984). Why, then, should we assume that women's social ties are severed by migration or that men necessarily assume the primary responsibility for building transnational networks?

Our findings suggest that in their efforts to ensure some level of economic security, both migrant *and* nonmigrant Garifuna women engage in building and maintaining transnational networks, much as they do at the local level in Belize. Therefore, it is critical to consider, not only intrahousehold relationships and negotiation in studies of migration decision making, but also the networks that link sending and receiving societies. Moreover, our findings indicate that transnational networks need *not* weaken over time and distance. On the contrary, social and economic pressures experienced by migrants in the United States can motivate them to strengthen their relationships with those back home.

GARIFUNA MIGRATION IN HISTORICAL CONTEXT

The Garifuna are a product of European colonial expansion into the Caribbean. Throughout their history, their economic fortunes have been inextricably linked to labor demands in the capitalist world-economy, and as a result, they exhibit a history of wage-labor migration extending back to the early nineteenth century. According to historical accounts, the Garifuna emerged as a distinct ethnic group after African slaves escaped the wreckage of two Spanish ships in 1635 and took up residence with the indigenous Carib Indians on the island of St. Vincent, in the eastern Caribbean. In 1797, after an unsuccessful uprising aimed at dislodging the island's British colonizers, the Garifuna were exiled to the Bay of Honduras and quickly began to migrate to the Central American mainland (Shephard, [1831] 1971). By 1800, they began to establish small settlements along the coast from Nicaragua to Belize, maintaining a peaceful, but uneasy, coexistence with the British colonists.

Their autonomy was short-lived, however. Following slave emancipation in 1834, chronic labor shortages in Belize made the Garifuna an attractive source of labor for British forestry and agricultural enterprises. Through a series of legislative measures that restricted their access to land, the British ensured Garifuna availability to the wage labor market (Bolland, 1977). However, by permitting the Garifuna to continue to occupy lands for traditional subsistence activities, the British reduced their labor costs substantially. During off-seasons in forestry and agriculture, the men returned to their home communities, where women provided support through their traditional horticultural activities.

Until the 1940s, male wage-labor migration was, by and large, temporary as men pursued seasonal employment in Central America's forests and plantations. However, World War II and resulting labor shortages in the United States created new employment markets for Garifuna men, who were recruited by the U.S. Labor Department to replace U.S. workers involved in the war effort. About half the men stayed on at war's end (Vernon, 1990), thus paving the way for a sustained flow of Belizeans to the United States.

As males began to travel farther and stay away longer, Garifuna women adapted their economic strategies to the changing patterns of male migration. Unable to maintain sufficient horticultural production without the assistance of men, they turned increasingly to marketing and domestic service in order to supplement their incomes. During the 1960s, however, structural changes in the U.S. economy resulted in a shift from a goods-producing to a service-based economy, creating a substantial demand for low-wage female labor (Tienda, Jensen, and Bach, 1984; Singlemann and Browning, 1980), and leading Garifuna women to quickly join their male counterparts in international wage-labor migration.

Garifuna men and women recall the 1960s and early 1970s as a boom period for both documented and undocumented workers seeking employment in Los Angeles. Not only were jobs plentiful, employers were relatively unconcerned about the immigration status of prospective employees. However, as restructuring in Los Angeles progressed, traditional blue-collar manufacturing jobs were largely replaced by downgraded manufacturing and low-wage service jobs. In the Los Angeles metropolitan area, some 75,000, mostly unionized, relatively high-wage manufacturing jobs disappeared due to plant closures and indefinite layoffs from 1978 to 1982 (Soja, 1987: 182), while garment-manufacturing and low-wage services that rely heavily on female immigrant labor made huge gains (Sassen, 1988; Soja, 1987).

Having grown accustomed to finding reasonably high-paying, blue-collar jobs with relative ease, Garifuna men found it difficult to adapt to the transformed labor market in Los Angeles, where the kinds of jobs they used to get (semiskilled factory and warehouse work and commercial maintenance work) were no longer available to them. Today, men arriving in Los Angeles often spend two or three months looking for employment and then are likely to find only low-paying, irregular work as parking lot attendants or security guards. Understandably, Garifuna migrants living in Los Angeles are more inclined to offer their assistance to women seeking to migrate, since these women are likely to be able to find work quickly and will not need to rely on the hospitality and financial resources of kin for extended periods of time after their arrival. James, a man in his mid-30s living in Belize, said, ''We keep getting the message from there, 'It's best you stay on your job where you are there than come here to waste time and live on somebody else's back.' '' As opportunities diminished, men began to relinquish their traditionally dominant role in the migration process to women, who continue to enjoy a strong demand for their labor in Los Angeles' low-wage service industry.

Since most Garifuna women who migrate to Los Angeles are relatively unskilled—and, as often as not, undocumented—their opportunities in Los Angeles are largely limited to low-wage, service-sector jobs. To understand why women actively seek jobs that most women in the United States would reject out of hand, a Garifuna woman in Belize explained, "You have to compare 'hard' in the States to 'hard' here [in Belize]." In the following section, we briefly describe the research setting and then examine the current economic situation in Belize and the narrow range of employment options available to women there.

WOMEN AND HOUSEHOLDS IN THE SOURCE COMMUNITY

Although Belize was initially a producer of forestry products, its economy is now primarily dependent on export agriculture. Sugar (grown in the northern districts) and citrus and bananas (from the south) constitute more than 70 percent of the total value of Belize's domestic exports. Employment opportunities and the earning power of Garifuna men is limited by the low-wage, mostly seasonal, labor demands of the citrus and banana industries, and also by longstanding ethnic discrimination in the Belizean labor market. The average wage of unskilled agricultural workers ranges between U.S. $.69 and U.S. $1.12 per hour (Labor Department, 1987).

Although there is no cultural resistance to women's employment outside the home and women are eager to take any available jobs, there are very few opportunities for them in the local wage-labor market. The unemployment rate of 38.8 percent for women in the district where the research was carried out is the highest in Belize. The women's high jobless rate is due, at least in part, to the preference of agricultural employers for male workers. A 1990 labor force survey indicated that males outnumbered females four-to-one in agricultural employment (Government Information Service, 1992).

The gender wage gap in Belize is also significant. Average wages for unskilled women range from $.58 to $.68 per hour, and even when they do the same work, women typically earn one-quarter to one-third less than their male counterparts (Bolland, 1986; Kerns, 1982). According to government estimates, in 1992, 59 percent of employed males earned less than $3,000 annually, compared to 75 percent of females (Government Information Service, 1992).[1] The employment difficulties experienced by women in Belize come into even sharper focus when we consider that one-third in Belizean households are headed by women (Government Information Service, 1992: 45). In the southern districts where Garifuna are concentrated, this figure has reached 40 percent (Ministry of Education, 1984: 15).

To further probe into employment and migration patterns, this section reports the findings of our study of a coastal settlement in Belize. Most contemporary Garifuna communities in Central America are coastal settlements, with small numbers of Creoles (descendants of the slave population), East Indians, and Chinese in residence. We use the fictitious name "Seaview" to refer to a town (population 7,000) where Professor Matthei did her Belizean fieldwork. A commercial and transportation hub, it serves as a major staging area for U.S.-bound migrants from throughout southern Belize.[2]

The dearth of full-time employment opportunities makes it necessary for most Garifuna to employ a strategy of "occupational multiplicity" (Comitas, 1973). That is, they work at several income-generating activities in order to make ends meet. For men, occupational multiplicity often involves migration between temporary formal-sector jobs in various areas of Belize supplemented by fishing and odd jobs during their stays in Seaview. The lack of formal-sector employment for women requires that they engage in a variety of informal-sector activities (e.g., taking in laundry, sewing, vending a variety of low-cost goods, and taking in boarders). Though women often devalue their activities, referring to them as simply "turning over a little cash," both men and women agree that women are particularly resourceful at generating cash in the informal sector. The local social-service officer estimates that women are the primary sources of household income in more than half of her town's households.

The composition of Garifuna households is fluid and flexible, and as a result, it is often difficult to determine to which household an individual does, in fact, "belong" at any given time. For instance, it is not uncommon for a man to carry on simultaneous relationships with two or more women, dividing his time (and economic contributions) among them (González, 1969). Moreover, though most men and women spend some part of their lives in one form of conjugal relationship or another, such unions are not necessarily regarded as permanent, and both men and women often have more than one marital partner during their lifetimes (González, 1969; Kerns, 1983). Households also expand and contract with the periodic comings and goings of adult kin who find themselves *between* marital relationships. Since conjugal relationships are often transitory, Garifuna men and women retain substantial autonomy in their domestic relationships. Even within stable households, marital partners maintain separate purses, and they only rarely hold property in common (Miller, 1992; Kerns, 1983). In Seaview, for example, an examination of applications for residential lots from 1959 through 1990 revealed that only 11 of 1,481 applications were made jointly (780 were made by individual males, and 690 by individual females) (Government Information Service, 1959–1990).

Although couples do typically contribute a portion of their incomes to meet household expenses, neither partner has direct access to the other's earnings, nor does one spouse necessarily know exactly how much the other earns (see Benería and Roldán, 1987, and Treas, 1991, on similar patterns in Latin America and the United States). The wife typically controls the pooled budget to purchase food and take care of daily household expenses, but any additional purchases are made on an individual basis (usually by the wife), without consultation between partners. Interviews with Garifuna women revealed that perceived inequities in household contributions are a common source of domestic conflict. They complain that men withhold substantial portions of their income for their personal use and fail to contribute adequately to the household (see Benería and Roldán, 1987). Thus, they argue that they must protect themselves and their children by maintaining control of their own incomes. For example, in explaining why she kept her own finances separate, one informant clearly called into question the assumptions of unity and solidarity proffered in typical household models: "Whatever women make stays in the home. Men have five or ten places for their money. It's us against them!"

Although the household model posits discrete, independent units, among the Garifuna relationships with extra domestic kin are frequently stronger and more enduring than marital ties (Kerns, 1983; González, 1969). For women in particular, relationships beyond the level of the household are vital sources of support during periods of crisis (cf. Wong, 1984). Most Garifuna women find themselves responsible for dependent children and without a mate more than once during their lifetimes (Kerns, 1983: 112), and they must often depend on relatives, either for child care when they are working or for temporary support and refuge when marital relationships end. However, because they themselves are often unemployed and in poor economic circumstances, the assistance that kin are able to provide is usually limited. To broaden their potential resource base, women in Seaview also forge cooperative relationships with female friends and neighbors. Food, clothing, small loans, and child care services are exchanged with the assumption that debts will be repaid at some point in the future. During periods of relative plenty, women share any surplus they may acquire within their networks, thus building accounts of social capital on which they can draw when circumstances demand.

Personal networks outside the household are particularly crucial to women, who depend on income-generating activities in the informal sector. With very limited financial resources and few formal skills, they must actively seek out opportunities. In Belize, Garifuna women frequently recruit five or six friends to pool their limited financial resources and labor in a variety of small income-generating enterprises. The networks also function as important conduits for information regarding potential employment opportunities elsewhere, and in addition to their local networks, women assiduously cultivate ties throughout Belize. The relatively recent introduction of telephone service in outlying areas greatly enhances the ability of individuals to maintain frequent contact with friends and relatives in urban centers like Belize City and Belmopan, the nation's capital, where domestic and commercial service jobs are more plentiful. Thus, women who are unable to find work locally often turn to their contacts in other communities for employment information and for temporary living quarters while they look for work.

Garifuna women's personal networks have traditionally served as channels for the exchange of material goods, services, and employment information in Belize, but they have also adapted their support networks to meet the exigencies of international migration. Expanded transnationally, these networks serve as vital conduits that facilitate migration, the exchange of employment information, and remittances. Conceptual models that arbitrarily define the household as the locus of migration decision making overlook the vital role that such extra domestic networks play in the migration process. Moreover, as the following section illustrates, it is often women who are the central actors in building and maintaining these networks.

TRANSNATIONAL NETWORKS OF GARIFUNA WOMEN IN BELIZE

The most obvious and immediate benefits of maintaining strong transnational ties are perhaps clearest for nonmigrant women seeking to ensure a regular flow of remittances from migrant kin. Among the Garifuna, ties between mothers and daughters are particularly strong, as women must often seek maternal aid when their marital relationships fail. Even though daughters may migrate, these bonds tend to remain strong. In Los Angeles, the Garifuna women interviewed named their mothers as recipients of their remittances more frequently than any other kin, including children. Though most daughters remit to their mothers, in many cases a migrant daughter's obligation is reinforced because she has left her children in the care of her mother in order to seek work in the United States. Thus, children often serve as critical links in women's transnational networks and ensure a regular flow of remittances (cf. Soto, 1987).

Although children are most often placed with their maternal grandmothers, other female kin (usually sisters) also actively seek the opportunity to "foster" the children of migrants. In most cases, the caretaker receives some sort of remittance (either cash or material goods) in exchange for her child care services. However, there are other potential benefits as well—a woman who fosters the children of migrants builds a reservoir of social capital on which she can draw in the future. Mutual obligation is implicit in the fostering relationship, and it is understood that the woman for whose children she has cared is obligated to help should she or a member of her family seek to come to the United States at some point. In some cases, women who migrate have jobs waiting for them upon their arrival in the United States. In others, migrant women meet their obligations to nonmigrant kin through what might be described as "job sharing." If the mother of fostered children works as a domestic in the United States (a common pattern of employment among Garifuna women), she will sometimes arrange for their caretaker to travel, at her expense, to the United States to fill in at her job while she returns to Belize to spend time with her children. In addition to the money she earns, the foster mother gains some useful domestic experience that she may well use should she herself migrate in the future.

Nonmigrant women's roles as critical anchors in the transnational networks that link sending and receiving communities secure for them significant control in migration decision making. Because they maintain the ties that link potential migrants to opportunities in the United States, they ultimately hold a good deal of power in determining which members of their household will be selected for migration. Presented with the opportunity to launch the migration of one of her children, for example, a woman will, more often than not, elect to invest her network resources in a daughter, who will "remember" her with remittances, rather than a son who, it is assumed, will eventually transfer his affections and earnings to his wife and her family.

As in other source communities, migration to the United States becomes an important means of escape for women who find themselves in unhappy conjugal relationships. Under these circumstances, a woman's access to transnational ties is crucial. Typically, the woman makes the decision to migrate and organizes the move surreptitiously, with the cooperation and financial assistance of kin in the United States.

Nonmigrant women's transnational ties serve much the same function as the ties that they use on a day-to-day basis in Belize. In addition to helping them to meet immediate economic needs, reciprocal ties to migrant kin also serve as investments in the future. The mutual obligations of close kin are implicit in the relationship, although the ties can be strengthened through child fostering and the transnational exchange of goods and services. Women may tap into their networks to facilitate their own migration, or they may transfer their social capital to their daughters so that they both may benefit: the daughters through employment in the United States, and the mother through the remittances sent home.

Those who stress the role of households in migration decision making may fail to recognize that the decision to migrate is often conditioned by prospective migrants' ability to marshal the support and assistance of kin already settled in the receiving country. As migration opportunities became more accessible to Garifuna women, they actively worked to build systems of support in the United States. As a result, they now play a central role in organizing their own, and their children's, migration.

MIGRANT WOMEN'S TRANSNATIONAL NETWORKS

In general, scholars argue that as migrants accumulate time in sending societies, they put down increasingly deeper social and economic roots, so that over time, there is a gradual weakening of ties to their home communities as they begin to view themselves as "settlers" rather than "sojourners" (Chávez, 1991; Massey et al., 1987). However, among the Garifuna, even women who have lived in Los Angeles for 25 to 30 years generally maintain close ties to their home communities through remittances, periodic visits, and economic investments in homes and businesses. It might be argued that as the traditional "kin keepers,'' women feel stronger emotional bonds to the kin who are left behind, but our findings suggest that social and economic pressures also induce Garifuna women to foster strong relationships with those back home.

Although some women establish careers as teachers, clerical workers, and nurses in Los Angeles, most arrive with few skills and spend their years working in the informal sector as domestics, nurse's aides, and nannies. For the latter group, retirement pensions are nonexistent, and they must eventually either return to Belize to take advantage of the lower cost of living or find a way to supplement their U.S. earnings. With this in mind, most women set aside a portion of their earnings to buy or build houses in their home communities in Belize.[3] Others invest their earnings in businesses back home. In 1990, for example, Matthei found that a hotel, two clothing stores, and a restaurant in Seaview were owned by migrant women living and working in the United States (see Portes, Chapter 8 of this volume, for similar findings).

Social pressures in the United States also motivate women to nurture their links to Belize. The Garifuna are concentrated in South-Central Los Angeles, an area that in recent years has become a national symbol of the economic decay and unrest plaguing America's inner cities. As economic conditions in the South-Central area have worsened over the years, crime rates (especially those associated with gangs and drugs) have soared, and the area has the highest homicide rate in the city (Silverstein and Brooks, 1991). In response to an open-ended question regarding what they disliked most about living in Los Angeles, 34 of 51 (67 percent) Garifuna men and women identified gangs, drugs, and drive-by shootings as the major drawbacks (Miller, 1992). As the levels of drug activity and gang violence have intensified over the years, Garifuna parents have grown increasingly wary of raising children in Los Angeles. Some have extended the period of time that their children remain in Belize, and others sent offspring born in Los Angeles back to be raised by kin. Still others send adolescent sons to Belize ''under punishment'' because they have gotten involved in gang-related activity in Los Angeles.

Although a few families have acquired the financial means to move their families out of South-Central Los Angeles, most have not. Unskilled, single women with children find it nearly impossible to leave the area. They lack the financial resources to pay the much higher rents in other parts of the city, and few enjoy the job security needed to commit to long-term leases. Under these circumstances, the availability of kin in Belize who are willing to take on child care responsibilities is critical.

Contrary to findings that suggest that migrants' ties to their home societies wither as they accumulate time abroad, our research suggests that geographic separation and the resulting decrease in frequency of contact need not lead to a weakening of ties. The extraordinary stresses associated with life in South-Central Los Angeles motivate Garifuna migrants to foster their links to Belize even after absences of decades. Given the social and economic instability that characterizes their lives in Los Angeles, women are particularly unwilling to burn their bridges to Belize. Indeed, most carefully nurture their transnational ties, which provide potential "safety nets" for them and their children and which may, for some at least, pave the way for their eventual return migration.

CONCLUSION

A growing body of migration research documents the increasing participation of women in international labor migration as a consequence of global economic restructuring and the "feminization" of low-wage labor markets in the United States (e.g., Simon and DeLey, 1986; Sassen, 1988; Pedraza-Bailey, 1991). Even in Latin America, where migration streams have long been dominated by males, there is a clear trend toward greater female participation in labor migration to the United States (Donato, 1994; Fernández-Kelly, 1988). Though migration research is beginning to acknowledge women as an increasing "presence" in international migration, we still know relatively little about them as "actors" in the migration process.

Much of the blame for this blindness to female agency is caused by a misplaced theoretical emphasis on households as the unit of analysis in migration studies. As currently conceived, this model fails to take into account the variability of household forms cross-culturally, and thus lacks empirical validity. It presents us with assumptions regarding how households *should* operate, but fails to consider a large body of empirical evidence suggesting that household behavior is far more complex than suggested by the model. Moreover, by treating the household itself as a social actor, important intrahousehold conflicts and divisions based on gender are hidden from view.[4] However, feminist approaches that cast women as powerless victims of the migration process are problematic, too, as they tend to overlook the ways in which women build significant bases of informal power through personal networks extending beyond the household.

It is time that migration studies move away from facile assumptions regarding gender roles in international labor migration. We claim that women, as anchors of extradomestic and transnational networks, play a significant role in determining which of their household members are selected for migration. Although labor migration may once have been the relatively exclusive domain of males, this is no longer the case. We must begin to consider the broader implications of a trend in which women migrate and men are increasingly the ones "left behind." Moreover, as migration becomes institutionalized over time and a substantial proportion of individuals in sending societies gain access to ties in the United States, the transnational network, rather than the household, becomes the primary locus of migration decision making.

There may be an even more general lesson in this chapter. In recent essays, both Ward (1993) and Böröcz and Smith (1995) have decried the lack of dialogue between researchers working from a feminist "women in development" approach and world-system analysis. At least part of the problem involves a preference for different levels and modes of analysis. Feminists tend to favor ethnographic views of women's everyday lives, while world-system analysts opt for macrostructural, political-economic explanations. A focus on the gendered structure of the everyday networks making up the sinews of particular transnational communities could provide an important theoretical bridge between these scholarly camps. Smith-Lovin and McPherson have presented an interesting argument (though implicitly based on advanced industrial societies) to the effect that the socialization processes and webs of interpersonal relationships in which people find themselves create differences in behavior and outlook that lead to "dramatic levels of gender segregation and inequality" (1993: 223). Our research reveals distinct male and female networks for migration and job seeking among Garifuna men and women, too. We believe that these Garifuna patterns are quite *different* in nature from those Smith-Lovin and McPherson described, and that this is due to the particular macrohistorical context of this community, including the way in which it was incorporated into the modern world-system and how it currently experiences global restructuring. To fully understand the "embedded" nature of transnational communities, we need to arrive at synthetic views that capture *both* the micro/everyday aspects of personal relationships *and* the macro/historical dynamics of global political-economy.

NOTES

    Linda Miller Matthei gratefully acknowledges the research support provided by a National Science Foundation dissertation grant (BNS–8918803) and by a Rockefeller Foundation Post-Doctoral Fellowship at the Institute of Latin American Studies, University of Texas, Austin.

    1. Women are not only paid less than men, they also work for a shorter portion of their lives. Most full-time employment in Belize carries a mandatory retirement age of 55 for both sexes, but traditional employment practices make it nearly impossible for women to find any sort of waged employment past the age of 50 (Kerns, 1982).

    2. A fictitious name is used for this town, which is a major staging area for both documented and undocumented migration to the United States.

    3. A social worker estimated that since the 1960s, women had built 65 percent of the new homes in the town where the research was done. The perception that women are more likely to build homes than men is held by both sexes. In fact, men's tendency to burn their bridges with their home communities is a topic of jokes, folktales, and music in the community. In Los Angeles in 1990, a Catholic bishop visiting from Belize chastised migrant men during his sermon for failing to maintain ties and build homes as women have done.

    4. Moser made a similar argument, claiming that constructive attempts to formulate policies must "disaggregate households and families on the basis of gender" (1993: 15). While we limit our focus to migration, the scope of her thesis is broader, with generic implications for policies and planning for Third World development.

REFERENCES

Ashcraft, Norman. 1973. *Colonialism and Underdevelopment: Processes of Political Economic Change in British Honduras.* New York: Teachers College Press, Columbia University.

Bach, Robert L., and Lisa A. Schraml. 1982. "Migration Crisis and Theoretical Conflict." *International Migration Review* 16, 2: 320–341.

Benería, Lourdes, and Martha Roldán. 1987. *The Crossroads of Class and Gender: Industrial Housework, Subcontracting and Household Dynamics in Mexico City.* Chicago: University of Chicago Press.

Blumberg, Rae Lesser, ed. 1991. "Introduction: The 'Triple Overlap' of Gender Stratification, Economy and the Family." In *Gender, Family, and Economy: The Triple Overlap,* ed. Rae Lesser Blumberg, pp. 7–32. Newbury Park, CA: Sage Publications.

Bolland, O. Nigel. 1977. *The Formation of a Colonial Society: Belize, from Conquest to Crown Colony.* Baltimore: Johns Hopkins University Press.

———. 1986. *Belize: A New Nation in the Making.* Boulder, CO: Westview Press.

Böröcz, József, and David A. Smith. 1995. "Introduction: Late Twentieth-Century Challenges to World-System Analysis." In *A New World Order? Global Transformations in the Late Twentieth Century,* ed. David A. Smith and József Böröcz, pp. 1–15. Westport, CT: Greenwood.

Boyd, Monica. 1989. "Family and Personal Networks in International Migration: Recent Developments and New Agendas." *International Migration Review* 23, 1: 638–670.

Central Statistical Office. 1990. *Abstract of Statistics, 1990.* Belmopan, Belize: Central Statistical Office.

Chávez, Leo R. 1991. "Outside the Imagined Community: Undocumented Settlers and Experiences of Incorporation." *American Ethnologist* 18, 2: 257–278.

———. 1992. *Shadowed Lives: Undocumented Immigrants in American Society.* Fort Worth, TX: Harcourt Brace Jovanovich College Publishers.

Comitas, Lambros. 1973. "Occupational Multiplicity in Jamaica." In *Work and Family Life: West Indian Perspectives,* ed. Lambros Comitas and David Lowenthal, pp. 157–174. Garden City, NJ: Anchor Press.

Donato, Katharine M. 1994. "U.S. Policy and Mexican Migration to the United States, 1942–92." *Social Science Quarterly* 75, 4: 705–729.

Fapohunda, Eleanor R. 1988. "The Nonpooling Household: A Challenge to Theory." In *A Home Divided: Women and Income in the Third World,* ed. Daisy Dwyer and Judith Bruce, pp. 143–154. Stanford, CA: Stanford University Press.

Fernández-Kelly, Maria Patricia. 1981. "Mexican Border Industrialization, Female Labor Force Participation, and Migration." In *Women, Men, and the International Division of Labor,* ed. June Nash and Maria Patricia Fernández-Kelly, pp. 205–223. Albany: State University of New York Press.

Foner, Nancy. 1986. "Sex Roles and Sensibilities: Jamaican Women in New York and London." In *International Migration: The Female Experience,* ed. Rita James Simon and Caroline B. Brettell, pp. 133–151. Totowa, NJ: Rowman and Allanheld.

Georges, Eugenia. 1990. *The Making of a Transnational Community: Migration, Devel-*

opment and Cultural Change in the Dominican Republic. New York: Columbia University Press.

González, Nancie. 1969. Black Carib Household Structure. Seattle: University of Washington Press.

————. 1984. "Rethinking the Consanguineal Household and Matrifocality." Ethnology 23, 1: 1–12.

Gordon, Elizabeth. 1978. The Women Left Behind: A Study of Migrant Workers in Lesotho. World Employment Program Working Paper. Geneva, Switzerland: International Labor Office.

Government Information Service. 1959–1990. Government Gazette. Belize: Government Printery.

————. 1992. "Women in the Workforce." Belize Today (Government Information Service, Belmopan, Belize) 6 (October): 44–46.

Grasmuck, Sherri, and Patricia R. Pessar. 1991. Between Two Islands: Dominican International Migration. Berkeley: University of California Press.

Grieco, Margaret. 1987. Keeping It in the Family: Social Networks and Employment Chance. London: Tavistock.

Guyer, Jane I., and Pauline E. Peters. 1987. "Introduction." Development and Social Change 18, 2: 197–214.

Kerns, Virginia. 1982. "Structural Continuity in the Division of Men's and Women's Work Among the Black Carib (Garifuna)." In Sex Roles and Social Change in Lower Central American Societies, ed. Christine A. Loveland and Franklin O. Loveland, pp. 23–43. Urbana: University of Illinois Press.

————. 1983. Women and the Ancestors: Black Carib Kinship and Ritual. Urbana: University of Illinois Press.

Labour Department. 1987. Annual Report of the Labour Department. Belmopan, Belize: Government Printery.

Lee, Everett S. 1966. "A Theory of Migration." Demography 3, 1: 47–57.

Massey, Douglas S., Rafael Alarcón, Jorge Durand, and Humberto González. 1987. Return to Aztlán. Berkeley: University of California Press.

Meillasoux, Claude. 1972. "From Reproduction to Production." Economy and Society 1, 1: 93–105.

Miller [Matthei], Linda R. 1992. "Bridges: Garifuna Migration to Los Angeles." Ph.D. dissertation, University of California, Irvine.

Ministry of Education. 1984. Belize Today: A Society in Transformation. Belmopan, Belize: Sunshine Books.

Morokvasic, Mirjana. 1983. "Women in Migration: Beyond the Reductionist Outlook." In One Way Ticket: Migration and Female Labour, ed. Annie Phizacklea, pp. 13–31. London: Routledge and Kegan Paul.

Moser, Caroline O. N. 1993. Gender Planning and Development: Theory, Practice and Training. New York,: Routledge.

Neuhouser, Kevin. 1989. "Sources of Women's Power and Status among the Urban Poor in Contemporary Brazil." Signs 14: 685–702.

Peattie, Lisa. 1977. "Migrants and Women Who Wait: Introduction." In Women and National Development, ed. Wellesley Editorial Committee. Chicago: University of Chicago Press.

Pedraza, Silvia. 1991. "Women and Migration: The Social Consequences of Gender." Annual Review of Sociology 17: 303–325.

Pessar, Patricia. 1982. "The Role of Households in International Migration and the Case of U.S.-Bound Migration from the Dominican Republic." *International Migration Review* 16: 342–364.

Piore, Michael J. 1979. *Birds of Passage: Migrant Labor and Industrial Societies.* London: Cambridge University Press.

Portes, Alejandro, and Robert L. Bach. 1985. *Latin Journey: Cuban and Mexican Immigrants in the United States.* Berkeley: University of California Press.

Portes, Alejandro, and John Walton. 1981. *Labor, Class, and the International System.* Orlando, FL: Academic Press.

Sanford, Margaret. 1971. "Disruption of the Mother-Child Relationship in Conjunction with Matrifocality: A Study of Child-Keeping among the Carib and Creoles of British Honduras." Ph.D. dissertation, Catholic University of America.

Sassen, Saskia. 1988. *The Mobility of Labor and Capital: A Study in International Investment and Labor Flow.* Cambridge: Cambridge University Press.

Sassen-Koob, Saskia. 1981a. "Labor Migration and the New Industrial Division of Labor." In *Women, Men, and the International Division of Labor,* ed. June Nash and María Patricia Fernández-Kelly, pp. 175–204. Albany: State University of New York Press.

———. 1981b. "Towards a Conceptualization of Immigrant Labor." *Social Problems* 29, 1: 65–85.

Shephard, Charles. [1831] 1971. *An Historical Account of the Island of St. Vincent.* London: Frank Cass and Company.

Silverstein, Stuart, and Nancy Rivera Brooks. 1991. "South L.A. Shoppers Need Stores." *Los Angeles Times,* November 24.

Simon, Rita J., and Margo C. DeLey. 1986. "Undocumented Mexican Women: Their Work and Personal Experiences." In *International Migration: The Female Experience,* ed. Rita J. Simon and Caroline B. Brettel. Totowa, NJ: Rowman & Allanheld.

Singlemann, Joachim, and Harley Browning. 1980. "Industrial Transformation and Occupational Change in the U.S., 1960–1970. *Social Forces* 59: 246–264.

Smith, Joan, Immannuel Wallerstein, and Hans Dieter Evers, eds. 1984. *Households and the World-Economy.* Beverly Hills, CA: Sage Publications.

Smith-Lovin, Lynn, and Miller McPherson. 1993. "You Are Who You Know: A Network Approach to Gender." In *Theory on Gender/Feminism on Theory,* ed. Paula England, pp. 223–251. New York: Aldine De Gruyter.

Soja, Edward W. 1987. "Economic Restructuring and the Internationalization of the Los Angeles Region." In *The Capitalist City: Global Restructuring and Community Politics,* ed. Michael Peter Smith and Joe R. Feagin, pp. 178–198. New York: Basil Blackwell.

Soto, Isa Maria. 1987. "West Indian Child Fostering: Its Role in Migrant Exchanges." In *Caribbean Life in New York City: Sociocultural Dimensions,* ed. Constance R. Sutton and Elsa M. Chaney, pp. 131–149. New York: Center for Migration Studies.

Stivens, Maila. 1984. "Women, Kinship and Capitalist Development." In *Of Marriage and the Market: Women's Subordination Internationally and its Lessons,* ed. Kate Young, Carol Wolkowitz, and Roslynn McCullagh, pp. 178–192. London: Routledge and Kegan Paul.

Tienda, Marta, Leif Jensen, and Robert L. Bach. 1984. "Immigration, Gender and the

Process of Occupational Change in the United States, 1970–1980." *International Migration Review* 18: 1021–1044.

Treas, Judith. 1991. "The Common Pot or Separate Purses? A Transaction Cost Interpretation." In *Gender, Family, and Economy: The Triple Overlap*, ed. Rae Lesser Blumberg, pp. 211–224. Newbury Park, CA: Sage Publications.

Vernon, Dylan. 1990. "Belizean Exodus to the United States: For Better or For Worse." In *SPEAR Reports 4: Second Annual Studies on Belize Conference*, pp. 6–28. Belize City: Society for the Promotion of Education and Research (SPEAR).

Ward, Kathryn. 1985. "Women and Urbanization in the World-System." In *Urbanization in the World-Economy*, ed. Michael Timberlake, pp. 305–323. New York: Academic Press.

———. 1993. "Reconceptualizing World-System Theory to Include Women." In *Theory on Gender/Feminism on Theory*, ed. Paula England, pp. 43–68. New York: Aldine De Gruyter.

Wolf, Diane L. 1988. "Father Knows Best About All in the Household: A Feminist Critique of Household Strategies." Paper presented at the Sex & Gender Session of the American Sociological Association Meetings, August.

———. 1992. *Factory Daughters: Gender, Household Dynamics, and Rural Industrialization in Java*. Berkeley: University of California Press.

Wong, Diana. 1984. "The Limits of Using the Household as a Unit of Analysis." In *Households and the World-Economy*, ed. Joan Smith, Immanuel Wallerstein, and Hans Dieter-Evans, pp. 56–63. Beverly Hills, CA: Sage Publications.

Wood, Charles. 1982. "Equilibrium and Historical-Structural Perspectives on Migration." *International Migration Review* 16: 298–319.

Yanagisako, Sylvia Junko. 1977. "Women-Centered Kin Networks in Urban Bilateral Kinship." *American Ethnologist* 3: 207–226.

8

TRANSNATIONAL COMMUNITIES: THEIR EMERGENCE AND SIGNIFICANCE IN THE CONTEMPORARY WORLD-SYSTEM

Alejandro Portes

The aphorism, "capital is global, labor is local," sits at the base of an edifice built relentlessly during the last half century. From different theoretical quarters, this edifice has been celebrated as the final triumph of free trade and economic rationality as well as denounced as the tomb of proletarian rights and national liberation. Whatever the outlook, the narrative that follows portrays an increasingly bound global economy in which capital criss-crosses the earth in search of accumulation. The success of these initiatives correlates inversely, in most cases, with the economic autonomy achieved by national states and the economic prerogatives of local labor. For the most part, however, the momentum acquired by global capitalist expansion tends to sweep away everything in its path, confining past dreams of class equity and autonomous national development to the dustbin of history.

The process of capital going abroad in search of valorization is, of course, nothing new; it is, indeed, the cloth from which numerous accounts of the growth of the modern world-system have been fashioned. What is new at present are the modalities and intensity of the process, which today are driven by technological improvements in communications and transportation. Today, instantaneous investments and disinvestments are made in the bourses of remote Asian and Latin American countries and, as Castells (1980) puts it, a garment design conceived in New York can be transmitted electronically to a factory in Taiwan and the first batches of the product received in San Francisco in a week's time. The advantages of the process seem to be entirely on the side of those able to avail themselves of the new technologies, thus turning globalization into the final apotheosis of capital against its adversaries, be they state managers or organized workers.

However, as sociologists we are professionally trained to look at the dialectics of things and hence, understand that a social process of this magnitude cannot be all one-sided. By its very momentum, the process is likely to trigger various reactions giving rise to countervailing structures. In the end, the technology-driven revolution that we are witnessing at century's end may not usher in the era of unrestrained global capitalism after all, but rather a new form of that age-old struggle of exchange versus use values or, put differently, of the formal rationality of law versus the substantive rationality of private interests.

As a contribution to this analysis, I attempt here to give theoretical form to the concept of *transnational communities*, as a less noticed, but potentially potent, counter to the more visible forms of globalization described in the recent literature. I embark on this task with some hesitation since the concept of trans-nationality, like that of globalization itself, threatens to become part of one of the passing fads that grip social scientist's attention for a while, only to then fade into oblivion. I believe, however, that there is enough real substance here to make the effort worthwhile. If successful, the concept may actually perform double duty as both part of the theoretical arsenal with which we approach the modern world-system and as an element of a more neglected enterprise, namely, the analysis of the everyday networks and patterns of social relationships that develop in and around that system. The latter goal belongs in the realm of a mid-range theory of social interaction, which I will seek to outline after considering two past initiatives in the same general direction.

FAILED MID-RANGE EFFORTS: LABOR STANDARDS AND FLEXIBLE SPECIALIZATION

From policy and academic quarters, there have already been efforts to come to terms with the new mobility of capital by finding ways to rein in its footloose ways. One of these efforts has seen institutional economists, industrial sociologists, and trade unionists deplore the consequences of deindustrialization in the developed world and call for governmental measures to reverse it. This approach pits the regulatory capacity of national states against the global opportunities for profit created by new technologies drawing on vast differentials in wage levels. The result has been the Labor Standards movement, which seeks to restrict imports produced under conditions that violate the labor rights commonly accepted in the First World. In the words of one of the movements' most prominent academic supporters:

[N]ew communication technologies have virtually eliminated international barriers to trade. They have brought the most extreme income disparities in the world into play, and this change has happened very rapidly. . . . If you let the market play itself out, it could undermine our capacity to redeploy the economy towards high-wage productive strategies. We can't get to the high-wage business strategy because it . . . is continually being undermined by the attraction of essentially a Third World system. (Piore, 1990: 48–49)

This contest of domestic and globalized interests has so far produced some interesting ironies such as North American industrialists, formerly notorious opponents of organized labor, becoming ardent advocates of trade unions and workers' rights abroad. Spearheaded by such powerful organizations as the International Labour Office, the effort to reproduce the achievements of two centuries of labor struggles in Europe and North America in the newly industrialized countries of the periphery has met with some notable *formal* successes.

Since the mid-1980s, for example, the United States Congress has enacted four different laws that make access to the U.S. market contingent on respect of "internationally recognized labor rights." The United States has also sought to introduce the issue of international labor rights into multilateral trade agreements. In the European Union, workers' rights were taken up in 1989 in the community's Charter of Fundamental Rights of Workers. Although provisions vary widely, they are all guided by the same premise: that poor working conditions in one country will adversely affect labor and competitiveness in others (Lawyers Committee for Human Rights, 1991).

These impressive declarations contrast markedly with their failure to alter conditions on the ground. The fundamental reason is that the task of enforcing such lofty goals falls on peripheral governments that are seldom keen to do so. Officials in these nations know that excessive zeal in applying imported labor standards will only lead to the exodus of foreign investments to an adjacent labor-surplus country. Their position is buttressed by arguments about the long-term consequences of labor-intensive export industrialization. Linda Y. C. Lim, a Chinese Singaporean economist, puts this argument succinctly:

While initially low labor standards may be one of the factors attracting investors, export manufacturing itself tends to raise these standards. . . . In Thailand, as in other developing countries, successful export manufacturing has rapidly expanded the industrial proletariat and labor organization, arguably at an earlier stage of development than occurred historically in the developed countries themselves. (Lim, 1990: 93)

The attempt to impose First World standards on less-developed countries leads to another perverse consequence, namely, the transfer of many productive activities to the informal sector. Though well-concealed from public view, informal subcontracting and off-the-books hiring represent important mechanisms in labor-surplus economies by which to escape costly state regulation. Formal industry and commerce in these countries commonly avail themselves of this strategy, creating in the process a working class segmented between a relatively high-paid and protected minority and a mass of unprotected workers employed in numerous informal activities (Benería and Roldán, 1987; Castells and Portes, 1989).

In these contexts, the "underutilization" of labor by the formal sector is, in many cases, more apparent than real. The literature documents a number of instances in which the problem is not the absorptive capacity of the modern economy, but the ways in which it utilizes labor in order to bypass relatively advanced regulatory structures (Fortuna and Prates, 1989; Birbeck, 1979; Davies, 1979). A dense network of formal-informal relations is characteristic of peripheral economies with extensive rules and indicates, in turn, the futility of attempting to equalize labor market conditions on the basis of externally imposed standards. By the same token, this situation points to a theoretical dead end, namely, the effort to apprehend a global process on the basis of normative structures designed to regulate national economies.

A second mid-range approach to productive globalization was pioneered by economists Michael Piore and Charles Sabel, who theorized the experience of the small-firm economy of central Italy into a new model of industrial organization. In their view, the old model of mass production based on Taylorist principles is being superseded by new forms of flexible production based on smaller units, which are better able to adapt to changes in the world-market. This structural change coincides with the globalization process and makes use of the same technologies. It is precisely through these technologies that formerly centralized assembly-line production can be parceled out to smaller units and thereby made more flexible (Piore and Sabel, 1984; Sabel, 1982, 1986).

Simultaneously, flexible specialization opens up new opportunities for artisans and small producers to insert themselves into the networks of global trade. This is what happened in the central Italian region of Emilia Romagna, where networks of skilled workers and artisans managed to create a competitive export economy based on technological prowess and cooperative relations. Italian students of this experience have been skeptical about the possibility of reproducing in other national contexts the industrial know-how and bounded solidarity on which it is based (Capecchi, 1989; Brusco, 1982). Nevertheless, Piore and Sabel forged ahead, defining the process as universal and identifying numerous other "industrial districts" where, in their view, it is also taking place. Sabel went as far as suggesting that informal activities in Latin America and other Third World regions may be converted, under certain conditions, into models of flexible specialization, thus reproducing the small firm successes in central Italy. In his words:

The second surprising setting in which flexible specialization might emerge is the immeasurably vast and poorly understood informal sector in Latin American economies. . . . It would not be the first time that such a thing happened: many of the small firms in the Third Italy that today vaunt their numerically controlled machines and foreign customers had their start when large firms decentralized production in the early 1970s to avoid growing union control. (Sabel, 1986: 48)

The problem with this optimistic scenario is that it finds few instances of empirical support. Examples of communities of successfully integrated producers and exporters are exceptional; they are particularly rare in Latin American countries. The global wave of industrial restructuring has not substituted Fordist production in the deindustrializing areas of the advanced countries for flexibly specialized districts in the backward ones. Instead, restructuring has, for the most part, merely transplanted assembly-line production that is organized along typical Taylorist lines to export zones in the Third World. The production regime in these zones can be every bit as harsh and mind-numbing as those documented at the height of assembly-line production in the industrialized countries (Fernández-Kelly, 1983; Deyo, 1989; Pérez-Sainz, 1994).

Back in the First World, there is evidence that the experiences of successful small firms do not so much oppose as complement the long-term plans of large corporations. Although portrayed as organizational dinosaurs by some advocates of flexible specialization, many corporations have proven quite adept at appropriating the ideas of small innovators. As Bennett Harrison (1994) noted in his recent critique of the flexible specialization school, such appropriation can occur either through the direct acquisition of successful small companies or through copying and internalizing their technological breakthroughs. Although the founders of the raided small companies can benefit from these transactions, their activities do not provide a systemic counter to the dominance of large-scale capital.

In fairness to Piore and Sabel, they show themselves quite aware of the depredations of runaway industries in the periphery as well as of the ability of some large firms to implement flexible and innovative production arrangements in the advanced countries (Piore and Sabel, 1984; Sabel, 1986). However, if their analysis were limited to these points, it would be no different from the many reports of global restructuring or competition among factory regimes in North America, Europe, and Japan. The core point that makes their argument attractive is the vision of an emerging opportunity for grassroots economic actors to gain a niche in an expanded global system (Harrison, 1994). Unfortunately, this is also the most doubtful part of their story.

Hence (like the effort to stop the excesses of transnational capitalism with nationally imposed labor standards), the promise of a new economic order where the coordinated activities of artisans and small entrepreneurs can outcompete the corporate giants falls short. Although one perspective comes from the practical realm of trade unions and the other from the academic field of institutional economics, the two coincide in keeping labor local while conceding globality to large-scale capital ventures. Neither national laws nor cooperative efforts of small producers are enough by themselves to counterbalance that age-old tool of the moneyed class: complete mobility, which permits it to identify profitable options worldwide and seize them or buy out those initially profiting from them. To be effective, any social reaction to current trends must have some of the same elements of geographic mobility and, more important, it must be driven by the same forces promoting industrial restructuring rather than running counter to it.

THE ONSET OF TRANSNATIONAL NETWORKS

The popular response to the globalization of capital has been more subtle than the imposition of labor standards and more widespread than the emergence of flexible industrial districts. It consists of the gradual growth of communities that sit astride political borders and that, in a very real sense, are "neither here nor there." The economic activities that sustain these communities are grounded precisely on the differentials of advantage created by political boundaries. In this respect, they are no different from the large global corporations, except that these enterprises emerge at the grassroots level.

A group of well-informed social anthropologists has pioneered the identification of this phenomenon in the attempt to make theoretical sense of it. In their words:

We define "transnationalism" as the processes by which immigrants forge and sustain multi-stranded social relations that link together their societies of origin and settlement. We call these processes transnationalism to emphasize that many immigrants today build social fields that cross geographic, cultural, and political borders. . . . An essential element . . . is the multiplicity of involvements that transmigrants sustain in both home and host societies. We are still groping for a language to describe these social locations. (Basch, Glick Schiller, and Blanc-Szanton, 1994: 6)

Their puzzled attitude toward this emergent phenomenon is understandable when we begin to grasp the array of activities that it comprises and the potential for social and economic transformation that it holds. The existing literature suggests three tentative theoretical points: (1) The emergence of these communities is tied to the logic of capitalism itself. (2) While following well-established sociological principles of the development of social structures, these communities represent a distinct phenomenon at variance with traditional patterns of immigrant adaptation. (3) Because the phenomenon is fueled by the dynamics of globalization itself, it has greater growth potential and offers a broader field for popular initiatives than alternative social structures.

Let us begin by looking at the origins of these communities. As the preceding quote indicates, they are composed of immigrants and their friends and relatives. Public opinion in the advanced countries has been conditioned to think that contemporary immigration stems from the desperate quest of Third World peoples seeking to escape poverty at home. In fact, neither the poorest of the poor migrate, nor is their move determined mainly by individualistic calculations of advantage.[1] Instead, contemporary immigration is driven by twin forces that have their roots in the dynamics of capitalist expansion itself. These are, first, the labor needs of First World economies, and second, the penetration of less-developed countries by the productive investments and consumption standards of the advanced societies.

Contrary to widespread perceptions, immigrants come to the wealthier nations less because they want to than because they are needed. A combination of social and historical forces has led to acute labor scarcities in these economies. In some instances, these are real, absolute scarcities such as the dearth of industrial workers in Japan and the deficit in certain professions, such as nursing and engineering in the United States. In other instances, however, the scarcity stems from the culturally conditioned resistance of native-born workers to accept the low-paid, menial jobs commonly performed by their ancestors (Piore, 1979; Gans, 1992; Portes and Guarnizo, 1991). The list of such stigmatized occupations is large and includes, among others, agricultural labor, domestic and other personal services, and garment sweatshop jobs (Sassen, 1989).

By 1990, the foreign-born population of the United States had reached almost 20 million, the largest absolute total in the century (Fix and Passel, 1991; Rumbaut, 1994). The legislated loopholes of the Immigration Reform and Control Act (IRCA) of 1986, plus new, generous provisions in the 1990 Immigration Act, virtually guarantee that this absolute number and the proportion that immigrants represent in the total U.S. population will increase significantly by the century's end.[2] In Germany and France, despite the official termination of the foreign guestworker program in the 1970s, immigrant communities have continued growing through a variety of legal loopholes and clandestine channels (Zolberg, 1989; Bade, 1995). Today, Germany has a foreign population of 7 million, or roughly 9 percent of the total, which is quite similar to that in the United States (Münz and Ulrich, 1995; Rumbaut, 1994). Even in ethnically homogenous Japan, labor scarcity has prompted a variety of legal subterfuges, including the use of foreign-company "trainees" and visa overstayers to perform line-industrial jobs. By 1990, the foreign-born population of Japan numbered about 1.1 million. This is still an insignificant proportion of the total, but the number was expected to double during the decade (Cornelius, 1992).

The other side of the equation involves the effects of the globalization process in the supply of potential immigrants. The drive of multinational capital to expand markets in the Third World and, simultaneously, to take advantage of its reservoirs of labor has had a series of predictable consequences. Among them are the remolding of popular culture on the basis of external forms and the introduction of consumption standards bearing little relation to local wages (Alba, 1978). The process presocializes prospective immigrants about life abroad and encourages them to move because of the gap between local realities and imported consumption aspirations. Paradoxically, this process does not so much affect the very poor as the working- and middle-class sectors, which are frequently the most exposed to marketing messages and cultural symbols beamed from the advanced world (Grasmuck and Pessar, 1991; Portes and Bach, 1985).[3]

The fundamental point is that contemporary, First World–bound immigration is not a contingent process, but one driven by the very dynamics of global capitalism. For this reason, the immigration flow to the developed world can be confidently expected to continue in the years ahead. This foreign population provides, in turn, the raw material out of which transnational communities develop.

THE RISE OF TRANSNATIONAL ENTERPRISE

Immigrant workers attracted by the growing demand in the advanced countries for fresh sources of low-wage labor soon become aware that the pay and labor conditions in store for them do not go far in promoting their own economic goals. To bypass the menial, dead-end jobs that the host labor market assigns them, they must put into play their networks of social relationships. Immigrant social networks display two characteristics that those among domestic workers generally lack. First, they simultaneously are dense and extend over large geographical distances, and second, they often generate high levels of solidarity by virtue of uncertainty. The sociological principle that exchange under conditions of uncertainty creates stronger bonds among participants applies particularly well to immigrant communities (Kollock, 1994). Their economic transactions in the receiving country tend to occur with little initial information about the trustworthiness of exchange partners and the character and reliability of state regulation. This high uncertainty creates the need to remain loyal to trustworthy partners, regardless of tempting outside opportunities (Guarnizo, 1992).

Geographically extended and solidary networks among immigrants can be put into play for a number of strategic initiatives. A first initiative, discussed by Sassen (1994), leads to long distance, cross-national labor markets where job opportunities in far-away locations are identified and appropriated. A second, described by Zhou (1992), leads to living arrangements designed to lower consumption costs and produce savings for business or real estate acquisition abroad. A third, which has been extensively studied by Light (1984; Light and Bonacich, 1988), leads to the emergence of credit associations where pooled savings are allocated on a rotating basis. A fourth initiative, which is the present topic of inquiry, consists of appropriating the price and information differentials between sending and receiving countries through the creation of transnational enterprises.

Grassroots transnational enterprise benefits from the same set of technological innovations in communications and transportation that underlie large-scale industrial relocations. A class of immigrant entrepreneurs who shuttle regularly across countries and maintain daily contact with events and activities in them could not exist without these new technologies and the options and lower costs that they make possible. Put more broadly, these grassroots initiatives do not rise in opposition to global restructuring or technological innovation, but are driven by them. Through this strategy, labor (initially, immigrant labor) joins the circles of global trade by imitating, often in ingenious ways, the initiatives of large corporate actors.

This parallel between the strategies of corporations and immigrant entrepreneurs is only partial. Though both make extensive use of new technologies and depend on price and information differences across borders, corporations rely primarily on their financial muscle to make such ventures feasible, while immigrants must depend entirely on their social networks (Guarnizo, 1992; Zhou and Bankston, 1994). The long-distance ties that underlie the viability of such initiatives are constructed through a protracted, and frequently difficult, process of adaptation to a foreign society, which gives them their distinct characteristics. In turn, the onset of this economic strategy strengthens such networks. Hence, transnational entrepreneurs expand and thicken, in a cumulative process, the web of social ties that originally made their activities possible.

THE CONSTRUCTION OF TRANSNATIONAL COMMUNITIES

The cumulation of activities across national borders by former immigrants may lead eventually to a qualitatively distinct phenomenon. This qualitative leap, which has been adumbrated by the recent experience of a few immigrant groups, is what the concept of transnational community attempts to capture. Before discussing its formal characteristics, a few examples from the recent literature are presented to flesh out these abstract considerations.

There exist today in the Dominican Republic literally hundreds of small and medium enterprises that are founded and operated by former immigrants to the United States. They include small factories, commercial establishments of different types, and financial agencies. What makes these enterprises transnational is not only that they are created by former immigrants, but that their existence depends on continuing ties to the United States. A study of 113 such firms conducted in the late 1980s found that their mean initial capital investment was only $12,000, but that approximately half continued to receive periodic capital transfers from abroad, averaging $5,400. Monies were remitted by kin and friends who remained in the United States and were partners or co-owners of the firm. In addition to capital, many firms received transfers in kind, producer goods, or commodities for sale (Portes and Guarnizo, 1990: 16).

In the course of fieldwork for this study, we found a second mechanism for capital replenishment, namely, owners' periodic trips abroad to encourage potential new immigrant investors. Such promotions may take place directly, through existing kin and friendship networks, or through the mediation of Dominican-owned financial and real estate agencies in New York City. These trips are also used by factory owners and managers to sell part of their production abroad. Proprietors of small garment firms, for example, regularly travel to Puerto Rico, Miami, and New York to sell their wares. It is common practice to have a prearranged verbal agreement with buyers abroad, including small clothing stores. On their way back to the Dominican Republic, the informal exporters fill their empty suitcases with inputs needed for business, such as garment designs, fabrics, and needles.

To the untrained eye, these loaded-down international travelers appear as common migrants visiting and bearing gifts for their relatives back home, but in reality, they are engaged in a growing form of transnational informal trade. The information requirements for this traffic are invariably transmitted through kin and friendship networks spanning the distance between places of origin and destination. By the same token, it is clear that the men and women who operate these firms are not "return immigrants" in the traditional sense of the term. Instead, they make use of their time abroad to build a base of property, bank accounts, and business contacts from which to organize their return home. The result is not final departure from the United States, but rather a cyclical, back-and-forth movement through which the transnational entrepreneur makes use of differential economic opportunities spread across both countries (Portes and Guarnizo, 1990: 21–22).

A similar story, but with a unique cultural twist, is told by David Kyle (1994) in his study of the Otavalan indigenous community in the highlands of Ecuador. Traditionally, the region of Otavalo has specialized in the production and marketing of clothing, developing and adapting new production skills since the time of the colonial period under Spain. During the last quarter of a century or so, Otavalans have taken to traveling abroad to market their colorful wares in major cities of Europe and North America. By so doing, they appropriate the exchange value pocketed elsewhere by middlemen between Third World indigenous producers and final consumers. After years of traveling abroad, they have also brought home a wealth of novelties from the advanced countries, including European and North American wives. In the streets of Otavalo, it is not uncommon to meet these women attired in traditional indigenous garb.

During the same period, semipermanent Otavalan enclaves began to appear abroad. Their distinct feature is that their members do not make their living from wage labor or even local self-employment, but from the sale of goods brought from Ecuador. They remain in constant communication with their hometown in order to replenish supplies, monitor their *telares* (garment shops), and buy land. The back-and-forth movement required by this trade has turned Otavalans into a common sight, not only at the Quito airport, but also in street fairs in New York, Paris, Amsterdam, and other large cities. According to Kyle (1994), Otavalans have even discovered the commercial value of their folklore and groups of performers have fanned throughout the streets of First World cities.

The sale of colorful ponchos and other woolens accompanied by the plaintive notes of the *quena* flute have been quite profitable. The economic success of these indigenous migrants is evident in their near-universal refusal to accept wage labor abroad and in the evident prosperity of their town. Otavalo is quite different in this respect from other regions in the Andean highlands. Its indigenous entrepreneurs and returned migrants comprise a good portion of the local upper stratum, reversing the traditional pattern of dominance by white and mestizo elites.

A third variant involves immigrants of considerably greater economic power. For example, the growth of Asian communities in several U.S. cities has created opportunities for moneyed entrepreneurs from Taiwan, Hong Kong, and South Korea to invest profitably in the United States and, in the process, themselves become part of the transnational community. Smith and Zhou (1995) explained, for example, how the rapid growth of Chinese home ownership in the New York City suburb of Flushing has been largely financed by new Chinese banks established with Taiwanese and Hong Kong capital. Members of the rapidly growing Chinese population in Flushing and adjacent cities in the borough of Queens are very motivated to acquire their own homes but lack the knowledge of English and the credentials needed to seek credit from mainstream institutions. To meet the burgeoning demand for housing loans processed in the immigrants' own language, local entrepreneurs went to Taiwan and Hong Kong to pool capital for new banks, and new investors came to the United States bearing the necessary resources. As a result, Chinese-owned banks in Flushing proliferated. Although small by conventional standards, they serve simultaneously the economic interests of the immigrant community and those of overseas investors.

Three thousand miles to the west, the city of Monterey Park, California, has been transformed into the "first suburban Chinatown," largely by the activities of well-heeled newcomers (Fong, 1994). Many Taiwanese and Hong Kong entrepreneurs established businesses in the area, less for immediate profit than as a hedge against political instability and the threat of a Chinese communist takeover. Opening a new business in the United States facilitates obtaining permanent residence permits, and as a result, many owners are able to bring their families along to live in Monterey Park, while they themselves continue to commute across the Pacific.

The activities of these "astronauts" (as they are dubbed in Chinese in reference to the frequency of their air travel) adds a new layer of complexity to the transnational community. In this instance, returned immigrants do not invest U.S.-accumulated savings in enterprises at home; instead, immigrants bring new capital to invest in firms in the United States. The birth of a child on American soil guarantees the offspring U.S. citizenship and securely anchors the family in their new setting. As a result of the twin processes of successful investments and citizenship acquisition, Chinese immigrants have moved swiftly from the status of marginal newcomers in Monterey Park to the core of the city's business class (Fong, 1994).

A fourth instance of transnationalization illustrates another facet of the process, namely, the political and social influence that immigrant groups can acquire over the sending communities. The example is based on Smith's (1992) study of a small farming community in the Mixteca region of Mexico, near the city of Puebla. Smith described the excitement of members of the Ticuani Potable Water Committee on learning that new tubing had arrived, and with it, the long-awaited solution to the town's water problem. They immediately made plans to go inspect the new materials and organize their installment. Smith commented:

> On first sight, this is no more than an ordinary civic project. . . . Yet when we consider certain other aspects of the scene, the meaning becomes quite different. The Committee and I are not standing in Ticuani, but rather on a busy intersection in Brooklyn. . . . The Committee members are not simply going to the outskirts of the town to check the water tubes, but rather they are headed to JFK airport for a Friday afternoon flight to Mexico City, from which they will travel the five hours overland to their pueblo, consult with the authorities and contractors, and return by Monday afternoon to their jobs in New York City. (1992: 1)

As it turns out, the potable water project was only the latest of a series of public works in Ticuani to be initiated and paid for by its New York immigrants. For this particular project, the expatriate community contributed more than $50,000, which was gathered in donations of $100 or less. The waterworks also marked the twentieth anniversary of the successful completion of the first transnational public project, and for this occasion, the New York Committee unveiled a new seal, to be used in all future correspondence and public events. It reads: *"Por el Progreso de Ticuani: Los Ausentes Siempre Presentes. Ticuani y New York"* ("For the Progress of Ticuani: The Absent Ones, Always Present. Ticuani and New York") (Smith, 1992: 1–2).

I have dwelled on these examples at some length to give credibility to a phenomenon that, when initially described, strains the imagination. A multitude of similar examples could have been used, as illustrated in the pioneering collection by Basch and her collaborators (Basch, Glick Schiller, and Blanc-Szanton, 1994). The central point that these examples illustrate is that once started, the phenomenon of transnationalization can acquire a cumulative character, expanding not only in numbers, but also in the qualitative character of its activities. Hence, while the original wave of these activities is economic and their initiators can be properly labeled transnational entrepreneurs, subsequent activities encompass political, social, and cultural pursuits as well.

Alerted by the initiatives of immigrant entrepreneurs, political parties and even governments have established offices abroad to canvass immigrant communities for financial and electoral support. Not to be outdone, many immigrant groups organize political committees to lobby the home government or, as in the case of the Mexican community studied by Smith, influence the local municipality on various issues. To provide yet another example, Colombian and Dominican immigrants in New York City organized during the 1970s and 1980s to demand the right to vote in elections in their respective countries and to obtain the support from their home governments to combat negative stereotypes in the U.S. media (Sassen, 1979).

Churches and private charities have joined the traffic between home country and immigrant community with a growing number of initiatives involving both.

Finally, the phenomenon can acquire a cultural veneer as home performers and artists use the expatriate communities as platforms to break into the First World scene and returnee artists popularize cultural forms learned abroad.[4] The end result of this cumulative process is the transformation of the original pioneering economic ventures into transnational communities, which are characterized by dense networks across space and by an increasing number of people who lead dual lives. Members are at least bilingual, move easily between different cultures, frequently maintain homes in two countries, and pursue economic, political, and cultural interests that require a simultaneous presence in both. It bears repeating that the onset of this process and its development are nurtured by social forces unleashed by contemporary global capitalism. Paralleling Marx's description of the proletariat as created and placed into the historical scene by its future class adversaries, today's roaming capitalist ventures have given rise to the conditions and incentives for the transnationalization of labor.

THE STRUCTURE AND LONG-TERM CONSEQUENCES OF TRANSNATIONALIZATION

If conditions confronting today's U.S.-bound immigrants bore some similarity to those faced by their European predecessors at the turn of the century, one could wager that today's immigrants would not have moved so decisively in the direction of transnationalization. That earlier era featured two conditions significantly different from today: a plethora of relatively well-paid wage jobs in industry and the limitations imposed by the costly and time-consuming nature of long-distance transportation. The first condition militated against widespread entrepreneurial ventures and gave rise over time to stable working-class ethnic communities. For example, most Poles and Italians in the United States became workers and not entrepreneurs because labor market opportunities in the industrial cities where they arrived made this an attractive option. By contrast, today's uncertain and minimally paid service-sector jobs strongly encourage immigrants to seek alternative automonous paths.

Second, communications and transportation technologies were such as to make it prohibitive for turn-of-the-century immigrants to make a living out of bridging the cultural gap between countries of origin and destination or to lead simultaneous lives in both. No trans-oceanic commuting was possible, and thus, no means were available for Polish peasants to check how things were going at home over the weekend and be back in their New York jobs on Monday.

Contemporary transnational communities are distinguished from comparable activities of earlier immigrant waves by three features: First, the instantaneous character of communication across vast geographic distances; second, the large numbers involved in these activities; and third, the tendency for these activities to become normative in the immigrant community, driven by the numbers who take part and the dearth of alternative opportunities in the host society. Just as in the past migration abroad became the norm in certain regions of the Third

World (Massey and Garcia España, 1987), today, participation in transnational enterprises is turning into "the thing to do" among certain groups of immigrants.

It must be emphasized that transnational communities do not emerge in opposition to global capitalism, nor is there anything in their operation that is set explicitly against the designs of large corporations. In this sense, the analogy with Marx's account of the emergence of the industrial proletariat breaks down. Grassroots transnational enterprises and the manifold social and political activities that follow them are not necessary for the structures of global capital accumulation; they represent instead the means through which some members of the working class escape the hold of these structures.

Over time, however the process can acquire novel characteristics and lead to unexpected consequences. As more and more common people become involved in transnational activities, they come to subvert one of the basic premises of contemporary capitalist globalization, namely, that labor stays put and that its reference point for wages and work conditions remains local. Immigrant workers who become transnational entrepreneurs not only deny their own labor to businesses abroad and at home, they become conduits for information about different labor conditions and novel economic opportunities. The growth of socio-political and -economic ties across national borders can also provide a measure of protection for immigrant workers against the vulnerability of cultural isolation and an inferior legal status in the developed world. Flows of capital from newly industrialized countries of Asia to North American cities work in the same direction by facilitating home ownership and a swift move into self-employment in the immigrant community.

The significance of transnationalization is already apparent in the smaller labor-exporting countries. In the peripheral nations of the Caribbean Basin, as well as those Asian countries with long ties to the United States (such as Taiwan, South Korea, and the Philippines), the entire economy has been remolded by the twin processes of corporate globalization and immigrant transnationalization. Scarcely a family exists that does not have a relative abroad, and the back-and-forth movement of people, information, and investment has become integral to family economic strategies. Consumption patterns and lifestyles are shaped as much by the global media as by the activities of former immigrants who have been transformed into transnational entrepreneurs. Even governments get into the act by seeking, as in the case of President Jean Bertrand Aristide of Haiti, to transform the immigrant community into a symbolic "10th Department" (in addition to the existing nine) in search of its contributions and political support (Glick Schiller, Basch, and Blanc-Szanton, 1992).

It is still too soon to predict the long-term implications of the process of transnationalization. While in smaller peripheral countries it already has great importance, in larger labor-exporting nations, such as Mexico, its visibility and significance remain limited. Nonetheless, as the process continues, it may become a significant factor in modifying a strategy of capitalist accumulation based on wage differentials and information asymmetries between different regions of the world. The main reason for this expectation is that, unlike labor standards or flexible specialization, the emergence of transnational communities places everyday people in the same plane as the corporate actors who are engaged in global restructuring. The level of information and expertise thus acquired may partially neutralize the power of First World employers to simultaneously exploit Third World populations at home and their immigrants abroad. Whether the process comes to acquire this systemic consequence or not, the spectacle of common people criss-crossing the world in search of opportunities that are otherwise denied to them possesses enough intrinsic appeal to deserve attention.

EDITOR'S NOTE

This chapter was the keynote address delivered at the nineteenth annual conference on the Political Economy of the World-System, "Latin America in the World-Economy," North-South Center at the University of Miami, April 21, 1995.

NOTES

1. This statement cannot be fully justified here without derailing the reader's attention from the central focus of the analysis. The argument has been documented fully in several earlier writings. See Portes (1978) and Portes and Böröcz (1989).
2. Some 2.5 million formerly unauthorized aliens were legalized under IRCA. Subsequent legislation contained generous provisions for newly legalized immigrants to bring their relatives. More importantly, IRCA retained a large loophole allowing for the continuation of the unauthorized flow by requiring employers to check prospective workers' documents but not to establish their validity (Portes and Zhou, 1995).
3. Sassen (1988) has developed a variant of this argument whereby runaway industries located in peripheral export zones stimulate outmigration by presocializing their work forces in First World cultural practices. Most of the labor force in these industries is formed by young people, who are commonly dismissed after a few years. The combination of the skills and aspirations learned during their employment with their economic redundancy converts them into a ready pool for future migration. Sassen provided little empirical evidence, but subsequent research in a number of Latin American countries indicates that Sassen's thesis has some validity (see Pérez-Sainz, 1994; Itzigsohn, 1994).
4. Latin American artists have taken to using the city of Miami, Florida, in this way because of its large and diversified Spanish-speaking community, which is anchored by the Cuban ethnic enclave. Latin-owned recording studios, galleries, and theaters, plus a large resident artist community, offer newcomers access to opportunities that are unavailable elsewhere in the United States (Sassen and Portes, 1993).

REFERENCES

Alba, Francisco. 1978. "Mexico's International Migration as a Manifestation of Its Development Pattern." *International Migration Review* 12 (Winter): 502–551.
Bade, Klaus J. 1995. "From Emigration to Immigration: The German Experience in the 19th and 20th Centuries." Paper presented at the German-American Migration

and Refugee Policy Group, American Academy of Arts and Sciences, Cambridge, MA, March 23–26.

Basch, Linda G., Nina Glick Schiller, and Cristina Blanc-Szanton. 1994. *Nations Unbound: Transnational Projects, Post-colonial Predicaments, and De-territorialized Nation-States.* Langhorne, PA: Gordon and Breach.

Benería, Lourdes, and Marta I. Roldán. 1987. *The Crossroads of Class and Gender: Homework, Subcontracting, and Household Dynamics in Mexico City.* Chicago: University of Chicago Press.

Birkbeck, Chris. 1979. "Garbage, Industry, and the 'Vultures' of Cali, Colombia." In *Casual Work and Poverty in Third World Cities*, ed. R. Bromley and C. Gerry, pp. 161–183. New York: John Wiley.

Brusco, Sebastiano. 1982. "The Emilian Model: Productive Decentralization and Social Integration." *Cambridge Journal of Economics* 6, 2 (June): 167–184.

Capecchi, Vittorio. 1989. "The Informal Economy and the Development of Flexible Specialization." In *The Informal Economy: Studies in Advanced and Less Developed Countries*, ed. A. Portes, M. Castells, and L. A. Benton, pp. 189–215. Baltimore: Johns Hopkins University Press.

Castells, Manuel. 1980. "Multinational Capital, National States, and Local Communities." Institute of Urban and Regional Development working paper. University of California, Berkeley.

Castells, Manuel, and Alejandro Portes. 1989. "World Underneath: The Origins, Dynamics, and Effects of the Informal Economy." In *The Informal Economy: Studies in Advanced and Less Developed Countries*, ed. A. Portes, M. Castells, and L. A. Benton, pp. 11–37. Baltimore: Johns Hopkins University Press.

Cornelius, Wayne A. 1992. "Controlling Illegal Immigration: Lessons from Japan and Spain." Working paper. University of California, San Diego, Center for U.S.-Mexico Studies.

Davies, Rob. 1979. "Informal Sector or Subordinated Mode of Production? A Model." In *Casual Work and Poverty in Third World Cities*, ed. R. Bromley and C. Gerry, pp. 87–104. New York: John Wiley.

Deyo, Frederic C. 1989. *Beneath the Miracle, Labor Subordination in the New Asian Industrialism.* Berkeley: University of California Press.

Fernández-Kelly, M. Patricia. 1983. *For We Are Sold, I and My People: Women and Industry in Mexico's Frontier.* Albany, NY: State University of New York Press.

Fix, Michael, and Jeffrey S. Passel. 1991. "The Door Remains Open: Recent Immigration to the United States and a Preliminary Analysis of the Immigration Act of 1990." Working paper. The Urban Institute and the Rand Corporation.

Fong, Timothy P. 1994. *The First Suburban Chinatown: The Remaking of Monterey Park, California.* Philadelphia: Temple University Press.

Fortuna, Juan Carlos, and Suzanna Prates. 1989. "Informal Sector versus Informalized Labor Relations in Uruguay." In *The Informal Economy: Studies in Advanced and Less Developed Countries*, ed. A. Portes, M. Castells, and L. A. Benton, pp. 78–94. Baltimore: Johns Hopkins University Press.

Gans, Herbert. 1992. "Second-generation Decline: Scenarios for the Economic and Ethnic Futures of the Post-1965 American Immigrants." *Ethnic and Racial Studies* 15 (April): 173–192.

Glick Schiller, Nina, Linda Basch, and Cristina Blanc-Szanton. 1992. "Transnationalism:

A New Analytic Framework for Understanding Migration." *Annals of the New York Academy of Sciences* 645: 1–24.

Grasmuck, Sherri, and Patricia Pessar. 1991. *Between Two Islands: Dominican International Migration.* Berkeley: University of California Press.

Guarnizo, Luis E. 1992. "One Country in Two: Dominican-Owned Firms in the United States and the Dominican Republic." Ph.D. dissertation, Department of Sociology, The Johns Hopkins University.

Harrison, Bennett. 1994. *Lean and Mean: The Changing Landscape of Corporate Power in the Age of Flexibility.* New York: Basic Books.

Itzigsohn, Jose A. 1994. "The Informal Economy in Santo Domingo and San Jose: A Comparative Study." Ph.D. dissertation, Department of Sociology, The Johns Hopkins University.

Kollock, Peter. 1994. "The Emergence of Exchange Structures: An Experimental Study of Uncertainty, Commitment, and Trust." *American Journal of Sociology* 100 (September): 313–345.

Kyle, David. 1994. "The Transnational Peasant: The Social Structures of Economic Migration from the Ecuadoran Andes." Ph.D. dissertation, Department of Sociology, The Johns Hopkins University.

Lawyers Committee for Human Rights (LCHR). 1991. "Protection of Workers' Rights." Draft. LCHR, New York.

Light, Ivan. 1984. "Immigrant and Ethnic Enterprise in North America." *Ethnic and Racial Studies* 7 (April): 195–216.

Light, Ivan, and Edna Bonacich. 1988. *Immigrant Entrepreneurs: Koreans in Los Angeles 1965–1982.* Berkeley: University of California Press.

Lim, Linda Y. C. 1990. "Singapore." In *Labor Standards and Development in the Global Economy,* ed. S. Herzenberg and J. Perez-Lopez, pp. 73–95. Washington, DC: U.S. Department of Labor.

Massey, Douglas, and Felipe García España. 1987. "The Social Process of International Migration." *Science* 237: 733–738.

Münz, Rainer, and Rolf Ulrich. 1995. "Changing Patterns of Migration, the Case of Germany, 1945–1994." Paper presented at the German-American Migration and Refugee Policy Group, American Academy of Arts and Sciences, Cambridge, MA., March 23–26.

Pérez-Sainz, Juan Pablo. 1994. *El dilema del Nahual.* San José, Costa Rica: FLACSO Editores.

Piore, Michael. 1979. *Birds of Passage.* Cambridge: Cambridge University Press.

———. 1990. "Labor Standards and Business Strategies." In *Labor Standards and Development in the Global Economy,* ed. S. Herzenberg and J. Perez-Lopez, pp. 35–49. Washington, DC: U.S. Department of Labor.

Piore, Michael J., and Charles F. Sabel. 1984. *The Second Industrial Divide.* New York: Basic Books.

Portes, Alejandro. 1978. "Migration and Underdevelopment." *Politics and Society* 8: 1–48.

Portes, Alejandro, and Robert L. Bach. 1985. *Latin Journey: Cuban and Mexican Immigrants in the United States.* Berkeley: University of California Press.

Portes, Alejandro and József Böröcz. 1989. "Contemporary Immigration: Theoretical Perspectives on Its Determinants and Modes of Incorporation." *International Migration Review* 23 (Fall): 606–630.

Portes, Alejandro, and Luis E. Guarnizo. 1990. "Tropical Capitalists: U.S. Bound Immigration and Small Enterprise Development in the Dominican Republic." Working paper no. 57. Commission for the Study of International Migration and Cooperative Economic Development, Washington, DC.

———. 1991. "Tropical Capitalists: U.S.-Bound Immigration and Small Enterprise Development in the Dominican Republic." In *Migration, Remittances, and Small Business Development: Mexico and Caribbean Basin Countries*, ed. S. Díaz-Briquets and S. Weintraub, pp. 101–131. Boulder, CO: Westview Press.

Portes, Alejandro, and Min Zhou. 1995. "Divergent Destinies: Immigration, Poverty, and Entrepreneurship in the United States." In *Poverty, Inequality, and the Future of Social Policy*, ed. K. McFate, B. Lawson, and W. J. Wilson, pp. 489–520. New York: Russell Sage Foundation.

Rumbaut, Rubén G. 1994. "Origins and Destinies: Immigration to the United States Since World War II." *Sociological Forum* 9, 4: 583–621.

Sabel, Charles. 1982. *The Division of Labor in Industry*. Cambridge: Cambridge University Press.

———. 1986. "Changing Modes of Economic Efficiency and Their Implications for Industrialization in the Third World." In *Development, Democracy, and Trespassing: Essays in Honor of Albert O. Hirschman*, ed. M. S. McPherson, A. Foxley, and G. O'Donnell, pp. 27–55. Notre Dame, IN: Notre Dame University Press.

Sassen, Saskia. 1979. "Formal and Informal Associations: Dominicans and Colombians in New York." *International Migration Review* 13 (Summer): 314–332.

———. 1988. *The Mobility of Labor and Capital: A Study in International Investment and Labor Flow*. New York: Cambridge University Press.

———. 1989. "New York City's Informal Economy." In *The Informal Economy: Studies in Advanced and Less Developed Countries*, ed. A. Portes, M. Castells, and L. A. Benton, pp. 60–77. Baltimore, MD: Johns Hopkins University Press.

———. 1995. "Immigration and Local Labor Markets." In *The Economic Sociology of Immigration: Essays in Networks, Ethnicity, and Entrepreneurship*, ed. A. Portes, pp. 87–127. New York: Russell Sage Foundation.

Sassen, Saskia, and Alejandro Portes. 1993. "Miami: A New Global City?" *Contemporary Sociology* 22 (July): 471–477.

Smith, Christopher, and Min Zhou. 1995. "Flushing: Capital and Community in a Transnational Neighborhood." Manuscript. Russell Sage Foundation, New York.

Smith, Robert C. 1992, October. "Los ausentes siempre presentes: The Imagining, Making, and Politics of a Transnational Community between New York City and Ticuaní, Puebla." Manuscript. Columbia University, Institute for Latin American and Iberian Studies.

Zhou, Min. 1992. *New York's Chinatown: The Socioeconomic Potential of an Urban Enclave*. Philadelphia: Temple University Press.

Zhou, Min, and Carl L. Bankston. 1995. "Entrepreneurship." In *The Asian American Almanac: A Reference Work on Asians in the United States*, ed. S. Gall and I. Natividad, pp. 511–528. Detroit: Gale Research, Inc.

Zolberg, Aristide R. 1989. "The Next Waves: Migration Theory for a Changing World." *International Migration Review* 23 (Fall): 403–430.

9

REVOLUTIONARY TERRORISM IN THE PERIPHERY: A COMPARATIVE ANALYSIS OF THE SHINING PATH AND THE KHMER ROUGE

Bruce M. Podobnik

The particularly brutal form of revolutionary violence that continues to haunt Peru and Cambodia is a forceful reminder of the dangers inherent in a global system characterized by growing inequality and the increasing marginalization of vast segments of the population of peripheral societies. Caught in an international context marked by wrenching economic restructuring, chronic austerity, and the apparent collapse of alternative development strategies, entire generations of youth in less-developed countries such as Peru and Cambodia face futures of grinding poverty and social dislocation. While the majority of the youth of these countries continue in their attempts to survive within the framework of the contemporary capitalist world-system, small but determined groups of Shining Path and Khmer Rouge guerrillas have chosen to reject any accommodation with such a system, and instead have embarked on radical projects of autonomous socialist development.

An examination of the recent history of the Shining Path and the Khmer Rouge, however, highlights the dangers involved when revolutionary forces within peripheral nations attempt to undertake policies of autarkic development. In both Peru and Cambodia, transitory periods of popular support for guerrilla campaigns against oppressive elites or occupying military forces gave way to widespread resistance in the face of the destructive policies of autarky and social reconstruction imposed by Shining Path and Khmer Rouge guerrillas. Imbued with an apparently limitless faith in the accuracy of their revolutionary analyses, Shining Path and Khmer Rouge cadre refused to accommodate their policies to existing realities and instead systematically assassinated representatives of virtually all state institutions, peasant leaders, labor organizers, and most other activists who would not submit to the radical demands of their movement. In a pattern that resembles those of other recent revolutionary conflicts, the struggles of the Shining Path and the Khmer Rouge degenerated into increasingly incomprehensible, and ultimately self-defeating, orgies of violence and terror.[1]

The comparative analysis that follows is intended to shed light on the conditions that produced movements willing to employ violence against virtually all social groups in their efforts to achieve revolutionary transformations. As this chapter will argue, structural problems common to most peripheral societies led to the emergence of a generation of youth in Peru and Cambodia with few viable employment opportunities in either rural or urban areas. Although mentioned in passing in previous writings on peripheral revolutions, my analysis emphasizes the key role of such youth in the contemporary revolutionary struggles of Peru and Cambodia.[2] In addition to examining the emergence of these strata of detached youth, I investigate specific social, political, and cultural conditions that led dissident elite groups within each country to adopt extremist, uncompromising stances toward existing political and social structures. The institutional settings in which such leadership factions could engage in the intensive ideological training of alienated rural and urban youth are then described, followed by an analysis of the regional political and social vacuums into which embryonic radical parties could expand and generate wider bases of social support.

THE EMERGENCE OF A GENERATION OF DETACHED YOUTH

The penetration of capitalist enterprise into rural areas in Cambodia and Peru has led to the disruption of local subsistence economies, the concentration of landownership, and the growth of a sector of the peasantry that is compelled to migrate in search of employment. Combined with the destructive impact of regional wars and internal civil conflict, these pressures have led to the dislocation of large segments of the rural populations of both countries. Demographic growth, spurred by the introduction of modern health services, has served to heighten the social tensions inherent in contexts of increasing class inequality and foreign exploitation, while the urban industrial sectors have proven incapable of providing avenues out of poverty for the majority of the citizens of either country. These, I will argue, are the structural roots of the emergence of revolutionary terrorist movements in Cambodia and Peru.[3]

The imposition of French colonial rule over Cambodia in 1863 marked the definitive end of that country's political autonomy and the beginning of its incorporation into an expanding capitalist world-system as an exporter of agricultural commodities. Plantations established by the French in the Mekong Delta had, by the 1930s, transformed Cambodia into an important exporter of rubber and cotton, while an influx of foreign capital from France, the United States, the Soviet Union, and China in the years following World War II financed the expansion of port facilities and transportation systems and allowed for steady increases in Cambodian agricultural production during the period of 1950–1966 (Chandler, 1991: 89).

When measured in terms of its export sectors' performance, the Cambodian economy appeared to be relatively dynamic into the mid-1960s. Modest successes in Cambodia's export performance, however, masked growing internal structural imbalances. The expansion of large landholdings and plantations in the country's most fertile regions brought about the dislocation of rural populations, so that during the period 1950–1970, the percentage of Cambodians forced to work as sharecroppers or landless migrant laborers grew from 4 to 20 percent (Kiernan, 1982: 4). Rapid demographic expansion produced high rates of rural out-migration in Cambodia as well. It is interesting to note that while approximately 590,000 people resided in urban areas in 1962, by 1967 that number had risen to 880,000 (Banister and Johnson, 1993: 107). By the late 1960s, a sizable class of impoverished rural inhabitants with few ties to the land had emerged. As in other peripheral societies, it was precisely this confluence of structural changes that provoked serious social conflict in rural Cambodia.

The first revolutionary tremors broke out in April 1967, with the beginning of the Samlaut Rebellion in the central rice plains of Cambodia. Located in Battambang province, the Samlaut region was the site of increasing land pressure during the 1950s and 1960s as fruit and cotton plantations encroached on peasant holdings. What appears to have begun as a largely spontaneous peasant revolt sparked off by these multiple threats to local subsistence activities had, by 1969, expanded to become the most extensive outbreak of violence seen since anti-French uprisings had swept through Cambodia following World War II.

While tensions were growing in those parts of central Cambodia that were most integrated into the national and international market systems, conditions in the country's peripheral mountain and jungle regions were deteriorating as well. Inhabited primarily by non-Khmer tribal minorities, the remote areas of northeastern, southwestern, and eastern Cambodia remained largely untouched by commercial influence into the 1960s. In the mid-1960s, however, the central government began moving lowland Khmer peasants into the northeastern zone in an apparent attempt to "Khmerize" the independent hill tribes, and thus establish some control over the region. The threats to local ethnic customs and subsistence activities posed by these new colonists provoked a series of tribal revolts throughout the northeast in 1968 and 1969, eventually leading many of the non-Khmer minorities to join the Khmer Rouge's war against lowland, urban Cambodia (Burgler, 1990: 23).

By the late 1960s, in short, both the central and the more remote regions of the country were already exhibiting most of the social tensions characteristic of societies undergoing processes of peripheral development. The expansion of the Indochina War into Cambodia brought profound disruptions to the society and accelerated revolutionary processes within the country. In an effort to shut down the North Vietnamese supply lines that stretched along Cambodia's eastern frontiers, the United States initiated covert bombing raids into the country in early

1969. The bombing campaign expanded relentlessly, so that by the time the U.S. Congress halted military operations in Cambodia in August 1973, approximately 500,000 tons of explosives, or more than three times that dropped on Japan during all of World War II, had been unleashed on the nation (Markusen, 1992: 159). In addition to killing an estimated 275,000 Cambodians, the U.S. bombing campaign destroyed most of the country's rural infrastructure, disrupted agricultural production, and generated an immense refugee population. As a result, by 1975, the population of the country's capital city, Phnom Penh, had surged to approximately 3 million, or over 40 percent of Cambodia's entire population (Banister and Johnson, 1993: 107). It was precisely in this context of rural collapse and widespread destruction that the Khmer Rouge was able to recruit a young cadre to perpetuate its revolutionary war.

Although Peru has avoided provoking the direct wrath of a core state in the contemporary period, its initial mode of incorporation into the modern world-system was itself an extremely violent process. The impact of European military campaigns, enslavement, and contagious diseases provoked an Andean demographic collapse of dramatic proportions, while the exploitation of Peru's mineral and agricultural resources during the ensuing centuries further threatened Andean societies. It is estimated that only about 6 percent of Peru's land mass is suitable for agriculture, and although indigenous communities developed networks of exchange in order to integrate distinct ecological niches into sustainable systems, such subsistence economies have proven vulnerable to the expansion of capitalist markets, predatory landowners, and demographic pressures.

The penetration of railroads and other transportation networks into the central Andes during the 1940s and 1950s precipitated structural changes that, over the long term, undermined these Andean subsistence economies (Slater, 1989). The availability of improved transportation systems encouraged large landowners to bring fertile land into intensive production for urban markets, which meant driving segments of the peasantry off their land. Even those indigenous communities that managed to retain control over communal lands began to experience growing internal pressures as the spread of public health services generated a demographic expansion throughout the central Andes in the postwar period. That a growing number of peasants were desperate for land is evidenced by the wave of land invasions that began in the mid-1950s and which, by 1968, had involved the participation of over 300,000 peasants (García-Sayán, 1982: 13).

A further indication of the poverty and subsistence crises sweeping through the countryside can be found in an analysis of rates of out-migration. During the 1940–1981 period, out-migration rates from the central Andean provinces of Ayacucho, Apurimac, Ancash, and Huancavelica were consistently the highest in the nation (Degregori, 1990: 32). In this period, in fact, Peru underwent a fundamental transition: whereas in 1940, only 17 percent of the nation's population resided in urban areas, by 1980, this percentage had grown to 65 percent.

In 1980, fully one-quarter of the country's 17 million people resided in the capital city of Lima.

By invading marginal urban land, constructing homes, and then organizing to demand the provision of such services as water and electricity, Lima's new residents managed to begin a process of achieving limited upward mobility during the 1950s, which lasted into the 1970s. A portion of the city's working class was absorbed by expanding formal industrial enterprises, while the rest sought employment in an informal sector that flourished in Lima's streets and neighborhoods. Moreover, for the children of these new migrants, state-funded education offered a new avenue toward upward mobility: while in 1960 there were only 30,000 university students nationwide, by 1970 there were 109,000, and by 1982 the number had expanded to 305,000 (Cotler, 1986: 110).

Migrating to Lima and other urban areas resulted in better living conditions and employment prospects for most individuals into the 1970s. However, the onset of a protracted economic crisis in 1976 began to undermine the capacity of Peru's lower classes to generate alternative forms of limited upward mobility. The increasing saturation of urban spaces and the urban informal economy led to intensified competition among impoverished residents for shrinking resources (Stein and Monge, 1988). Meanwhile, a collapse of formal industrial employment severely limited the ability of high school and university graduates to find adequate employment. As a result of this collapse, by 1982, fully 63.4 percent of Lima residents aged 15 to 24 were either underemployed or unemployed (Cotler, 1986: 114).

By 1980, in sum, structural inequalities and demographic pressures in rural and urban areas were undermining the future prospects of an entire generation of Peruvians. Much as in Cambodia, processes of uneven development in Peru were resulting in the emergence of a class of youth with few attachments to the land and also with limited opportunities for upward mobility in urban areas. These conditions resulted in heightened levels of political and social turmoil over the following decades.

THE CONSOLIDATION OF SECTARIAN LEADERSHIP GROUPS

In addition to producing a generation of rural and urban youth with few employment opportunities, the particular forms of uneven development that have taken place in Cambodia and Peru produced exclusionary social systems that failed to incorporate newly emergent classes of professionals and educated individuals into meaningful political participation.[4] It was precisely out of these marginalized strata that the core leadership factions of the Khmer Rouge and the Shining Path emerged.

From 1941 until 1970, the Cambodian political system was dominated by the idiosyncratic rule of one individual, Prince Norodom Sihanouk. Although nominally democratic parliamentary procedures were instituted in the mid-1950s,

Sihanouk ensured that most of his chosen candidates ran unopposed in elections during the subsequent decade. A new class of entrepreneurs in Phnom Penh found itself shut out of the Cambodian political arena, while a growing number of young university graduates encountered few opportunities for suitable employment as the Cambodian economy stagnated (Chandler, 1991).

This closed political and social order came under increasingly severe criticism from a select group of Cambodians who studied together in France in the early 1950s and then returned to their native country, only to find most avenues of upward social mobility blocked.[5] Saloth Sar (who later adopted the guerrilla name Pol Pot), Ieng Sari, Son Sen, and Khieu Samphan were sent to Paris for technical training but became immersed in the radical political environment created by a large Asian expatriate community in the French capital. Upon their return to Phnom Penh, a series of elements converged to further intensify the political extremism of this faction. First, throughout the 1950s and 1960s, Prince Sihanouk appropriated much of the moderate left's political rhetoric by adopting an anti-imperialist, anti-American stance, and by supporting the Non-Aligned Movement. Pol Pot and his allies initially echoed Sihanouk's critiques of exploitative international powers, but they eventually went further and demanded a complete cut in ties with virtually all foreign powers.

In 1963, following widespread protests mounted by students and disaffected urban residents, Sihanouk unleashed his military on the Cambodian Communist Party, thereby driving the entire Khmer Rouge leadership into the remote northeastern mountains. From 1963 until 1975, Pol Pot and his faction lived among the isolated hill tribes of this northeast region, depending on the assistance of these tribal people for their very survival (Burgler, 1990: 17). This experience more than any other nurtured the anti-urban, Maoist orientation of the original Khmer Rouge leadership, thus producing a revolutionary group that was fundamentally different from any other oppositional faction in Cambodia. In sum, by the 1960s, a closely knit, ideologically distinct Khmer Rouge leadership group had coalesced within a context marked by closed political and social institutions, a violent and repressive central government, and a sustained immersion in rural Cambodian society.

A very similar set of conditions produced an equally sectarian, extremist leadership group in the Andean highlands of Peru. Although the modern political history of Peru is more complex than that of Cambodia in part because elected civilian governments alternated with de facto military regimes throughout the century, a few constants can nevertheless be identified. First, until very recently the central government itself has been dominated by a *criollo* elite, with cultural roots in Lima as well as economic ties to key export sectors linking Peru to the world-economy. This political and economic orientation toward the coast produced a second constant in Peruvian politics and society: the neglect of the marginally productive, culturally isolated central Andean regions. Well into the twentieth century, sections of the Andean highlands remained largely outside the sphere of influence of the Peruvian central government; instead, large landowners exercised ideological, economic, and political domination over the regional populations. In a uniquely Andean phenomenon termed *gamonalismo*, the indigenous populations of such provinces as Ayacucho, Apurimac, and Huancavelica were subjected to intense forms of coercion by powerful hacendados who, in addition to imposing feudalistic obligations on the peasants they employed, frequently controlled local municipalities, legal officials, and even church clergy (Manrique, 1990: 82).

Within this oppressive political and social context, an emergent mestizo class of provincial university professors and students began to elaborate critiques of the inequalities embedded in Andean society.[6] Key among this elite group of dissidents was Abimael Guzmán Reynoso, a professor of philosophy who arrived in Ayacucho in 1962 and soon distinguished himself as a particularly dogmatic activist within the local political scene. A visit to China during the height of the Cultural Revolution intensified Guzmán's ideological extremism, and by late 1969, he and a small group of allies, including key future leaders such as Oscar Morote, Julio Mezzich, and Antonio Díaz Martínez, had split from another local Maoist party to form the Peruvian Communist Party–Shining Path (Gorriti, 1990).

The sectarian nature of the Shining Path began to reveal itself immediately. Labeling all other splinter groups in Ayacucho "revisionists," the group proceeded to argue that there was no possible accommodation with the "bureaucratic capitalist, fascist state" that they claimed ruled Peru. Drawing on Mao Tse-tung's theory of guerrilla warfare, Guzmán called the mobilization of the peasantry in a massive assault on urban society the only correct strategy for true revolutionaries in Peru (Peruvian Communist Party, 1982). Militants of the Shining Path physically attacked members of other radical parties in Ayacucho who rejected such a strategy, accusing these more moderate activists of confusing the masses with revisionist doctrines (Gorriti, 1990: 32–33).

Aside from the possible psychological idiosyncrasies of the core leadership of the Shining Path, there are specific social and political conditions that pushed the party to adopt such uncompromising positions. Much like Prince Sihanouk in Cambodia, the reformist military regime of Juan Velasco Alvarado, which seized power in Peru in 1968, appropriated the moderate left's political agenda by attacking U.S. business interests, denouncing foreign imperialism, and instituting an agrarian reform. The failure of most of these reforms, which was evident by 1976, lent added weight to the Shining Path's attacks on all versions of political revisionism. Additionally, the abortive guerrilla struggles waged in Ayacucho in 1965 by a handful of Cuban-inspired urbanites convinced Shining Path militants that long-term efforts would be required to establish the rural connections necessary for carrying out a peasant-based guerrilla war in the Andes.

Much like the Khmer Rouge, therefore, the original leaders of the Shining Path consolidated their position within a context of closed political and social systems, a heritage of pervasive local oppression, and long-term interaction with rural populations. Moreover, like the Khmer Rouge, the Shining Path leadership came to reject reformist policies in favor of a strategy of peasant-based guerrilla warfare.

INSTITUTIONAL CONTEXTS

Having examined the emergence of populations of detached youth in Cambodia and Peru, along with the consolidation of extremist leadership factions in each country, I now turn to an analysis of the institutional contexts in which these two social groups came into sustained contact with each other. Particular attention will be directed toward identifying precisely which kinds of individuals responded to the political messages being advanced by the leaders of the Khmer Rouge and the Shining Path.

The core leaders of what was to become the Khmer Rouge were able to begin the long-term task of recruiting militants on their return from Paris in the 1950s, when they assumed positions within key universities in Phnom Penh. In 1956, Pol Pot took a teaching position in the private Chamraon Vichea (Progressive Study) school, while Khieu Samphan and Ieng Sari joined the faculty at Kambubot College, an institution that had already earned a reputation as a site of radical political activity. The success of the original leadership of the Khmer Rouge in mobilizing support within these university contexts is revealed by Chandler:

The roles played by teachers at Kambubot and Chamraon Vichea are crucial to the development of Cambodian radicalism. . . . By the late 1960s, when a Communist-led rebellion had broken out in much of Cambodia, many guerrilla bands were made up in part of former teachers and their students who had followed them into the forest. (1991: 110–111)

Frustrated by the closed nature of Cambodia's political system and class structure, teachers and students in Phnom Penh became actively engaged in oppositional activities by the late 1950s. Prince Sihanouk responded by clamping down on the Communist Party, forcing Pol Pot and his key allies to flee into the remote northeast provinces of the country in 1963. In 1967, a renewed crackdown on urban Maoists in Phnom Penh drove hundreds of young students and intellectuals into the jungle, facilitating the expansion of Khmer Rouge influence in rural areas. By 1968, the Khmer Rouge had established a network of contacts throughout the country that allowed them to begin their armed struggle against the Cambodian state.

Although the Khmer Rouge received little support from the middle peasantry located in the central rice plains and along the Mekong River, they did gain adherents among the impoverished hill tribes where for years, party members had worked the land, dug irrigation canals, and provided basic medical care. Young peasants with no access to land in these peripheral regions became the movement's main converts (Frieson, 1993: 37). Indeed, the party found the young to be the most committed revolutionaries. Party documents indicate that by 1970, efforts were being made to organize special military- and political-training camps for the poorest peasant youth in Khmer Rouge base areas (Etcheson, 1984: 161). Once sent to the front lines to battle government troops, these youth were isolated from their families, and their dependence on the party thus became complete. The harshness of the war, including saturation bombing of the countryside by U.S. B-52 bombers, had a profound psychological impact on these youth, inuring them to brutality and generating hatred for the members of the urban elite who were orchestrating the destruction of rural Cambodia.[7] It was precisely these young cadres who marched into Phnom Penh in April 1975, ready to carry out the radical policies of the Khmer Rouge leadership.

The history of the Shining Path shares striking similarities to that of the Khmer Rouge, though there are important differences as well. As with the Khmer Rouge, the leadership of the Shining Path was able to initiate its recruitment efforts in a university context. Unlike the Khmer Rouge, however, the Shining Path did not find bases of support solely among the poorest segments of the peasantry. Instead, the movement's most consistent militants were provincial and urban youth with relatively high levels of education but few viable opportunities for upward social mobility.

One of the sad ironies of Peruvian history is that changes that were fundamentally progressive often resulted in heightened social conflict over the long term. Thus, although the Agrarian Reform of 1969 succeeded in eradicating an exploitative class of rural landowners, these same measures undermined investments in Andean agriculture and led to an intensification of the subsistence crisis assailing the central sierra. Similarly, while the reopening of the University of San Cristóbal de Huamanga in the provincial capital of Ayacucho in 1959 brought new educational and professional opportunities to an impoverished region, this same university also became the epicenter of the most violent guerrilla movement in Peru's history.

From 1969 until 1973, the Shining Path dominated key institutions within the University of San Cristóbal. With Guzmán installed as director of university personnel and Díaz Martínez as director of student affairs, the party was able to exercise control over hiring and admissions decisions regarding professors and students. With the partial support of university resources, Shining Path activists began their own outreach programs into the surrounding Andean countryside in the early 1970s, spending long periods of time providing rudimentary medical, teaching, and technical services to impoverished rural inhabitants. In contrast to other leftist factions, which remained encased within urban areas, by the late 1970s, Shining Path militants had dispersed themselves throughout Ayacucho and neighboring provinces, thus extending the influence of the party into rural communities (Degregori, 1990: 184).

In 1976, Guzmán resigned from the University of San Cristóbal and returned to Lima. The Shining Path slowly increased its influence in the capital, especially within the University of San Marcos. As an institution, San Marcos provided a safe haven for radical political activism in the capital, since under the legal autonomy enjoyed by all Peruvian universities, police and military personnel are prohibited from entering the grounds without a warrant. As early as 1965, Maoists had won student elections at San Marcos, and the student body proved receptive to the radical critique of Peruvian society advanced by Shining Path militants in the 1970s (Montoya, 1992).

From their positions within universities in Ayacucho and Lima, Shining Path leaders undertook long-term efforts at recruiting larger numbers of militants. A study by Chávez de Paz (1989), which examined the background of 183 individuals imprisoned in Lima for terrorist acts during the period 1983–1986, provides one snapshot of the social characteristics of these early Shining Path members. According to his findings, 60 percent of those arrested on terrorist charges had been born in the rural provinces. Furthermore, whereas only 7.7 percent of Peru's total population had achieved some university education, a full 35.5 percent of the accused terrorists had attained that educational level or higher. An unusually large number of the prisoners were women, and the educational levels attained by these female accused terrorists were generally much higher (including graduate and postgraduate studies) than those of male accused terrorists or the general Peruvian population (Chávez de Paz, 1989: 34–43).

These findings generally support the conclusion that the Shining Path recruited the majority of its core militants from the ranks of male and female provincial university students. Culturally alienated from their rural communities through their educational experiences, these youth found few avenues for upward social mobility in a society characterized by an enduring economic crisis and persistent racism. By the late 1970s, networks of extremely dedicated militants recruited from this social strata had been established in the regions surrounding Ayacucho, and in the capital of Lima as well. It was this organizational strength that encouraged the Shining Path to begin its armed struggle in 1980, just as Peru was returning to democratic rule.

EXPANSION INTO REGIONAL POLITICAL AND SOCIAL VACUUMS

The final task in this comparative analysis is to describe the expansion of the armed struggles of the Khmer Rouge and the Shining Path. Both guerrilla movements were able to take advantage of political and social vacuums in order to impose military control over wide segments of Cambodia and Peru. While ideologically committed cadres of the Khmer Rouge and the Shining Path proved effective in carrying forward such military struggles, the totalitarian characteristics of each party's revolutionary policies alienated rural and urban populations. Organized civilian resistance in the face of such policies provoked an increasingly violent response from Khmer Rouge and Shining Path cadres, leading to the escalation of terrorism and the eventual weakening of each party's revolutionary projects.

The large-scale bombing of Cambodia carried out by the United States had been designed both to disrupt North Vietnamese supply lines and to prop up a Cambodian state that was faltering in the face of the guerrilla campaign being waged within the country. Rather than reinforce the Cambodian state, however, this massive deployment of military firepower had the unintended consequence of forging what had been a fractured nationalist/communist insurgency into an extremely radical, Khmer Rouge-dominated revolutionary army (Etcheson, 1984: 118). Although backed by massive U.S. financial and military assistance, the Cambodian military was decimated in 1970 and had to withdraw from most of northeastern Cambodia. By 1973, the Cambodian state had essentially disintegrated and its leaders were confined to Phnom Penh, which was itself subjected to repeated attacks by Khmer Rouge forces.

On April 17, 1975, Khmer Rouge forces took control of Phnom Penh. Reports indicate that most party cadres appeared to be under fifteen years of age and were illiterate, and although many technicians and educated urban citizens offered their assistance to the party, such conciliatory advances were rejected by the Khmer Rouge. Armed cadres instead began evacuating Phnom Penh and other cities, so that within two months, between 2 and 3 million people had been forced into the Cambodian countryside.

Once in the countryside, people found themselves in a radically transformed environment dominated by the Khmer Rouge's network of party members and sympathizers. Money was abolished, markets were closed, most personal property was confiscated, and virtually everyone was forced to don the black clothing traditionally worn by peasants. Religious orders, including Buddhism, Islam, and Catholicism, were suppressed, and concerted efforts were made by the Khmer Rouge to dismantle the traditional Cambodian family structure by separating children from their parents and sending relatives to work in different regions. A 1976 party document graphically summarized the central aim of the Khmer Rouge in the following terms:

All the exploiting classes who had previously been beaten down were beaten and cut down again. . . . As for individualism, whether of feudalists, capitalists, or of other classes not particularly poor, such as independent farmers, independent workers, and independent manual laborers, we have dug down and uprooted even more of this in 1976. We won't allow individualism to rise again. (Communist Party of Kampuchea, 1976: 182)

In 1976, the Khmer Rouge leadership inaugurated a four-year plan of economic development that involved the collectivization of all agriculture and the undertaking of massive irrigation projects. Malnutrition increased throughout 1976, however, and by 1977–1978, famine conditions became widespread as poorly planned irrigation systems silted up, agricultural machinery broke down, and Khmer Rouge confiscations of rice supplies intensified. The policies of complete autarky imposed on Democratic Kampuchea by Pol Pot and his key allies led to the rejection of all foreign humanitarian and technical assistance, bringing about the collapse of the country's mechanical infrastructure and an expansion of malaria during this period.

The totalitarian regulations imposed by the Khmer Rouge led hundreds of thousands of Cambodians to seek refuge in neighboring countries, while many who were trapped inside the country attempted to resist Khmer Rouge policies. Dissent and criticism were not tolerated in Democratic Kampuchea, however, and teenage cadres began executing peasants, workers, and intellectuals. Conditions became so extreme that by late 1976, a number of provincial Khmer Rouge leaders came to the conclusion that Pol Pot and his advisors were bringing about the destruction of Democratic Kampuchea, and attempts were apparently made on Pol Pot's life. In response, the hard-line group led by Pol Pot began to carry out internal purges within the Khmer Rouge. As a result, between 1976 and 1978, as many as 20,000 party members were interrogated, tortured, and then killed in Tuol Sleng, a former school in Phnom Penh (Etcheson, 1984: 178). In addition, purges directed against party members in Cambodia's eastern provinces claimed approximately 100,000 lives.

In an apparent attempt by the Khmer Rouge leadership to deflect internal criticism by inciting xenophobic hatred of an old adversary, military raids were initiated against Vietnamese villages in 1977. The attacks eventually provoked a full-scale invasion by the Vietnamese army, however, and an estimated 30,000 Khmer Rouge troops proved no match for the well-equipped Vietnamese forces. By January 1979, the Vietnamese army had surrounded Phnom Penh, forcing Pol Pot to flee by helicopter and bringing about the downfall of the Khmer Rouge regime.

Although a core group of Khmer Rouge leaders and cadres succeeded in imposing their revolutionary agenda on the Cambodian people during the period 1975–1978, the totalitarian nature of such transformations, which in the end led to the death of over a million Cambodians, alienated most of the population and many within the party's own ranks, thus fatally weakening the Khmer Rouge. Interestingly, a similar pattern emerged in many of the rural and urban areas that fell under the influence of the Shining Path of Peru.

The central Andean departments of Ayacucho, Andahuaylas, and Huancavelica were the site of the Shining Path's first extensive military campaigns. Shining Path guerrillas began threatening and killing police, judges, and other government officials in 1980, so that by 1982, many rural regions in the central Andes had been "liberated." Peasant accounts of what transpired in "liberated" villages during this period have been recorded by anthropologists, and such testimonies consistently describe the same general pattern of events.[8] Shining Path militants typically entered villages and, based on their familiarity with specific communities, executed cattle thieves, hacendados, or government officials who were particularly hated by local peasants. Party members also imposed strict codes of behavior on these villages, punishing individuals who drank to excess, committed adultery, or abused family members. This imposition of social order in communities that had suffered long histories of abuse at the hands of local landlords and corrupt officials was initially welcomed, and rural support for the Shining Path grew during the early stages of the party's military campaign.

However, in accordance with its Maoist-inspired guerrilla strategy of surrounding urban areas and strangling them, the Shining Path began closing down peasant markets and prohibiting all commerce between villagers and nearby towns. Such policies generated widespread opposition, but when peasant leaders voiced disagreement, they were accused of being in collaboration with the government and threatened or killed by Shining Path cadres. From 1981 through 1983, increasingly bloody confrontations took place between organized peasants and the Shining Path in the central sierra (Gorriti, 1990: 254).

These early attempts by Andean communities to expel the guerrilla movement were completely subverted by the arrival of the Peruvian military in late 1982. Instead of targeting actual guerrilla cadres, state security forces from the coast proceeded to carry out indiscriminate assaults on the Andean peasantry itself. As a result of this state-sponsored terrorism, the death toll in the Peruvian civil war rose abruptly; whereas in 1982 there were 170 confirmed deaths as a result of political violence, by 1983 this number had risen to 2,807, and it jumped to 4,319 in 1984 (Americas Watch, 1992: 14).

Although the military occupation of Ayacucho and surrounding departments led to the massacre of entire peasant communities and the generation of a large population of displaced persons, it did not halt the expansion of the Shining Path. Guerrillas moved into the strategically important Mantaro Valley in Junin (a key source of hydroelectric power and agricultural products for Lima), and also penetrated deep into the upper Huallaga Valley, a center of Peruvian coca production. By the mid-1980s, electrical power in Lima was regularly disrupted by Shining Path dynamite attacks, and in 1987 the guerrillas dramatized their presence in the Huallaga Valley by launching widespread attacks on police stations and halting traffic on most roads in the jungle region (Gonzáles, 1992: 109).

While the Shining Path's ability to project its military influence into these new regions was certainly impressive, the party's political success at the village level was more qualified. Peasant communities in the Mantaro Valley, which have experienced some economic progress by selling agricultural products in Lima's central markets, have consistently resisted the Shining Path's attempts to sever all commerce with the capital (Kent, 1993). Similarly, attempts by the Shining Path to expand into the southern department of Puno were met with resistance from moderate, progressive political and church organizations, which favored more peaceful forms of protest (Berg, 1992). By the late 1980s, both the Mantaro Valley and the regions surrounding Puno had become the site of intense confrontations between peasants and insurgents, indicating again the deep-seated resistance among wide sectors of the Peruvian lower and middle peasantry to the revolutionary policies that the Shining Path was attempting to impose.

The final front in the Peruvian civil war has been fought in the capital, Lima. Beginning in 1989, the Shining Path dramatically escalated its military actions in the capital, and by 1991 more than half the nation's incidents of political violence were occurring in the city (Kent, 1993: 452). From May to September 1992, the Shining Path conducted a terrorist offensive in Lima that included the regular detonation of large explosive devices, spreading fear throughout the city's civilian population. This deployment of violence, however, concealed underlying weaknesses in the Shining Path's bases of support in the capital. Although the party had generated some sympathy in isolated shantytowns by spearheading a number of land invasions, most of the city's community organizations rejected the violent and dogmatic behavior of Shining Path militants. The fact that the Shining Path had assassinated many of Lima's most respected progressive leaders and killed hundreds of citizens at random in car bomb attacks further undermined urban support for the movement.

Due to its increasingly indiscriminate use of violence in both rural and urban areas, the Shining Path came under attack from peasant and urban groups that might otherwise have formed the social basis for a future expansion in the party's guerrilla war. Instead, as Degregori (1994: 89) noted, by 1993 approximately 300,000 peasants had joined civic defense committees and, armed with an estimated 10,000 rifles provided by the Peruvian military, were engaged in driving Shining Path columns away from their communities. Meanwhile, throughout Lima's shantytowns, neighborhood watch groups have attempted to protect their own activists by expelling Shining Path militants. The September 1992 capture of Abimael Guzmán and most of the Shining Path's Central Committee severely shook an already-fragile guerrilla movement, terminating whatever slim chance the party had of overthrowing the Peruvian state and imposing its unpopular revolutionary agenda.

CONCLUSION

This comparative analysis of the Khmer Rouge and the Shining Path reveals a fundamentally problematic feature of the contemporary world-system. On the one hand, growing numbers of rural and urban youth throughout the periphery face futures of poverty and social dislocation. The disruption of rural subsistence economies, whether as a result of wartime destruction in Cambodia, demographic pressures in Peru, or environmental degradation in many other regions is accelerating, while urban industries continue to prove incapable of providing young men and women with stable employment. The global expansion of educational systems in the postwar era has done little to improve the employment opportunities for youth in peripheral societies, and may instead increase relative levels of frustration and political radicalism.[9]

Although many requisite elements are in place to foster new social upheavals in specific countries in Latin America and throughout the periphery, the experiences of the Shining Path and the Khmer Rouge highlight the destructive paths that can be taken by isolated, sectarian groups in the name of revolution. As world-system theorists have long argued, the constraints imposed by the capitalist world-economy and the rules enforced by advanced industrial states make it exceedingly difficult for individual parties in dependent nations to seize state power and carry out lasting, progressive transformations.[10] When reformist, quasi-socialist regimes such as those of Sihanouk in Cambodia and Velasco in Peru fail to bring about real change, political and ideological spaces are opened for extremist parties that espouse total revolution of one kind or another.

The Shining Path and the Khmer Rouge may represent, therefore, instances of a kind of revolutionary violence that may become increasingly common in peripheral societies. Faced with the collapse of reformist regimes on a global level, segments of the youth of Latin America and the periphery appear to be turning to messianic political or religious movements that claim to offer new alternatives to harsh social realities. The best hope for reducing the danger of the emergence of new revolutionary terrorist movements in such a global context lies in the efforts spearheaded by progressive groups to increase popular participation in decisions made regarding political, economic, and social matters. It may only be through such grassroots campaigns for participatory democracy that the populations most susceptible to extreme political radicalization—the youth of the world who are subjected to unrelenting economic shocks—may be integrated into constructive revolutionary struggles rather than the self-destructive, totalitarian forms of revolutionary terrorism represented by the Shining Path and the Khmer Rouge.

NOTES

I would like to thank Bill Smith, Beverly Silver, Mahua Sarkar, and Dag MacLeod for comments on earlier versions of this chapter. I am especially indebted to Mirella Podobnik for her assistance during my research in Peru and in the following years.

1. A partial list of movements with roughly similar histories would include Renamo of Mozambique, the Naxalite movement of India, and the Tamil Tigers of Sri Lanka.

2. While Wolf (1969: 281) noted the increasing difficulty of contemporary peasant societies in absorbing new generations of youth, and Wickham-Crowley (1992: 29) empirically documented the prevalence of youth in Latin American guerrilla movements during the postwar era, the role of peasant or urban youth in revolutionary struggles remains largely unexamined.

3. My understanding of the structural roots of revolution draws on the work of such theorists as Goldfrank (1979), Paige (1975), Walton (1984), and Wolf (1969).

4. Goodwin and Skocpol's (1994) analysis of the regime types that appear most susceptible to revolutionary overthrow sheds light on the experiences of Cambodia and Peru. Cambodia typifies the neopatrimonial state, which they identify as being most vulnerable, while Peru highlights the greater resiliency of quasidemocratic regimes, even in the face of strong guerrilla uprisings.

5. The most sophisticated of these Khmer Rouge critiques is that of Samphan (1959).

6. See Díaz Martínez (1985) for the Shining Path's interpretation of Peru's developmental problems.

7. While crucially important in explaining the viciousness of Khmer Rouge cadre, the experience of being subjected to sustained aerial bombardment must be seen as only one of the necessary conditions that produced the revolutionary terrorist movement in Cambodia. The inhabitants of Laos, after all, were subjected to a higher per-capita level of bombing than were their Cambodian neighbors, but the Pathet Lao, who took power in 1975, manifested few of the totalitarian characteristics of the Khmer Rouge. A more detailed comparison of the Khmer Rouge and the Pathet Lao remains to be carried out.

8. See Isbell (1992), Manrique (1990), and Smith (1992) for particularly good descriptions of Shining Path behavior in peasant communities.

9. John Meyer and Michael Hannan (1979) have documented the expansion of global education systems.

10. See the volume edited by Boswell (1989) for an introduction to a world-systems approach to understanding revolutions.

REFERENCES

Americas Watch. 1992. *Peru under Fire: Human Rights since the Return to Democracy.* New Haven, CT: Yale University Press.

Banister, Judith, and Paige Johnson. 1993. "After the Nightmare: The Population of Cambodia." In *Genocide and Democracy in Cambodia*, ed. Ben Kiernan, pp. 65–139. New Haven, CT: Yale University, Southeast Asia Studies Program.

Berg, Ronald. 1992. "Peasant Responses to Shining Path in Andahuaylas." In *The Shining Path of Peru*, ed. David Scott Palmer, pp. 83–104. New York: St. Martin's Press.

Boswell, Terry, ed. 1989. *Revolution in the World-System.* Westport, CT: Greenwood Press.

Burgler, Roeland. 1990. *The Eyes of the Pineapple: Revolutionary Intellectuals and Terror in Democratic Kampuchea.* Saarbrucken, Germany: Verlag Breitenbach Publishers.

Chandler, David. 1991. *The Tragedy of Cambodian History: Politics, War, and Revolution Since 1945.* New Haven, CT: Yale University Press.

Chávez de Paz, Dennis. 1989. *Juventud y terrorismo: Características sociales de los condenados por terrorismo y otros delitos.* Lima, Peru: Instituto de Estudios Peruanos.

Communist Party of Kampuchea. 1976. "Report of Activities of the Party Center According to the General Political Tasks of 1976." Translated and reprinted in *Pol Pot Plans the Future: Confidential Leadership Documents from Democratic Kampuchea, 1976–1977*, ed. David Chandler, Ben Kiernan, and Chanthou Boua, pp. 177–212. New Haven, CT: Yale University Southeast Asia Studies.

Cotler, Julio. 1986. "The Political Radicalization of Working-Class Youth in Peru." *CEPAL Review* 29: 107–118.

Degregori, Carlos. 1990. *Ayacucho 1969–1979: El surgimiento de Sendero Luminoso.* Lima: Instituto de Estudios Peruanos.

———. 1994. "Shining Path and Counterinsurgency Strategy since the Arrest of Abimael Guzmán.'' In *Peru in Crisis: Dictatorship or Democracy?* ed. Joseph Tulchin and Gary Bland, pp. 81–100. Boulder, CO: Lynne Rienner Publishers.

Díaz Martínez, Antonio. [1965] 1985. *Ayacucho: Hambre y esperanza.* Reprint. Lima: Mosca Azúl Editores.

Etcheson, Craig. 1984. *The Rise and Demise of Democratic Kampuchea.* Boulder, CO: Westview Press.

Frieson, Kate. 1993. ''Revolution and Rural Response in Cambodia, 1970–1975.'' In *Genocide and Democracy in Cambodia,* ed. Ben Kiernan, pp. 33–50. New Haven, CT: Yale University, Southeast Asia Studies Program.

García-Sayán, Diego. 1982. *Tomas de tierras en el Peru.* Lima: Centro de Estudias y Promoción del Desarrollo.

Goldfrank, Walter. 1979. ''Theories of Revolution and Revolution without Theory: The Case of Mexico.'' *Theory and Society* 7, 1 (January–May): 135–165.

Gonzáles, José. 1992. ''Guerrillas and Coca in the Upper Huallaga Valley.'' In *The Shining Path of Peru,* ed. David Scott Palmer, pp. 105–125. New York: St. Martin's Press.

Goodwin, Jeff, and Theda Skocpol. 1994. ''Explaining Revolutions in the Contemporary Third World.'' In *Social Revolutions in the Modern World,* ed. Theda Skocpol, pp. 259–278. Cambridge: Cambridge University Press.

Gorriti, Gustavo. 1990. *Sendero: Historia de la guerra milenaria en el Peru.* Lima: Editorial Apoyo.

Isbell, Billie. 1992. ''Shining Path and Peasant Responses in Rural Ayacucho.'' In *The Shining Path of Peru,* ed. David Scott Palmer, pp. 59–81. New York: St. Martin's Press.

Kent, Robert. 1993. ''Geographical Dimensions of the Shining Path Insurgency in Peru.'' *Geographical Review* 83, 4 (October): 441–454.

Kiernan, Ben. 1982. ''Introduction.'' In *Peasants and Politics in Kampuchea, 1942–1981,* ed. Ben Kiernan and Chanthou Boua, pp. 1–28. New York: M. E. Sharpe.

Manrique, Nelson. 1990. ''Formas de acción de sendero y su relación con el campesinado.'' In *Las condiciones de la violencia en Peru y Bolivia,* ed. Heidulf Schmidt and Carlos Toranzo, pp. 75–87. La Paz: ILDIS.

Markusen, Eric. 1992. ''Comprehending the Cambodian Genocide: An Application of Robert Jay Lifton's Model of Genocidal Killing.'' *Psychohistory Review* 20, 2 (Winter): 145–169.

Meyer, John, and Michael Hannan, eds. 1979. *National Development and the World System: Educational, Economic, and Political Change, 1950–1970.* Chicago: University of Chicago Press.

Montoya, Luis. 1992. *El lado oscuro de la luna: Las percepciones de los jóvenes en los 70 y 90.* Lima: Centro de Estudios y Promoción del Desarrollo.

Paige, Jeffery. 1975. *Agrarian Revolution: Social Movements and Export Agriculture in the Underdeveloped World.* New York: Free Press.

Peruvian Communist Party (Shining Path). 1982. ''Desarrollemos la guerra de guerrillos!'' Clandestine mimeograph.

Samphan, Khieu. [1959]. *Cambodia's Economy and Industrial Development.* Reprint and translation. Ithaca, NY: Cornell University, Southeast Asia Program, Department of Asian Studies.

Slater, David. 1989. *Territory and State Power in Latin America: The Peruvian Case.* London: Macmillan.

Smith, Michael. 1992. "Taking the High Ground: Shining Path and the Andes." In *The Shining Path of Peru*, ed. David Scott Palmer, pp. 15–32. New York: St. Martin's Press.

Stein, Steve, and Carlos Monge. 1988. *La crisis del estado patrimonial en el Perú*. Lima, Peru: Instituto de Estudios Peruanos.

Walton, John. 1984. *Reluctant Rebels: Comparative Studies of Revolution and Underdevelopment*. New York: Columbia University Press.

Wickham-Crowley, Timothy. 1992. *Guerrillas and Revolution in Latin America: A Comparative Study of Insurgents and Regimes since 1956*. Princeton, NJ: Princeton University Press.

Wolf, Eric. 1969. *Peasant Wars of the Twentieth Century*. New York: Harper and Row.

10

GLOBAL RESTRUCTURING AND THE
ENVIRONMENT IN LATIN AMERICA

J. Timmons Roberts

> Controversy over development of heavy oil reserves in Ecuador's Oriente
> rain forests has escalated to the point where environmentalist and native
> groups have routinely picketed company offices in Quito, Ecuador's capital,
> and used mass fund raiser mailings in North America. Other major industry/
> environment conflicts are taking shape in Brazil and Peru, and in Venezuela
> the state oil company has initiated the kind of broad environmental initia-
> tives usually seen among U.S. and European multinational petroleum firms.
>
> Oil and Gas Journal (July 6, 1992: 46)

> I don't think we can afford to have the [nature] reserve anymore—we need
> jobs. We're a third-world country with first-world environmental laws.
>
> Carlos Estrada, Mexican Land Developer, 1995

As Latin America turns from strongly protected and state-regulated economies
to economies more open to market forces, are environmental conditions likely
to improve or decline? Can the impacts of increasing export production be mit-
igated by the growing number of international treaties and business initiatives
concerning the environment? What forces generate pressure to protect the environment in Latin America, and how durable and significant are they?

The goal of this chapter is to introduce Latin American environmental questions to world-systems scholars and to incorporate the insights of the world-
system perspective in our understanding of environmental problems in the
region. While globally, a virtual consensus is emerging that assessments of national development cannot ignore issues of ecological sustainability, writings in
the world-system tradition have remained nearly silent on issues of the natural
environment (see Smith, 1993; Grimes, Roberts, and Manale, 1993; Chew,

1995). Quite simply, we cannot understand Latin America's place in the world-economy without examining what has too long been treated as an externality by neoclassical and Marxian economic analysis alike: the environment (Bunker, 1985).

In spite of this silence, the world-system perspective has significant potential to provide insights into the interaction between national actors and the international forces implicated in environmental issues. For example, world-systems research has focused on how ties to the world-economy—through historical patterns of colonial conquest, productive investments, and external debt, to name a few—influence national class structures, social movements and types and levels of government repression. Grimes, Roberts, and Manale (1993) have argued that, therefore, a nation's links to the world-economy have critical implications for its environment and for the likely success of environmental social movements.

Some environmental impacts are characteristic of countries at one position in the global stratification (core, semiperiphery and periphery) and others of countries moving up or down in the hierarchy.[1] In simple terms, the pollution of poverty is different than the pollution of affluence, as was pointedly remarked at the United Nations Conference on the Environment, held in Stockholm, Sweden, nearly a quarter century ago. Of course, many factors are operating to subtly influence the relationship between position in the international system and environmental degradation, such as efficiency of production, level of infrastructure, internal political struggles, and norms of consumption, all of which vary with global region and culture. My intent here is to examine how changes in national links to the world-economy and world-system influence the direction of environmental conditions in the Latin American periphery and semiperiphery.

Latin America is taken here in its broadest sense, including Caribbean nations as well as those countries south of the United States without Iberian origins. This region is tremendously diverse in cultural and ecological terms; in world-system terms, it ranges from lower periphery (Haiti) to upper semiperiphery (Argentina, Venezuela, Brazil, Mexico). As the next section describes, environmental issues vary tremendously by country, but overall, conditions are serious and deteriorating throughout the region. How can we account for those differences and predict the direction of environmental conditions with respect to current changes in the world-system?

To assess the influence of international forces on environmental conditions in Latin America, we need to analyze trends in three separate areas as well as the effects of their convergence: the shift to export-oriented strategies of growth, the internationalization of the environmental movement, and the internationalization of environmental regulation.

First, quite apart from the widespread devastation to the environment associated with import-substitution industrialization (ISI), Latin American countries have turned from inward-focused development strategies to policies of free trade and export promotion as a consequence of oil shocks, massive external debt, and persistent economic crises. In order to minimize imports, countries often continued to employ inefficient, domestically produced technologies long after "cleaner-tech" versions were available elsewhere. Pollution controls and impact statements were often neglected in pursuing projects of national development. Subsidized energy prices were kept so low that they eventually favored terrible inefficiencies (World Bank, 1992). ISI policies were also heavily urban biased, and they left a legacy of poverty, deforestation, and soil erosion in the rural environment.[2] However, much the same can be said for the effects of export projects in the region during the postwar period, as well as many current export initiatives.

Throughout Latin America, plantation agriculture designed for export often forced peasants out of fertile lowlands onto more marginal soils or into cities. The region became attractive as a site for core-based firms wishing to avoid labor and environmental regulations and penetrate new markets. Environmentalists have increasingly tied foreign direct investment (FDI) to air pollution, toxic contamination, and worker exposure throughout the region. They have also criticized chemically intense agriculture; sloppy oil extraction, mining, lumbering and ranching projects; and highly polluting factories in the region's cities and across the *maquiladora* belt along the U.S.-Mexican border.[3] Export initiatives often require the exploitation of resources in the national hinterlands, and this, in turn, requires infrastructure such as roads, highways, and railroads. These "rainforest corridors" frequently bring lumberers, miners, ranchers, and squatters along their penetration routes.[4]

With this in mind, it can be said that in the post-ISI era, Latin America's relationship with the world-economy is becoming both more intense and more complex. Some countries have diversified their export profiles to include "nontraditional" products, but small nations have been far less able to substitute manufactured imports, and most countries continue to be dependent on a fairly narrow range of "traditional" exports such as coffee, bananas, cacao, oil, and minerals.[5] The region's economies (with a few exceptions) have grown in absolute terms over the last fifteen years, albeit sporadically. While a point may be reached at which Latin American countries can afford greater pollution controls, it appears that for most nations, economic growth will pose a multitude of urgent environmental problems.[6] Several authors also argue that increasing openness to trade is likely to intensify precisely the *type* of growth that is driven by foreign productive technologies and brings with it unsustainable imported consumption values (e.g., Serbin, De Lisio, and Ortiz, 1993; Barkin, 1995).

To consider only economic forces, however, would be to miss what I will argue is the main engine driving environmental initiatives of all types in Latin America: the internationalization of the environmental movement. Nongovernmental organizations (NGOs) dedicated to environmental causes mushroomed in number and in size during the years leading up to the UN 1992 Conference on Environment and Development in Rio de Janeiro (also known as UNCED, the Earth Summit, or EcoRio). The official and unofficial meetings that took place at the conference brought together representatives of hundreds of countries and thousands of nongovernmental organizations. Across the region, and around the world, the movement has sagged somewhat since Rio, and the significance and permanence of its accomplishments remain an open question. However, most observers believe that the event, as well as the proliferation and growth of electronic networks (such as ECONET, BIODIV-L, and ELAN), have helped "globalize" the environmental movement by allowing NGOs of many types to interact and build communications and support networks. There is little doubt that overall, internationalization has strengthened the position of many Latin American environmental movements by providing them new leverage vis-à-vis the transnational corporations and their own states. Besides examining the potential of the international environmental movement to react effectively to the restructuring of capital, we need to examine how global connections between environmental NGOs affect the direction and durability of the "green" movement in Latin America.

Finally, we cannot ignore the growing number of international environmental agreements that have been advanced, on their own and also in conjunction with the explosion of free-trade agreements, both in the region and around the world. Thirty years of major environmental treaties include the Montreal Protocol on chlorofluorocarbon (CFC) emissions, the CITES treaty on the endangered species trade, and the UN Framework Convention on Climate Change. Each of these treaties has important implications for economic growth in noncore countries and raises specific environmental enforcement problems for Latin American states. Their impact is unclear: while signing an environmental treaty certainly can be no more than an empty promise, efforts for their enforcement are gaining strength. Ironically, more may be at stake in economic integration treaties such as the North American Free Trade Agreement (NAFTA), the General Agreement on Tariffs and Trade (GATT), the Caribbean Basin Initiative, MERCOSUR, and the Pact of the Americas. Environmental issues constantly arise during these negotiations. World-systems research must consider whether these political initiatives, in combination with those begun by the business community itself in response to demand for "green" products, have the potential to create global environmental standards that could establish limits on capital's attempts to flee regulation.

In attempting to gauge the interaction of these three currents, this chapter first reviews the origins and scope of environmental problems in Latin America. It then examines the role of Latin American public opinion concerning environmental questions and the strength and direction of environmental movements in the region. Finally, the chapter analyzes environmental treaties, side agreements to trade treaties, and industrial initiatives. Because its scope is so wide, this chapter constitutes, by necessity, an exploratory effort at synthesizing the environmental impacts of a diverse set of globalizing influences.[7] The task has elements of crystal ball gazing: with Latin American development paths, environmental social movements, and global agreements on the environment changing so rapidly, we can use current and past trends only to project possible future scenarios. The picture that emerges is of a world-economy and state system exerting complex, and often contradictory, pressures on the environment and environmental social movements in Latin America.

THE SCOPE OF ENVIRONMENTAL PROBLEMS IN LATIN AMERICA

The environment in Latin America is beset by a series of dire threats, although there is little agreement on which issues are most important. Popular concern from outside the region has focused almost entirely on the destruction of the rainforest, especially the Amazon.[8] Common local concerns focus on more immediate hazards to human health, such as sewage treatment and urban air and water pollution (Roberts, 1994; Keck, 1995).

The acuteness of these urban environmental problems is reflected in emergencies leading to driving bans and the closure of factories on days with high pollution inversion in Mexico City, São Paulo, Santiago, Bogotá, and Caracas (World Health Organization and UN Environment Program, 1992). Comparative urban air-pollution data is not available outside these cities, but estimates of per capita emissions of carbon dioxide (presented in Table 10.1) demonstrate that Trinidad, Venezuela, Suriname, Mexico, and Argentina are the biggest emitters in Latin America relative to their populations.

The recent cholera epidemic affecting Peru, Ecuador, Colombia, and Brazil drew attention to the fact that sewage treatment and safe drinking water are currently the exception rather than the norm in the region. For example, in São Paulo, the continent's most powerful industrial center (with more than 15 million people and over a quarter of Brazil's entire gross national product), more than 80 percent of the population lacks sewage treatment.[9] The situation is similar or worse in most other Latin American cities; across the region 20 to 80 percent of national populations officially lacked sewage treatment in 1990.[10]

Many chemicals banned long ago in the United States continue to be used in the region, some of which are exported from the United States itself or produced by U.S. firms in Latin America. Poor training and equipment for handling toxic chemicals are responsible for dangerous exposures to humans and the environment in industry and agriculture throughout the region. This is reported to be especially true in export agriculture and in assembly and chemical factories, such as in the *maquiladora* belt along the U.S.-Mexico border.

Land degradation is severe, especially of the marginally arid and hilly farming and grazing lands, and particularly in Mexico and Central America. The Sonoran, Patagonian, and Atacama deserts are at risk of spreading due to continued unsustainable land use, and the northeast of Brazil is in a severe and extended drought (World Wildlife Federation, 1990: 54–55). Most countries have over half their land classified by Conservation International and the World Resources Institute as "disturbed by human action." Recent reports are that 40 percent of

Table 10.1
Indicators of Environmental Policies and Conditions in the Americas

Country	(1) % w/ Sanit- ation Urban 1990	(2) % w/ Sanit- ation Rural 1990	(3) Fossil Fuel CO$_2$ per capita 1991	(4) Defor- estation Rate 1981-90	(5) % Land w/medium or high disturb. 1993	(6) # Env'l treaties signed (of 9) 1963-89	(7) % CITES treaty require- ments met 1990	(8) % of Land in Pro- tected Areas 1993
Argentina	100	29	3.6	..	64	4	82	3.4
Belize	76	22	1.4	0.2	64	..	55	12.7
Bolivia	38	14	0.8	1.1	22	3	62	8.4
Brazil	84	32	1.4	0.6	33	5	41	3.3
Canada	..	..	15.2	..	7	7	100	5.0
Chile	100	6	2.4	..	44	6	65	18.1
Colombia	84	18	1.8	0.6	33	4	64	8.2
Costa Rica	100	93	1.1	2.6	88	4	76	12.1
Cuba	100	68	3.2	0.9	98	2	50	8.1
Dom. Republic	95	75	0.8	2.5	82	4	80	21.5
Ecuador	56	38	1.6	1.7	53	3	76	39.3
El Salvador	85	38	0.5	2.1	100	1	20	0.9
Guatemala	44	17	0.4	1.6	75	6	83	7.6
Guyana	97	81	1.1	..	2	1	53	0.3
Haiti	44	17	0.1	3.9	95	1	na	0.3
Honduras	89	42	0.4	1.9	68	4	29	4.8
Jamaica	14	..	1.9	5.3	100	1	na	0.1
Mexico	85	12	3.9	1.2	77	6	100	5.1
Nicaragua	32	..	0.6	1.7	68	3	80	7.3
Panama	100	68	1.5	1.7	..	8	86	17.2
Paraguay	31	60	0.4	2.4	16	3	60	3.6
Peru	76	20	0.9	0.4	40	5	59	3.2
Suriname	64	36	4.7	0.1	9	5	100	4.5
Trin. & Tobago	100	92	14.7	1.9	50	4	67	3.4
United States	..	..	19.5	0.1	75	8	88	10.5
Uruguay	60	65	1.4	..	100	6	59	0.2
Venezuela	97	72	6.2	1.2	100	5	79	30.2

Sources: sewage disposal: World Resources Institute (WRI) (1994). Note that definitions may vary (some include pit toilets, others only flush toilets); CO2 per capita: WRI (1994); deforestation and levels of human disturbance: WRI (1994: 307, 319); environmental treaties: Dietz and Kalof (1992: 360); CITES treaty (trade in endangered species) requirements met: WRI (1994: 327); protected areas: WRI (1994: 317).

the land in Central America and Mexico has seen its productivity reduced by erosion; this figure reaches a frightening 77 percent in the case of El Salvador.[11] Coastal pollution and the destruction of mangroves and reefs are less well known problems, which carry critical ramifications for the ecology and for the fishing and tourism industries.

Finally, deforestation and other habitat loss has wiped out about 70 percent of Central America's rain forests and almost 93 percent of Brazil's Atlantic Coast forest. Small remnant forests in Trinidad, Jamaica, Haiti, Costa Rica, the Dominican Republic, and Paraguay are disappearing rapidly (Rudel and Roper, 1994). Meanwhile, some of the rain forest areas were, until recently, considered relatively "safe" with respect to deforestation, due to their size or inaccessibility. However, the most recent estimates for the Amazon region (both in Brazil and in the other eight countries that contain Amazon forests) show continuing deforestation, although about 80 to 90 percent remains uncleared overall (Skole and Tucker, 1993; Kasa, 1993). As South and East Asian countries deplete their supplies of lumber, they have increased their reliance on Latin American suppliers. Reports are now coming out of the Guyanas (Suriname, French Guiana, and Guyana) of huge lumber concessions to Korean, Indonesian, and Malaysian companies (Linden, 1995). Timber deals involving exports have also been reported in Nicaragua, Panama, Honduras, Guatemala, and Peru. Assuming that 5 million species inhabit the tropical moist forests of the world (the majority of which are in Latin America), E. O. Wilson (1988) estimated that 17,500 species are being driven to extinction each year by deforestation.

War, poverty, and the increasing concentration of landholdings have combined to drive refugees and profiteers into the region's remaining wild lands to farm, lumber, grow and smuggle coca, drill for oil, and pan for gold (Faber, 1993; Butler, 1985; Hecht and Cockburn, 1990). Indigenous populations have suffered these incursions in the form of disease, degraded environments, and cultural loss. Because of peoples' desperation and the difficulty of policing, areas that are officially "protected" in national, indigenous, or extractive reserves are often nothing but "paper parks."[12] On average, about 8 percent of the land in Latin American countries is now officially "protected" in parks and other reserved areas. National variation is great, however: while Belize, Costa Rica, Dominican Republic, Panama, Chile, Venezuela, and Ecuador have over 10 percent of their land in protected areas, Jamaica, Uruguay, Haiti, Guyana, and El Salvador have protected less than 1 percent.

Tracing the roots of all these environmental problems in Latin America is beyond the scope of this chapter (see Hajek, 1991; Maguire and Brown, 1986), but some points can be made. Latin America's incorporation into the world-system was essentially in the role of an extractive periphery (Bunker, 1985; Cardoso and Faletto, 1979). As such, the region's mineral and agricultural resources have been devastated for centuries by colonial and, later, neocolonial powers. While a few parts of the region were settled in earnest, others were considered only temporary stopping places from which to make one's fortune and return to the homeland. Often, the export of its natural resources left precious little by way of an integrated social infrastructure capable of absorbing the impact of subsequent waves of capital expansion, extraction, and contraction (Wolf and Hansen, 1972; Bunker, 1985). Concern was seldom paid to the sustainability of production under such conditions.

Twentieth-century efforts by Latin American states to integrate their national territories and substitute imports with locally made products were precisely attempts to break with the negative pattern typical of extractive peripheries. In order to accumulate sufficient capital to fund these efforts, many countries adopted state-led strategies and borrowed heavily from overseas. Large loans from foreign banks and multilateral agencies, such as the International Monetary Fund (IMF) and the World Bank often went to fund development mega-projects. One dramatic example of the relation between mega-projects and debt was the massive Itaipú Dam in Brazil, which cost that nation U.S. $20 billion, one-fifth of its foreign debt at the time (Green, 1991). Mega-projects have also included airports, highways, industries, and mining, colonization, agribusiness, and ranching projects. Many of these projects have combined an export orientation with essentially ISI objectives such as opening bottlenecks in national infrastructure or heavy industry.

Poverty and economic crisis, worsened by the pressure of debt-service payments, have certainly sharpened the logic of searching for quick export commodities that may ultimately damage the environment. Mega-projects are easy to begin, but because weak states have extreme difficulty in enforcing environmental regulations, environmental and social calamities may spin out of control.[13] Many mega-projects have had devastating environmental consequences, and some have been strongly criticized for their questionable benefits for human welfare. Corruption as well as class and urban biases have been widely reported, and many externally financed mega-projects are thought to have benefited mainly political elites and well-connected government subcontractors. The complexity of environmental enforcement for such mega-projects is shown by the Brazilian case: environmental impact analysis was formally adopted by the nation in 1986, but the biggest projects, with the greatest potential environmental impacts, are government directed, and the government exempts itself from preparing environmental impact statements. Strong political pressure from environmentalists has been necessary for any credible impact analyses to be carried out.

ENVIRONMENTAL SOCIAL MOVEMENTS: THEIR SUPPORT AND LINKAGES

The impact of export-led development strategies on Latin America's environment will depend substantially on the extent to which its citizens express opinions and mobilize in favor of environmental causes. The shape, strategy, and direction of environmental movements depend, in turn, on their class makeup and their relations with national elites and international environmentalists.

Environmental social movements in core nations have often been characterized as elitist, and while support for environmental causes crosses class lines, activists in the mainstream groups tend to be highly educated, urban, and of above-average income (Morrison and Dunlap, 1986).[14] While Leff (1986) pointed out the complexity of the environmental movement in Latin America and its potential to bridge social strata, Viola's (1992) research has suggested that Brazilian environmental activists tend to be urban professionals.[15] The groups are well connected with universities, government agencies, policy networks, and international financial institutions. Highly educated technicians and administrators are leading these advocacy and research organizations, increasingly making the movement a professional one.[16] Supporting this view is a recent poll in Brazil showing that the degree of interest in the environment "increases proportionally to education and family income" (MAST/CNPq, 1992: 5).

How widespread is environmental concern in the broader populations of Latin America? Cross-national research on environmental concern and participation in environmental groups has been scarce, but the Gallup Institute's 1992 "Health of the Planet Survey" asked a series of questions to national samples in 24 nations, including Mexico, Brazil, Chile, and Uruguay (cited in Dunlap, Gallup, and Gallup, 1993). Over the 1990–1993 period, the World Values Survey asked a consistent battery of questions to national samples in 43 nations, including the same Latin American countries as the Dunlap/Gallup study (except that Uruguay was replaced by Argentina) (Ingelhart, 1995). Both studies are biased in favor of the countries in the region with the highest world-system positions, but they provide the only existing cross-national data. The surveys show that approval of the environmental movement and concern about the environment both reach levels that are, in some places, even *higher* than in core countries. This is especially true for local environmental issues such as air and water pollution. According to the Dunlap/Gallup poll, the most serious local issue for respondents in all four countries was inadequate sewage treatment. In this poll, concern over global issues was at a level similar to that for the core countries.

There is also some evidence that a majority of citizens in these semiperipheral countries might value environmental protection over economic gain. Given the choice between placing a priority *either* on protecting the environment *or* promoting economic growth, 64 percent of Chileans and Uruguayans and 71 percent of Mexicans and Brazilians chose protecting the environment, at levels *higher* than found in the United States (Dunlap, Gallup, and Gallup, 1993). Over half of respondents in each country said they were "willing to pay higher prices to protect the environment."[17] Rates of reported "green consumerism" (that is, avoiding certain products that harm the environment) were low in the region, however, and the percent of the population saying they were active in environmental groups varied from 4 percent in Brazil to 10 percent in Chile (one of the world's highest rates).[18] While these polls must be taken extremely cautiously, they do show why environmental NGOs in Brazil have grown in number from just 2 groups in 1971 and about 40 in 1980 and over 1,000 in 1992 (Viola, 1992; Movimento Ecológico Mater Natura, 1992; Landim, 1992). Other nations have seen substantial, albeit less spectacular, rates of growth; in particular, Costa Rica and Ecuador have especially strong environmental movements.

Some grassroots groups, such as those made up of rubber tappers, small farmers, and shantytown dwellers, have also taken up environmental causes. These groups differ in their approach and interests from mainstream environmental groups in much the same ways as U.S. grassroots and environmental justice groups differ from the big national groups such as the Sierra Club: they tend to be interested more in health, social justice, and/or economic welfare issues rather than habitat preservation (Bullard and Wright, 1992; Freudenberg and Steinsapir, 1992). These grassroots groups also often prefer direct action, such as protests and education campaigns, rather than lobbying and legal work. These findings are supported by a 1992 survey by the Brazilian Institute for Public Opinion Research (IBOPE), which found that overall levels of *interest* in environmental issues did not vary significantly by class or education (although profiles of public supporters and activists did tend to differ). The IBOPE survey found that less-educated respondents are more practical and interested in the conservation of local resources, while higher education people are "more idealistic" and interested in national and international environmental issues (Pedro Leitão, interview, June 22, 1993).

Environmental NGOs in Latin America share a common problem. In North America and Europe, hundreds of thousands of dues-paying members provide independence, power, and legitimacy to their environmental leaders, but in Latin America there is a smaller potential constituency of dues-paying members. While the World Wildlife Fund in Britain has 1,200,000 members, each donating varying amounts, a nationwide publicity campaign by Brazil's largest group, S.O.S. Mata Atlántica, only recruited 1,000 new members (although this represented a doubling of the membership, to 2,000).[19] The World Wildlife Fund in Brazil itself has virtually no dues-paying members in the sense of U.S. or European groups.

Thus, Latin American NGOs are forced to look for other sources of funding, primarily from international groups, corporate sponsors, or government contracts (Roberts, 1994). Each option opens new doors at the cost of a certain loss in autonomy (Viola, 1992: 62–63). An undeniable result of the UNCED conference was the massive presence of NGOs at official and unofficial parallel events. When these links involve money, they have sometimes obliged Latin American groups to focus on issues distant from their own priorities, for example, species or habitat preservation instead of urban pollution and the environmental effects of poverty. In short, due to their greater dependence on overseas funding, some Latin American environmental groups may be forced to focus on preserving large, "charismatic" species that sell calendars and bring in pledge money in the United States and Europe.

"The whole world is watching" is a common cry of protest movements, and with the expansion of electronic networks (which include both Latin American and northern environmentalists, academics, and journalists), this is increasingly true. Action alerts have been disseminated across Internet services such as ECONET and the Environment in Latin America Network on pressing environmental issues from the Ecuadoran Amazon and the Galapagos to Mexico's southern and northern border regions, as well as in Guatemala, Costa Rica, Venezuela, and Brazil. Usually these alerts call for letter writing, phone calls, and other forms of outside pressure on corporations, funding agencies, and Latin American states to protect the environment. Their success at generating this pressure has not been studied, but even the circulation of information often prevents a state from so easily committing environmentally and socially degrading actions.

The effect of the exchange of information between Latin American environmentalists and their colleagues in the core can be seen in two examples from the Brazilian Amazon, both of which were pivotal in redirecting the lending strategy of the World Bank. First, a photograph of the western Amazon taken one evening from the U.S. space shuttle showed over 5,000 fires. That photo covered an area of the state of Rondônia, where a huge colonization project funded by the World Bank and Inter-American Development Bank, called Polonoroeste, was underway. In 1985, after a public outcry and a campaign by environmentalists to stop the project, the World Bank halted money for the project, the first time it had ever done so for environmental reasons.

A second example is the huge Carajás project. With the help of the World Bank, the Brazilian state planned to turn the massive Carajás iron deposits in the eastern Amazon into an immense regional development project (Bunker, 1989). The most controversial part of the plan involved 22 pig-iron factories that were to run on charcoal from the native rainforest (Anderson, 1990). In fighting the projects, international environmentalists worked with local groups, such as peasant leagues and indigenous peoples, to focus attention on the international press, the United States Congress, and other lenders such as the European Economic Community (EEC) and the Inter-American Development Bank. Hearing of the potential devastation through pressure from environmentalists, who dubbed the Carajás project potentially one of the world's five worst ever, the EEC boycotted Carajás iron and the World Bank issued warnings about future funding for Brazil. Later, after the struggles with Chico Mendes's group of rubber tappers and peasant farmers, funds for the paving of a critical highway in Acre were also suspended several times.

Battles over a number of projects related to the Carajás complex still continue, but since 1985, the environmental evaluation components of these loans have pressured Latin American states to more actively enforce *some* environmental laws and even to expand their areas under preservation (Gross, 1990).[20] The continuing importance of the environment to the international banks remains clear in the 1990s. For example, the U.S. deputy assistant secretary for inter-American affairs reported that the United States has encouraged multilateral lenders to increase their focus on the environment (Gelbard, 1992). As an indicator of change in what is now the world's largest creditor nation, the Japan Development Bank has begun "directing its efforts toward solving worldwide environmental problems" (Amano, 1993: 20). Whether bank pressures inspire genuine efforts or empty gestures merely "for the English to see" (as the Brazilian saying goes) is hotly debated. This tension—between the appearance of protection and actual action—was revealed in a statement about the Amazon by Brazil's president, Fernando Henrique Cardoso, shortly after he assumed office in 1995. Cardoso observed that Brazil would not be able to obtain low-cost loans from such sources as the World Bank "if we don't have a sense that we are responsible before the rest of mankind for preserving nature, for preserving indigenous culture" (Reuters News Service, March 31, 1995).

Outside pressure over environmental issues provoked a sometimes-strident nationalist backlash in Latin America. For a long time, Brazil's government claimed that outside pressure was part of a plot to keep Brazil from becoming a developed country.[21] These backlashes typically come from the political right, business interests, and militaries of Latin America, but they often gain the support of much wider segments of the population. Such appeals invoke sentiments of national sovereignty and reveal a weakness in externally imposed and top-down environmental regulations and activism, such as their external cash dependency and heavy reliance on (and pressure from) outside funding and regulatory agencies.

In sum, then, public opinion appears to have "greened" significantly in those Latin American nations for which survey data is available. The region's many environmental groups have made significant advances, but many remain tied to, and dependent on, northern environmental groups. These ties provide leverage that local groups can use in their battles with their states and with transnational corporations. Their links provide leverage, of course, only to the extent that they represent the genuine threat of poor publicity for governments and firms, which depends directly on the extent to which they can generate mobilization in the wealthier nations. Their ability to mobilize those letters, phone calls, protests, and boycotts in the North will generally be limited to issues that inspire Northerners. This circuitous route of pressuring Latin American states and high-polluting transnational firms, however, does not provide much leverage over national firms (especially those that do not export to the core).

INTERNATIONAL AGREEMENTS AND INITIATIVES

Beyond considering economic restructuring and the expansion of the role of environmental NGOs, when assessing the influence of international forces on environmental conditions in Latin America we must consider the effects of treaties and other types of multinational agreements. What explains the rapid proliferation of these accords? Do these pacts have the potential to create globally standardized environmental regulations, eliminating disparities and thereby modifying the trajectories of capital movements?

Four types of international environmental agreements must be examined: binational agreements, multilateral treaties, side agreements to trade pacts, and industry's own initiatives to create "green" standards. Binational agreements tend to be limited in scope, attempting to resolve disputes such as transboundary air or water pollutants between neighboring countries. However, they have often provided frameworks for the initial discussion of issues that later are incorporated into wider, regional pacts. Multilateral environmental treaties such as those on ozone protection, climate change, endangered species, and nuclear testing attempt to create a consensus among the largest possible number of nations on issues considered most critical to humanity's collective survival. Since so many environmental issues are global in scope (Stern, Young, and Druckman, 1992), solving them requires that a majority of nations sign. While these treaties are normally proposed and drafted by core nations, Third World nations have some bargaining power since they can threaten to deny drafters the consensus they see as necessary for their success (Miller, 1995a, 1995b).

Latin American nations vary tremendously in their level of participation in environmental treaties such as those just mentioned.[22] Of the nine major global treaties negotiated over the 1963–1987 period, Haiti, Guyana, El Salvador, and Jamaica had signed only one of the nine treaties by 1992, while Panama, Guatemala, Chile, Mexico, and Uruguay signed six or more, with the other nations falling in between (see Table 10.1).[23] Elsewhere I have reported that worldwide, there is a strong positive relation between a country's position in the world-system (or its GDP per capita) and the likelihood that it signed the nine treaties (Roberts, 1996). This is true also for Latin America, which demonstrates that the wealthier semiperipheral states tend to be more interested in, or able to participate in, global eco-diplomacy.[24] The actual importance of these treaties is unclear for several reasons, including the fact that many countries sign and then proceed to flaunt them, and also because of the weakness of their enforcement and dispute-resolution mechanisms (Biggs, 1993). Moreover, even when they possess the political will, Latin America's governments may, in fact, not be *able* to effectively enforce the protection of their environments, especially in the face of recent efforts to "shrink the state." I return to this issue in the concluding section.

Meanwhile, the opening of Latin American economies and the explosion of free-trade agreements across the region are the harbingers of both greater environmental perils and of new leverage for enforcing protection. For example, the environmental side agreement to the North American Free Trade Agreement (NAFTA) includes explicit directives regarding the "harmonization" of environmental protection in Canada, the United States, and Mexico. In the years just prior to January 1, 1994, when NAFTA took effect, Mexico substantially increased environmental regulations and spending, as well as the enforcement of environmental laws. A considerable official oversight structure is being put into place along the border and in Washington, Mexico City, and Ottawa, bringing together government officials, academics, and activists.[25] The success and permanence of these efforts remains to be seen, especially as national and international attentions shift elsewhere. The crisis in Mexico involving devaluation of the peso and the land developer's quote at the outset of this chapter show how a pact can restructure trade and the deeper structures of production, the consequences of which can far outlive popular support for, and watch-dogging of, environmental safeguards.

While many environmentalists have decried the lack of solid protection for the environment under the NAFTA treaty, it is the best agreement drafted so far in this hemisphere. Negotiations for the other economic integration treaties in the region—the Caribbean Basin Initiative, CARICOM, MERCOSUR, the Group of Three, the Andean Pact, Amazon Pact, and the future Pact of the Americas—have all raised some environmental issues but have not incorporated protections in formal mechanisms. The General Agreement on Tariffs and Trade (GATT) is, in many ways, the worst of all treaties for environmentalism since it prohibits nations from excluding imports because of environmental considerations on how they were produced (Biggs, 1993). The GATT approach, however, answers the greatest fears of many Latin American leaders who worry that environmental restrictions on imports will become a new camouflage for protectionism of core markets (see, for example, Alsogaray, 1993; Ominami, 1993).

Finally, in discussing the environmental impact of the emergent pattern of integration of Latin America in the world-economy, it is also important to mention the potential roles of industry environmental initiatives, "green marketing," and new international quality-control standards. Though normally greeted with cynicism by environmentalists and progressives, efforts by business to incorporate environmental protection should be carefully examined and not hastily or summarily written off.

Most obviously, the new "environmental technologies" industry has grown surprisingly quickly in the past two decades: a 1994 survey by German market researchers projected global purchases of $374 billion in "green-tech" products in 1995 (Rubin, 1994).[26] "Green" firms are obviously interested in regulations and treaties that will drive the demand for their products.[27] As ex-Chilean economy minister Carlos Ominami pointedly stated, these restrictions probably will increase Latin America's technological dependency: "It is common for the same country imposing the restrictions to offer the technology or expertise necessary to satisfy them" (1993: 149).

Driven by demand for "green products" and the integration of the EEC, international quality-control standards are being developed so that industrial purchasers will know what they are buying in an increasingly global marketplace. Some of these standards are beginning to include quality control, not only for the final products, but also for the *process* by which they are produced. Standards might include worker health, some aspects of labor relations, and conformity to environmental standards, especially of emissions (Heller, 1993). An official for a major transnational chemical company, Joel Charm of Allied Signal Corporation, stated that these initiatives increase "the probability that there will be one world environmental standard," and noted that "they are likely to become law in Europe and provide a transparency for how to conduct business in the Third World" (Heller, 1993: 31). In Latin America, it appears that these standards will have the greatest initial impact on suppliers of raw materials and intermediate products such as minerals and chemicals to overseas manufacturers, especially in Europe. Small firms and the informal sector will probably continue to produce with little concern for environmental regulations. However, the linkages between informal producers and multinational export firms (Portes, Castells, and Benton, 1989) suggest that quality control and "green labeling" may force some small-scale producers to pay closer attention to environmental effects. Again, Ominami pointed out that these standards are "biased toward vertical integration" (1993). In world-system terms, consumers looking for "green labels" on products are likely to shift profits back to brand names and up the commodity chain to core distributors providing them, thus reducing markets for Latin American national brands.

CONCLUSION

This chapter's central question is whether environmental conditions in Latin America are likely to improve or erode further as nations move from strongly protected and regulated economies to ones more open to market forces. A balanced perspective must consider both positive and negative forces.

On the positive side, free-trade advocates project that if aging and inefficient ISI factories are shut down and replaced by competitive and more efficient facilities for exports, the region's air may become somewhat cleaner, while incomes will rise. For this to occur, countries will require huge infusions of (presumably foreign) capital, and decades to replace old capital equipment.

One could emphasize that global integration is bringing, albeit in fits and starts, some level of international standardization of environmental regulations. This is occurring in several ways beyond international treaties on the environment. Following side agreements in economic integration treaties such as NAFTA, the Caribbean Basin Initiative (CBI), and MERCOSUR, future trade pacts (at least those that include the United States will almost certainly incorporate environmental protection provisions into the main treaty or a side agreement.[28]

The very globalization of commerce and the demand for "green products" have forced core-based firms to create standardized quality-control guidelines, which are now spreading around the world. These guidelines, which will most affect export-oriented firms and their suppliers in Latin America, increasingly incorporate health, safety, and environmental-management systems at global levels.

Together, these elements will increase global standardization, but it is unlikely that they will reach more than 25 to 50 percent of the economy—namely, the large-scale and export sectors. National industries and the informal sector are likely to avoid increasing environmental regulations as long as possible (which could be indefinitely). This will depend largely on the growth and strength of environmental pressure from within Latin American nations.

In this regard, while external debt played a key role in the origin of environmentally destructive mega-projects between the 1960s and early 1980s, more recently, the necessity of attracting low-interest loans from multilateral sources has actually driven some Latin American countries to beef up their environmental protection efforts since 1985 (Sanderson, 1993; Roberts, 1994). Attention by these agencies to environmental issues is likely to continue only as long as the pressure on politicians and banks continues from core environmentalists who are, in turn, linked to Latin American groups. To understand the likelihood that this dynamic will continue, we need a solid understanding of both northern and southern environmental movements, and especially their class roots and public support. The internationalization of environmental and social justice NGOs strengthens the movement in the short term but might risk local support if Latin American groups must bend to international desires to the detriment of local chapters, or if core environmentalists ignore the urban, public health, and social justice–related environmental issues that inspire wider popular support in Latin America.

On the negative side, some would argue that global integration is not conducive to environmental protection because cutthroat international competition can drive nations to neglect safeguards and because austerity programs and the economic crises associated with the transition to market-centered models of accumulation create a desperation that drives poor people to unsustainable uses of their resources (Barkin, 1995; Serbin, De Lisio, and Ortiz, 1993). To correct exchange rates, control inflation, and lower tariff barriers, global integration and export orientation have been linked with drastic programs of privatization and "state shrinking" in Latin America. As the state shrinks, however, respect for the rule of law often weakens, as does confidence in environmental protection agencies.[29] Even if those agencies are well funded by outside financing, in times of austerity, many people may see them as increasingly alien and irrelevant in times of desperate hardship. Desperate times tend to favor short-term thinking, not sustainable development.

With the demise of government social programs and substantial public-sector employment, most researchers also envision greater income inequality and poverty throughout the region. An important question, then, will be whether income inequality leads to wasteful consumption with greater environmental damage without commensurate social gains (Sanderson, 1993). The direct implication of these questions is that too rapid a liberalization and "modernization" of the state risks dire environmental crisis.

Finally, if greater openness to trade brings economic growth to Latin America, it may provide the opportunity for greater spending on sanitation and urban air-pollution control. However, with economic expansion, carbon dioxide emissions and many other pollutants are almost bound to increase (from new autos, factories, mines, agrochemicals, dumping, etc.).[30] These conclusions suggest that the only force with the capacity to change the relationship between economic growth and pollution in Latin America is strong pressure brought on governments and on transnational *and* national firms through lobbying, boycotts, and direct action, all supported by cross-border links.

NOTES

Helpful comments were provided by Amy Bellone, David Barkin, Alvaro Díaz, Peter Grimes, Daniel Hilliard, Ellen Mitchell, Timothy Power, Mike Renning, Orlando San

Martín, Marc Stern, Thomas Rudel, Bill Smith, and Roberto Patricio Korzeniewicz. This research was funded by the Mellon Foundation, the Fulbright Commission, and the National Science Foundation.

1. See Grimes, Roberts, and Manale (1993), Roberts (1996), Grimes and Roberts (1995), as well as note 5 below.

2. As Orlando San Martín of the Norwegian Institute of International Affairs (NUPI) usefully pointed out, "the social costs [of ISI] that caused higher levels of income concentration [also] encouraged short-sighted approaches to resource exploitation by the rural poor" (personal communication, March 12, 1995).

3. However, subsequent empirical analyses have produced mixed results in testing whether firms are fleeing tighter environmental regulations in the core and moving to "pollution havens" in the periphery (Low and Yeats, 1992; Leonard, 1988; Pearson, 1987). Perhaps contrary to the hypothesis that firms are moving to the most unregulated locations, and contrary to my own prediction, I found in a recent analysis of global data that FDI is *positively* related to a country's likelihood to have signed international environmental treaties such as the Montreal Protocol for Ozone Protection and the endangered species treaty (Roberts, 1996). This suggests that the best "business climate" may not be found in areas of the least regulation, an idea that is supported by analyses comparing regulation and economic growth in the 50 U.S. states (Freudenberg 1990; Meyer, 1992; Hall, 1994). The causality may work in both directions, however, since the desire for positive trade relations has driven some countries to sign treaties. For the 27 Latin American nations for which there was data, levels of FDI (flows, not stocks) were not directly correlated with the environmental outcomes listed in Table 10.1.

4. This problem has been documented in Brazil, Ecuador, Peru, Bolivia, Costa Rica, and Venezuela. However, there are many cases of ISI or national integration projects also opening such corridors, and often these corridors are oriented in ways that more directly draw population from major centers.

5. By 1990, two-thirds of Latin America's exports were still fuels, minerals, metals, and other primary commodities, while only 30 percent of exports of the East and South Asian countries were (World Bank, 1992). More than their Asian counterparts, then, Latin American nations have struggled to ascend in the global system of stratification while continuing to export primary commodities, raising important questions about the viability of this route to the semiperiphery (Cicantell, 1994; Roberts, 1992). Korzeniewicz and Martin (1994) confirmed for the past few decades Wallerstein's (1974, 1979) central structural postulate: that while a few countries can move up or down in the world stratification system, the structure itself remains largely unchanged. Further, while Latin America, and the peripheral states in general, are exporting more transportation and electronics products, the relative value of their exports remains low because they continue to be excluded from the research, innovation, and marketing stages of global commodity chains. For additional discussion, see the contributions in Gereffi and Korzeniewicz (1994).

6. As Grossman and Krueger (1995) and the World Bank (1992) have pointed out, some pollutants increase in concentration with level of development (e.g., carbon dioxide, nitrogen oxides, municipal waste), while others tend to improve steadily with income levels (e.g., percent of population with basic sanitation, potable water, etc.). The relation for carbon dioxide (CO_2) emissions has been borne out with very few exceptions in world history, and as "development" proceeds, it appears that each increment in economic growth brings wider ecological impacts (Grimes and Roberts, 1995). Most interesting, perhaps, is the fact that other pollution problems tend to be worst for nations at

the middle levels of income and for both poorer and wealthier countries (e.g., problems with urban particulates, sulphur dioxide, and a series of water pollutants). Grimes, Roberts, and Manale (1993) discovered that findings forming a similar inverted-U curve also exist for the CO_2 emissions *efficiency* of nations. We explain this trend as the result of inefficient machinery and infrastructure and high deforestation in the upper peripheral and rising semiperipheral countries.

7. Its scope is comparative and regional, but my experience in Brazil means that I rely most heavily on examples from there.

8. As the cynical Brazilian saying has it, concern for the Amazon rain forest seems to be directly proportional to one's distance from it.

9. While 64 percent of São Paulo households have sewage *pipes*, about 85 percent of waste water goes untreated (Gunn, 1993).

10. Columns 1 and 2 of Table 10.1 show the percentage of households with sanitation services (World Resources Institute, 1994; Economic Commission on Latin America [ECLA] 1990, 1993). This includes pit toilets and other types of sanitation not considered by the ECLA figures.

11. This is widely cited as an underlying reason for the "Soccer War" (Durham, 1979; Faber, 1993; Green, 1991).

12. A graphic example is the fact that, fifteen years after their establishment, Brazil still has not "delimited" most of its indigenous reserves in the Amazon. Only 39 percent of these reserves had been demarcated by 1995, two years after the deadline established in Brazil's 1988 constitution (Rainforest Action Network, 1995).

13. This is especially true outside the official project's boundaries: for example the Carajás railroad and its buffer zone were carefully reseeded and protected. However, just outside that area there has been a flood of land clearing and contamination in ranches, farms, and gold mines (Becker, 1990; Roberts, 1992).

14. The environmental racism/justice movement and the NIMBY (Not in My Backyard) groups are important variants (see Dunlap and Mertig, 1992).

15. This was confirmed for the Brazilian case in interviews with environmentalists Arturo Deiges (June 19, 1993) and Beth Grimberg (June 21, 1993). For other Latin American nations, see Hochstetler (1995), Prell (1995), Price (1995), and Christen (1995).

16. See Viola (1992: 61). Political scientist Steven Sanderson (interview, November 29, 1993) made similar observations.

17. The World Values Survey found similar results for Argentina (about 50 percent). However, for their reverse-coded question, which forced pro-environment respondents to disagree with the statement that "it shouldn't cost me any money" to reduce pollution, variation was much greater. Seventy-two percent of Argentines (among the highest in the world) agreed, as did 65 percent of Brazilians, 57 percent of Chileans, and 40 percent of Mexicans.

18. Some pollsters, however, insist that *volunteered* responses of environmental concern are the best indication of the *salience* of the issue (Dunlap, 1992). Because economic and crime problems are most critical in most people's lives, only 2 to 3 percent of Uruguayans and Brazilians *volunteered* environmental problems as "the most" important problem facing their nation. However, 20 percent of Chileans and 29 percent of Mexicans did (levels far above the United States and Canada).

19. Interview, Flávio de Mattos Franco, World Wildlife Fund, June 22, 1993.

20. Marc Stern of University of California at San Diego pointed out that most envi-

ronmental loans by the World Bank since 1989 have actually been in the area of urban infrastructure, such as for water and sewage (personal communication, February 17, 1995). That the March 1995 UN Conference on Social Development in Copenhagen saw activists still pushing for social aspects of development projects to be included in decision making suggests that environmentalists have been somewhat more effective at raising their issues than were social activists.

21. Speaking to a meeting of the Amazon basin's nine nations in 1989, for example, senior Brazilian diplomat Paulo Flecha de Lima described accusations about Brazil's poor environmental record in the region as part of "a campaign to impede exploitation of natural resources in order to block [Brazil] from becoming a world power." *O Liberal* (Belém), November 14, 1989.

22. From nuclear weapons in the early 1960s to the current debate over the terms of the UN Framework Convention on Climate Change, a series of global agreements have been drafted, debated, and signed. Dietz and Kalof (1991) compiled an index of "state environmentalism" based on which of the nine treaties had been signed during the period 1963–1987 (see Table 10.1). The treaties were the Nuclear Test Ban Treaty (1963); Wetlands (Ramsar, 1971); Biological and Toxic Weapons (1972); World Cultural and Natural Heritage (1972); Ocean Dumping (1972); Endangered Species (CITES, 1973); Ship Pollution (1978); Migratory Species (1979); Law of the Sea (1982); Ozone Layer, Vienna (1985); CFC Control, Montreal (1987); and Hazardous Waste Movement (1989) (Dietz and Kalof, 1992: 355).

23. Environmental Sociologist Thomas Rudel pointed out that poorer nations are often unable to send delegates to treaty drafting sessions (personal communication, December 3, 1994). This does not prevent them from later formally agreeing to the treaty's terms.

24. This is shown in the fact that I found no statistical relationship between GDP per capita and the percentage of requirements on endangered species trade (under the CITES treaty) that the Latin American nations had met by 1990. Elsewhere I have presented a cross-sectional analysis comparing the ability of external and internal influences to predict participation in environmental treaties for a global sample (Roberts, 1996). That analysis suggested that the hierarchical world-system position (WSP) and levels of foreign investment were positive predictors of the likelihood of signing environmental treaties, while debt service, dependence on one trading partner, regime repressiveness, and military spending all had significant negative impacts. Replicating the reduced final model from that analysis for this work on Latin America, I found that only WSP was significantly tied to state environmentalism (however, the much smaller sample size was problematic).

25. This includes the Border Environmental Cooperation Commission (BECC), North American Development Bank (NADBank), the Border Ecology Project (BEP), university research centers, state government agencies, and NGO groups.

26. An earlier Organization for Economic Cooperation and Development (OECD) study estimated the market for environmental equipment and services at around U.S. $200 billion and growing at over 5 percent per year (Stevens, 1993).

27. Karliner (1994) pointed out that they often stress the cleanup rather than prevention of pollutants.

28. In cases with imbalances in regulations, it is not certain whether environmental regulations will "harmonize" at the core or peripheral levels; for example, in the case of NAFTA, Mexico is having to do the most work to "get up to speed."

29. However, through the late 1980s economic crisis, IBAMA, Brazil's environmental

protection agency continued to expand, largely through funding from the World Bank and other external sources.

30. See note 6 above.

REFERENCES

Alsogaray, María Julia. 1993. "International Trade and the Environment: A View from Argentina." In *Difficult Liaison: Trade and the Environment in the Americas*, ed. Heraldo Muñoz and Robin Rosenberg, pp. 153–158. New Brunswick, NJ: Transaction.

Amano, Hidetake. 1993. "Globalization of the Economy and the Response of the Japan Development Bank." *Japan 21st* v. 38 (December): 20–21.

Anderson, Anthony B. 1990. "Smokestacks in the Rain Forest: Industrial Development and Deforestation in the Amazon Basin." *World Development* 18: 1191–1205.

Barkin, David. 1995, March. "Wealth, Poverty, and Sustainable Development." Working Paper. Cambridge, MA: Lincoln Institute.

Becker, Bertha K. 1990. *Amazônia*. São Paulo, Brazil: Editora Ática.

Biggs, Gonzalo. 1993. "The Interrelationship between the Environment and International Trade in Latin America: The Legal and Institutional Framework." In *Difficult Liaison: Trade and the Environment in the Americas*, ed. Heraldo Muñoz and Robin Rosenberg, pp. 167–204. New Brunswick, NJ: Transaction.

Bullard, Robert D., and Beverly H. Wright. 1992. "The Quest for Environmental Equity: Mobilizing the African-American Community for Social Change." In *American Environmentalism: The U.S. Environmental Movement 1970–1990*, ed. Riley E. Dunlap and Angela G. Mertig, pp. 39–50. Philadelphia: Taylor and Francis.

Bunker, Stephen G. 1985. *Underdeveloping the Amazon: Extraction, Unequal Exchange, and the Failure of the Modern State*. Urbana: University of Illinois Press.

———. 1989. "The Eternal Conquest." *NACLA Report on the Americas* 23, 1: 27–35.

Butler, John R. 1985. "Land, Gold and Farmers: Agricultural Colonization and Frontier Expansion in the Brazilian Amazon." Ph.D. dissertation, University of Florida, Gainesville.

Cardoso, Fernando H., and Enzo Faletto. *Dependency and Development in Latin America*. Berkeley: University of California Press, 1979.

Chew, Sing C. 1995. "Environmental Transformations: Accumulation, Ecological Crisis, and Social Movements." In *A New World Order? Global Transformations in the Late Twentieth Century*, ed. David A. Smith and József Böröcz, pp. 201–215. Westport, CT: Praeger.

Christen, Catherine. 1995. "Field Scientists and Park Administrators: Environmental Conservation Initiatives in Costa Rica 1960s–1970s." Latin American Studies Association 19th international congress, September 28–30, Washington, DC.

Cicantell, Paul. 1994. "The Raw Materials Route to the Semiperiphery: Raw Materials, State Development Policies and Mobility in the Capitalist World-System." American Sociological Association annual meetings, August, Los Angeles, CA.

Dietz, Thomas, and Linda Kalof. 1992. "Environmentalism among Nation-states." *Social Indicators Research* 26: 353–366.

Dunlap, Riley E. 1992. "Trends in Public Opinion toward Environmental Issues: 1965–1990." In *American Environmentalism: The U.S. Environmental Movement*

1970–1990, ed. Riley E. Dunlap and Angela G. Mertig, pp. 89–116. Philadelphia: Taylor and Francis.

Dunlap, Riley E., George H. Gallup, Jr., and Alec M. Gallup. 1993. *Health of the Planet: Results of a 1992 International Environmental Opinion Survey of Citizens in 24 Nations*. Princeton, NJ: George H. Gallup International Institute.

Dunlap, Riley E., and Angela G. Mertig, eds. 1992. *American Environmentalism: The U.S. Environmental Movement 1970–1990*. Philadelphia: Taylor and Francis.

Durham, W. 1979. *Scarcity and Survival in Central America: The Ecological Origins of the Soccer War*. Stanford, CA: Stanford University Press.

Economic Commission on Latin America (ECLA). 1990. *Statistical Yearbook for Latin America and the Caribbean*. Santiago, Chile: ECLA.

———. 1993. *Statistical Yearbook for Latin America and the Caribbean*. Santiago, Chile: ECLA.

Faber, Daniel. 1993. *Environment under Fire: Imperialism and the Ecological Crisis in Central America*. New York: Monthly Review Press.

Freudenberg, Nicholas, and Carol Steinsapir. 1992. "Not in Our Backyards: The Grass-roots Environmental Movement." In *American Environmentalism: The U.S. Environmental Movement 1970–1990*, ed. Riley E. Dunlap and Angela G. Mertig, pp. 27–38. Philadelphia: Taylor and Francis.

Freudenberg, William R. 1990. "A 'Good Business Climate' as Bad Economic News?" *Society and Natural Resources* 3: 313–331.

Gelbard, Robert. 1992. "Environment for the Americas: 'No Country Will be Able to Enjoy Economic Prosperity without Protecting the Environment That All Countries Share." *U.S. Department of State Dispatch* 3 (February 24): 142.

Gereffi, Gary, and Miguel Korzeniewicz, eds. 1994. *Commodity Chains and Global Capitalism*. Westport, CT: Praeger.

Green, Duncan. 1991. *Faces of Latin America*. London: Latin America Bureau.

Grimes, Peter E., and J. Timmons Roberts. 1995. "Oscillations in Atmospheric Carbon Dioxide and Long Cycles of Production in the World Economy, 1790–1990." American Sociological Association annual meetings, August, Washington, DC.

Grimes, Peter E., J. Timmons Roberts, and Jodie Manale. 1993. "Social Roots of Environmental Damage: A World-Systems Analysis of Global Warming." American Sociological Association annual meetings, August, Miami, FL.

Gross, Anthony. 1990. "Amazonia in the Nineties: Sustainable Development or Another Decade of Destruction?" *Third World Quarterly* 12, 3 (July): 1–24.

Grossman, Gene M., and Alan B. Krueger. 1995. "Economic Growth and the Environment." *Quarterly Journal of Economics* 110 (May): 353–377.

Gunn, Philip. 1993. "The Tietê Project." Lecture at the University of São Paulo, June 14.

Hall, Bob. 1994. "Gold and Green: Can We Have Good Jobs and a Healthy Environment?" *Southern Exposure*, Fall, pp. 4–6.

Hajek, Ernest R., ed. 1991. *La situación ambiental en América Latina: Algunos estudios de casos*. Buenos Aires, Argentina: Centro Interdisciplinario de Estudios sobre Desarrollo Latinoamericano (CIEDLA).

Hecht, Susanna, and Alexander Cockburn. 1990. *The Fate of the Forest: Developers, Destroyers and Defenders of the Amazon*. New York: Harper Perennial.

Heller, Karen. 1993. "ISO 9000: Stepping-Stone on the Road to a Global Economy:

Environmental Standards Take Center Stage.'' *Chemical Week*, February 10, pp. 30–32.

Hochstetler, Kathryn. 1995. ''Environmental and Popular Coalitions in Local Environmental Politics in Brazil and Venezuela.'' Latin American Studies Association 19th international congress, September 28–30, Washington, DC.

Inglehart, Ronald. 1995. ''Political Support for Environmental Protection: Objective Problems and Subjective Values in 43 Societies.'' *PS: Political Science and Politics* 23, 1: 57–72.

Karliner, Joshua. 1994. ''The Environment Industry Profiting from Pollution.'' *Ecologist* 24, 2: 59–63.

Kasa, Sjur. 1993. ''Environmental Reforms in Brazilian Amazonia under Collor and Sarney: Explaining some Contrasts.'' Working paper. Center for International Climate and Energy Research-Oslo (CICERO).

Keck, Margaret E. 1995. ''Parks, People and Power: The Shifting Terrain of Environmentalism.'' *NACLA Report on the Americas* 28, 5: 36–41.

Korzeniewicz, Roberto P., and William Martin. 1994. ''The Global Distribution of Commodity Chains.'' In *Commodity Chains and Global Capitalism*, ed. Gary Gereffi and Miguel Korzeniewicz, pp. 67–92. Westport, CT: Praeger.

Landim, Leilah, ed. 1992. *Sem Fins Lucrativos: As Organizações Não-Governamentais no Brasil*. Rio de Janeiro: Instituto de Estudos da Religião.

Leff, Enrique. 1986. ''Notas para un análisis sociológico de los movimientos ambientalistas.'' In *Politica ambiental y desarrollo: Un debate para América Latina*, ed. Marta Cárdenas, pp. 115–126. Bogotá: FESCOL/INDERENA.

Leonard, H. Jeffery. 1988. *Pollution and the Struggle for the World Product: Multinational Corporations, Environment, and International Comparative Advantage*. Cambridge: Cambridge University Press.

Linden-Paramaribo, Eugene. 1995. ''Chain Saws Invade Eden.'' *Time*, August 29.

Low, Patrick, and Alexander Yeats. 1992. ''Do 'Dirty' Industries Migrate?'' In *International Trade and the Environment*, ed. Patrick Low, pp. 89–104. World Bank Discussion Papers. Washington, DC: International Bank for Reconstruction and Development/World Bank.

Maguire, Andrew, and Janet Welsh Brown. 1986. *Bordering on Trouble: Resources and Politics in Latin America*. Bethesda, MD: Adler and Adler.

Meyer, Stephen M. 1992. ''Environmentalism and Economic Prosperity: Testing the Environmental Impact Hypothesis.'' Mimeo. Massachusetts Institute of Technology Project on Environmental Politics and Policy.

Miller, Marian A. L. 1995a. ''Globalization and Interdependence: The Third World in the Evolution of Environmental Regimes.'' International Studies Association annual meetings, February 21–26, Chicago, IL.

———. 1995b. *The Third World in Global Environmental Politics*. Boulder, CO: Lynne Rienner.

Morrison, D. E., and Riley E. Dunlap. 1986. ''Environmentalism and Elitism: A Conceptual and Empirical Analysis.'' *Environmental Management* 10: 581–589.

Movimento Ecológico Mater Natura. 1992. *Cadastro Nacional de Instituições Ambientalistas*. Curitiba, Brazil: World Wildlife Fund/Mater Natura.

Museum of Astronomy and Related Sciences/National Council for Scientific and Technological Development (MAST/CNPq). 1992. ''What Brazilians Think of Ecology.'' Mimeo.

Ominami, Carlos. 1993. "International Trade and the Environment: A View from Chile." In *Difficult Liaison: Trade and the Environment in the Americas*, ed. Heraldo Muñoz and Robin Rosenberg, pp. 147–151. New Brunswick, NJ: Transaction.

Pearson, Charles S. 1987. "Environmental Standards, Industrial Relocation, and Pollution Havens." In *Multinational Corporations, Environment, and the Third World: Business Matters*, ed. Charles S. Pearson, pp. 113–128. Durham, NC: Duke University Press.

Portes, Alejandro, Manuel Castells, and Lauren A. Benton, eds. 1989. *The Informal Economy: Studies in Advanced and Less Developed Countries*. Baltimore: Johns Hopkins University Press.

Prell, Renae. 1995. "Class, Education and Cultural Perspectives of Mexican and Mayan Environmentalists in the Yucatan." Latin American Studies Association 19th international congress, September 28–30, Washington, DC.

Price, Marie. 1995. "Venezuela's Environmental Voices and Actors." Latin American Studies Association 19th international congress, September 28–30, Washington, DC.

Rainforest Action Network. 1995. "Brazil Backslides on Land Demarcation." *World Rainforest Report*, July–September (electronic edition).

Roberts, J. Timmons. 1992. "Forging Development, Fragmenting Labor: Subcontracting and Local Response in an Amazon Boomtown." PhD dissertation, Johns Hopkins University.

———. 1994. "Economic Crisis and Environmental Policy [Brazil]." *Hemisphere* 6, 1: 26–30.

———. 1996. "Predicting Participation in Environmental Treaties: A World-System Analysis." *Sociological Inquiry* 66, 1: 38–57.

Rubin, Debra K. 1994. "Firms Gear up to Think Globally, Link Locally, Focus on Environment." *Engineering News-Record* 232 (February 21): 42.

Rudel, Tom, and Jil Roper. 1994. "People, Roads, and Tropical Forests: Cross-National Patterns of Tropical Deforestation, 1975–1990." Paper presented at the annual meetings of the American Sociological Association, August 5–9, Los Angeles, CA.

Sanderson, Steven E. 1993. "International Trade, Natural Resources, and Conservation of the Environment in Latin America." In *Difficult Liaison: Trade and the Environment in the Americas*, ed. Heraldo Muñoz and Robin Rosenberg, pp. 53–78. New Brunswick, NJ: Transaction.

Serbin, Andrés, Antonio De Lisio, and Eduardo Ortiz. 1993. "The Environmental Impact of International Trade and Industry: Reflections on Latin America and the Caribbean." In *Difficult Liaison: Trade and the Environment in the Americas*, ed. Heraldo Muñoz and Robin Rosenberg, pp. 127–145. New Brunswick, NJ: Transaction.

Skole, David, and Compton Tucker. 1993. "Tropical Deforestation and Habitat Fragmentation in the Amazon: Satellite Data from 1978 to 1988." *Science* 260: 1905–1910.

Smith, David A. 1993. "Uneven Development and the Environment: Toward a World-System Perspective." Paper presented at the Korean Sociological Association International Conference on Environment and Development, November, Seoul.

Stern, Paul C., Oran R. Young, and Daniel Druckman, eds. 1992. *Global Environmental*

Change: Understanding the Human Dimensions. Washington, DC: National Academy Press.

Stevens, Candice. 1993. "Organization for Economic Cooperation and Development Framework for the Discussion of Trade and Environment Concerns." In *Difficult Liaison: Trade and the Environment in the Americas,* ed. Heraldo Muñoz and Robin Rosenberg, pp. 161–166. New Brunswick, NJ: Transaction.

Viola, Eduardo J. 1992. "O Movimento Ambientalista no Brasil (1979–1991): Da Denúncia e Conscientização Pública para a Institucionalização e o Desenvolvimento Sustentável." In *Ecologia, Ciência e Política,* ed. Mirian Goldenberg, pp. 49–75. Rio de Janeiro, Brazil: Editora Revan.

Wallerstein, Immanuel. 1974. *The Modern World-System I: Capitalist Agriculture and the Origins of the European World-economy in the Sixteenth Century.* Vol. 1. New York: Academic Press.

———. 1979. *The Capitalist World-Economy.* New York: Cambridge University Press.

Wilson, E. O. 1988. "The Current State of Biological Diversity." In *Biodiversity,* ed. E. O. Wilson, pp. 3–18. Washington, DC: National Academy Press.

Wolf, Eric R., and Edward C. Hansen. 1972. *The Human Condition in Latin America.* London: Oxford University Press.

World Bank. 1992. *World Development Report 1992.* New York: Oxford University Press.

World Health Organization (WHO) and United Nations Environment Program. 1992. *Urban Air Pollution in Megacities of the World.* Oxford, UK: Blackwell Reference.

World Resources Institute (WRI). 1994. *World Resources 1994–95.* New York: Oxford University Press.

World Wildlife Fund (WWF). 1990. *Atlas of the Environment,* ed. Geoffery Lean, Don Hinrichsen, and Adam Markham. New York: Prentice Hall Press.

11

DISORDERLY DEMOCRACY: REDEFINING PUBLIC SECURITY IN LATIN AMERICA

A. Douglas Kincaid and Eduardo A. Gamarra

News reports from Latin America in the mid-1990s have brought word repeatedly of soldiers in the streets. Military units have been on patrol in the major cities of Honduras and El Salvador; the Bolivian army enforces a state of siege; Brazilian troops have occupied shantytowns in Rio de Janeiro; demonstrations and riots in the Dominican Republic have been suppressed by the army; and in Venezuela, the defense ministry has presented to the president a contingency plan for the military to take control of Caracas. Unlike in past decades, however, this activity has not been accompanied by coups and dictatorships. It is all at the initiative of elected civilian presidents rather than generals.

The policy arena of public security has been largely ignored or taken for granted in debates about contemporary challenges facing the national state. This applies to both the literature on national security, which is dominated by discussions of the transformations of sovereignty and international conflict in the post–Cold War era (e.g., Mandel, 1994), and analyses of global political economy, which are concerned with state roles and constraints amid increasingly transnational economic forces (Centeno, 1993; Evans, 1995). In part, this may stem from the perception that the maintenance of internal order is a core function under even the most minimalist concept of the state, and hence is not in question, while war making and economic functions are.

It is our contention, however, that these occurrences are not isolated events but rather form part of a regional pattern of state formation and government responses to what are perceived as crises of public security. One of the principal defining characteristics of this pattern is a recourse to military intervention in support, or in place, of normal police responsibilities. Such action, in and of itself, is neither unusual from a comparative international perspective, nor necessarily nefarious with respect to democratic norms. Much depends on the circumstances and conditions under which the decisions are made and policies are implemented. Here, we focus on three specific cases—Bolivia, Brazil, and Honduras—as a means to consider some of the consequences of these actions, with respect both to public security and to the processes of democratization now underway in Latin America. In our conclusion, we argue that these actions are suggestive of a new model of public security that is emerging in Latin America in response to world-systemic, international, and domestic pressures—a model with significant and unfavorable implications for the institutions and practices of democracy.

CONCEPTS OF SECURITY AND REGIONAL PATTERNS

The backdrop for this analysis is a region where police and military institutions and missions were closely intertwined during recent decades, especially under military authoritarian rule. This relationship has been changing since the return to elected civilian governments during the 1980s, a dynamic that is a necessary point of reference in our analysis of contemporary patterns.

First, however, the discussion may be enhanced by a delineation of some basic concepts of security and their relationship to police and military forces. While *security* is an extremely broad term that varies according to the qualities it denotes and the object to which the qualities apply, we focus here on security in terms of linkages between the state, society, and citizenry. From this standpoint, we may usefully distinguish between three types of security for which modern states typically assume primary responsibility. These are national defense, public security, and citizen security.

By national defense, we refer to the upholding of the sovereignty of the national state and territory against external threats, which usually, although not exclusively, emanate from other states. Public security refers to the maintenance of public order and the enforcement of laws. Citizen security, finally, concerns the guarantees of specific rights pertaining to citizens as such, including both civil and political rights. All three types of security, along with institutional responsibilities and jurisdictions, are usually spelled out in national constitutions and elaborated within legal frameworks.

Military and police forces are examples of state institutions that are specialized to address security needs. They are not the only agencies responsible for security, of course; court systems, intelligence agencies, and a number of other state actors are likely to play significant roles as well. The military and the police are of particular interest, however, in that their ranks are trained, organized, and authorized to employ physical force in defense of security. In Max Weber's terms, they share the state's monopoly of the legitimate use of coercive force. Thus, the rules and norms governing police and military actions—as well as their interactions—are especially important, and their subordination to elected civilian authority is one of the defining features of democratic political systems.

As a general rule, military forces are given the primary responsibility for

Figure 11.1
Basic Model of Police and Military Roles in the Modern State

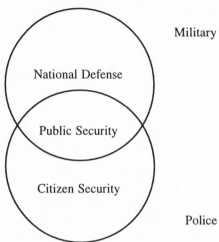

national defense, while police institutions are charged with upholding public security as well as, on a less exclusive basis, citizen security. Virtually everywhere in the world, however, the military are given some public-security functions as well—most commonly, the capacity to intervene to restore and maintain public order in case of conditions (such as large-scale riots or natural disasters) that surpass the limits of police capabilities. The typical domains of police and military institutions can thus be graphically portrayed as overlapping circles (see Figure 11.1).

Some further observations can be made concerning this division of labor. As one consequence, military and police institutions are likely to be characterized by fundamental differences of organization, doctrine, training, and deployment, among other traits. These differences bear strongly on the nature of their involvement in the realm of public security. There is an obvious potential conflict, even within the bounds of constitutionally sanctioned practices, between the maintenance of public order and the defense of citizen security. Indeed, some rights of citizens are defined as restrictions on what the state may legitimately do to them. Thus, police forces face a permanent tension in the enforcement of laws that may well represent competing collective and individual rationalities. By contrast, military forces charged with national defense and prepared for the conduct of war are necessarily centered on collective interests, and their entry into public-security functions is likely to be accompanied by the suspension or downgrading of some citizen rights.

This is an abstract portrayal of military and police institutions within modern states; in practice, there are wide variations between countries as to how these responsibilities are defined and how the boundaries of institutions are maintained (not to mention how the domains of state prerogatives and citizen rights are constitutionally provided for). As a whole, Latin America stands out in world comparisons for its history of close structural and functional linkages between the military and the police, albeit with important subregional and national variations (Bayley, 1993).

Under the authoritarian regimes that predominated in the region from the mid-1960s to the early 1980s, the reigning doctrine of national security centered on anticommunism led to more cross-national similarity than difference in these relationships. As military governments linked external defense to internal control and confrontation with domestic actors identified as enemies, police institutions and functions were increasingly subordinated to direct military control. In terms of the distinctions made in Figure 11.1, this pattern of development can be described as the militarization of the police and the recasting of public security missions as national defense, to the severe detriment of citizen security. In the wake of democratic transitions throughout the region since 1980, efforts to dislodge police institutions from military control have assumed great importance in the reform of civil-military relations (Kincaid and Gamarra, 1994). Latin American military leaders have been grudging in their acquiescence to these reforms, but the general pattern is one of substantial progress over the last decade toward the structural separation of police and military institutions.[1]

With regard to functional differentiation, however, there is a curious trend that seems to be running in the opposite direction. We can label this trend (a bit awkwardly, but symmetrically) the "policization" of the military, which involves increasing the public security functions of the armed forces. In the following sections of this chapter, we discuss three contemporary cases of military involvement in the public security arena.[2]

OPERATION RIO: THE WAR ON CRIME IN BRAZIL

On October 31, 1994, President Itamar Franco signed an emergency agreement with the governor of the state of Rio de Janeiro. The accord provided for the Brazilian military to oversee a joint command of police forces in the city of Rio de Janeiro, provide operational support to the police, and attempt to counter illegal drug and arms trafficking. This initiative was a response to increasingly vocal public frustration over what was perceived as a rising tide of crime and violence.

Murder in Rio had reached a rate of about 8,000 a year, and totaled 70,000 victims during the last decade. Illegal drug trafficking and drug-related crime seemed to be growing unchecked. The news was dominated by highly visible crimes, such as kidnappings of wealthy executives, youth gangs sweeping along the famous Rio beaches and robbing beachgoers en masse, and other gangs blockading the tunnels leading out of Rio during the afternoon rush hour and robbing commuters. Partly as a result, the city's important tourist economy suffered a disastrous drop, declining by 50 percent between 1989 and 1994, a period in which tourism revenues for Brazil as a whole were rising (Brooke, 1994).

Two aspects of the spiral of violence stood out in the dynamic leading to military intervention. One was the domination of a number of Rio's *favelas* (shantytowns) by organized criminal gangs, fueled primarily by illegal lotteries (the famous *jogo de bicho*) and, more recently and with much more nefarious consequences, narco-trafficking. The gangs increasingly were functioning as a parallel state, with local bosses (estimated to number some 300) controlling access to neighborhoods, regulating commerce, imposing curfews, and granting permission for candidates to campaign for public offices. This system rested on a combination of corruption and coercion—local police and public officials were paid off for their tolerance or active involvement, while rivalries, resistance, and disobedience were settled summarily and violently.

The other crucial element was a discredited police force, which had come to mirror the gangs in its tendencies toward corruption and violent action.[3] Brazil's police forces have long had a reputation for extralegal violence, which is in part a legacy of the military authoritarian period (Pinheiro, 1991). Brazil has two police systems that operate locally: a civilian police and a military police, both of which are organized at the state level. There is also a federal (national-level) police force, with primarily investigative responsibilities. In 1969, along with other measures to institutionalize authoritarian rule, the military police forces were placed under centralized army control and given major counterinsurgency and repressive responsibilities. Over the course of the 1970s, the military police gradually assumed a greater role in confronting common crime, evolving parallel capabilities with those of the civil police only with greater resources, and operating with the total impunity of the military justice system. By the 1980s, Brazil had become known for the application of "dirty war" practices—death squads, disappearances, and summary executions—to the control of common crime.

The adoption of a new constitution in 1988, following the return to civilian rule, marked a partial reform of police structures (Zaverucha, 1994). The military police remained part of the armed forces but were placed under the authority of civilian state governors, who also command the civil police forces. The military police's armaments, intelligence, and logistical support come from the army ministry; salaries are paid by the state governments. The civil and military police still constitute parallel organizations with overlapping functions of maintaining order, conducting investigations, serving arrest warrants, and so on.

President Franco had two options for bringing in the military to conduct police operations in Rio. One was to declare a "state of defense" (the Brazilian term for state of exception), under which the president could order a federal takeover of a state or local government for 30 days. This required the approval of the congress. The second option was to have the state governor request federal intervention for the restoration of public order, with the governor remaining in nominal control. With an election pending, and preferring not to suspend constitutional guarantees under his own responsibility, President Franco persuaded Rio's governor to request federal intervention. On November 1, Brazilian military commanders assumed responsibility for coordinating joint action among the local civil and military police, the federal police, and their own troops.[4]

Direct operations in the *favelas* began on November 19. The typical operation was for some 1,500 to 2,000 troops to cordon off a particular neighborhood, attempt to serve standing arrest warrants, search for drugs, and detain everyone who was not carrying identification. Controversy arose almost immediately, as complaints were filed with human rights groups over the soldiers' abusive treatment of those that were detained, as well as over the fact of detention itself, since carrying identification is not required under Brazilian law. Defending the actions of his forces, the army general in charge of "Operation Rio" said, "I recognize that some civil liberties have been restricted, but we are not a battalion of social workers. It is impossible to avoid excesses." A week after the operations began, a priest and a nun claimed to have witnessed soldiers torturing detainees, using electricity and near-drownings, in one *favela* operation. Following an investigation, the attorney general's office announced that it would seek prosecution of the soldiers involved ("Brazil," 1994: 2).

The operations went on periodically through December, and on January 3, 1995, newly inaugurated President Fernando Henrique Cardoso and Rio's new governor, Marcello Alencar, agreed to extend the military's authorization. The biggest operation of the entire campaign, involving 4,000 troops, was carried out during January 10–12, following an outbreak of fighting among rival gangs. When the authorization expired on February 1, the governor asked the military to withdraw but remain "on call" should further action be necessary. The call was not long in coming; in late March, following renewed violent clashes between police and gangs, Governor Alencar announced that he would be recalling the military to action at the beginning of April following consultation with President Cardoso.

"Operation Rio II" began on April 4 under the authority of the army and the state security council. Provisionally, military units were assigned to patrol major streets and points of access to the city, and to provide training for police in the use of military weapons. Raids on the shantytowns were ruled out except in backup support of police actions. On the same day the new military intervention was announced, armed gangs burned down a police station and robbed a bank.

As of mid-1995, there was little evidence that the introduction of military forces had proved an effective strategy in reducing the wave of violence in Rio. If anything, crime statistics suggested the opposite. After a temporary drop-off in November and December, the first two months of military action, Rio's homicide rate soared. The toll for the first three months of 1995 was 2,121 deaths, more than double the homicides reported for the same period in 1994 (Ellison, 1995; Latin American Newsletters, 1995). Police casualties for 1995 stood at

67 by mid-May. A few of the most wanted gang leaders were killed or captured, but drugs continued to be plentiful, and kidnappings and bank robberies also were reported on the rise.

Undaunted, Governor Alencar vowed to get tougher. In May, he appointed a retired army general, Nilton Cerqueira, as head of public security, a position giving him command of the combined Rio police forces and military backup. Cerqueira, a veteran of counterinsurgency operations who had been accused of torture by human rights groups during the military regime, ordered a new set of large-scale police incursions into the *favelas*, employing a "shoot first" policy (Ellison, 1995). Meanwhile, the governor announced plans to increase police armaments, including the acquisition of helicopter gunships. The war on crime in Rio seemed to be increasingly just that.

RECLAIMING THE STREETS: NEOLIBERAL AUSTERITY AND PUBLIC SECURITY IN BOLIVIA

Bolivia has a long and complex history of periodic attempts by the armed forces to subordinate the police under its command. These have generally been in the context of replacing or supplementing the role of the police forces in maintaining public order (Gamarra and Barrios, 1993). This pattern has taken many forms and cuts across regime types. The common feature, however, has been a recourse to states of exception (states of siege, as they are called in Bolivia), under which military units patrol city streets, carry out arrests, and generally enforce the law. Under military regimes, states of siege were declared primarily to deal with perceived threats from the left and organized labor. These actions were largely motivated by Cold War notions of national security, and the armed forces often took over all public security matters and relegated the police to a support capacity.

In the 13 years since the transition to democracy, the armed forces have been called on to break labor strikes, lift road blockades, and arrest striking union leaders. The common denominator has been worker resistance to the imposition of austerity measures. In the country's ten-year attempt to deepen structural reforms, Bolivia has become an extreme case of a society coping with the collateral effects of neoliberal adjustment.

Bolivia also stands out because of the proliferation of the coca-cocaine economy, which has led to civil unrest in the country's coca growing regions. Since the early 1980s, coca growers have organized, joined the principal labor confederation, and attempted to resist the imposition of coca-crop eradication programs. By joining forces with organized labor, peasant coca growers have also been the target of repression, especially under states of siege. While the phenomenon is primarily rural, the coca growers' marches have been defined as a public security problem when they have targeted the cities.

Significantly, every time the armed forces have been mobilized to control worker unrest, popular support for the government's actions was high among certain sectors. Two reasons account for this sentiment. First, the actions of striking workers generally disrupted life in the major cities. As strikes proliferated and the actions of workers grew more radical, popular support for them decreased, and cries for the reestablishment of order followed.

Typically, support for the measures of exception has been closely tied to social class identification. Members of the business sector, and the middle classes in general, have welcomed states of siege because they have enabled them to carry on their daily activities, while worker unrest disrupts business. In their view, striking workers constituted a public-security problem. For obvious reasons, support for strikers has generally been greater among those groups at the bottom of the socioeconomic scale, which have been most affected by the process of economic reform.

Support for austerity measures has been high because of what might be termed the *hyperinflation syndrome*.[5] This is a collective sense among the upper and middle classes that giving in to workers' demands or retreating from neoliberal programs could set off a new economic crisis. Demands for higher salaries have been characterized by successive governments as attempts to destroy the tenuous economic stability established in 1985.[6] This view has been widely accepted. In the remainder of this section we examine the dilemmas of public security and neoliberalism through one specific instance in which a democratically elected government launched a state of siege in order to deepen the process of market-oriented reform.

In April 1995, Bolivia faced a new general strike by the country's largest labor organization, the Confederación Obrera Boliviana (COB), as well as a teachers' strike over the government's educational policy, an incipient separatist movement from the southernmost department of Tarija, and a potential insurrection by coca-growing peasants in the Chapare Valley.[7] Responding to these pressures, President Gonzalo Sánchez de Lozada (the principal author of the Paz Estenssoro administration's 1985 stabilization plan) declared a state of siege on April 18, suspending all constitutional guarantees for a 90-day period. Shortly before midnight on April 18, the military and police arrested hundreds of union leaders and confined them to remote jungle and *altiplano* (highland) towns ("Estado de Sitio," 1995). These issues had paralyzed the Sánchez de Lozada government for six weeks prior to the enactment of the state of siege. Demanding that the government rescind an educational reform law that would ostensibly leave them unemployed, striking teachers erected roadblocks, threw dynamite sticks at police, and generally paralyzed life in the capital city. In the Chapare, coca growers' unions organized a movement to resist the government's attempts to enforce the coca-eradication program.[8] The COB, in turn, was in its thirteenth day of a general strike to protest low salaries and the government's refusal to give in to demands for higher levels of social spending. Finally, after staging a march with thousands of supporters, civic leaders in the city of Tarija threatened to secede from Bolivia unless the central government altered a decentralization law that would limit local government autonomy.

Throughout most of Bolivia, public opinion had little or no sympathy for the striking workers and teachers. Most Bolivians wondered if and when the government would take decisive action to end the strikes that prevented them from going to work or walking the streets without dodging tear gas, rubber bullets, and rocks. President Sánchez de Lozada's attempts at establishing a dialogue with the strikers—with the mediation of the Catholic Church—were seen mainly as a reflection of the government's weakness and indecisiveness.

On April 19, the day after the state of siege was declared, public opinion in general favored President Sánchez de Lozada's decision to mobilize the armed forces and arrest labor leaders. Media interviews with average citizens reflected a sense of relief and support for the reestablishment of order. Most did not question why the rules of exception had been implemented; instead, they wondered why the government had taken so long to react. A taxi driver captured this generalized sentiment and highlighted an all-too-common reaction throughout Latin America: "What we need is a Fujimori who will ensure, as in Peru, that authority is respected, put things in their place, and resolve the country's problems without political deals" ("Incertidumbre," 1995).

Predictably, the principal opposition political parties expressed their outrage at the imposition of a state of siege, alluding mainly to the threat to democracy and civil rights. The Catholic Church warned against human rights violations and underground union leaders announced clandestine resistance. If the past serves as a guide, then labor unions will be weakened temporarily, later to resurface to contest the process of neoliberalism that the government has promised to sustain for the rest of the century. The likelihood of greater unrest is high, however, as this is the first time that any government—military or civilian—has simultaneously targeted coca growers, unions, and civic committees. All three sectors have claims that will not disappear with repression.

President Sánchez de Lozada, in a speech at the military academy given a day after launching the measures of exception, stated that the role of the armed forces in a modern democracy was to sustain the legally constituted regime ("Incertidumbre," 1995). If this is a sign of things to come, then Bolivia can expect to require continued reliance on the military in order to enforce public security.

WHICH WAY TO THE BARRACKS? THE CASE OF HONDURAS

The evolution of police-military relations in Honduras presents an interesting counterpoint within the regional pattern (Kincaid and Juhn, 1994). On the one hand, under a lengthy period of military rule (1963–1980), police and military institutions were unified within the command structure of the armed forces. Nonetheless, after the return to civilian rule, both police and military forces exercised a more repressive role during the 1980s under civilian presidents than they had under the military regime of the preceding decade. This ambiguity of the Honduran transition process has persisted; in 1995, with civil-military relations undergoing their most fundamental reform in the last half-century, the most reform-minded of recent presidents, Carlos Roberto Reina, called the troops out to patrol the streets of Tegucigalpa and San Pedro Sula.

Following the coup that established military government in 1963, the National Police of Honduras were renamed the Special Security Corps and transferred from the Ministry of Government to the Ministry of Defense.[9] This shift reflected the military's determination to monopolize the state's coercive power and consolidate its autonomy with respect to civilian political interests. Twelve years later, in 1975, the formal subordination of the police to the military was strengthened under a new constitutive law of the Honduran military. Now called the Public Security Force (FUSEP), the police were made the fourth branch of the Honduran armed forces.

The Honduran version of the national security doctrine came late; it was implanted under a civilian president after the Honduran military had relinquished the executive office in 1980. Surrounded by the civil wars of El Salvador, Guatemala, and Nicaragua, and supported by both President Roberto Suazo Cordova and the Reagan administration, the Honduran military unleashed its own repressive model during the early 1980s. FUSEP was fully integrated into local counterinsurgency operations, despite the absence of a credible Honduran guerrilla movement. The National Directorate of Investigation (DNI), the investigative arm of the FUSEP, was responsible for more than 100 disappearances and deaths over the course of the decade. This was a small figure by Central American standards, but it was a sharp departure from prior Honduran practices.

During this period, for reasons related to the privileging of national security affairs over routine police work, public security was converted into a private commodity. Concerned over rising crime rates, a group of private-sector leaders requested that FUSEP provide their enterprises with security guard services in exchange for a payment covering the salaries of participating police agents and leaving a profit for the institution. The arrangement rapidly gained popularity and, by the 1990s, it had become a multimillion-dollar enterprise for the armed forces, into whose coffers the income went directly without passing through the national treasury. This dedication of active duty police agents to private interests has come under sharp criticism from other sectors of the population as public concern with FUSEP's inability to deal with crime has mounted.[10]

Toward the end of the 1980s, a number of civilian political leaders, supported by a variety of business, labor, and other social groups, began to call for the dissolution of the DNI and the creation of a new investigative police force, to be attached to the Ministry of Justice. With this proposal they sought two objectives. One was to strengthen the administration of justice system, which was seriously handicapped by the weak investigative capabilities of the DNI; the other was to eliminate the institution responsible for the worst abuses of citizen security during the authoritarian period.

The initial response of the military was to roundly reject any dilution of their control over the police, including the DNI. However, with peace accords putting an end to the conflicts in Nicaragua and El Salvador, and under strong pressure from the U.S. embassy (which reversed its policy of blind support during the 1980s), the Honduran military high command found itself on the defensive. In 1992, President Rafael Callejas named an ad hoc commission to study the situation of the DNI, and in March 1993, the commission reported back to the president, recommending that the DNI be immediately purged of corrupt and abusive officials and that preparations be made to turn its responsibilities over to civilian hands in the justice ministry.

In the course of this process, the attitude of the military high command shifted from open opposition to tacit acceptance—or, perhaps, tactical acceptance, as it was apparently motivated by the notion that the reform of the DNI might reduce pressure for more profound challenges to military prerogatives. In late 1993, President Callejas announced that a new cabinet-level entity, the Public Ministry, was to be created, and that it would control two new police entities, the Department of Criminal Investigations (DIC)—replacing the DNI—and the Counter-Narcotics Police, all under civilian control.

In January 1994, Carlos Roberto Reina was sworn in as president; as a candidate, he had promised to complete the restoration of civilian control over the military. With the support of the legislature, the president initiated efforts to do away with the military draft and pursue investigations to establish responsibility for the worst human rights abuses during the 1980s. In the midst of concessions that would have been virtually unthinkable only two or three years previously, the military high command acceded, in mid-1994, to the gradual separation, in principle, of FUSEP from the armed forces. In the latter decision, they may have been prodded by the idea of diverting toward civilian authorities a rising tide of public criticism over police inability to counteract increasingly violent criminal activity.

The DIC was finally inaugurated on January 23, 1995, after months of delays that seemed to indicate the lack of civilian preparedness to assume security functions previously carried out under military authority. On April 6 the Honduran legislature abolished the draft on a vote of 127 to 1; the measure was accompanied by a pay raise of 800 percent (from roughly US $5.50 to $77.00 monthly) to allow for a professional voluntary force. Later that month, the legislature began consideration of a constitutional reform bill for converting FUSEP back to a civilian-led National Police.

All this suggests substantial progress toward a more democratic model of police-military relations and public security. Against this measured pace of reform, however, the pressure to act more directly against violent crime has created a separate dynamic. In 1994, the FUSEP inaugurated a program of support for civilian "community watch" groups, with the objectives of forestalling crime and assisting the police. On April 3, 1995, one of the leading Honduran newspapers published an account of one such group in a town near San Pedro Sula. Calling themselves "Los Lobos," they wore masks, were armed with rifles and automatic weapons, and carried police communication equipment—with the mission of dispensing vigilante justice. Under pressure from the government's human rights commissioner, FUSEP commanders ordered the group disbanded, claiming that "Los Lobos" had no authorization to carry heavy weapons ("En proyecto," 1995; "FUSEP," 1995).

In February 1995, in another initiative addressed to the issue of crime, President Reina named the Archbishop of Tegucigalpa to head the nation's Ad Hoc Commission for the Prevention of Crime and Violence. In May the commission released its first report with a set of recommendations for short-term measures to confront rising crime rates ("Urge freno," 1995). Among the policy recommendations was congressional action to accelerate the separation of FUSEP from the armed forces, the creation of an externally administered emergency fund to improve FUSEP's operational capacity, and reforms to the penal code and judicial system. The commission also promised a second report that would analyze the root causes of crime and violence and propose long-term solutions.

During the same period, a different anticrime effort got underway. Prodded by the legislature, the president authorized the deployment of military forces to begin patrolling the country's major cities. In March and again in May, army troops were ordered into action on police patrol. Announcing the first deployment, the commander of the Honduran army said, "I have all the soldiers [available] in the streets and gradually they will be going out into the whole country. For each policeman, there will be five soldiers" (Reuter, 1995).

CONCLUSION

On the face of it, democracy in Latin America is a disorderly business. The demise of authoritarian military regimes and efforts to restore or create democratic political institutions have been accompanied by a widely perceived crisis of public security. One consequence of this situation has been that civilian presidents have felt compelled to assign military forces a major part in the response.

In the three cases we have described, the deployment of military forces in public security roles is of two types. One is to maintain public order under a state of constitutional exception (enacted in Bolivia and considered in Brazil), and the other is to combat crime and violence (enacted in Brazil and Honduras).[11] A first level of evaluation of these actions should be conducted in terms of intended effects.

Does the declaration of a state of exception and the deployment of troops bring about the restoration and maintenance of public order? In the short run it clearly does, in the absence of any force capable of directly challenging military force. This is a situation for which practically all states provide on an emergency basis. The question raised by the Bolivian experience (and perhaps reflected in Peru under Alberto Fujimori as well) is whether at some point, the exceptional will become the rule and the state of full constitutional guarantees will become the exception (Loveman, 1994). In such a case, the policy represents more a strategy of governance than one of emergency management.

Does assigning military units to support the police have an impact on crime and violence? The evidence here leads us to be skeptical. The deployment of military units on the streets has an obvious, immediate deterrent effect. It may also serve as a temporary arrangement to facilitate purging or reforming existing police institutions, or to create new ones. There is little evidence from the cases we have looked at, however, to suggest that the deterrence is more than temporary, and no reason to expect that military forces will be able to carry out any police functions beyond purely reactive and repressive ones. In Brazil, military intervention has failed to dismantle Rio's criminal gangs, which seem to have simply diversified their activities in adjustment to the military presence. In Honduras, where the recent wave of crime and violence has taken place while the police are still administered on a military model as a branch of the armed forces, there is even less room for optimism.

It should be emphasized that all the military interventions described in this chapter have taken place within legal, constitutional frameworks, and in response to the initiatives of elected civilian leaders. In a sense, these actions have demonstrated the achievement of the subordination of military institutions to civilian leadership, which is a key democratic tenet. In the current debates about security in the region, there is little evidence of any efforts to revive the military authoritarian models of the 1960s and 1970s.

Nonetheless, a serious threat is posed to democratic institutions by these policies. Both the recourse to states of exception and the deployment of troops to police the streets and chase criminals pose a deterioration of citizen security— of the enjoyment of basic political and civil rights. Moreover, in the characteristics of the cases we have described, we can discern the outlines of a new Latin American model of public security in the context of disorderly democracy. This model has three noteworthy features:

- a *militarization* of the provision of public security for large sectors of the population, wherein large-scale disorder is repressed but crime may well flourish, and where citizen security will be minimal;
- a simultaneous *informalization* of some public-security functions, whether provided in the form of paramilitary neighborhood groups, as have appeared in Honduras, or the "parallel state" of shantytown criminal organizations, as have sprung up in Rio; and
- a *privatization* of "public" security for those who can afford to pay for it, as a commodity to be directly purchased.[12]

To characterize these processes as a "Latin American model" is to assert both a significant generalization across a diverse array of countries and a particular causal pattern that has contributed to this outcome. We do not pretend to suggest that the militarization, informalization, and privatization of public security extend uniformly across the region, nor that all three elements will co-vary across cases.[13] We do contend, however, that these are related phenomena that are sufficiently widespread to warrant speaking of them as an emergent regional model.

There are two distinct causal explanations for the emergence of this model. One is that it represents an aspect of what Guillermo O'Donnell (1994) has called the "crisis of the state" in Latin America. By this, he referred to the contemporary interaction of neoliberal economic policies and the specific historical formations of states and political systems. From this perspective, the shrinking of the state, which is prescribed as part of the neoliberal orthodoxy by international financial institutions and embraced with varying degrees of enthusiasm by Latin American governments, undermines state capacities for extending the effectiveness of the rule of law in an equitable manner across both territory and social order. These constraints help to explain the set of government actions (and inactions) that constitute the new model of public security.

The second explanatory factor is the transnational economy of illegal drugs. This has been aptly described as a new, perverse form of integration into the world-economy for national and local economies and for social actors (Castells and Laserna, 1994). Much attention has been paid to the challenges to the state posed by the vast, unregulated flow of commodities and currencies across national boundaries. What is equally evident at this point is that the linked characteristics of illegality, high profitability, and violence create a continual political challenge as well, which is manifested in situations as diverse as those of Bolivian coca growers and Brazilian *favela* gangs.[14]

In sum, the dynamics of illegal drug trafficking interact with those of the weakened Latin American state to fuel the contemporary crisis of public security. Against this generally pessimistic scenario, some other trends and alternatives may be noted. Technical reforms, such as efforts to improve police professionalism in conformity with the rights of citizens, are underway in many countries throughout the region. These are unlikely, however, to alter the basic dynamics underlying the crisis we have described. In our view, more far-reaching changes are necessary to promote a more democratic model of public security.

One of the necessary changes will be to mitigate the popular toll exacted by neoliberal economic policies over the last decade. A number of governments have launched social emergency programs to deal with unemployment and declining standards of living. Deeper reforms to provide increased funding for social policies while maintaining adequate levels of growth may reduce unrest and minimize the deterioration of public security.[15] A second change concerns the nature of national and international law-enforcement efforts with respect to illegal drugs, and consideration of alternative options. While there are few positive trends to be cited in this regard, we would argue that policies oriented to demilitarizing efforts to cope with the transnational drug economy should be considered as a means to reducing the levels of violence associated with it.[16]

Without such bold initiatives, increasing disorder may prove the undoing of democracy in Latin America.

NOTES

This chapter draws extensively on research carried out with support from grants by the Heinz Endowment, North-South Center, Arias Foundation, and U.S. Institute of Peace, which, of course, bear no responsibility for the results. We thank Jairo Valverde for his assistance, and Bill Smith and Roberto Patricio Korzeniewicz for their helpful comments.

1. The most persistent structural ties between police and military appear to be in those countries where armed guerrilla movements remain active, as in Guatemala (Aguilera Peralta, 1993), Colombia (Leal, 1994), and Peru (Degregori and Rivera, 1993).

2. Data concerning these breaking events are drawn primarily from newspaper and wire-service reports and must be regarded with the usual caution. Our interpretations, however, are based on a regional comparative analysis grounded in a set of empirical case studies of police-military relations carried out under our direction in 1992–1993.

3. At the point when the troops were called in, military intelligence sources reported that 70 percent of the civil police and 20 percent of the military police were involved in criminal activities ("Brazil," 1994). A poll found that 58 percent of Rio residents agreed with the statement that police and criminals were the same "breed" (Harris, 1994).

4. The president's move met with widespread approval. Public opinion polls taken in Rio shortly after his decision showed more than 85 percent support for military action, and more than 50 percent in favor of direct military occupation of the *favelas* ("Brazil," 1994). The intervention was endorsed by then-presidential candidate Fernando Henrique Cardoso.

5. By *hyperinflationary syndrome* we refer to a pattern where recent memories of high levels of inflation legitimized profound structural adjustment measures despite their high social cost.

6. For an account of the 1985 stabilization program and societal responses, consult Gamarra (1994).

7. The Bolivian government faced a U.S. ultimatum that called either for the eradication of 1,750 hectares of coca leaf and the signing of an extradition treaty by June 30, 1995, or a suspension of all U.S. assistance. Using the ultimatum as an excuse, the government intensified the eradication campaign.

8. The prevailing policy that the armed forces should take a leadership role in the fight against narcotics only if the police were overrun by the traffickers was reversed by the launching of the state of siege. Under the emergency measures, troops moved into coca-growing regions and arrested the union leaders, including Evo Morales, the best known and most controversial of them.

9. Our account of police-military relations during the 1970s and 1980s is based on the work of Leticia Salomón (1994).

10. It was reported that in 1995, 6,000 police officers were being "rented" by private firms ("*Ejército*," 1995). Since this figure would encompass practically the entire national police force, it is no doubt exaggerated, but it does indicate the widespread nature of the practice.

11. We have also alluded to a third, related type of military action that concerns public

security: the military role in counter-narcotics efforts. This issue has been analyzed in more detail elsewhere; suffice it to say that the characteristics of military involvement in that sphere parallel those we have discussed here (Kincaid and Gamarra, 1994; Gamarra, forthcoming).

12. In this work we have focused almost exclusively on the first of these features, the use of military forces. Both the informalization of public security (reflecting, de facto, the absence or partial withdrawal of the state from particular zones) and privatization (in the form of private security firms mushrooming across Latin America), represent emergent phenomena that deserve serious attention.

13. It should also be obvious that we are not using the term *model* in a normative sense, as a set of behaviors to be emulated.

14. Thomson (1995) argued that undermining a state's capacity to enforce its laws constitutes a much more serious attack on the basis of national sovereignty than the reduction of the state's ability to regulate transnational economic activity.

15. For a discussion of how such programs may be implemented see Bresser, Maravall, and Przeworski (1994).

16. We have developed this argument in greater depth elsewhere (Gamarra, forthcoming). For contending views on this issue, see Bagley and Walker (1994).

REFERENCES

Aguilera Peralta, Gabriel. 1993. "Función policíaca y transición a la democracia: El Caso de Guatemala." Paper presented to the conference entitled, "Between Public Security and National Security: The Police and Civil-Military Relations in Latin America," October 21–22, Washington, DC.

Bagley, Bruce, and William O. Walker III, eds. 1994. *Drug Trafficking in the Americas*. New Brunswick, NJ: Transaction Publishers.

Bayley, David. 1993. "What's in a Uniform? A Comparative View of Police-Military Relations in Latin America." Paper presented to the conference entitled, "Between Public Security and National Security: The Police and Civil-Military Relations in Latin America," October 21–22, Washington, DC.

"Brazil: Controversy Explodes over Military Anti-Crime Operations in Rio Slums." 1994. *NotiSur: Latin American Political Affairs* (University of New Mexico), December 2.

Bresser, Luiz Carlos, José María Maravall, and Adam Przeworski. 1994. "Economic Reforms in New Democracies: A Social-Democratic Approach." In *Latin American Political Economy in the Age of Neoliberal Reform*, ed. William C. Smith, Carlos H. Acuña and Eduardo A. Gamarra, pp. 181–212. New Brunswick, NJ: Transaction Publishers.

Brooke, James. 1994. "Crime Reigns in the City Renowned for Romance." *New York Times*, October 25, p. A4.

Castells, Manuel, and Roberto Laserna. 1994. "The New Dependency: Technological Change and Socioeconomic Restructuring in Latin America." In *Comparative National Development: Society and Economy in the New Global Order*, ed. A. Douglas Kincaid and Alejandro Portes, pp. 57–83. Chapel Hill: University of North Carolina Press.

Centeno, Miguel. 1993. "The New Leviathan: The Dynamics and Limits of Technocracy." *Politics and Society* 22, 3: 307–336.

Degregori, Carlos I., and Carlos Rivera. 1993. "Peru 1980–1993: Fuerzas Armadas, subversión y democracia." Documento de Trabajo no. 53. Instituto de Estudios Peruanos, Lima, Peru.

"Ejército hondureño combate a delincuentes." 1995. *El Nuevo Herald* (Miami, FL), May 26, p. 1B.

Ellison, Katherine. 1995. "In Rio, All's Fair in Desperate War on Soaring Crime." *Miami Herald*, May 25, p. 22A.

"En proyecto: FUSEP a manos civiles." 1995. *Inforpress Centroamericana* (Guatemala), April 27, p. 15.

"Estado de Sitio: La punta de un ovillo." 1995. *Informe R.*, April 28, pp. 8–9.

Evans, Peter. 1995. *Embedded Autonomy: States and Industrial Transformation.* Princeton, NJ: Princeton University Press.

"FUSEP incapaz de controlar criminalidad." 1995. *Inforpress Centroamericana* (Guatemala), May 18, p. 13.

Gamarra, Eduardo. 1994. "Market-oriented Reforms and Democratization in Bolivia." In *A Precarious Balance: Democracy and Economic Reforms in Latin America*, ed. Joan Nelson, pp. 21–94. Washington DC: International Center for Economic Growth and Overseas Development Council.

———. Forthcoming. *Dictators, Democrats, and Drugs: A Brief History of U.S.-Bolivia Counternarcotics Policy.* Pittsburgh: University of Pittsburgh Press.

Gamarra, Eduardo, and Raúl Barrios. 1993. "Seguridad ciudadana y seguridad nacional: Relaciones policía-miltiares en Bolivia." Paper presented to the conference entitled, "Between Public Security and National Security: The Police and Civil-Military Relations in Latin America," October 21–22, Washington, DC.

Harris, Ron. 1994. "Brazil Orders Military to Combat Crime in Rio." *Los Angeles Times*, November 2, p. A1.

"Incertidumbre por estado de sitio en Bolivia." 1995. *El Nuevo Herald* (Miami, FL), April 20, p. 2B.

Kincaid, A. Douglas, and Eduardo Gamarra. 1994. "Police-Military Relations." In *Hemispheric Security in Transition: Adjusting to the Post 1995 Environment*, ed. L. Erik Kjonnerud, pp. 149–167. Washington, DC: National Defense University Press.

Kincaid, A. Douglas, and Tricia Juhn. 1994. "La seguridad pública en America Central: Perspectivas sobre las relaciones policía-militares." In *Los retos de la democracia*, ed. Leticia Salomón, pp. 33–56. Tegucigalpa Centro de Documentación de Honduras.

Latin American Newsletters. 1995. "New Security Chief Named by Alencar." *Latin American Regional Reports* (Brazil), June 8, p. 6.

Leal, Francisco. 1994. *El oficio de la guerra: La seguridad nacional en Colombia.* Bogotá: TM Editores.

Loveman, Brian. 1994. "Protected Democracies' and Military Guardianship: Political Transitions in Latin America, 1979–1993." Paper presented to the 18th international Congress of the Latin American Studies Association, March 10–12, Atlanta, GA.

Mandel, Robert. 1994. *The Changing Face of National Security: A Conceptual Analysis.* Westport, CT: Greenwood Press.

O'Donnell, Guillermo. 1994. "The State, Democratization, and Some Conceptual Problems." In *Latin American Political Economy in the Age of Neoliberal Reform:*

Theoretical and Comparative Perspectives for the 1990s, ed. William C. Smith, Carlos H. Acuña, and Eduardo A. Gamarra, pp. 157–180. New Brunswick, NJ: Transaction Publishers.

Pinheiro, Paulo Sérgio. 1991. "Police and Political Crisis: The Case of the Military Police." In *Vigilantism and the State in Modern Latin America: Essays on Extralegal Violence*, ed. Martha Huggins, pp. 167–188. New York: Praeger.

Reuter. 1995. "Honduran Troops to Combat Crime." Reuter News Service, Central and South America, March 20.

Salomón, Leticia. 1993. *Policias y militares en Honduras*. Tegucigalpa: Centro de Documentación de Honduras.

Thomson, Janice E. 1995. "State Sovereignty in International Relations: Bridging the Gap between Theory and Empirical Research." *International Studies Quarterly* 39, 2: 213–233.

"Urge freno a la violencia." 1995. *Inforpress Centroamericana* (Guatemala), June 8, pp. 4–5.

Zaverucha, Jorge. 1994. *Rumor de Sabres: Tutela Militar ou Controle Civil?* São Paulo, Brazil: Editora Atica.

12

REBUILDING STATE CAPACITY IN CONTEMPORARY LATIN AMERICA: THE POLITICS OF TAXATION IN ARGENTINA AND MEXICO

Sergio Berensztein

During the 1980s and the early 1990s, Argentina and Mexico underwent a sweeping reformation of their public revenue systems, ultimately leading to the strengthening of both state capacity and enforcement mechanisms. The public's perceptions and attitudes toward taxation have changed dramatically. Under the previous tax system, compliance was considered foolish, and both firms and individuals tried to evade paying taxes as much as possible. In contrast, under the new system, as the tax base has been enlarged and enforcement mechanisms substantially improved, payment is now considered—at the very least—inevitable. Due to this institutional transformation, state capacity in both countries has been greatly improved.[1]

Historically, the two dominant approaches to the study of Latin American economic restructuring lead us either to encourage and embrace, or to expect and fear, the existence of a weak state. Neoliberalism asserts that since the market is the most efficient mechanism for allocating resources, economic reforms should aim to reduce state interventionism significantly and curtail most of its regulatory capabilities.[2] By the same token, excessively broad assessments of the impact of structural adjustment and/or ideologically driven, melancholic judgments opposing economic reforms argue that the reforms have been causing the destruction of the state and the dismantling of its vital institutions. Moreover, it is argued that a supposedly powerless state apparatus would not only be ineffective in checking the behavior of powerful private interests, but would also be incapable of avoiding "market failures." The new state, therefore, would ultimately provoke negative effects for economic development, social justice, and political stability.[3]

This Manichean debate surrounding neoliberalism precludes a theoretically more illuminating, empirically relevant, and politically crucial issue: *the actual institutional design of the states emerging from economic restructuring.* Such a focus allows us to move beyond this narrow debate and identify instead the specific kinds of state institutions that, in fact, are emerging in the wake of market-driven strategies of structural adjustment. Moreover, focusing on the nature and logic of institutional reforms, as well as on the emerging design of the state, clarifies the changing role of the state in an era of rapid globalization.

Many studies argue that due to the impact of financial liberalization, nation-states no longer have the state capacity or the resources to regulate their economy. Although this may indeed be the case with regard to capital flows and short-term portfolio investments, this chapter will show that the experiences of both Argentina and Mexico suggest that states still have an important role to play. They retain the ability to reform themselves and transform economic and political institutions, and therefore to affect economic and political outcomes. As always, local actors engage in the creation and refashioning of institutions in ways that change the distribution of political, symbolic, and material resources, even at times when the landscape in which these actors operate seems to be altered primarily by the shifting climate of an expanding global economy.

This chapter presents findings on the politics of taxation in Argentina and Mexico since 1982.[4] In both countries, the debt crisis triggered a long, complex, and conflictive process of deep fiscal reform regarding revenue and expenditure.[5] These reforms were implemented during the wave of stabilization and structural adjustment programs monitored by international financial institutions (IFIs) such as the International Monetary Fund (IMF) and the World Bank (International Monetary Fund, 1990; World Bank, 1991). The argument unfolds in three sections. First, I analyze the politics of taxation in both countries prior to the 1980s. Second, I focus on the emerging tax structure and analyze the material and symbolic transformations inherent in the emergent tax systems in both Argentina and Mexico. Finally, I address the spillover effects that the new tax systems may provoke and their implications for the emerging political matrices in both countries.

THE POLITICS OF TAXATION PRIOR TO THE 1980s

Before the wave of fiscal reforms that began in the 1980s, Argentina and Mexico (as well as many other Latin American countries) relied only partially on taxation as a way to extract resources from their societies; other means of collection, such as tariffs on imports and exports, foreign and domestic debt, and the inflationary tax, were considered to be politically less costly for governments than obtaining revenue through a workable, efficient tax system. Although there existed a myriad of taxes on income, sales, and property, very inefficient administrative procedures and enforcement mechanisms rendered taxation almost irrelevant. As was the case in many other sectors of the state apparatus, it became very easy for private interests to locate and take advantage of veto points through which to create and/or defend opportunities for rent seeking. Corruption was generalized, tax agencies and their personnel had extremely bad reputations, and many failed attempts to change this situation gave the impression that having a sound tax system was indeed an utopian dream.

Measures of tax collection as a proportion of GDP show the weakness of formal taxation in Argentina and Mexico (see Tables 12.1 and 12.2). However, revenue statistics tell only part of the story, as it is not only important to consider how much revenue a state can extract from its citizens and subjects, but also its methods of extraction. Indeed, the institutional framework that regulates taxation has profound consequences in terms of financial equilibrium, income redistribution, savings, investment, and economic growth (Steinmo, 1993). In Argentina and Mexico, the prevailing tax institutions operated in a vicious circle to create the wrong incentives for societal actors. The state proved to be weak, and therefore incapable of creating an efficient tax system, or even enforcing existing regulations. Thus, taxpayers found it both easy and safe to evade and/or elude their responsibilities. Although individually this was a rational act, the aggregate effect of such behaviors was suboptimal and very harmful for society, thus presenting a textbook case of a collective action problem.

Fragile public-finance structures caused macroeconomic instability and inflationary spirals, primarily in cases of external shocks. Subsequently, interest rates began to rise, making the financial cost of compliance much higher. Uncertainty and the expected drop in economic activity prompted cautious crisis-management strategies on the part of both firms and individuals. Both individuals and firms were, therefore, driven to evade their taxes in order to avoid liquidity and cash-flow problems. A lack of effective enforcement capabilities and the certainty of eventual tax "forgiveness" provided further incentives for such behavior. The only possible risk that a firm incurred was having its business inspected by revenue agents. This risk usually proved minimal, however, as corruption was rampant and businesspeople often found ways to "persuade" the tax agent to overlook the records. Since paying taxes was anything but a priority, firms and individuals allocated their money to safer, more profitable endeavors, such as the purchase of hard currency or speculation in the risky, but lucrative, domestic financial system. Bureaucrats and the rich and powerful members of society dominated this game, relegating the state and ordinary citizens to a secondary, and largely passive, role.

These complex and deficient tax systems were not merely consequences of poor implementation or faulty technical design; private actors also played a role as they found it possible to lobby in order to protect their interests in the context of "permeable" political regimes. Moreover, taxation was just one of the means through which private interests could create and perpetuate lucrative rent-seeking opportunities; other means included trade, financial, monetary, and social policies. Under the ideological umbrellas of nationalism, protectionism, infant industry arguments, and the like, both labor and capital utilized their political and economic power to mobilize public opinion as a tool to pursue their constituents' interests as well as protect their own corporatist privileges.

Problems such as improper institutional designs, administrative incapability, and poor enforcement mechanisms began to affect other areas of state involvement. As Cavarozzi (1991, 1992, 1994) has argued, since the 1980s, the more industrialized Latin American countries have been suffering a crisis of the state-centric economic and political matrix (SCM) that had emerged in the 1930s and 1940s. In this matrix, the state managed social conflicts by playing a major role as the agent of accumulation, redistribution, modernization, and incorporation of new social and political actors. A complex, and sometimes chaotic, web of economic and political institutions was established by the state and controlled by both the new and old political elites, depending on each country. The SCM remained basically unchanged under both authoritarian and democratic regimes. The matrix was able to survive as long as the state had sufficient political and economic resources to respond to domestic social demands as well as to changes in the international system (including external shocks). These resources included the capacity to finance expenditures through inflationary taxation, debt, and the improper use of public assets, funds, and savings earmarked for other purposes (e.g., the public retirement system in Argentina; oil-generated revenue in Mexico). Although the SCM began to display obvious signs of exhaustion by the mid-1970s, it was the 1982 debt crisis that delivered the final coup de grâce.[6] Until then, the SCM had proven quite resilient and resistant to change as entrenched groups and dominant actors managed to successfully reproduce their interests. In this type of inflationary environment, there was a concentration of income benefiting the wealthiest strata of the population, combined with a perverse transfer of resources away from fixed-income sectors (e.g., labor, retirees).[7]

Inflationary financing replaced taxation as a central tool for collecting revenues. Labyrinthine tax laws and inadequate enforcement mechanisms gave impetus to a vicious circle that, along with the debt crisis, eventually ended in dramatic fiscal disasters. In hindsight, not only did the state suffer the consequences of high inflation, but politicians and public-sector elites also helped to perpetuate it. As Olivera (1967) and Tanzi (1977, 1978) have demonstrated, lags in tax collection strongly influenced the level of real, inflation-adjusted levels of revenues due to the constant depreciation of the currency and the lack of sound mechanisms for indexation. In addition, the state's inability to improve tax administration was a key factor in reproducing its own weakness, especially due to the lack of effective enforcement and the ubiquity of unscrupulous inspectors. There were clear incentives for inspectors to behave in this particular manner, and for people to behave illegally, as well. Salaries were low, no one really supervised the inspectors' conduct of their duties, and consequently, the profession was altogether lacking in prestige.[8]

The state nourished this vicious circle, not only through its inflationary financing and inability to improve enforcement institutions, but also by engendering the personnel in charge of administering the perverse system: the certified public accountants (CPAs). CPAs played a crucial role in this game, which was not limited solely to the prosperous business of advising firms on the best way to evade taxes. The practice of "double-accounting" became very popular and quite sophisticated. Double-accounting meant having the administration of a business divided between "white" (or legal and taxable) activities and "black" activities, which violated the tax codes. In order to operate in this manner, a double financial system was needed, including banking accounts, stub books, receipts, and so forth.[9] In many cases, CPAs completely falsified the figures reported on tax returns.[10]

Until the 1980s, attempts to change this system failed repeatedly. Political and social actors involved in the tax process found it more convenient simply to leave the existing tax system in place, despite its inefficiency. Ruling elites, both authoritarian and democratic, seemed to prefer the inflationary tax to any other, more open and formal, revenue-collection strategy. If elites were obliged to change course and follow a different strategy, this usually meant the implementation of stabilization policies in the context of economic emergencies. These policies frequently failed, however, due to intense opposition from political and social actors. In any case, ruling elites transferred the costs of their revenue strategies to future generations, which was a logical decision in unstable political environments like the ones prevailing in Latin America. Attempts to organize a sound, efficient, and fair tax system were considered pointless, and in any case, were hardly appealing to those actors whose priorities were defined in terms of short-term goals and the pursuit of quick rewards.

Firms and individuals also preferred inflationary taxation because the alternatives were perceived to be more costly. As long as levels of inflation were not extremely high (i.e., no hyperinflation) and economic growth continued despite (and, to some extent, thanks to) inflation, there were weak or nonexistent incentives for economic agents to risk modifying their behavior. In fact, agents developed quite sophisticated strategies to deal with inflation (e.g., the indexation of contracts and other ingenious financial tricks), reducing the costs of operating in such environments. However, when inflation and macroeconomic instability spun completely out of control, all the sophisticated strategies proved to be ineffective, and the actors' preferences began to change. Until that point was reached, however, anti-inflationary policies were unpopular, preventing both democratic and authoritarian regimes from actively pursuing stabilization.

Since the onset of the debt crisis, the resulting (and unprecedented) fiscal crisis of the state completely altered the prevailing politico-economic scenarios in both Argentina and Mexico (Acuña, 1994; Heredia, 1994). During the 1980s, first in Mexico and then in Argentina, a new set of perceptions, values, options, constraints, and priorities gained momentum as inflation, for the first time in the contemporary history of both countries, came to be considered truly harmful to society.[11] Moreover, macroeconomic stability came to be recognized as a public good, and the steep social costs and political risks entailed were seen as simply the unavoidable price to be paid for achieving monetary stability. As fiscal responsibility became a crucial electoral issue, political elites, which had become separated from their previous ideological preferences, found themselves obliged to rebuild the state apparatus virtually from scratch. They started the rebuilding process by dismantling the most burdensome parts of the state apparatus (e.g., state-owned enterprises, industrial promotions schemes, and other subsidies, including, not only social spending, but also many subsidies benefiting the capitalists). This gargantuan task inevitably involved redefining—one is tempted to say "reinventing"—basic institutions such as tax agencies and the attendant tax legislation.

UNTOUCHABLES AND TERRORISTS

As a consequence of these neoliberal reforms, a very different situation now prevails in both Argentina and Mexico. A wave of tax reforms has dramatically affected people's attitudes about taxation. Former perceptions regarding the weakness of the state and, in particular, the lack of integrity of tax inspectors have quickly vanished. Changes in staff recruiting, training, wage policy and promotions have significantly bolstered inspectors' espirit de corps and modified their behavior. They have now developed a new group identity and a new loyalty to their agencies. Tax inspectors have become portrayed as crusaders of public finance, the shock troops of the modernization.[12]

Symbolic changes and mass media campaigns have helped to create a new sense of transparency and visibility for the countries' tax institutions. For instance, in Argentina the new headquarters of the national internal revenue service, the Dirección General Impositiva (DGI), is now located directly on the Plaza de Mayo, Buenos Aires's main square. (According to Spanish tradition, the headquarters of the most important institutions of society are to be located around the city's main square.) In addition to its new location, the DGI has acquired a new elite corps of inspectors and investigators that has become the special weapons and tactics (SWAT) team of tax enforcement. This group is commonly referred to as "the Untouchables," a name taken from the celebrated story about the Chicago mafia and the group of honest law enforcers led by Elliot Ness. The label itself is interesting, as it strongly suggests, not only a need for eternal vigilance, but the fact that Argentina, much like Chicago in the 1930s, is threatened by organized crime. This select group has developed a solid reputation in Argentina: it is now respected and even feared.

Tax agencies are struggling to further reduce evasion and identify the sectors of society still committing fraud and other crimes. Progress is indeed being made in both Argentina and Mexico. The traditional notions that taxation is not important, that inspectors can be easily bought, and that the tax administration is a mess have begun to disappear. As important as the increase in tax revenues generated through these changes is the fact that tax authorities and institutions are now very visible in society. The public has developed a new awareness of the tax burden, and realizing this, political parties and social actors are focusing on taxation as an electoral issue. The very idea that tax policy can become a hot electoral issue signals what may be the harbinger of an authentic revolution in the political culture of both countries.

Actual revenues generated by these reforms are of great importance. In Argentina, as Durán and Gómez Sabaini (1994) reported, tax collection increased 200 percent in real terms between the third quarter of 1991 and the fourth quarter of 1993. Table 12.1 reports that in less than three years, the deficit of the public sector (4.2 percent of GDP in 1989) turned into a surplus (0.3 percent of GDP in 1992). By 1992, total revenues reached a peak of 17.5 percent of GDP, the highest level in ten years.

Gil Díaz (1993) reported that in Mexico, the tax burden increased as much as 30 percent from 1988 to 1991, as tax revenues (excluding oil) grew from 9.3 percent of GDP in 1988 to 10.8 percent of GDP in 1991. During that period, the number of taxpayers increased 31.7 percent, primarily through the incorporation of members of the liberal professions, merchants, and service sector employees. Excluding employees and considering only these new "independent" taxpayers, the tax base grew an impressive 87.2 percent compared to the period prior to the reform (Gil Díaz, 1993).[13] Table 12.2 corroborates these findings and demonstrates that by 1991, not only was the deficit eliminated, surpluses were achieved.[14]

The omnipresence attained by the Argentine and Mexican tax agencies in recent years has been maintained primarily through media and mass-mailing campaigns, and of course, by the threat of stepped-up inspections. Tax agencies in both countries have even gone so far as to publish lists of firms and individuals that are under investigation and subject to prosecution for tax fraud. Although judicial processes are still very slow and extremely intricate, investigations have resulted in the incarceration of many tax dodgers, and numerous firms have been forced to pay their unpaid taxes. The aggressive policies of the Argentine and Mexican tax agencies have produced obvious results, although some people naturally complain that the "visible hand" of the tax collector has become too heavy and meddlesome.

Some critics argue that investigations are not carried out properly and that inspectors and tax agencies fail to correctly observe pertinent regulations. The states' "authoritative" procedures have, in many instances, become increasingly arbitrary and authoritarian in operation. There is clearly room for improvement in the new system, as numerous procedural flaws remain.[15] Despite the persistence of some degree of wrongdoing in the new system, however, the bottom line is that the strengthening of state institutions has prompted serious resistance from many of the affected sectors. For example, in 1989, following the enactment of new taxes in Mexico, powerful business associations publicly accused Francisco Gil Díaz, the civil servant then serving as the undersecretary of public finance, of "fiscal terrorism" because of his attempt to enforce the new legislation approved by Congress. Gil Díaz had drafted a new law that taxed firms' existing assets in such a way as to increase revenue, although the primary purpose was to verify the profitability of firms at a moment when many enterprises

Table 12.1
Argentina: Selected Macroeconomic Indicators

	1983	1984	1985	1986	1987	1988	1989	1990	1991	1992
% Growth of GDP	3.7	1.8	-6.6	7.3	2.3	-1.9	-6.2	0.1	8.9	8.7
Investment as % of GDP	-0.7	-3.4	-17.8	15.2	14.0	-2.0	-24.4	-9.9	25.1	30.9
% Annual inflation (CPI)	433.6	686.8	385.4	81.9	174.8	387.7	4,923.3	1,343.9	84.0	15.6
Total Revenues as % of GDP	12.1	12.2	16.8	15.6	14.7	13.1	14.0	13.4	15.4	17.5
Total Expenditures as % of GDP	22.3	18.1	20.4	19.5	20.8	17.8	16.9	15.3	17.4	19.1
Deficit as % of GDP	10.1	5.7	3.1	3.2	5.7	4.0	2.7	1.4	1.1	0.3
Tax burden as % of GDP	18.4	18.2	22.5	23.5	21.6	19.7	18.9	19.5	---	---
Tax revenue as % of total revenue	82.7	83.1	83.8	89.3	91.1	92.1	93.1	92.1	92.2	93.0
Non-tax revenue as % of total revenue	17.3	16.9	16.2	10.7	8.9	7.9	6.9	7.9	7.8	7.0
Direct taxes as % of GDP	1.3	0.9	1.4	1.6	1.7	1.8	1.2	1.0	1.1	1.5
The VAT as % of GDP	2.2	1.9	2.4	2.5	1.8	1.8	1.6	2.3	3.5	6.3

Note: VAT = value-added tax.
Sources: Inter-american Development Bank (1993); Duran and Sabaini (1994); Damill and Frenkel (1992).

Table 12.2
Mexico: Selected Macroeconomic Indicators

	1983	1984	1985	1986	1987	1988	1989	1990	1991	1992
% Growth of GDP	-4.2	3.6	2.6	-3.7	1.6	1.4	2.9	4.3	3.5	2.6
Investment as % of GDP	17.6	17.9	19.1	19.4	18.4	19.1	---	---	---	---
Annual Inflation (CPI)	80.8	59.2	63.7	105.7	159.2	51.7	19.7	30.0	19.6	10.5
Total Revenues as % of GDP	17.8	16.9	16.9	15.9	17.0	16.7	17.6	16.9	20.2	20.4
Total Expenditures as % of GDP	25.9	24.1	24.4	28.9	31.2	26.3	22.6	19.7	16.9	15.9
Deficit as % of GDP	8.2	7.2	7.6	13.0	14.2	9.6	5.0	2.8	-3.3	-4.5
Tax burden as % of GDP	20.1	19.1	19.1	17.5	17.8	21.5	---	---	---	---
Tax revenue as % of total revenue	57.4	61.0	60.5	70.4	62.9	72.2	67.5	67.2	57.5	58.9
Non-tax revenue as % of total revenue	42.6	39.0	39.5	29.6	37.1	27.8	32.5	32.8	42.5	41.1
Direct taxes as % of GDP	4.2	4.2	4.1	4.3	3.9	4.8	---	---	---	---
VAT as % of GDP	2.8	2.7	2.8	2.7	2.8	3.0	3.0	---	---	---

Sources: Inter-american Development Bank (1993); Carciofi et al. (1992).

237

were filing tax returns claiming bankruptcy. If a terrorist is defined as "one who favors or uses terror-inspiring methods of governing" (*The Concise Oxford Dictionary of Current English*, 1959: 1316), then it is understandable that business associations regarded the new legislation as "terror-inspiring." Gil Díaz was certainly breaking an accepted code that had been in place in Mexico for decades. More important, such "odd behavior" by a state functionary had obvious material consequences for those who were now obliged to honor their responsibility to pay taxes.

There is evidence that the informal "black" economy has shrunk significantly as enforcement capabilities have expanded, although informality and the resulting tax evasion still remain a significant problem in many large urban areas. The role of the CPA has also changed as a result of the new regulations. CPAs are now the key link between the state and the taxpayers, and are responsible for the communication of pertinent client information to the various tax agencies. In both Argentina and Mexico, taxpayer information must now be delivered on computer-readable forms, thus facilitating more rapid and accurate scrutiny. Moreover, in both countries, CPAs are now held legally responsible for the truthfulness of the information provided to authorities on behalf of their clients and could be forced to forfeit their licenses (or even be incarcerated) if fraud were to be proven.

In short, tax reform on the revenue side has generated new institutional arrangements by changing tax laws and enforcement mechanisms, enhancing revenue-collection agencies, and improving administrative procedures. Consequently, tax reforms must be understood as a part of an overall, and very ambitious, strategy aimed at the elimination of direct and indirect subsidies that have grossly protected large sectors of the economy. Though by no means through a smooth, linear process, successive tax reforms in both Argentina and Mexico ultimately led to: (1) the broadening of the tax base, thus incorporating large sectors that had previously been able to avoid paying taxes; (2) the reduction of the nominal tax burden for income taxes, the elimination of ineffective taxes, and the overall simplification (in relative terms, as it is claimed that the regulations can be further simplified) of administrative procedures for taxpayers; (3) the increased reliance on indirect taxation, namely, the value-added tax (VAT), as a crucial policy tool; and (4) the tightening of tax regulations, as well as improvement in the agencies in charge of collecting and overseeing taxation through the incorporation of up-to-date technology and new personnel, thus bringing about a substantial improvement of efficiency and capabilities in tax collection.

There are broader consequences of these reforms. First, tax reforms have helped achieve macroeconomic stability. They have drastically changed the allocation of the tax burden by incorporating people that have been traditionally out of the system, especially the middle-class sectors, professionals, and the self-employed. Second, by increasing revenues and reducing fiscal imbalances, these reforms have made a modest contribution toward greater equity by curbing the regressive distributional impact of the so-called "inflation tax."[16]

Third, taxation is currently an important electoral issue, and thus there is a novel concern regarding the allocation of resources by governments. There is not yet a "party of taxpayers" in Argentina and Mexico. The new awareness of fiscal questions may, however, prompt further changes in the electoral agenda and programmatic platforms of the political parties.[17] Finally, strengthening state capabilities in the area of taxation may eventually produce long-term "spillover" effects in upgrading state capacity in other important policy arenas (e.g., alleviating poverty, combating environmental degradation, promoting competition and antitrust regulation in the context of the privatization of public enterprises, etc.).[18]

TAX REFORM AND INSTITUTIONAL DESIGN

How was it possible to undertake such drastic reform of the tax institutions in Argentina and Mexico? Who was in charge of designing and implementing these significant policy changes? What were the roles of opposing groups and affected sectors? The findings reported in this chapter indicate that success in the implementation of the new tax strategies was an outcome of the prevailing structural economic crisis and the resulting transformation of societal preferences and strategies.

The economic crisis of the 1980s dramatically changed people's social preferences as macroeconomic stability became the major priority, even if this meant sacrificing (at least temporarily) well-entrenched symbols and ideological discourses concerning social justice, economic sovereignty, and political independence. The concomitant crisis of the SCM impeded the social and political actors associated with that matrix from articulating a sound and feasible alternative to neoliberalism. This was due to the impossibility of maintaining the state as a mobilizing mechanism and to the fact that atomized, individual strategies were substituted for collective ones as the legitimacy of those actors associated with the SCM was drastically reduced.[19] In addition to these factors, the debt crisis, the fiscal crisis of the state, and the need to bargain with private lenders all served to strengthen the role of the international financial institutions (IFIs) in Latin American societies. The new tax strategies in both Argentina and Mexico were very similar to the strategy advocated by the International Monetary Fund, the World Bank, and the Inter-American Development Bank. As the financial situations of both Argentina and Mexico continued to deteriorate, the international financial institutions capitalized on this opportunity to strongly influence domestic policy choices. The capacity of the IFIs to influence domestic economic policy has increased since 1982 due to crisis of the SCM and the myriad of societal and political changes that the crisis brought about. In sum, the change in domestic coalitions, societal preferences, state elites' strategies and capabilities, and the role of IFIs (all of which are closely related to the debt crisis and its aftermath) have combined to facilitate the transformation of tax institutions in Argentina and Mexico.[20]

However, the key players in reforming tax institutions have been state actors. Although the international financial institutions and other domestic actors have also been involved, a new breed of so-called "technopols"—comprised of the leading members of the "economic teams" and other new recruits to key posts in the executive branch—have largely displaced more traditional technocrats, who were affiliated with entrepreneurial interests or the political parties, and assumed a preeminent role in articulating the ideological discourse that attempts to legitimate the neoliberal revolution to citizens who are increasingly afflicted by plummeting living standards.[21] In evaluating the role of these technocrats, of course, it is important to consider that the presidency has been substantially reinforced under both Carlos Menem in Argentina and Carlos Salinas in Mexico. These stronger presidencies have facilitated the effective implementation of economic-restructuring policies, and particularly tax reform.[22]

Claiming that state capacity in Argentina and Mexico has increased is contradictory to both the neoclassical and the (more-or-less radical) neostructuralist paradigms.[23] Both these paradigms, their theoretical and normative differences notwithstanding, generally assert that the state should be, or will be, weakened in the process of neoliberal reform, and that there will be a tendency for markets to assume a more dominant role in the allocation of resources. However, due to tax reforms, in both Argentina and Mexico the state has increased its capacity and ability to extract and distribute resources. In addition, asserting that state actors have been the key players in reforming tax institutions challenges the argument that stabilization and structural reform packages (including tax reforms) were imposed by international financial agencies and creditors and that local actors lacked the capacity to decide how, when, and what to reform. Even though it is impossible to ignore the role of international actors, it is nevertheless the case that local actors, coalitions, and political processes (in other words, the political mechanisms behind economic reforms) are the dominant actors in the reform process.

As part of the policies of economic restructuring, a contingent coalition formed by incumbents, technocrats, private actors, and representatives of the international financial institutions both design, and participate in, the implementation of the tax reforms. This coalition may eventually experience internal struggle over particular issues, leading reformers to strengthen the tools that can dissuade real or potential adversaries and prevent less-than-enthusiastic members of the reform coalition from straying. For instance, the use of decrees, executive orders, and the threat of veto power of the executive can discipline the behavior of both supporters and opponents of reform. The core of the coalition ("the reformers") may also eventually employ some informal tools to secure compliance among its members.[24]

The tax reforms themselves can be used as a tool to encourage support for the larger neoliberal reform strategy, particularly among those sectors that had borne much of the tax burden under the previous revenue structure (i.e., high-income individuals, big local conglomerates, etc.). These sectors could conceivably have been targeted to increase the direct taxation of corporations and wealthy individuals. However, while direct taxes affecting these interests have risen slightly, current reforms have emphasized indirect taxation as the primary means to increase revenues. Moreover, by increasing the number of taxpayers and reducing the nominal burden, the reformers discouraged the development of opposing coalitions.

The experience of both Argentina and Mexico suggests that when dealing with potential opponents, reforming coalitions can also: (1) enlarge the tax base for both direct and indirect taxes; (2) expand the relative and absolute importance of the value-added tax; and (3) attempt to compensate the losers of the new scheme through enacting appropriate compensatory social policies directed toward the victims of reform or by hailing the positive consequences for the overall welfare of the citizenry of such general policy outcomes as price stability.[25] Consequently, even though specific private interests may eventually oppose particular policies (according to the particular actor's interests and relative political and economic resources), such partial opposition would not be likely to jeopardize the continuation of economic reforms. Finally, the particular dynamic of economic restructuring (i.e., its complexity, scope, and the lack of information about actual or probable consequences) helps to frustrate the emergence of coalitions espousing rival strategies.

The preceding explanation of reforming coalitions challenges a series of partial (and generally accepted) interpretations regarding particular aspects of economic restructuring. First, it is usually argued that uncertainty generates defensive strategies. However, my argument is that uncertainty, coupled with the positive initial results of restructuring policies, can help prevent defensive behaviors. Second, it is generally assumed that the reforming coalition is coherent and harmonious because its members share common interests in pursuing economic restructuring. My argument, however, is that the internal dynamics of the reforming coalition are seldom as melodious as is usually assumed. This is especially true for the so-called technocrats, a group that plays a crucial role in creating (and reinventing) incentives for the principal actors to help them persevere in their support of economic restructuring. In this sense, fiscal and monetary policies can also be interpreted as tools for reformers to use to keep the coalition together. In sum, the political engineering behind economic reforms is as important as the content itself of some policies and their apparent coherence (or lack thereof) vis-à-vis the overall economic strategy.[26]

CONCLUSION

How permanent are the recent policy and institutional reforms, including those affecting taxation, wrought by neoliberal restructuring in Latin America? Have the macroeconomic and political conditions that reduce uncertainty and allow actors to lengthen their time horizons become firmly institutionalized? At the macroeconomic level, if the permanence of recent transformations is not assured, speculative movements of internationally mobile capital in so-called emerging markets can challenge the efforts of states and international financial institutions, resulting in recessions and unstable political and economic scenarios. At a rather more microeconomic level, a rise of domestic or international interest rates could motivate a new surge of tax evasions.[27] After all, for taxpayers to continue complying with the law, their payoffs must not only exceed the costs of compliance, there must be certainty that in the medium to long term, no backsliding or return to the previous situation of free-riders and pervasive rent seekers will take place. Furthermore, given the fragility of the party systems in Latin America, the logic of electoral competition could eventually initiate a bidding war for taxpayer support; incumbents seeking reelection could find it electorally costly to attempt to sanction noncompliance behavior.[28]

Various "routes to the past" are possible, with predictably disastrous economic consequences and troubling implications for the consolidation and deepening of democratic institutions and practices. The story of tax reform remains open-ended; the course of future economic policy in both countries is also quite indeterminate. Moreover, it still remains to be seen whether the process of reconstructing state capacity will broaden beyond taxation to include other significant arenas of state policy. It is always logical—even imperative—to think of the possibility of a future tax reform, perhaps with a quite different orientation. These caveats notwithstanding, the transformations in Argentina and Mexico that were highlighted in this analysis lead to one certain conclusion: the script and the leading protagonists of the drama have changed. The Untouchables are now in town—and they are here to stay.

NOTES

1. By state capacity, I mean the state's ability to implement its own goals (including the creation and restructuring of political and social institutions) in the face of opposing societal actors and adverse macroeconomic conditions (Nordlinger, 1981; Skocpol, 1979; Knight, 1992).

2. Constrast Williamson's (1990) first statement of the "Washington Consensus" with his more recent position (1994), which is characterized by a greater recognition of the importance of state regulation and the strengthening of civil society.

3. As Acuña and Smith (1994) have maintained, this approach is certainly much less homogeneous. The main point that critics have in common is the rejection of neoclassical economic principles; principally, the idea that market mechanisms, by themselves, in the present international context are capable of promoting economic growth and development without state intervention (Borón, 1991; Evans, 1992; Fanelli et al., 1990; O'Donnell, 1992; Sunkel, 1993).

4. Haggard and Kaufman (1994) also recognized the strengthening of state capacity as a result of tax reform in the context of the instrumentation of neoliberal economic policies.

5. To have a more thorough understanding of this issue, considerations about the expenditure side must also be included. However, for the purpose of this chapter, I focus solely on the revenue side of fiscal reform, stressing especially those institutional and policy changes that led to the strengthening, thus leaving out other important problems such as the distributional and power consequences for different sectors (see the comments on this issue in note 23 below). For a further understanding of the politics of economic reform, see Haggard and Kaufman (1992), and Smith, Acuña, and Gamarra (1994a, 1994b). On taxation and tax reform, see Bird (1992); Carciofi et al. (1992); Durán and Gómez Sabaini (1994); Elizondo (1994, 1995); Gil Díaz (1993); Gillis (1989); and World Bank (1991).

6. See McCoy and Smith (1995) for an extension of Cavarozzi's discussion of the SCM to incorporate Venezuela's petro-state model of rentier capitalism.

7. Unions usually tried to get raises by renegotiating salaries after the official figure of inflation was released. However, it proved difficult for labor to get increases sufficient enough to counterbalance inflation. Moreover, the consumer price index (CPI) included a number of goods and services that did not necessarily correspond to what an average household actually consumed.

8. The social status of inspectors was as low as any other ordinary state employee for whom citizens had little respect. Working for the state was perceived to be synonymous with laziness and incompetence. Though this was a prejudice, people's daily experience justified this perception: any simple transaction at a public (not just a tax) agency or state enterprise required interminable waits in seemingly endless lines. Complicated procedures, proliferating regulations, and irrational instructions often turned objectively uncomplicated issues into inordinately time-consuming endeavors.

9. For instance, employees would receive part of their salaries "in white" (i.e., the minimum stipulated by the law) and part of them "in black" (i.e., a complementary and nontaxable amount). Therefore, contributions to social security would be calculated taking into consideration only the "white" part of the salary. Under this system, employees would get more money than they would if the system was just "white." Since the pension system was also mismanaged, workers had no incentive whatsoever to give more money to the pension system.

10. The regular procedure consisted of finding out how much money the owner of the firm (since they were primarily family businesses), or the financial manager, was willing to pay. Then, the equation was inverted. CPAs had to do their job in such a way as (a) to satisfy owners' greed (as they were ultimately the bosses) and/or make things compatible with the firm's overall double system and financial constraints; and (b) to avoid calling the attention of the tax collector by reporting tiny profits or figures inconsistent with previous years.

11. Before the 1980s, some efforts to modernize the tax structure were attempted in both Argentina and Mexico (as well as elsewhere in Latin America and other developing countries). However, as the core of the SCM remained very solid, achievements were only partial and generally proved ephemeral.

12. The notion of crusaders is not just allegorical. Carlos Tacchi, the current undersecretary of public revenue and the major actor involved in the new tax policy in Argentina, very recently stated in a celebrated TV show:

I owe God three very important things. I owe Him my own existence. He saved my son when he suffered a terrible accident riding a horse. And, third, He allowed me to continue living even though

I have cancer. For those reasons, I promise God just one thing: I'm going to exterminate people who evade taxes. I'm going to screw them all. ("Tiempo Nuevo," April 12, 1995)

13. For a further discussion of fiscal reform in Mexico, see Aspe Armella (1993); Bazdresch et al. (1993); López (1994); and Lustig (1992).

14. The financial collapse of late 1994 has, of course, seriously undermined macroeconomic stability and will make it difficult for the Zedillo government to sustain the progress of previous years.

15. For instance, since the wages of inspectors are partially related to the fines they collect, minor mistakes or technical violations might be used as an excuse to levy fines. Moreover, the complexity of the tax laws and other regulations may lead to misunderstandings as taxpayers and their CPAs, as well as inspectors, commit accidental mistakes. The only way to resolve these problems is by further simplifying regulations. In both countries, there is an emergent consensus in this regard.

16. Similarly, although indirect taxes have actually increased, effective enforcement mechanisms helped to eliminate another source of inequality: the transfer of resources from consumers to the owners of firms. Under the previous system, final prices included the value-added tax (VAT), so consumers did not have the opportunity to evade payment; in contrast, firms (especially smaller firms) commonly were able to evade payment of the VAT tax. Moreover, the evasion of the VAT (and the "black" economy in general), created further inequalities within sectors by helping inefficient firms to compete. In turn, this situation (in a closed economy) discouraged investment, technological innovation, and so forth. Finally, broad sectors of the upper-middle class in both Argentina and Mexico, and especially the "liberal professions" (physicians, lawyers, CPAs, dentists, etc.), which were previously beyond the reach of the tax collector, now pay taxes. In short, although indirect taxes (which impact workers and salaried employees disproportionately) have actually increased, the overall operation of the reformed tax systems have complex consequences that are ill-captured by such linear notions as "progressive" or "regressive."

17. The recent economic crisis in Mexico also allows us to evaluate how much taxation has changed in both countries. Thus, in the context of ambitious stabilization policies, both governments have relied heavily on the VAT as a tool to increase revenue. Mexico increased the VAT by 50 percent (from 10 percent to 15 percent), while Argentina increased it by 11.7 percent (from 18 percent to 21 percent). Had tax reforms in both countries not occurred, it would have been unthinkable for the governments to even consider the VAT as a useful instrument. The Chilean experience in the 1990s also suggests that the state could assume a reformulated, but still vital, role in social policy, and that taxation could become an appropriate tool, not only for funding new social programs, but also for achieving macroeconomic stability (i.e., as a tool for applying restrictive fiscal policies if inflationary trends are detected). See Berensztein (1994) for further analysis of these questions.

18. Although the process of state reform clearly still has a long way to go, some positive signs are already visible. Thus, in Mexico, migration agencies are learning from tax agencies' experience on how to improve administration, incorporate computer systems, train personnel, and so forth. In Argentina, the DGI is now in charge of the pension system, leading to a notable improvement in collection and operational efficiency.

19. The impacts of the collapse of the SCM on labor and capital are different, however. Indeed, the consequences of structural reforms within sectors are perhaps as im-

portant as those between them. In particular, the main divide seems to be between tradable and nontradable goods. Among the producers of nontradable goods, some sectors can better resist economic liberalization due to their capacity to obtain special protectionist policies (e.g., the auto industry). However, as a general rule, it could be argued that even though the emerging matrix seems to offer few opportunities for the exercise of veto powers compared to the SCM, capital obviously retains its ability to exercise market power, and particularly the capacity to determine the level of investment. Moreover, market power, and particularly control over the level of investment, is currently much more important than during the SCM era, as the public sector has been forced by the exigencies of fiscal equilibrium into a relatively passive role regarding investment.

20. For general arguments relating the role of external constraints and actors such as the IFIs to a shift in the direction of market-oriented strategies, see Stallings (1992) and Acuña and Smith (1994).

21. For an articulate defense of the "technopols," see the essays in Williamson (1994).

22. In both countries, strong executives have been a major attribute of their political systems, and democratic traditions have been fragile in Argentina and notoriously weak in Mexico. Therefore, although it is apparent that the concentration of power in the executive has had detrimental consequences for democracy, this should be interpreted as a continuity of prevailing features of their political systems and relations between the state and civil society, rather than as peculiarities specifically associated with recent neoliberal reforms. What is new, however, is the kind of tax policy that is being implemented. State actors are now strengthening tax institutions, which is indeed a sign of fundamental change.

23. It is worth noting that although some important contributions have already underscored the need to go beyond these simple notions (e.g., Acuña and Smith, 1994, and the other chapters in this volume), these paradigms still have a notable popularity.

24. For example, these measures can be used to threaten local producers with a further reduction of trade barriers, should prices increase, or to threaten local banks with tightened banking regulations, should administrative costs not be reduced.

25. Distributive considerations have prevented reformers from increasing the relative importance of the VAT as much (and as quickly) as they really wanted.

26. See Acuña and Smith (1994) for general arguments about "Hobbesian" strategies and the incentives shaping the response of different actors during the process of neoliberal restructuring.

27. In fact, the recent Mexican crisis and the "Tequila effect" in Argentina seem to corroborate this speculation, as tax collection has declined in nominal and real terms in both countries since December 20, 1994.

28. It is worth noting that in the long run, both Argentina and Mexico may have to reduce the tax burden, mainly for business. The rigidity of the current monetary policy in Argentina, for example, may make the level of taxation the only modifiable cost (at least in the short term) able to promote domestic activity and exports. In Mexico, as Reyes Heroles (1991) correctly argued, the current tax burden for business is very high if public goods obtained as a result of paying taxes are considered. As security, infrastructure, labor skills, and the like are very deficient, firms must provide those goods and services by themselves, thus increasing transaction costs. Finally, the wave of market-oriented reforms undergone by numerous other countries with so-called emergent markets may also influence the level of taxation in Argentina and Mexico. Thus, in an increasingly

competitive international environment, where both countries badly need inflows of foreign investment, the tax burden could become a variable that is adjusted in order to encourage direct foreign investment.

REFERENCES

Acuña, Carlos H. 1994. "Politics and Economics in the Argentina of the Nineties (Or Why the Future No Longer Is What It Used To Be)." In *Democracy, Markets, and Structural Reform in Latin America: Argentina, Bolivia, Brazil, Chile, and Mexico*, edited by William C. Smith, Carlos H. Acuña, and Eduardo A. Gamarra, pp. 31–74. New Brunswick, NJ: Transaction.

Acuña, Carlos H., and William C. Smith. 1994. "The Political Economy of Structural Adjustment: The Logic of Support and Opposition to Neoliberal Reform." In *Latin American Political Economy in the Age of Neoliberal Reform: Theoretical and Comparative Perspectives for the 1990s*, ed. William C. Smith, Carlos H. Acuña, and Eduardo A. Gamarra, pp. 17–66. New Brunswick, NJ: Transaction.

Aspe Armella, Pedro. 1993. *El camino mexicano de la transformación económica*. México, D.F.: Fondo de Cultura Económica.

Bazdresch, Carlos, et al. 1993. *Mexico: Auge, crisis y ajuste*. México, D.F.: El Trimestre Económico.

Berensztein, Sergio. 1994. "Política, economía y transición a la democracia en Chile." *Revista Internacional de Sociología* 7: 145–179.

Bird, Richard. 1992. "Tax Reform in Latin America: A Review of Some Recent Experiences." *Latin American Research Review* 27, 1: 7–36.

Borón, Atilio. 1991. *Memorias del capitalismo salvaje*. Buenos Aires: Imago Mundi.

Carciofi, Ricardo, et al. 1992. *"Reformas tributarias en América Latina: Revisión de algunas experiencias de la década del ochenta."* Buenos Aires: Comisión Económica para América Latina.

Cavarozzi, Marcelo. 1991. "Más allá de las transiciones a la democracia en América Latina." *Revista de Estudios Políticos* 74: 85–111.

———. 1992. "Paths of Democratization and State-Shrinking in South America." Overseas Development Council, Washington, DC. Mimeo.

———. 1994. "Politics: A Key for the Long Term in South America." In *Latin American Political Economy in the Age of Neoliberal Reform: Theoretical and Comparative Perspectives*, ed. William C. Smith, Carlos H. Acuña, and Eduardo A. Gamarra, pp. 127–156. New Brunswick, NJ: Transaction.

The Concise Oxford Dictionary of Current English. 1959. London: Oxford University Press.

Damill, José María, and Roberto Frenkel. 1992. "Reestructuración democrática y política económica: Argentina, 1984–1991." Centro de Estudios de Estado y Sociedad, Buenos Aires, Argentina. Mimeo.

Durán, Viviana, and Juan Carlos Gómez Sabaini. 1994. *Lecciones sobre reformas fiscales en Argentina 1990–1993*. Buenos Aires, Argentina: Organización de los Estados Americanos, Centro Interamericano de Tributación y Administración Financiera.

Elizondo, Carlos. 1994. "In Search of Revenue: Tax Reform in Mexico under the Administrations of Echeverría and Salinas." *Journal of Latin American Studies* 26, 1: 159–190.

———. 1995. "The Politics of Tax Reform in Latin America." México, D.F.: Centro de Investigación y Docencia Económicas. Mimeo.

Evans, Peter. 1992. "The State as Problem and Solution: Predation, Embedded Autonomy, and Structural Change." In *The Politics of Economic Adjustment: International Constraints, Distributive Conflicts, and the State*, ed. Stephan Haggard and Robert Kaufman, pp. 139–181. Princeton, NJ: Princeton University Press.

Evans, Peter, Dietrich Reuschemeyer, and Theda Skocpol, eds. 1985. *Bringing the State Back In*. Cambridge: Cambridge University Press.

Fanelli, José et al. 1990. *Growth and Structural Reform in Latin America. Where We Stand*. Documento CEDES 57. Buenos Aires: Centro de Estudios de Estado y Sociedad.

Gil Díaz, Francisco. 1993. *Análisis y evaluación de las reformas tributarias en México: 1980–1992*. Santiago: Comisión Económica para América Latina.

Gillis, Malcolm, ed. 1989. *Tax Reform in Developing Countries*. Durham, NC: Duke University Press.

Haggard, Stephan, and Robert Kaufman, eds. 1992. *The Politics of Economic Adjustment: International Constraints, Distributive Conflicts, and the State*. Princeton, NJ: Princeton University Press.

———. 1994. "The Challenges of Consolidation." *Journal of Democracy* 5, 4: 5–16.

Heredia, Blanca. 1994. "Making Economic Reform Politically Viable: The Mexican Experience." In *Democracy, Markets, and Structural Reform in Latin America: Argentina, Bolivia, Brazil, Chile, and Mexico*, ed. William C. Smith, Carlos H. Acuña, and Eduardo A. Gamarra, pp. 265–296. New Brunswick, NJ: Transaction.

Inter-American Development Bank (IDB). 1993. *Progreso económico y social en América Latina*. Washington, DC: Inter-American Development Bank.

International Monetary Fund (IMF). 1990. *"The IMF and Tax Reform."* Washington, DC: IMF, Fiscal Affairs Department.

Knight, Alan. 1992. *Institutions and Social Conflict*. Cambridge: Cambridge University Press.

López, Julio, ed. 1994. *México: La nueva macroeconomía*. México, D.F.: CEPNA and Nuevo Horizonte.

Lustig, Nora. 1992. *Mexico: The Remaking of an Economy*. Washington, DC: Brookings Institution.

McCoy, Jennifer, and William C. Smith. 1995. "The Challenge of Democratic Reequilibration in Venezuela: Theoretical and Comparative Perspectives." In *Venezuelan Democracy under Pressure*, ed. Jennifer McCoy, William C. Smith, Andrés Serbin, and Andrés Stambouli, pp. 237–284. New Brunswick, NJ: Transaction.

Nordlinger, Eric. 1981. *On the Autonomy of the Democratic State*. Cambridge: Harvard University Press.

O'Donnell, Guillermo. 1994. "The State, Democratization, and Some Conceptual Problems (A Latin American View with Glances at Some Post-Communist Countries)." In *Latin American Political Economy in the Age of Neoliberal Reform: Theoretical and Comparative Perspectives for the 1990s*, ed. William C. Smith, Carlos H. Acuña, and Eduardo A. Gamarra, pp. 157–180. New Brunswick, NJ: Transaction.

Olivera, Julio. 1967. "Money, Prices and Fiscal Lags: A Note on the Dynamics of Inflation." *Banca Nazionale del Lavoro Quarterly Review* 20: 258–267.

Reyes Heroles, José. 1991. "El sistema fiscal como determinante de la competitividad en el contexto del tratado trilateral de libre comercio." Paper presented to the conference entitled, "Integración Económica y Tributación." September 26, Guadalajara, Mexico.

Skocpol, Theda. 1979. *States and Social Revolutions: A Comparative Analysis of France, Russia, and China.* Cambridge: Cambridge University Press.

Smith, William C., Carlos H. Acuña, and Eduardo A. Gamarra, eds. 1994a. *Democracy, Markets, and Structural Reform in Latin America: Argentina, Bolivia, Brazil, Chile, and Mexico.* New Brunswick, NJ: Transaction.

———. 1994b. *Latin American Political Economy in the Age of Neoliberal Reform: Theoretical and Comparative Perspectives for the 1990s.* New Brunswick, NJ: Transaction.

Stallings, Barbara. 1992. "International Influence on Economic Policy: Debt, Stabilization, and Structural Reform." In *The Politics of Economic Adjustment: International Constraints, Distributive Conflicts, and the State,* ed. Stephan Haggard and Robert R. Kaufman, pp. 41–88. Princeton, NJ: Princeton University Press.

Steinmo, Sven. 1992. *Taxation and Democracy: Swedish, British and American Approaches to Financing in the Modern State.* New Haven, CT: Yale University Press.

Sunkel, Osvaldo, ed. 1993. *Development from Within: Toward a Neo-Structuralist Approach for Latin America.* Boulder, CO: Westview.

Tanzi, Vito. 1977. "Inflation, Lags in Collection, and the Real Value of Tax Revenue." International Monetary Fund (IMF) Staff Papers, vol. 24.

———. 1978. "Inflation, Real Tax Revenue and the Case for Inflationary Finance: Theory with an Application to Argentina." International Monetary Fund (IMF) Staff Papers, vol. 25.

Williamson, John, ed. 1990. *Latin American Adjustment. How Much Has Happened?* Washington, DC: Institute for International Economics.

———. 1994. *The Political Economy of Policy Reform.* Washington, DC: Institute for International Economics.

World Bank. 1991. *Lessons from Tax Reform: An Overview.* Washington, DC: World Bank.

13

ECONOMIC DYNAMISM AND INSTITUTIONAL RIGIDITY IN CHILE: RISKS AND OPPORTUNITIES AT THE TURN OF THE TWENTIETH CENTURY

Alvaro Díaz

Shortly before the inauguration of the Frei administration (1964–1970), a distinguished Economic Commission on Latin America (ECLA) economist, Aníbal Pinto, pointed out that "the Chilean case has shown for quite a while relatively advanced forms of social organization and institutional forms that contrast with a relative absence of changes in its economic structure, a dissociation that has become wider during the last two decades" (1975: 246). From 1964 to 1990, that disparity compelled governments of the right, center, and left to implement radical political and structural reforms.

These reforms have managed to modify, from above, the fundamental contours of the nation. During the last twenty years, Chile's economy has experienced dramatic and profound transformations that irreversibly modified, not only its own structure, but also that of the country's fundamental underlying institutions. Indeed, the nature of private companies and economic groups, of markets, and of attendant networks in which business activities are coordinated, as well as the role of the state in the promotion of development, in regulation, in the field of social welfare, and in the provision of productive infrastructure, are all substantially different from twenty years ago (see, among others, Silva, 1992, 1993; Vergara, 1985; Valenzuela and Valenzuela, 1986).

Thirty years later, Chile is beginning to experience the inversion of Pinto's old asymmetry. With protectionist anti-oligarchic barriers out of the way, the Chilean economy is growing healthily within a context of considerable macroeconomic stability. Today, however, Chilean institutions that were shaped by almost two decades of authoritarian rule and preserved through the first half of the 1990s by virtue of a pacted transition exhibit signs of obsolescence, not only as pertains to democracy, but also in the prevalent socioeconomic institutional context (cf. Garretón and Espinoza, 1992; Garretón, 1994). In a country characterized by expanding opportunity, such an institutional rigidity is alarming. If not seriously tackled within the next five years, this rigidity may threaten Chile's economic development, and could even culminate in a new sociopolitical crisis.

Revisiting Pinto's argument from the early 1960s, the central hypothesis analyzed in this chapter is that there is a growing disparity between the liberalization of the Chilean economy and the continued rigidity of its socioeconomic and political institutions. This asymmetry is gradually generating persistent and worsening difficulties, that not only threaten economic expansion as the country has thus far experienced it, but also prevent the construction of a more democratic sociopolitical order capable of offering a better life for all Chileans. Within this context, I will discuss three models that permit a more sophisticated and generalizable analysis of the challenges posed by the globalization of the world-economy and internationalization of Latin American economies: an Asian Pacific model, a model of neoliberal restructuring, and a balanced model of export-oriented insertion in the world-economy.[1] Hence, although this chapter deals with the specific experience of Chile, its purpose is to use the Chilean experience to engage a larger debate on future development paths in Latin America.

ECONOMIC EXPANSION AND INSTITUTIONAL RIGIDITY

After a decade of continuous growth, it is important to assess the degree of development achieved by Chile's economy, since this constitutes the point of departure for determining the potential effects of the internationalization of trade and regional integration schemes, as well as the possibility of Chile's entrance into the North American Free Trade Area (NAFTA) or even broader free trade agreements. As Table 13.1 demonstrates, Chilean development has moved into a *second exporting phase* (SEP), characterized by five basic tendencies: (1) the diversification of a core nucleus of enterprises oriented toward exports (a core that is no longer merely confined to copper but now includes a greater variety of products and destination markets); (2) the growth of an industry of "industrially processed raw materials" (IPRMs), which are experiencing a notable technological improvement; (3) the unexpected growth of manufacturing exports (not based on national IPRMs), which increased seven-fold between 1987 and 1994; (4) the rise of service exports, which grew by twenty times over during the last decade; and (5) the significant increase of direct Chilean investment in neighboring countries (surpassing U.S. $2 billion in the case of Argentina).[2]

The "real" SEP is, in fact, much broader than was depicted by theorists in the late 1980s. It is not merely limited to the manufacturing area, nor does it imply a complete rupture with the traditional phase of export-led growth. On the one hand, it is clear that Chile will not cease to be an exporter of raw materials such as minerals and forestry products. On the other hand, the SEP favors the growth of nontraditional exports, including goods, services, and capital. It therefore makes more sense to compare Chile with Sweden, Finland,

Table 13.1
Chilean Goods and Service Exports, 1987–1994 (Millions of Dollars FOB)

Exports	1987	1990	1994	% variation 1987-1994
Raw Materials % Participation in X_t	$3,614 57%	$5,587 54%	$6,422 44%	8.6%
Processed Raw Materials % Participation in X_t	$1,410 22%	$2,167 21%	$3,815 26%	15.3%
Manufactures % Participation in X_t	$200 3%	$569 6%	$1,410 10%	32.2%
Services % Participation in X_t	$1,085 17%	$2,001 19%	$2,860 20%	14.9%
Total	$6,309	$10,323	$14,507	12.8%

FOB: Free on Board (Port of Shipment price).
X_t: Exports for year in question.
Source: Raw Data from Banco Central (Chile). Estimates for 1994 are preliminary. Methanol is included as an industrial commodity.

Denmark, and New Zealand—countries with intensive export capacity in regard to processed raw materials—than with Taiwan and South Korea. What is peculiar about Chile, however, is its highly segmented mode of international insertion: although exports of processed raw materials generally flow toward Asia, Europe, and the United States, manufactured goods and a large share of services are oriented toward other Latin American markets.

The consolidation of the SEP faces three major problems: the so-called Dutch syndrome, asymmetrical income distribution, and politico-institutional rigidity.

The *Dutch syndrome* entails a drop of real exchange rates—at least in the middle term—that results from the success of primary exports and influx of foreign investment (which in Chile's case is channeled chiefly into the mining sector). In addition, real salaries persistently tend to rise due to the tension created by a labor market that is segmented into tradable and nontradable sectors.[3] When combined, these tendencies may adversely affect the gains made by

Table 13.2
Household Participation in Income Distribution in Chile

	Lowest 40%	Middle 40%	Top 10%	Equity Lowest 40% Top 10%
Chile				
1968	13.7	35.4	34.4	0.40
1978 (a)	14.5	34.5	35.0	0.41
1988	13.4	30.8	41.9	0.32
1990	14.5	29.6	42.2	0.34
1993	15.1	31.0	40.0	0.38
Sweden	21.2	41.9	20.8	1.02
Japan	21.9	40.6	22.4	0.98
Germany	19.5	41.9	23.4	0.83
Spain	19.4	40.5	24.5	0.79
U.S.	15.7	42.4	25.0	0.63
Hong Kong	16.2	36.8	31.3	0.52
Singapore	15.0	36.0	33.5	0.45
Malaysia	13.9	35.5	34.8	0.40
Venezuela	14.3	36.3	33.2	0.43
Mexico	12.7	33.1	38.1	0.33
Brazil	7.0	25.7	51.3	0.14

Sources: All calculations by the author. Chilean data provided by the Instituto Nacional de Estadística. For other countries, see World Bank (1975–1993).

the manufacturing sector and the growth of spinoff industries and other production linkages. This has not yet occurred, which underscores the considerable amount of competitive resources enjoyed by this sector. However, it is far from clear whether it could withstand prolonged exposure to these tendencies. This vulnerability, coupled with the possible obsolescence of the system of promotion of nontraditional exports and the lack of effective safeguards against disloyal competition, suggests the possibility of a future involution of the SEP and a return to a more traditional export model based on primary products. This would, in turn, provoke a new wave of defensive rationalizations on the part of the industrial sector, a rise in unemployment, and the loss of previously accumulated exporting experience.

Asymmetrical income distribution is another problem of the SEP. Despite obvious improvements in the standard of living of its population, the data in Table 13.2 reveal that, in comparison with other countries, Chile has not experienced changes in its highly skewed income distribution between 1968 and 1993. Although income distribution improved slightly between 1988 and 1993, it is even more skewed than it was in 1968, when it was already significantly asymmetrical.[4] Indeed, Chile is far from attaining the income equity levels found in developed countries, even lagging behind the "Asian Tigers" (e.g., South Korea, Singapore, Hong Kong). Among late-developing economies, only Mexico and Brazil have more uneven income distribution structures.[5]

A cursory comparative reading of data from 1988 and 1993 could suggest that there is increasing income equity in Chile, with progress being slowed and conditioned by the economy's capacity to sustain high growth rates with low inflation. However, the evidence does not yet support this claim. For example, the Gini coefficient was 0.46 in 1991, 0.49 in 1992, and 0.47 in 1993, showing no clear tendency. Moreover, Chile's integration into global markets could stimulate combined expansion/decline cycles, which in the industrial and agricultural sectors would manifest themselves through a stagnation of employment levels, new rationalizations of firms, and even increased disparity between productivity and salaries.

There are institutional and structural variables that explain the persistence of a highly uneven income distribution. Institutional variables include the specific nature of factory regimes and the organization of work along Taylorist lines, the existence of unregulated labor markets, and the absence of "safety net" mechanisms designed to protect the temporarily unemployed. Most important, structural variables include a high degree of economic concentration (70 percent of exports are concentrated among eighteen large companies and trading firms).[6] Uneven income distribution is only one manifestation of the large power asymmetries present throughout Chilean society.

A final difficulty associated with the SEP involves *politico-institutional rigidity*. The politico-institutional model that emerged under the authoritarian aegis between 1975 and 1985 has not been significantly altered. Furthermore, there currently are no social and political conflicts on the horizon that might be capable of initiating an overhaul of existing institutional arrangements. A specific political regime, with a certain institutional configuration and specific compliance mechanisms, has taken root. Within this matrix, the rightist opposition defends the status quo and seeks to preserve a particular modernizing strategy, while the center-left political forces controlling the central government aim at modifying the existing order and instituting a different strategy. The center-left coalition government has the support of most of the population, although with the disadvantage that Chilean civil society is still largely silent and disorganized, expressing itself through relatively few public actors. Thus, the government has as its main reference the world of "public opinion," which is chiefly voiced through mass communications media that are almost overwhelmingly controlled by economic elites and conservative forces.

All attempts at reforming socioeconomic regulatory mechanisms invariably collide with a conservative senate in which the rightist opposition is over-represented as a result of a system designed in part during the previous military regime (including the appointment of "designated," nonelected senators and a cameral electoral scheme). As a consequence of these electoral arrangements, the postauthoritarian democratic governments have found it difficult to propose significant reforms and instead tend to move toward the adoption of policies that are "administrative" in nature, appearing resigned to operate within the context of a "frozen" political system whose features cannot be revamped.

There is thus a growing asymmetry in Chile between two great forces that are reshaping the country: on the one hand, internationalization and democratic transition, and on the other, the rigidity and obsolescence of the political and economic institutions inherited from the previous authoritarian regime and its neoliberal economic policies. This constitutes an inversion from the dissociation that characterized the country prior to 1973. That disparity led to radical attempts at transforming and modernizing the economic structure between 1964 and 1990, transformations that were carried out by governments of the center (Eduardo Frei Montalva from 1964 to 1970), the left (Salvador Allende between 1970 and 1973), and the right (the neoliberal dictatorship of General Augusto Pinochet from 1973 to 1990).

The contemporary asymmetry is very different, however. The Chilean economy is undoubtedly growing by leaps and bounds. This vertiginous growth is rapidly modifying the economic structure of the country. However, this growth contrasts with a noticeable lag in the evolution of socioeconomic institutions. If this rigidity continues unchanged, the Chilean state may be left powerless to confront the important challenges of the future.[7]

THE (APPARENT) SILENCE OF CIVIL SOCIETY

Chile is notable for the apparent silence and docility of its civil society, in stark contrast with countries such as Mexico, Brazil, and Argentina (Tironi and Lagos, 1991; Acuña and Smith, 1994; Smith and Acuña, 1994). True, Chile has clearly experienced greater improvements in the standard of living of millions of its citizens. Even though income concentration has not changed, the number living in poverty has declined. Salaries have risen, and formal employment has expanded. Chileans today consume much more than at any point in the past. Nevertheless, there remain considerable insecurity and dissatisfaction with working and living conditions. In this sense, the "silence" of civil society might seem a mere appearance, as civil society expresses itself in many ways, sometimes openly and at other times in a more veiled manner. However, regardless of the modes of these expressions, the current situation is in clear contrast with the first half of the 1980s, when large public protests against the dictatorship were commonplace. The current silence is not simply felt in the streets; it has also taken root at a cultural level. Chile has not become a more open society. Instead, it seems that conservative tendencies, and even an authoritarian culture, have become stronger and more deeply embedded.

Table 13.3

Social Destructuring and Restructuring in Chile, 1972–1992

Transformations in Occupational Structure (% of economically active population).	Year		
	1972	1982	1992
Unemployment	4.3%	19.6%	4.4%
Wage Earners	60.2%	39.2%	60.4%
Service Workers	50.9%	61.8%	51.5%
Informalization	22.9%	22.7%	25.1%
Emergency Employment	0.0%	11.0%	0.0%
Public Employment	12.0%	8.0%	6.0%

Source: Calculated by author using data supplied by the Ministerio de Planificación y Cooperación (MIDEPLAN).

The explanation for this silence can only be found in the analysis of the events of the last two decades. From 1972 to 1982, Chilean society was characterized by the disarticulation of the old social structure, the chief manifestations of which were a rise of unemployment, wage loss, growth of informal urban labor, an increase of spurious tertiary employment, and general impoverishment. Subsequently, from 1983 to 1993, a new social structure, which was distinguished by a rapid decrease of unemployment levels, wage increases, relative shrinkage of the informal sector, a decline of spurious tertiary employment coupled with the emergence of a new tertiary labor sector, and a general reduction of poverty levels (especially between 1988 and 1992), began to emerge. The changes have been well documented (Díaz, 1991); they are summarized on Table 13.3, which depicts the relevant peaks of the 1972–1982 period.

In 1982, at least 50 percent of Chilean workers were unemployed, subscribed to emergency employment programs, or were part of the informal sector. This proportion changed drastically ten years later, when only three out of ten Chilean workers operated under the same conditions. In short, the labor force grew from 3.8 million in 1982 to 4.8 million in 1992, but the number of unemployed or underemployed workers declined from 2 million to 1.5 million. In addition, salaries rose and informal unemployment rates fell, indicating the emergence of a new social structure.

The data in Table 13.3 can be interpreted in terms of a superimposed sequence of three distinct social cycles.[8] The first cycle was characterized by the erosion of the social structure associated with the import-substitution industrialization model, with an attendant increase in the social costs of authoritarian repression. During the second cycle, the social structure associated with neoliberal reform took form only to subsequently enter into a process of decomposition, leading to mass protests and the emergence of antisystemic social movements. Finally, the third cycle, which is now emerging, entails the consolidation of new social structures linked to the expansion of an export-based economy and is characterized by the ascendancy of systemic social actors that are more fully incorporated into production, the market, and institutionalized forms of political participation.

What is interesting about the Chilean case is that, in contrast with other Latin American cases (such as Mexico), it included two *successive* phases of social disarticulation and rearticulation.[9] Chileans suffered massively during the 1973–1983 period, but they also enjoyed the benefits of the post-1984 recovery, particularly after 1990. This entailed the transformation and recomposition of the social bases that gave rise to the urban protest movement of the first half of the 1980s. New social actors, which are still in process of constitutive maturation, emerged during this period of social transformation.

The combination of destructuring and restructuring features is a phenomenon that has only been clearly discernable since the early 1990s, when certain production areas (e.g., coal, textiles, and some others) underwent processes of reconversion. In Chile, however, there are sharp sectoral and regional inverse relationships linking the degree of social activism to the level of economic growth. Industries affected by recession or decline (and the geographic regions in which they are based) have better-organized social actors. In contrast, those sectors of production that are in a process of expansion have inchoate collective social actors that are still in process of formation.[10]

This asymmetry is common to a number of Latin American societies. It is a by-product of a style of capitalist modernization characterized by strong private appropriation of benefits coupled with a socialization of losses and other negative effects. One of the most serious consequences of this asymmetry is that it poses major obstacles to dialogue between progressive, center-left political elites that subscribe to a modernizing view of society, and the popular sectors, who feel the most negative effects of that type of modernization. The result is a cleavage that alienates political parties (especially those concerned with governing) from the representatives of the subaltern strata of civil society.

THE CHALLENGE OF INTERNATIONALIZATION

The Chilean government has frequently reiterated its goal of inserting the country into a variety of trade blocs as a strategy designed to consolidate the level of diversification and international insertion thus far achieved. This strategic goal is congruent with the features of Chile's already-diversified international trade structure. It is for this reason that, having abandoned unilateral liberalization, the Chilean government has placed its bets on free-trade agreements rather than customs unions. It is for the same reason that, having made considerable inroads in the area of bilateral treaties, it also bets simultaneously on the North American Free Trade Agreement (NAFTA) and MERCOSUR, the Common Market of the Southern Cone, without losing sight of the potential represented by the Asian Pacific Economic Community (APEC) and agreements with the European Union.

This free-trade discourse is not mere rhetoric. It reflects significant efforts made by various cabinet ministries (finance, foreign relations, and economy) along many trade fronts, with a clear emphasis of the ministry of finance on NAFTA, and of the ministry of foreign relations on MERCOSUR. This represents a shift from the 1990–1993 period, when all efforts centered on achieving Chile's entrance into NAFTA, to the detriment of trade agreements with neighboring countries. The current strategy aims at correcting the strategic error of underestimating the dynamism of MERCOSUR, a policy error that underscores the perils of institutional rigidity. The Chilean leadership simply did not have sufficient margins of flexibility at the time when MERCOSUR was created, which precluded Chile's alignment with that bloc at its inception.

Many analysts overestimate the advantages of the "strategic anchor" that membership in NAFTA presumably will provide, while ignoring the fact that South America is an important market for a large part of Chile's industry and important segments of its agricultural and service sectors. It is important to ensure that Chile does not blindly follow the model implemented by the former Spanish Prime Minister Felipe González, who was the first to devise a "strategic anchor" policy that relied on membership in the European Economic Community (EEC) as the key to the consolidation of Spain's democracy and the modernization of its market economy.

However, a harmonious integration of Chile into NAFTA and MERCOSUR (as well as other trade blocs) constitutes a strategy that can only succeed if and when either (1) the entire world-economy becomes fully integrated, or (2) the Americas become a free-trade area. Neither of these scenarios is likely in the immediate future. This has a number of consequences. First, it is important to acknowledge that there is strong tension between the NAFTA and MERCOSUR options, as the concessions that Chile could offer within the context of NAFTA are not the same it could offer to MERCOSUR.[11] Second, the Chilean government faces uncertainties that will be difficult to overcome, regardless of political will. It cannot prematurely place all its bets in favor of one treaty to the detriment of the other, because *both* strategic options offer advantages, and also because events are largely beyond its control. Third, the government faces negotiations along two fronts: one with international trade blocs, and the other with domestic actors and pressure groups that present increasingly insistent demands of a corporatist nature. Finally, the government risks becoming trapped between the pressure exerted by state institutions (given the sensitivity of the various cabinet ministries to sectoral pressures) and the fissures produced by the division of labor among the cabinet ministries (reflected by the preference of the Ministry of foreign relations for MERCOSUR and the Ministry of Finance for NAFTA, for example). Thus far, these pressures have not exceeded certain bounds. However, as the negotiations progress (or stagnate), new uncertainties and difficulties will render the elaboration of a coherent strategy increasingly problematic.

What will be the consequences of this next phase of economic restructuring? Several propositions can be advanced. First, every process of integration generates benefits and costs that inevitably are unevenly distributed geographically and by area of occupation. Second, although trade agreements focus on commercial exchanges, a synergy occurs with the integration of financial markets, which are much more integrated and difficult to regulate.[12] Third, all integration agreements have social consequences.

Taking these propositions into consideration, integration is likely to bring along changes that will be massive and traumatic. Even though Chile probably will be able to maintain an annual GDP growth rate of between 5 and 6 percent, the expansion of some economic areas will be counterbalanced by the deterioration of other industries, geographic regions, and social actors. We already have seen many examples of this. For example, while the telecommunications industry thrives, coal production declines and textile and shoe production are in a difficult process of reconversion. Such complex scenarios probably will become much more commonplace during the next few years. Likewise, following integration into NAFTA, MERCOSUR, and the new General Agreement on Tariffs and Trade (GATT) regime, it will be difficult for Chile to sustain the levels of economic growth and social welfare of the 1990–1994 period in the absence of significant institutional changes, including, for example, the establishment of unemployment insurance and a better worker-training system.[13] Finally, contemporary processes of economic integration tend to induce an export-oriented dynamic favoring large-scale industrial endeavors. Despite its immediate benefits, this dynamic will exacerbate environmental pollution and require significant investment and regulation to promote the recycling of industrial waste and protect the environment, while ensuring the quality of life of the population.

In sum, internationalization will further stimulate Chile's economy, but it will also generate new economic and social disequilibria. If the benefits of globalization are regressive and very unevenly distributed, globalization will exert a destabilizing influence. The presence of both winners and losers will not neutralize the ensuing conflicts, as some observers might erroneously imagine. To the contrary, social tensions may rise in direct proportion to the deepening of social differences associated with sequential phases of economic restructuring.

Compounding these problems, governability might become increasingly problematic. Several analysts have noted that, regardless of intent, trade policy is being built as a substitute for an industrial policy that is oriented to the promotion of specific sectors of production. Such an avenue appears attractive, as policy makers face many obstacles in attempting to design a development strategy but few in negotiating a free-trade accord. However, herein lies one of the most serious flaws of the current strategy. Trade negotiations will not emerge from a strategic plan designed and agreed on by domestic sectors. Rather, trade deals will result from an uncertain and complex bargaining process. Domestic and external pressures, as well as a combination of forces among blocs, may produce a relatively disorderly opening to the world-economy, increasing in the future the difficulties of governing.

One of the sources of consistency in any trade strategy is the transparency of the general development model, which should not be a rigid blueprint, but rather a flexible strategy that takes aim at clearly established objectives. Chile's development strategy is unclear and has not been designed consensually. Moreover, there are no signs that any relevant dialogue will take place anytime soon. If these trends continue, the current drive for integration increasingly runs the risk of undermining the benefits that have been thus far achieved.

THREE MODELS OF DEVELOPMENT AND INTERNATIONAL INSERTION

In view of the known positions espoused by Chilean political and intellectual elites, one can identify three alternative models to the SEP. Although many of their main components remain largely implicit, these models reflect current debates on the issues at hand. As depicted in Table 13.4, these models reflect different social interests, are expressed through divergent economic policies, and entail different state configurations.

The *Asian Route* (Model I) has as its point of reference the East Asian paradigm (Japan, South Korea, and Taiwan). It seeks to mobilize surpluses from the primary and tertiary sectors to assemble a large-scale export industry. This requires the presence of an active state with a "market-friendly" industrial policy promoting exports of relatively high technological content.

Even leaving aside cultural differences, it is debatable whether this model could be applied to Chile. First, the country is endowed with resources of a different nature. It has a small population and vast natural resources (the opposite is true in Japan and South Korea). Second, the powerful Asian states of the 1950s emerged from a historical reality quite different from that of Chile,

Table 13.4
Three Strategies to "Deepen" the Second Exporting Phase

Model	I: Asian Route	II: Neoliberal Route	III: Balanced Development
Principal Sectors	Secondary exporting sector transferring surpluses from the primary and tertiary sectors	Primary and tertiary, with adjustments to the manufacturing and agricultural sectors	Even development of the three sectors
Type of State	"Developmentalist" state of the East Asian variety	Neoliberal	New state geared to an export-led economy
Type of Economic Strategy	Industrial policy results in macro- and micro-level over-regulation	Increasing "self-regulation" of financial markets and trade liberalization	Macro- and micro-level regulation, with technological, infrastructure, education, and human development policies

where the postwar climate favored national unity and a strong state–private sector partnership. Finally, the present global and domestic historical context does not favor export-promotion policies, which require a powerful protectionist state.

The *Neoliberal Route* (Model II) seeks to maintain the growth of the primary exporting sector while favoring the service industry. In Chile, its advocates assume that the agricultural and secondary sectors are not competitive internationally because they require excessive subsidies from the state. They also assert that primary exports will regain importance in view of the volume of investment flowing toward the mining and forestry sectors. However, this analysis neglects the fact that agricultural and fishing exports are not going to grow at the rate of the 1980s. In addition, it assumes that the Dutch syndrome will not be a problem because it reduces the cost of imports and thus favors the consumer, thus overlooking its destructive effects on the industrial and agricultural sectors.

Last, but not least, the neoliberal model assumes—without proving it—that the Chilean financial sector will have sufficient competitive advantages to constitute a financial-services platform. Simply asserting that Chile can become another Switzerland or Panama is a risky venture, since there are no certainties, but only flexible specialization in some industrial and agricultural areas in international financial markets.

The neoliberal model considers NAFTA, APEC, and an accord with the European Union as the only reliable path of successful international insertion. It ascribes no importance to MERCOSUR. Since Chile has already entered the second exporting phase, however, the result could well be an involution of the secondary exporting sector and the return to primary sector specialization in exports. This could unleash a new wave of defensive industrial rationalizations, foster unemployment, and destroy accumulated exporting experience. The result would be an even more skewed pattern of income distribution.

The third option involves a *Balanced Model of Development* (Model III), which asserts that export-led development can be maintained by diversifying exports among the primary, secondary, and tertiary sectors.[14] This is the best path for achieving a more equitable and sustainable income distribution, while promoting the modernization of the country in a context of global integration. The goal is also feasible, since the second exporting phase has already been successful in inducing a relatively balanced development among the three exporting sectors thanks to economic policies that prevented rigid and excessive overspecialization.

To accomplish balanced, export-led development, envisioning the type of foreign trade that will be dominant during the next decade, it is necessary to replace the conventional concept of *intersectoral* export specialization for a greater emphasis on *intrasectoral* specialization. Chile's future does not lie in the exploitation of its primary-sector comparative advantages and the relegation of the rest of its economy under the headings "nontradable" or "import substitutes." The achievements of the 1990–1994 period suggest that Chile's future hinges instead on its ability to take advantage of comparative advantages that will vary across sectors and industries.[15]

A balanced development of Chilean exports of goods, services, and investment precludes either a pursuit of an "Asian route" (for example, efforts to increase manufactures until they reach 30 percent of all exports) or a return to a model of primary-sector export specialization. The alternative model would consolidate the level of primary exports that has already been achieved (between 10 and 15 percent), so as to ensure a growth rate similar to that enjoyed by the total of exports. This would facilitate the modernization of the industrial sector and encourage innovative efforts to capture competitive export niches.

CONCLUSION: BEYOND NEOLIBERAL RESTRUCTURING

Structural adjustment took place within neoliberal parameters in Mexico, Argentina, Chile, Colombia, and other Latin American countries. The relative strength and cohesion of the state was one of the most significant factors responsible for the degree of success achieved by neoliberal reform projects. The Chilean case offers important lessons in this respect. The experience of 1983–

1990 and the subsequent transformations show that the Chilean state had, and still has, a significant interventionist capacity. In fact, it is by virtue of this capability that the state was able to reorganize its economy during the authoritarian period. Perhaps never before had a Chilean state been so powerful in its reach. Far from a "minimalist" state, what existed during the 1973–1990 dictatorship was a strong, neoliberal interventionist state whose industrial and social policies were quite regressive but whose policies in the financial-fiscal sphere were very activist in seeking to control the most important macroeconomic variables. Even now, after most of the neoliberal project has been implemented, the state has by no means been dismantled, as it clearly continues to enjoy relatively wide margins of action.

Neoliberalism-as-discourse continues to be largely hegemonic in Chilean society. However, neoliberalism is largely spent as a force for transforming the society, economy, and polity, and it does not constitute a long-term option. The neoliberal model *has* been applied in its entirety, but Chile now is moving into a post-neoliberal phase, as the old model progressively recedes before the advance of the democratic transition and the emergence of new challenges that call for the opening of the national economy. This transformation is not unique to Chile; it is common throughout the hemisphere. The neoliberal phase is coming to an end in all of Latin America. Shortly, there will be no more state enterprises to privatize; unilateral economic liberalization has given way to negotiated arrangements. Moreover, deregulation and the dismantling of old legislation restricting markets and limiting the options of both management and labor are already nearing completion.

Chile, Mexico, and Argentina have already moved into the post-neoliberal period, albeit at different tempos and with varying consequences.[16] The most important privatizations have been completed, as has the deregulation of old market-control mechanisms. The most important factors now affecting these economies involve integration into the regional and global economies, which are processes that require new forms of action on the part of the state. The post-neoliberal state will need to be more proficient in the management of macroeconomic variables, since commercial integration exacerbates the financial and monetary exchange difficulties inherent in internationalization. New conditions also will demand more "market-friendly" industrial and technological policies that, nonetheless, will still entail a significant component of subsidies to firms and workers. What will be increasingly required is a state that is actively involved in the allocation of resources and performs a vital catalytic role in the economy. In fact, new forms of industrial policy are currently being designed and implemented, signaling an irreversible erosion of the old neoliberal orthodoxy and the imperative of combining growth with equity in the context of more democratic societies.

The neoliberal model of the past is proving increasingly inadequate to face the challenges of the future. The challenges imposed by the internationalization of the economy in the context of a democratic transition call for the creation of a new developmental state. This new state should be oriented toward developing markets and private enterprises, but it must also be capably engaged on educating, training, fostering technological advancement, regulating, and developing the country's infrastructure. A new basis of bargaining and compromise must be found between workers and entrepreneurs, as well as between peripheral regions and the core of the country. Moreover, a new welfare state must be constructed, which is circumscribed by current levels of fiscal discipline and firmly anchored on decentralized structures. This new system would at once stimulate private initiative and possess the effective regulatory capacity needed to ensure a reasonable level of flexibility in the productive sector without jeopardizing employment.

Modernization entails transformation. In the context of the increasing globalization of the world-economy and the dawning of a period of great changes, the strategic design of an open, export-led economy will not be viable except for a modern state geared toward achieving development, building domestic consensus in a climate of partnership and cooperation, and ensuring the welfare of the citizenry in a manner congruent with the realities of the new age. Ultimately, a modern, export-led economy cannot be sustained without a free civil society and a more representative and democratic political system.

NOTES

The author would like to thank Erick Bridoux for translating this chapter from Spanish, and Bill Smith and Roberto P. Korzeniewicz for their useful comments and editorial suggestions.

1. By *globalization* I refer to the sum of financial, commercial, cultural, and social processes that link Chile to ongoing transformations in the world-economy. By *internationalization* I mean the sum of decisions and strategic actions undertaken by governing elites to effect and regulate the economic liberalization. Although both terms seem to be synonymous, they operate in entirely different realms. Globalization is initially an exogenous and, later, endogenous process that accelerates, at various levels, certain changes that have been taking place for a number of centuries. Internationalization, for its part, is an endogenous process related to the actions of actors in a small, peripheral country such as Chile. These actors—state elites, national economic groups, transnational enterprises, and others—seek to channel the benefits of globalization, mitigate its more destructive and centrifugal effects, and obtain a more convenient place in the new international order.

2. It is interesting to note that this type of investment emerged entirely as a result of an industrial logic. It makes more sense for some Chilean companies to purchase and modernize Argentine companies than to attempt to double their capacity within Chile. The significance of these investments may *not* appear evident in examining Chile's trade balance but will be reflected in the capital ledger, and perhaps also in the balance of services (see Table 13.1).

3. Moreover, there is a possibility that countries such as Argentina and Brazil will attempt to resolve their balance-of-payments problems through currency devaluations (as in Mexico) or by erecting tariff or nontariff barriers. This would not affect the level of

raw material or industrial commodity exports but would alter the volume of manufactured exports to Latin America.

4. It is important to point out that the poorest 30 percent of the population increased its share of national income from 7.5 percent to 9.2 percent between 1988 and 1993. Nevertheless, this change is practically marginal and does not substantially modify the situation.

5. Of course, we are dealing with economies that are still undergoing structural adjustment, with considerable economic expansion a strong possibility.

6. These companies produce commodities in continuous- and semicontinuous-processing plants (celluloid, paper, fish meal, refined copper, etc.) that have high capital- and labor-intensive configurations. The economic viability of these ventures rests on the construction of "mega-projects," which can only be made possible through multinational enterprises, large domestic economic groups, or joint ventures capable of mobilizing resources and investments often exceeding a hundred million dollars.

7. Indeed, in less than a decade, certain export-promotion mechanisms (such as the system of simplified tax incentives for exports) will cease to exist in their present form and will have to be replaced by a new set of instruments to stimulate production and the diffusion of new technologies. The same is true for regulatory mechanisms (such as "antidumping" regulations), which will have to be adjusted to new GATT norms. Unless a new system of export promotion (based more on technology than direct subsidies) is crafted, Chile may be trapped in an institutional vacuum that will impede its ability to take advantage of opportunities and adequately face the challenges posed by increased integration into the global economy.

8. How are these structural changes related to transformations in collective social action? The hypothesis I advanced in a previous work is that the relative dynamism and/ or acquiescence of social actors between 1972 and 1992 can best be understood, at least in the first instance, from factors found in the sociopolitical sphere. However, the structural transformations *consolidated* a process that began as a radical project emerging from the sociopolitical arena. For example, the nature of resistance to the Pinochet dictatorship would have been different if it had proved possible to maintain employment in the key industrial sector at the same high levels characteristic of the previous decades of ISI. This did not occur, of course. The drastic decline of industrial employment between 1975 and 1980 shows that the cooptation of the labor movement was the result, not only of government repression, but also of something that went much deeper. The neoliberal reform and structural adjustment processes destroyed the social bases that had sustained the power of the labor unions and political parties of the left during the 1960s. Ten years later, in the same vein, the antigovernment resistance of 1985 would have been quite different had the economic crisis continued unabated, pushing unemployment upward and enhancing the importance of the informal sector—that is to say, propping up the social actors that were the main protagonists of the antiregime events. This, too, failed to take place. The economic recovery and resumption of growth slowly altered the social structure and diluted the social and cultural bases that had catalyzed the great mobilizations of 1983–1986.

9. See Díaz (1996) for a more complete theoretical elaboration of this argument. Torre's (1996) comments comparing the Mexican and Chilean cases argue in a similar vein.

10. For example, this situation contrasts with the case of the "new unionism" in the late 1970s in the São Paulo region, where this asymmetry was not present.

11. This is true especially as pertains to some agricultural and industrial sectors. This is precisely what Brazilian and Argentine negotiators protest, even though they agree to Chile's status as only an associate member (and therefore recognize that it should not be obligated to raise its tariffs, which are lower than those mandated by MERCOSUR rules).

12. Hence, judging by the recent Mexican financial collapse and its so-called "tequila effect" on the other regional economies, the problem is not merely one of exchange rate instability but also one of great sensitivity to short-term capital movement.

13. See Vergara (1990, 1994) for critiques of the limitations of labor market, social welfare, and human capital formation policies, which stress the element of continuity under democracy with the practices inherited from the Pinochet dictatorship.

14. This development strategy can ameliorate the effects of some tendencies (for example, declining exchange rates) without nullifying them in the long term.

15. The textile sector is an example of this. Between 1991 and 1994, textiles experienced a continuous process of industrial adjustment that reduced the number of firms and contracted employment. In fact, this sector no longer encompasses the entire production chain but rather now concentrates on segments such as commercialization, services, and the final assembly of knitted products. This translates into a significant increase of Chilean goods being exported, as well as of Chilean investment flowing to neighboring countries. The textile industry is by no means dying; it is simply adjusting and specializing in niche exports.

16. See Acuña and Smith (1994) and Smith and Acuña (1994) for a theorization of possible alternative future politico-economic scenarios envisioning different combinations of market-oriented reform, disarticulation and rearticulation of collective actors, and various modes of democratic consolidation. Chile, in their analysis, stands out as the most successful case of neoliberal reform, although its democratic transition is characterized as "incomplete" due to the authoritarian enclaves and institutional arrangements put in place under the previous military regime.

REFERENCES

Acuña, Carlos H., and William C. Smith. 1994. "The Political Economy of Structural Adjustment: The Logic of Support and Opposition to Neoliberal Reform." In *Latin American Political Economy in the Age of Neoliberal Reform: Theoretical and Comparative Perspectives for the 1990s*, ed. William C. Smith, Carlos H. Acuña, and Eduardo A. Gamarra, pp. 17–66. New Brunswick, NJ: Transaction.

Díaz, Alvaro. 1991. "Nuevas tendencias en la estructura social chilena (asalarización informal y pobreza en los ochenta." *Revista Proposiciones* 20 (August).

———. 1996. "New Tendencies toward Social and Economic Restructuring in Latin America." In *The Politics of Social Change and Economic Restructuring in Latin America*, ed. William C. Smith and Roberto P. Korzeniewicz. Boulder, CO, and London: Lynne Rienner.

Garretón, Manuel Antonio. 1994. "The Political Dimensions of Processes of Transformation in Chile." In *Democracy, Markets, and Structural Reform in Latin America: Argentina, Bolivia, Brazil, Chile, and Mexico*, ed. William C. Smith, Carlos H. Acuña, and Eduardo A. Gamarra, pp. 217–236. New Brunswick, NJ: Transaction.

Garretón, Manuel Antonio, and Malva Espinoza. 1992. "Reforma del Estado o cambio de la matriz socio-política?" *Estudios Sociales* 74.

Pinto, Aníbal. 1975. "Desarrollo económico y relaciones sociales en Chile." In *Inflación: Raíces estructurales*. México, D.F.: Fondo de Cultura Económica.

Silva, Eduardo. 1992. "The Political Economy of Chile's Transition to Democracy." In *The Struggle for Democracy in Chile, 1982–88*, ed. Paul Drake and Iván Jaksic. Lincoln: University of Nebraska Press.

———. 1993. "Capitalist Coalitions, the State, and Neoliberal Economic Restructuring in Chile, 1973–1988." *World Politics* 45, 4: 526–559.

Smith, William C., and Carlos H. Acuña. 1994. "Future Politico-Economic Scenarios for Latin America." In *Democracy, Markets, and Structural Reform in Latin America: Argentina, Bolivia, Brazil, Chile, and Mexico*, ed. William C. Smith, Carlos H. Acuña, and Eduardo A. Gamarra, pp. 1–28. New Brunswick, NJ: Transaction.

Tironi, Eugenio, and Ricardo Lagos. "Actores sociales y ajuste estructural." *Revista de la Cepal* 44 (November).

Torre, Juan Carlos. 1996. "The Politics of Transformation in Historical Perspective." In *The Politics of Social Change and Economic Restructuring in Latin America*, ed. William C. Smith and Roberto P. Korzeniewicz. Boulder, CO, and London: Lynne Rienner.

Valenzuela, Arturo, and Samuel Valenzuela, eds. 1986. *Military Rule in Chile: Dictatorship and Oppositions*. Baltimore, MD: Johns Hopkins University Press.

Vergara, Pilar. 1985. *Auge y caída del neoliberalismo en Chile*. Santiago: Facultad Latinoamericana de Ciencias Sociales.

———. 1990. *Políticas hacia la extrema pobreza en Chile*. Santiago: Facultad Latinoamericana de Ciencias Sociales.

———. 1994. "Market Economy, Social Welfare, and Democratization in Chile." In *Democracy, Markets, and Structural Reform in Latin America: Argentina, Bolivia, Brazil, Chile, and Mexico*, ed. William C. Smith, Carlos H. Acuña, and Eduardo A. Gamarra, pp. 237–262. New Brunswick, NJ: Transaction.

World Bank. Various years. *World Development Report*. Baltimore: Johns Hopkins University Press.

Zermeño, Sergio. 1991. "Desidentidad y desorden: México en la economía global y en el libre comercio." *Revista Mexicana de Sociología* 53, 2.

———. 1996. "State and Society in the Crisis of Dependent Neoliberalism: The Case of Mexico." In *The Politics of Social Change and Economic Restructuring in Latin America*, ed. William C. Smith and Roberto P. Korzeniewicz. Boulder, CO, and London: Lynne Rienner.

INDEX

About the Contributors

AMY E. BELLONE is a Ph.D. candidate in the interdisciplinary Latin American Studies program at Tulane University. Her major field of study is sociology, with minor fields in economics and political science. The main focus of her research is comparative urban development. Her dissertation fieldwork examines the impact of national policies, urban planning efforts, and trends in the world economy on individual households in Santa Cruz de la Sierra, Bolivia.

SERGIO BERENSZTEIN is a Ph.D. candidate in Political Science at the University of North Carolina, Chapel Hill. He is currently a Research Fellow at Centro de Investigación y Docencia Económicas (CIDE) in Mexico City. He has published articles on taxation and tax reform in Latin America in *Política y Gobierno* and *Revista Internacional de Sociología*.

ALVARO DÍAZ is a sociologist and economist. His professional and academic experience has been in Latin America (Chile, Costa Rica, Nicaragua, Argentina, and Brazil). He is currently Senior Research Associate at the Centro de Estudios Sociales SUR, Professor of Economic Sociology at the Universidad de Chile, and a consultant to the Economic Commission of Latin America and the Caribbean (ECLAC). Since 1991 he has been an advisor in the Chilean Ministry of Economics and is currently the executive director of the Program in Technological Development and Innovation coordinated by the Ministry of Economics.

EDUARDO A. GAMARRA is Associate Professor of Political Science and Acting Director of the Latin American and Caribbean Center at Florida International University. He is the author of *Dictators, Democrats, and Drugs: A Brief History of U.S.-Bolivian Counternarcotics Policy* (forthcoming), the coauthor of *Revo-*

lution and Reaction: Bolivia, 1964–1985 (1989), and the coeditor of *Latin American Political Economy in the Age of Neoliberal Reform* (1994) and *Democracy, Markets, and Structural Reform in Latin America* (1994). His current research interests focus on civil-military relations, legislatures and political parties, narcotics trafficking, and U.S.–Latin American relations.

JOSÉ ITZIGSOHN is Assistant Professor of Sociology at Brown University. He has recently published papers on remittances and development, grass-roots political participation, and urbanization in the Caribbean in *Social Forces, International Journal of Urban and Regional Research*, and *Latin American Research Review*. His current research focuses on the rise of ethnic economies in the United States and the informal economy in Latin America.

SUSANNE JONAS teaches Latin American and Latino Studies at the University of California, Santa Cruz. She is currently engaged in a major collaborative project on Salvadoran and Guatemalan immigrant/refugee communities in the Los Angeles and San Francisco Bay areas. Among her research interests and writing focuses are issues of structural change, immigration, and refugee policies of the United States and Mexico, and reconceptualizations of citizenship in the Americas. Her most recent books are *The Battle for Guatemala* (1991) and an edited volume, *Latin America Faces the 21st Century* (1994). She has published a recent article on peace negotiations in Guatemala in *Foreign Policy*.

A. DOUGLAS KINCAID is Associate Professor of Sociology and Research Director of the Latin American and Caribbean Center at Florida International University. He is the coeditor of several volumes, including *Americas: An Anthology* (1992) and *Comparative National Development: Society and Economy in the New Global Order* (1995). His articles on development theory, civil-military relations, and rural politics in Central America have appeared in several anthologies and in journals such as *Sociological Forum* and *Comparative Studies in Society and History*.

MIGUEL E. KORZENIEWICZ is Assistant Professor of Sociology at the University of New Mexico. He has published on emerging forms of economic organization in Latin America in several edited volumes and sociological journals. He is the coeditor of *Commodity Chains and Global Capitalism* (1994). His current research interests include postindustrial exports and corporate social responsibility on a global scale.

ROBERTO PATRICIO KORZENIEWICZ is Assistant Professor of Sociology at the University of Maryland in College Park. He is the coeditor of *The Politics of Social Change and Economic Restructuring in Latin America* (forthcoming), and his publications have appeared in *Sociological Forum, Latin American Research Review, Hispanic American Historical Review, Revista Mexicana de So-*

ciología, and the *Bulletin of Latin American Studies*. He is currently completing a book on labor, gender, and political identity in Argentina, 1886–1946.

LINDA MILLER MATTHEI is Assistant Professor of Sociology and Anthropology at East Texas State University, Commerce, Texas. Her research interests focus on gender and international labor migration, the political economy of the English-speaking Caribbean, and migration as a process of constructing transnational network building. Her article on gender and migration will appear in an upcoming issue of *Social Justice*.

BRUCE M. PODOBNIK is a Ph.D. candidate in Sociology at Johns Hopkins University. In addition to his continuing research on radical political movements in the periphery, he is working on a dissertation analyzing the energy foundations of the modern world-economy.

ALEJANDRO PORTES is Chair of Sociology and John Dewey Professor of Sociology and International Relations at Johns Hopkins University. His recent books include *Labor, Class, and the International System* (1981), *Latin Journey: Cuban and Mexican Immigrants in the United States* (1985), *Immigrant America: A Portrait* (1990), *City on the Edge: The Transformation of Miami* (1993), and several edited volumes, including *The Informal Economy: Studies in Advanced and Less Developed Countries* (1989) and *Comparative National Development: Society and Economy in the New Global Order* (1995).

J. TIMMONS ROBERTS is Assistant Professor of Sociology and Latin American Studies at Tulane University. His current research examines questions such as the value of world-system approaches in elucidating the social roots of environmental damage, the psychosocial effects of hazardous work, and the environmental initiatives of chemical industries in Latin America. His recent articles have appeared in *Sociological Inquiry, World Development, Economic Development and Cultural Change*, and *Social Problems*.

DAVID A. SMITH is Associate Professor of Sociology at the University of California, Irvine. He recently has published a series of articles on comparative urbanization and development, technology in the world-system, and network analysis of the global economy in *Urban Affairs Quarterly; Science, Technology, and Human Values*; and *Social Forces*. Among his ongoing research interests are studies mapping the world city system, tracing raw-material commodity chains, and examining Los Angeles as a global city.

WILLIAM C. SMITH is Professor of Political Science at the Graduate School of International Studies of University of Miami. He is the author of *Authoritarianism and the Crisis of the Argentine Political Economy* (1989) and the coeditor of several volumes, including *Latin American Political Economy in the Age of*

Neoliberal Reform (1994), *Democracy, Markets, and Structural Reform in Latin America* (1994), and *The Politics of Social Change and Economic Restructuring in Latin America* (forthcoming). His articles have appeared in journals such as *Revista Mexicana de Sociología, Desarrollo Económico, Dados, Journal of Interamerican Studies and World Affairs, Studies in Comparative International Development,* and *Political Power and Social Theory.*

DAVID SPENER is a postdoctoral research fellow with the Program in Border and Migration Studies of the Population Research Center of the University of Texas. As a sociologist, his main research interests include economic sociology, Latinos in the United States, and comparative international development. He is currently helping to direct a binational study of the effects of U.S.-Mexican economic integration on small businesses and labor markets in the Texas-Mexico transborder region. His doctoral dissertation, "Entrepreneurship and Small-Scale Enterprise in the Texas Border Region: A Sociocultural Perspective," was completed at the University of Texas in 1995.

Studies in the Political Economy of the World-System
(Formerly published as Political Economy of the World-System Annuals)

States versus Markets in the World-System
edited by Peter Evans, Dietrich Rueschemeyer, and Evelyne Huber Stephens

Crises in the Caribbean Basin: Past and Present
edited by Richard Tardanico

Rethinking the Nineteenth Century: Contradictions and Movements
edited by Francisco O. Ramirez

Racism, Sexism, and the World-System
edited by Joan Smith, Jane Collins, Terence K. Hopkins, and Akbar Muhammad

Revolution in the World-System
edited by Terry Boswell

War in the World-System
edited by Robert K. Schaeffer

Semiperipheral States in the World-Economy
edited by William G. Martin

Cities in the World-System
edited by Resat Kasaba

Pacific-Asia and the Future of the World-System
edited by Ravi Arvind Palat

Commodity Chains and Global Capitalism
edited by Gary Gereffi and Miguel Korzeniewicz

Food and Agrarian Orders in the World-Economy
edited by Philip McMichael

A New World Order?: Global Transformations in the Late Twentieth Century
edited by David A. Smith and József Böröcz

ISBN 0-313-29814-9